Homeschooling In Wisconsin:
At Home With Learning

Additional copies of this book are available from

Wisconsin Parents Association
Post Office Box 2502
Madison, WI 53701-2502
608.283.3131
www.homeschooling-wpa.org
wpa@homeschooling-wpa.org

Members of Wisconsin Parents Association receive a discount.
Contact us for information.

For ongoing information about homeschooling,
become a member of WPA. You will receive
the WPA newsletter and special bulletins as needed.

Homeschooling In Wisconsin:

At Home With Learning

Seventh Edition

Wisconsin Parents Association
Madison, Wisconsin

Wisconsin Parents Association
  Homeschooling in Wisconsin: at home with learning
  p.   cm.
  Includes bibliographical references and index.
  ISBN 978-0-9651864-3-8

  1. Homeschooling—Curricula—Handbooks, manuals. 2. Non-formal educa-
     tion—Curricula—Handbooks, manuals. 3. Parenting.
     Wisconsin Parents Association.

649.68
HO

This edition printed in the United States
of America.

Important note: Nothing in this book is
intended or should be taken as the giving of legal
advice. This book is not intended to substitute
for privately retained legal counsel.

CONTENTS

Acknowledgments

This book would not have been possible without the work of many, many people. Among them:

• The homeschoolers who have created Wisconsin Parents Association (WPA) as a strong, effective grassroots organization and who have worked together through WPA to develop and maintain a favorable climate for homeschooling in Wisconsin. Some of the most obvious work has been done to gain and maintain a reasonable homeschooling law. But far more important, and requiring far more work, has been the growth and development of homeschools by thousands of families. These homeschooling families are reclaiming and reshaping a traditional approach to learning and showing the world that homeschooling works.

• All the homeschoolers who have stood up to school officials and others when they made unreasonable demands, tried to increase state regulation of homeschools, unfairly criticized homeschoolers, and intentionally or unintentionally gave out incorrect information about homeschooling. Through seemingly minor actions by thousands of people, we are reclaiming and maintaining our rights and responsibilities.

• The people who helped gather and develop the information in this book. Many people have read, thought, researched information, attended hearings, worked through support groups, and shared their experiences and stories, all of which has been distilled into the information presented here.

• Those who participated in the production of this book by researching, writing, editing, proofreading, laying out text and graphics, and coordinating production. A special thank you to the artist whose woodcut prints throughout this book convey the solidity, spirit, and down-to-earth nature of homeschooling.

• The cooperative and generous souls who willingly cooked meals, washed dishes, ran errands, and offered endless support so the people listed above could build WPA and work on this book.

• Most important, the children who have given their parents and their communities the opportunity to discover the wonder of homeschooling; to reclaim learning, family bonds, and whole lives; and to demonstrate that even in a complex, fast-paced, highly technological society, people can have fun learning together at a gentle pace. Without these children with their courageous spirits and enthusiasm for learning, neither homeschooling, nor WPA, nor this book would be possible. We give them our heartfelt thanks and our love.

Introduction

The book you are holding has the information you need to homeschool in Wisconsin. Homeschooling families have created it by living courageously, holding to our principles and beliefs, and daring to be different. Some of us are quoted here; more have contributed.

This book is our gift to you. We want to share some of what we've learned and support and encourage you. We want to tell you not to be afraid to homeschool, even if people close to you question you. Go for it, even if doubts threaten to overwhelm you. We know homeschooling isn't the only way, but we can assure you it's a good way. Only you can decide what's best for your family, but if you decide to homeschool, you can do it.

Families homeschool for many different reasons. Some want their children to have a conventional education while learning in their own way, at their own pace. Some want their children to pursue special interests. Other parents choose to share more of their beliefs and values than attending conventional school would allow. Some seek academic excellence, while others can't find an acceptable alternative. Some children cannot learn well in a conventional school. Other parents do not want their children trapped by the academic and social pressures of conventional schools. Some prefer to learn from life experience. Opportunities to build a stronger family draw others. And some want to take charge of their own lives rather than surrendering them to conventional schools.

Homeschooling encompasses all these reasons and more. Whatever your reasons, you are not alone.

Homeschooling families are amazing. In a society dominated by conventional schools, we are learning in our homes and communities, reveling in discovery, growing in confidence. We are contributing to our communities, doing important work, and having fun. We are living in the present as surely as we are preparing for the future.

Our lives make much needed statements:
• Families matter.
• Ordinary parents can raise children without relying on "experts."
• Children who are given love, support, and guidance are eager to learn and good at it.
• Everyone benefits when families learn and grow together, when parents consider raising their children a high enough priority to arrange income and career advancement around it.
• Even a small minority can work through a grassroots organization to maintain its rights and responsibilities in the face of continuing challenges from powerful interest groups.
• People can create and maintain a space where children and families are free to learn and live.

Today's homeschoolers walk in the footsteps of pioneers and provide the trail for those who will follow. Chapter 20 outlines Wisconsin homeschoolers' rich legacy that includes one of the most reasonable homeschooling laws in the country. Actions that will enable us to keep our freedoms and pass them on are discussed in Chapter 21. What you do will affect the way you and others, maybe even your children and grandchildren, can homeschool. Please act carefully, boldly, courageously, and wisely. Welcome to homeschooling in Wisconsin!

About This Book

Part One covers how to begin homeschooling.

Part Two discusses daily life: curriculums and learning resources, using the library and the Internet, homeschooling children with special needs, recognizing and evaluating learning, record keeping, high school at home, diplomas, socialization, support groups, parenting, problem solving, and secrets of experienced homeschoolers.

Part Three presents reasons homeschooling works, stories from homeschooling families, the history of homeschooling in Wisconsin, and the role of Wisconsin Parents Association (WPA).

Part Four explains why we must take responsibility for maintaining our freedoms. Reasons and strategies in Chapter 21 are followed by specific ways in which homeschoolers can work effectively individually and together.

Details about Wisconsin's homeschooling law and others affecting homeschoolers and ways of working with the Legislature are in **Part Five.**

"Homeschooling in a Non-Homeschooling World," **Part Six,** includes minimizing the chances a truant officer will contact you, responding if they do, working with public schools (if you want to), protecting your family's privacy, and current developments that affect homeschoolers,

Appendix A contains texts of important Wisconsin statutes. **Appendix B** describes WPA, who we are and what we do. WPA resolutions in **Appendix C** offer important perspectives on issues.

How You Can Use This Book

Read it straight through or choose the most important parts, whether you are a new homeschooler, a veteran seeking fresh perspectives, a teen developing your credentials, or a grandparent surprised that your grandchildren are homeschooling. Take it in the spirit in which it is offered: use the parts that fit your family and leave the rest. Read with pen in hand: underline, cross out, add your ideas. Insert tabs for quick reference. Make it your own.

To make information accessible, the book is formatted as a manual with lists of ideas, options, and suggestions plus cross references. Some repetition is inevitable as it presents, in linear form, ideas that are interconnected.

If you need information not in this book, call the WPA Voice Mail at 608-283-3131; visit the website at www.homeschooling-wpa.org; write to WPA, P. O. Box 2502, Madison, Wisconsin 53701-2502; or contact your WPA Regional Coordinator, listed in the WPA Newsletter and on the website.

May your family's homeschooling adventure be rich and rewarding!

Guide to Finding the Help You Need

For Information on Homeschooling

→ My children's current school situation has become intolerable. I need to begin home-schooling now, but I'm not sure how to begin. See pages 20 and 39.

→ I want to continue homeschooling, but I feel tired, overwhelmed, confused, and dis-couraged. See pages 39, 121, 126, 128, and 133.

→ I've just decided to homeschool our children, but I don't know what to do next. See pages 20 and 39.

→ I want to homeschool my child who is currently enrolled in kindergarten in a public school? What do I this? Do I need to file form PI-1206? See page 32.

→ How do I file the required form PI-1206 with the Department of Public Instruction (DPI)? See page 26.

→ Can I begin homeschooling in the middle of the school year or do I have to wait until next fall? See pages 26 and 33.

→ It is after the October 15th deadline to send form PI-1206 to the DPI. Can I still begin homeschooling? See pages 26 and 33.

→ Where do I get the books? See page 39.

→ There are so many different curriculums and so many ways to homeschool. Which one is the best? See page 58.

→ I'm trying to decide whether our family should homeschool. See page 17.

→ I want to begin homeschooling. What is legally required? See page 23.

→ How old should my child be when I start sending in form PI-1206 for them? See page 31.

→ What is our family supposed to actually do to learn things when we start homeschool-ing? See pages See page 39.

→ How do I choose a curriculum? What choices do I have? Do I have to buy a whole curriculum? See page 44.

→ What qualifications do I need to homeschool our children? See page 18.

→ Can I homeschool my child with special needs even though I'm not trained in special education? See page 82.

→ Our children are already in high school. Is it too late to begin homeschooling? See page 92.

→ My teens don't like school work. How can I homeschool them? See page 92 .

→ Can homeschoolers get good student discounts on auto insurance? See page 98.

→ How can homeschoolers get high school diplomas? See page 102.

→ How do homeschoolers get into college or technical school and get scholarships? See page 107.

→ Is there any way to get college credit without enrolling in college? See page 68 and 109.

→ What records do I have to keep? See page 85.

→ I'm not sure that our kids are learning enough of the right stuff. How should I evaluate their progress? Should I have them tested? See page 84.

→ What about socialization? See page 109.

→ Our child has trouble with reading (or whatever). What can I do? See page 124.

→ Our close friends, extended family, or neighbors are questioning our homeschooling. What can I do? See page 196.

→ As a homeschooling parent, I just don't have enough time for myself. See page 121.

→ A newspaper reporter has asked to interview our family about homeschooling. Should I agree to this? How do I prepare for the interview? See page 199.

→ How can I help our children prepare to enter or re-enter a conventional school after homeschooling? See page 244.

→ I am involved in a custody dispute with my ex-spouse. Can you help me? See page 126.

→ I want to hire an attorney for a case involving homeschooling. How can I find a good one? See page 180.

If a Public Official Contacts You

→ The school census taker is at the door (or on the phone, or has sent me a letter) requesting the names and ages of our children. See page 229.

→ A social service worker is at the door (or on the phone). See page 235.

→ A truant officer is at the door (or on the phone). See page 239.

→ Someone at our children's school just told me that we should begin homeschooling. See page 34.

→ Our child has been diagnosed as "learning disabled," "hyperactive," as having "attention deficit hyperactivity disorder" (ADHD), or some similar label, and school officials are pressuring us to put him or her into special education. See pages 71 and 221.

→ I just received a letter telling me to bring in our 4 year old (or 3, 2, or 1 year old) for preschool screening. Should I go? Am I required by law to go? See page 223.

→ I have received a letter and a questionnaire from our local school district requesting information about our family because we are homeschooling. Should I fill it out and send it in? See page 230.

→ Should I get our children's school records from the time they attended public schools? How do I do this? See page 251.

→ Our children would like to take a course in the local public school. Is this possible? See page 247.

→ I would like my special needs child to get speech therapy or other services from the public school. Is this possible? How do I make the necessary arrangements? See page 247.

For Information about Homeschooling in Wisconsin

→ What does Wisconsin's homeschooling law require? See page 23.

→ How can I find out more about Wisconsin's homeschooling law and other laws that affect homeschoolers? See pages 205 and 210.

→ What was it like to homeschool in Wisconsin before the current law passed in 1984? See pages 137 and 146.

→ How many homeschoolers are there in Wisconsin? See page 188.

→ Are homeschools in Wisconsin private schools? See page 207.

→ I want to be a responsible homeschooler. What should I be doing? See page 159.

→ Is it legal for homeschooling parents to homeschool children from another family along with their own children? See page 208.

For Questions about Policy and Practical Action

→ What can we do as parents to reclaim and maintain our rights and responsibilities? See page 159.

→ What issues do homeschoolers face today? See page 182.

→ Should homeschoolers get tax credits or other benefits from the state or federal government? See page 184.

→ What is the difference between compulsory attendance and compulsory education? Why does this matter? See page 169.

→ How can I get in touch with my legislators? See page 214.

→ How can I participate effectively in a legislative hearing? See page 217.

→ Do I need to worry about protecting my family's privacy? If so, what should I do? See page 254.

→ Should homeschoolers support legislation supposedly designed to protect parental rights? See page 260.

→ Why does Wisconsin have such a good homeschooling law? See page 145.

→ Should I have my question my children screened? See page 223.

For Questions Not Answered in This Book

→ Email WPA at wpa@homeschooling-wpa.org or call the WPA Voice Mail at 608-283-3131.

→ Contact your WPA Regional Coordinator listed in the WPA Newsletter and on the WPA website at www.homeschooling-wpa.org.

→ Visit the WPA website at www.homeschooling-wpa.org.

PART ONE

STARTING
HOMESCHOOLING

Chapter 1

Deciding to Homeschool

- **Questions to Consider 17**
- **Reassuring Information for Parents Considering Homeschooling 18**
- **Am I Qualified to Homeschool My Children? 18**

The decision to begin homeschooling involves much more than where children will learn to read and do long division. Homeschooling is a big responsibility with far-reaching consequences. It is also an adventure. For many families, it becomes a way of life.

People decide to homeschool for many reasons and in many ways. Some make an intellectual decision that it will provide the best education for their children. Others are lead through prayer or feel in their hearts that it is right for them. There are parents who reluctantly choose homeschooling as the best alternative despite a lack of confidence in their own abilities. Whatever your reasons for homeschooling, you are not alone. Others have chosen to homeschool for reasons similar to yours.

Parents' feelings about homeschooling vary, too. Many embrace homeschooling joyfully and truly love it. Some begin out of a sense of duty and find they like it better than they had expected, while others persist mainly because they are convinced it is best for their children.

Questions to Consider

Many parents consider questions such as the following when deciding whether to homeschool:

• What effect would homeschooling have on our children? In what ways would homeschooling benefit them? Are there any ways it might be detrimental?

• How would having more time together and sharing more experiences strengthen our family and the relationships we have with each other?

• How would homeschooling affect:

—our family budget?

—our children's relationships with their friends?

—our relationships with people outside the family?

—the work being done by adults in the family?

• Would homeschooling or attending a conventional school be a better way for our children to learn each of the following:

—basic academic skills?

—how to learn?

—religious and moral values?

—how to get along with peers?

—how to get along with people older and younger than they are?

—how to be responsible members of a group?

—how to master skills that interest them?

—how to assume responsibility and get a job done?

—appreciation of natural beauty and the arts?

(Add other skills, qualities, etc. that you consider important.)

• Would homeschooling or attending a conventional school give our children a better opportunity to learn at their own pace, in ways that work well for them? Which would give them a better chance to pursue topics that especially interest them?

• What stresses and tensions would our children face in attending a conventional school? In homeschooling? Which would they be better able to handle? Where would they get the most support? Where would they have the best opportunity to mature socially?

• What are my biggest concerns or worries about homeschooling? With whom could I discuss them?

Reassuring Information for Parents Considering Homeschooling

• Many parents find that it is easier to parent children when they are homeschooling than when they are attending a conventional school. The time that homeschooling families spend together is more relaxed and enjoyable than the limited time before and after school, on weekends, and during school vacations. (See Chapters 15, 16, and 17.)

• Most parents find that life as a homeschooling parent is different from what they imagined before they started homeschooling. It is certainly different from the lives of parents whose children attend conventional schools. It is better, according to the vast majority of homeschooling parents. Since they have more control over their time, space, and energy, the inevitable challenges and frustrations in life are more manageable. Homeschooling is a big responsibility and can be a lot of work, but most parents find that homeschooling is definitely worth the effort. (See Chapter 16.)

• Many families homeschool inexpensively, using suggestions in this handbook, libraries, the Internet, CLEP and AP tests; purchasing used materials; sharing resources with other homeschoolers; creating their own learning materials; and in other ways.

• Meeting the requirements of Wisconsin's reasonable homeschooling law is not difficult. (See Chapter 3.)

• A decision to homeschool does not have to be a lifelong commitment. Many homeschooled children have entered or re-entered conventional schools without difficulty, richer for the homeschooling experiences they have had.

Am I Qualified to Homeschool My Children?

Yes! How can that statement be made so definitely? For a number of reasons, including the following:

• You are a parent who cares enough about your children to consider homeschooling. (It is important to realize that homeschooling, or even considering homeschooling, is obviously not the only way parents show that they care deeply about their children. But parents who homeschool obviously care about their children.) Parents who care about their children, are committed to doing the best they can for them, and love them, are well prepared to homeschool.

• If you are considering homeschooling, there's a good chance that your children have already learned to walk and talk. Think about that. They've learned two of the most complicated human skills. To walk, they've learned about balance, using muscles, choosing a direction, and more. Somehow, from all the sounds they've heard, your children have selected the ones that are part of our language, figured out what they mean, and learned to make them. With your help and support, your children have learned all this! Of course you can homeschool.

• Doubts don't mean you shouldn't homeschool. Conscientious parents have doubts and feel concerned at times, whether they send their kids to conventional or alternative schools or homeschool.

• Homeschooling parents sometimes make mistakes as they are parenting and helping their children learn. That's okay. One of the big advantages to homeschooling is that it gives families time to make mistakes, learn from them, make amends, and move on.

• You are a person who seeks out information and resources for things you are considering doing. If you weren't, you wouldn't be reading this book. So you not only know how to find resources; you use them once you've found them. People who are willing to admit that more information would help and have some idea of how to find it, and who listen to other people's experiences and use what will work for their families, are obviously prepared to get the information and support they need to homeschool.

At the same time, getting a pile of information is not difficult. People today are surrounded by information, overloaded by it. The problem is finding accurate information that can be trusted. People who choose this book are choosing information from experienced homeschoolers who have worked hard to reclaim and maintain families' rights to homeschool, and who have helped develop a climate of public opinion favorable to homeschooling. Information from other homeschoolers in the state where you live is more reliable and useful than is information from school officials, the Department of Public Instruction (DPI), publishers trying to market homeschooling curriculums, or national homeschooling organizations that have limited knowledge of and commitment to homeschooling laws and practices in individual states. It is far superior to information from professionals and experts in education who know very little about homeschooling and whose experience and commitment to conventional schools distort the information they present and make it inaccurate.

Therefore, you have what it takes to homeschool. This does not necessarily mean that you should homeschool. That's a separate question you need to answer for yourself. But it means you will be able to homeschool if that's what you decide to do. Remember this, especially during times of doubt that arise partly from living in a society that is so dominated by conventional schools and their approach to learning and living: You can homeschool.

Homeschooling stabilizes families, links generations, celebrates the individual history and personality of a family, and conveys a passion for learning to the next generation. What a priceless gift we offer to our own children and grandchildren and to a society hungry for these values.–From Opening Remarks, WPA Conference, 2006

Chapter 2

Getting Started: What Does It Take to Homeschool?

Starting homeschooling is exciting and challenging. Here are some suggestions.

• **First, take a deep breath.** Homeschooling has worked well for many families, and it can work for yours. There's no rush. You have time to decide how you want to homeschool, what curriculum to use, how to comply with the law, and all that. This handbook will help you enormously.

• **Learn what's required to homeschool in Wisconsin** and what's not required. See Chapter 3.

• **File form PI-1206 online with the Department of Public Instruction (DPI).** It is illegal to homeschool in Wisconsin without filing this form. See Chapter 4.

• **Take a break from school work.** This will be a big help in starting homeschooling. Take the pressure off yourself and your kids. Don't worry about textbooks, worksheets, or curriculums for at least a week, ideally a month. Instead, help the kids find constructive things to do, or, better yet, do things together. Ask the kids what they'd like to do. Think of things you've wanted to do but haven't had time for—until now. Don't worry about how you'll get the 875 hours required by statute. You will be amazed at how much the kids learn during this break, and you'll have plenty of time later for more formal academics, if that's the type of curriculum you choose.

A break gives your family an opportunity to come together, get to know each other better, improve communication, reduce tension, and just plain have fun. Kids unwind, get their feet on the ground, and relax. It's especially important for kids who have had difficulties in conventional school, whether because of academics, teachers, peer pressure, bullying, or whatever. Parents can focus on just parenting without worrying about teaching.

Good activities for the first days and weeks of homeschooling include:
- Reading what the kids choose, as long as you consider it acceptable.
- Watching appropriate movies.
- Sleeping. Many kids (and parents) do not get as much sleep as they need. Catching up on sleep often works wonders.
- Going for long walks or nature hikes.
- Playing at the park.
- Daydreaming.
- Going to the library and checking out fun stuff: DVDs, music, magazines, colorful books from the children's section, cookbooks, anything that looks appealing.

- Taking a trip: a day trip to a nearby city or park, an overnight to a favorite spot or a new one you want to explore, or, if you can afford the time and money, a real vacation. If you give the kids as much responsibility as possible for planning, preparing, and managing the trip, they will learn without your having to do lesson plans or motivate them.
- For more ideas, see Chapter 6.

Many parents find they need to limit or prohibit activities they feel are unacceptable or unhelpful, perhaps computer games, television, etc.

If your family would also like to do something academic each day, because you enjoy it or want to stay at grade level in one or more subjects or for whatever other reason, here are some suggestions.

Read each day, in whatever way works best for your family. Take turns reading aloud. Gather as a group and each read silently. Listen to books on tape. Stretch the definition of reading and watch a movie based on a book. Read anything that appeals to you: magazines, picture books (no matter how old you are), novels, stories about homeschooling, you name it.

Use one or more of the resources listed in "Possibility #2" in Chapter 6 or under "Build a Subject-Specific Purchased Curriculum" from the library. Choose an activity that looks interesting, and do "school" for as long as you want to.

Activities like these will give your children plenty of learning opportunities while you take your time choosing a curriculum that will work for your family. You don't need to do at home what your children would have done if they had been attending a conventional school. As you're doing activities from the books listed above, remember that anything we learn is helpful. If your kids learn something about math or science or whatever that isn't part of the standard curriculum for their grade, it won't be a waste, and it will help them learn the material for their grade when (or if) you go back to it.

- **Take your time in choosing a curriculum.** Read Chapters 6 and 7. Explore what's available and try some of the suggestions in this book before you buy a curriculum. Trying to get kids to use a curriculum that's not working creates tension and makes learning more difficult. You'll have time for the 875 hours of instruction required by law, even if you spend a month or two choosing a curriculum. If your children attended a conventional school for part of the school year, those hours count toward the 875. While you are deciding, consider doing some of the activities in Chapter 6, make up your own, or ask your kids. Recognizing what they are learning now will help you choose a curriculum that works for your family.

If your kids aren't particularly interested in school work, especially if they've had a difficult time in a conventional school, see "Working with Teens Who Don't Like School" in Chapter 11.

- **Learn more about libraries in your area.** Most homeschoolers rely heavily on libraries. You can save hundreds of dollars on curriculum by using the library for most of your learning resources. See Chapter 8 for details.

- **Get in touch with other homeschoolers**. They will give you information and support, and your kids will be glad to know they aren't the only homeschoolers around. Contact your WPA Regional Coordinator (listed in the current WPA newsletter and on the WPA website) or email WPA or call the WPA Voice Mail for information about support groups in your area. Visit as many as you reasonably can. Groups vary a lot, and it's worth spending some time to find one that works well for your family. If you can't find a group that meets your needs, consider starting one. (See Chapter 14.)

- **Expect some ups and downs.** Homeschooling is a big change; it takes time to adjust and feel confident. Expect to spend some time figuring out how you want to homeschool and gaining confidence. Then, just when you think you almost know what you're doing, things will change, and you'll need to adjust. Searching, trial-and-error, and mid-course corrections are all part of what makes homeschooling so exciting and why it works so well for so many different families. Just hang in there and you'll make it. See Chapter 16 for suggestions on how to solve problems that may arise.

• **Become a responsible homeschooler.** The present and future of homeschooling in Wisconsin depend on **you** and other homeschoolers. Actions of individuals like you are critical to maintaining our homeschooling freedoms. It's not difficult once you understand a few basic principles. See Chapter 21.

• **Join Wisconsin Parents Association (WPA).** WPA provides the support and information families need to homeschool. In addition, Wisconsin has one of the most reasonable homeschooling laws in the country. Homeschoolers working together through WPA got the law passed in 1984 and have worked hard to maintain it despite numerous challenges. (See Chapter 20.) WPA cannot do its work without members like you.

Chapter 3

What Wisconsin's Homeschooling Law Requires

■ **Understanding and Complying with Wisconsin's Homeschooling Law 23**
■ **Additional Considerations 24**
■ **Some Things Not Required 25**

Understanding and Complying with Wisconsin's Homeschooling Law

In Wisconsin statutes, homeschools are referred to as "home-based private educational programs." They are required to provide "at least 875 hours of instruction each school year" and "a sequentially progressive curriculum of fundamental instruction in reading, language arts, mathematics, social studies, science and health." (See Appendix A for the complete text of this law.) Homeschoolers need to understand what the statute does and does not require, especially because many school officials are either misinformed or uninformed about it.

1. The statute requires 875 hours of instruction, which can be 175 days of five hours each or some other schedule. This does not mean parents and children have to spend 875 hours at the kitchen table with textbooks and workbooks. Among the activities that can be counted as instruction:

- reading books, listening to other people read aloud, listening to books on tape;
- completing workbooks and exercise sheets where students develop and use skills like calculation and penmanship;
- doing hands-on experiments and observing things that give students a chance to make discoveries for themselves;
- using computers (with parental supervision, if necessary);
- using educational audio-visual materials (films, DVDs, CDs, etc.);
- participating in community activities, including field trips and volunteer service;
- learning practical skills such as cooking, cleaning, doing laundry, driving, gardening, sewing, and home maintenance;
- working part-time in ways that are similar to work-study programs in conventional schools;
- playing educational games;
- participating in individual and team sports, including community programs; and
- others.

2. The statute requires a "sequentially progressive curriculum." This is an educational plan in which new subject matter builds on what has previously been learned. Many different

curriculums are acceptable. Some families choose a standardized curriculum similar to those used in conventional schools, either purchasing a published version or developing their own. Some families develop their own curriculum based on their children's needs, interests, and abilities, being sure to include the subject areas required by law. (See Chapter 7.)

The required subject areas (reading, language arts, mathematics, social studies, science and health) are commonly understood and ensure that the educational program is well-balanced. However, the 875 hours can include other subjects a family chooses, such as art, religion, music, auto mechanics, computers, and household management.

3. Parents or guardians are required to file form PI-1206 with the Department of Public Instruction each year they are homeschooling, beginning the year their child turns six on or before September 1. They need to continue to file a form each year they homeschool until their child is no longer covered by the compulsory school attendance law. (See Chapter 4.)

4. In addition, the definitions section of the private school law states that, "An instructional program provided to more than one family unit does not constitute a home-based private educational program." Disobeying this provision would jeopardize the homeschooling law. (See Chapter 28.)

The four additional requirements of the statute (#5-8 listed below) are seldom a problem. However, parents need to be familiar with them and comply.

5. "The primary purpose of the program is to provide private or religious-based education."

6. "The program is privately controlled."

7. "The program is not operated or instituted for the purpose of avoiding or circumventing the compulsory school attendance requirement under s. 118.15(1)(a)."

8. "The pupils in the institution's educational program, in the ordinary course of events, return annually to the homes of their parents or guardians for not less than two months of summer vacation, or the institution is licensed as a child caring institution under s. 48.60(1)." (This provision applies to boarding schools and other such institutions and not to homeschools.)

These requirements for home-based private educational programs are exactly the same as those for any other private school. Home-based private educational programs are, in fact, private schools. This is clear from the statutes: "118.165 Private schools. (1) An institution is a private school if its educational program meets all of the following criteria: [those listed immediately above and listed on the form homeschoolers must file]." Homeschools are called "programs" in the statutes only to prevent them from receiving federal or state funds paid directly to schools for things like school lunch programs and school bus service. (See Chapter 28.) However, private school students, including homeschoolers, are eligible for services provided by public schools, including courses in special education and other subjects. (See Chapter 32.)

For more detailed information about Wisconsin's homeschooling law, see Chapter 28.

Additional Considerations

Homeschooling is a serious responsibility. In addition to complying with the law, homeschooling parents consider questions such as:

• What are our goals for our children's education? In addition to instruction in required subjects, many parents include topics like: learning to take responsibility, appreciating beauty in nature and the arts, running a household, participating in their community and assuming civic and social responsibility; developing religious and moral values; serving others; and using resources wisely.

• How will our children's progress toward these goals be evaluated? Many approaches to evaluation are available; flexibility is an asset. Observing children is one of the best approaches; homeschooling parents have many opportunities. A review of records that have been kept, along with samples of children's work, demonstrates progress. See Chapter 10 for more on evaluations and record keeping.

• How will the children be supervised? Usually at least one parent is at home full-time, but there are other options, depending on the age and abilities of the children, family circumstances, and other factors.

• How will we provide a social life for our children? Homeschooling makes it easier for children to have important contact with a variety of older and younger people. They get together with kids their own age through neighborhood activities, organized sports, home-schooling support groups, and youth organizations such as 4-H, church groups, and scouts.

Social life in conventional schools can be negative, including intense competition, bullying, and peer dependency. Many parents feel that the social aspects of a classroom setting need not be duplicated and in fact are best avoided. After all, school is the only place where people are required to interact with a group of people who are all the same age.

• What community resources are available and how will we use them? Much depends on opportunities available in the community; children's interests and abilities; and parents' imagination, time schedules, and willingness to chauffeur. Many parents seek opportunities for their children to serve as well as be served.

Some Things Not Required

Things not required by Wisconsin law and not necessary for homeschooling include:

• Having public school officials review and approve homeschooling families' curriculums and/or calendars is not required. See Chapter 31 for information on handling contacts from public school officials.

• Testing or other assessment of homeschooled children is not required, although some parents choose to have their children take standardized tests while others keep records or monitor their progress in other ways.

• A certified teacher, a parent with a high school or college diploma, a hired tutor, or other "professional educator" is not required.

• Homeschooling does not need to be expensive. With planning and imagination, many resources can be borrowed from the library or other places or obtained free or at minimal cost.

• Parents do not need to know everything children will need or want to learn. Parents and children can learn together, older children can work independently, tutors can be used, etc.

• A two-parent family is not required. There may be additional challenges for a single parent, such as scheduling and providing adequate supervision, but single parents can and do homeschool.

Chapter 4

Filing Form PI-1206 Online

- ■ Key Points to Keep in Mind 26
- ■ How to File the Form Electronically 28
- ■ Notifying Your Local School District 29
- ■ What to Do After You Have Filed Your Form 30

Key Points to Keep in Mind

Remember that filing the form means you are simply **reporting** that you are home-schooling. You are **not requesting** permission to homeschool. You are **not asking** the DPI to approve your curriculum. You are **not registering** your child. You are **not enrolling** your child in a homeschool. (Note: Your children are automatically enrolled in your homeschool when you start homeschooling. There is no special procedure for enrolling them and no form to fill out. If you enroll your children in a public virtual charter school, you are **not** homeschooling.)

It is illegal to homeschool without filing the form "on forms provided by the department [the DPI]," which now means filing online. The DPI will not provide paper copies of the form. The DPI encourages people who have religious or other objections to using electronic media to use computers in public libraries or to ask a friend for help.

Form PI-1206 serves as a signed affidavit of parents' compliance with the homeschooling law. It becomes an important document if your compliance is questioned.

For accurate information about homeschooling and Wisconsin's homeschooling law, contact WPA. Do not contact the DPI. Some of the information about homeschooling on the DPI's website is inaccurate and misleading; homeschoolers should not trust it. The DPI and the educational establishment have been opposing and misrepresenting the rights and responsibilities of homeschoolers since before the current homeschooling law was passed in 1984. Although they have grudgingly made certain corrections in the information they distribute, they still are not a trustworthy source of information about homeschooling.

To maintain our homeschooling freedoms, we need to do only the minimum required by law. Doing more than the minimum encourages public officials to increase requirements for homeschoolers and exceed the authority they have been granted by law. See Chapter 21. Here are important ways to do only the minimum required by the law concerning filing form PI-1206.

• **Only file a form with the DPI for children who are covered by the compulsory school attendance law,** that is, children who were six or older on or before September 1 of the current school year and have not yet completed the semester during which they turn 18. (See Appendix A for the text of this law.) Children younger than six should not be included on the form even if one or more of the following are true:

—Even if you are filing a form for older children in your family.

—Even if you are actively homeschooling children who are younger than six by following a purchased curriculum or doing learning activities you have chosen.

—Even if you enrolled your child in four- or five-year-old kindergarten in a public or conventional private school and now are planning to homeschool them. You do need to notify the school, preferably in writing, that you are withdrawing your child, but you do not need to and should not file Form PI-1206 unless your child had turned six on or before September 1 of the current school year. See Chapter 5 for information on starting homeschooling a child who has been attending kindergarten in a conventional school.

• **Unless your child is currently enrolled in a public or conventional private school, do not file the form until after the third Friday in September.**

If your child is currently enrolled in a public or conventional private school, you must file the form before you begin homeschooling to avoid being charged with truancy. But if, like most homeschoolers, your child is not currently enrolled, file it in early October, by October 15. Filing the form before the third Friday in September weakens homeschoolers' authority and freedom to operate a homeschool independent of the state and public school authorities. Here are some of the reasons:

—When some homeschoolers file their form early, it encourages local school officials to require all homeschoolers to do so, even though the statutes do not give officials the authority to do this. For example, officials could require that homeschoolers file their forms before September 1 so school officials know who will not be attending public school; then officials could pressure them to attend. It could also encourage officials to attempt to demand more of homeschoolers, such as details about the curriculums they are using, their calendars and daily schedules, etc.

—Wisconsin statutes require public and private schools (which include homeschools) to report to the DPI their enrollment as of the third Friday in September. Homeschoolers who file their forms after that date are emphasizing to school officials that they are simply reporting their enrollment along with other schools. They are not under the control of the public schools. They are not registering their homeschool with the DPI or requesting permission from the DPI to homeschool.

—Some homeschoolers may be tempted to file their form before the third Friday in September to get it taken care of. They may think this will prevent local public school officials from contacting them. If their children attended a public or conventional private school last year, they may think it's easier to file the form than to call or write to the school, as a courtesy, to inform them that their children will not be attending this year.

—Filing the form early becomes a substitute for knowing and exercising our homeschooling rights and, if necessary, standing up for them. Instead it is used to shield us from dealing with public school officials. When we use the form in this way to shield us from dealing with public school officials, they gain power over homeschoolers, power they didn't have before homeschoolers gave it to them.

• **Don't file the form before the third Friday in September unless you are sure your child is now in fact officially enrolled in a public or conventional private school.**

Obviously, a child who is currently attending a public or conventional private school is officially enrolled in that school, so parents of the child are legally required to file form PI-1206 before they begin homeschooling. It doesn't matter whether it is before or after October 15.

School districts sometimes claim children are officially enrolled although parents haven't registered them. Districts increasingly seem to want to claim that a child who has attended a school in the past continues to be enrolled until the child is formally withdrawn, which school officials sometimes claim requires that a parent sign an official withdrawal form. But such practices assume that the school rather than the parent has control over a child during the summer and, more importantly, that the public school is where the child should be during public school hours unless the child is formally withdrawn. On this basis, conventional schools sometimes claim that children who attended a school the previous school year are "officially enrolled" for the coming school year even though the parents haven't registered the children for the coming year. To maintain our rights, we can and should understand and make clear to others that "officially enrolled" means we have formally registered our child for the coming school year and/or sent our child to school when it opened in the fall.

If you begin homeschooling at the beginning of a school year and wait until early October to file your PI-1206 form, the school your children attended during the previous year may contact you and claim that your children are truant because they are officially enrolled in the school and not attending. WPA suggests that you explain that you have not officially enrolled your children in their school for the current year and that you are now homeschooling and will file the required form with the DPI by October 15. If you need help, email WPA, call the WPA Voice Mail, or contact your Regional Coordinator.

How To File the Form Electronically

You can file the form from any computer with Internet access, including your home computer, a friend's, or one at your local public library. You do not need an email account to file or to receive confirmation that the DPI has received your form.

Go to the WPA website at http://homeschooling-wpa.org/ and click on the instructions for filing the form and then on the link to the DPI web site. There the DPI recommends that you read "the information in the navigation bar at the left of this page." WPA recommends that you NOT read this information because some of it is misleading and inaccurate. If you have questions, read the rest of this chapter, consult the WPA website, email WPA, or call the WPA Voice Mail or your Regional Coordinator.

Follow the instructions on the DPI website. First, you need to "set up an ID and password," This is similar to establishing an account with an online business. WPA suggests that you NOT use your email address or your name as your ID to protect your privacy. If you use it, your local school district may contact you by email to request more information (which they are not authorized to collect), encourage you to enroll in the public school, offer you special favors, etc. Also, databases including contact information too often are misused and/or given to other government agencies and researchers. If you have already used your email address or your name as your ID and want to change it, sign in to the DPI website and follow the instructions for changing it.

Instead, make up a user ID, which can be a random combination of letters and numbers, your pet's name, your hobby, your favorite food or flower, whatever. Then create a password. It is often recommended that a password be a random combination of letters and numbers, not your name or a familiar word. An easy way to create one is to think of a sentence, and use the first letter of each word. For example, if you use the sentence, "I have been homeschooling my 3 kids for 2 years," your password would be Ihbhm3kf2y. Write your password down, and then enter it in the box and re-enter it where it says "Retype password." (If you filed a form last year, you can use the same ID and password.) Record your ID and password on paper or in your computer so you can update your form if necessary (because your address or the number of children you are homeschooling changes) or so you can print additional copies of your completed form.

Once you have created an ID and password, sign in. Fill in the form completely. The electronic form is the same as paper forms used before 2010 except that the questions are on separate pages. You will be asked to report the number of children of each gender in each grade or the number who are "Ungraded 1-8" or "Ungraded 9-12."

To protect your privacy, the form does not require your children's names, birthdates, ages, social security numbers, or other information. Since 1984, homeschoolers have worked hard through WPA to prevent this information from being required. Please do not provide any information that is not required.

If you don't fill in any boxes that are required, you will see a red asterisk and the message "Required." You need to fill them in before you can continue. (Note: At one point the DPI asked for phone numbers, but in response to a request from WPA, the DPI has removed this.)

Finally, you will be asked whether you are in compliance with Wisconsin's homeschooling statute. To indicate that you are, "sign" the form electronically by checking a box that says "By checking this box, I agree that the home-based private educational program meets all of the following criteria." (The criteria listed are those in the homeschooling statute. See Chapters 3 and 28 and Appendix A.} Nothing else is required for your signature. You do not need to scan it in, type your name, provide your social security number or any other identifying number, or anything else.

As soon as you have clicked on the box that says, "Submit Enrollment Data," you will see a page that says, "Congratulations! Your PI-1206 Homeschool Report has been successfully received. What To Do Next." Click on "Print a copy of your Homeschool Report data." Note that in the upper right hand corner of the form you printed, it says, "To the Parent: Your PI-1206 Homeschool Report has been submitted and received by the DPI. Your confirmation number is 000." This statement is the equivalent of a letter of acknowledgement from the DPI and is what you will need for proof that you filed your form.

Notifying Your Local School District

When a parent or guardian files a PI-1206 form, the DPI sends a copy to the local school district in which they reside. If your child is not currently enrolled in a public or conventional private school when you file your form, you do not need to notify your local school district. The copy of your form from the DPI is all they need or are entitled to under Wisconsin law.

However, if your child was officially enrolled in a public or conventional private school when you filed your form, don't be surprised if you are contacted by a school official even though you have filed your form correctly. School officials are often less familiar with the homeschooling law than homeschoolers are, partly because dealing with homeschoolers is such a small part of their job. Or they may have been misinformed. Or a copy of your form may not have been forwarded to the school. In addition, school officials see themselves and are accustomed to being seen by others as authority figures, so they expect to be able to give orders that people will obey without question. Finally, a few school officials may be unreasonable and will use their power to intimidate homeschoolers into doing more than the law requires or tell them that they are not allowed to do what the law in fact says they can do.

To minimize the risk of being contacted by school officials and perhaps charged with truancy, WPA recommends that you take responsibility yourself and notify the school. A good way to do this is to make two extra copies of your PI-1206 form. Draw four lines on each for a school official to sign and label them Name, Title, Signature, and Date. Take both copies to the school or schools your children have been attending. Explain to the person you talk with, preferably the principal, that you are now homeschooling, and ask them to remove your children from their rolls. When they have signed and dated both forms, leave one with the school and keep the other one for your records.

WPA suggests that you not complete a student withdrawal form even if the school asks you to. The compulsory attendance law states that a parent shall cause a child to attend a school. It is up to the parent or guardian to decide which school and to ensure that the child attends. The legal requirements and penalties have to do with whether a child is attending a school, not whether a child has been formally withdrawn from a school. Homeschoolers sometimes begin homeschooling in the middle of the school year. Filing the PI-1206 form is all that is necessary for this to happen. Filing the form establishes that the parent is responsible for their child in accordance with the statutes, which do not require that parents sign a withdrawal form. Please inform WPA if your local school officials claim your child is officially enrolled simply because they attended a public school last year or if they insist that you sign an official withdrawal form before beginning homeschooling.

What To Do After You Have Filed Your Form

• Keep your copy of your form on paper or store it as a PDF or in some other way in your computer. Copies are sometimes required by school officials, employers, colleges, Social Security officials, military recruiters, and others.

However, if you need another copy of the PI-1206 form you filed for the current school year and some past years, you can sign in on the same DPI web page you used to file your form, using the ID and password you created. On the next page, which says "Review Sign-In Data," you will now see a box that says, "Click here to reprint your current PI-1206 Homeschool Report data."

• Update your form, if necessary. During the school year, if your name, address, or the number of children you are homeschooling changes, update your online form. To do so, sign in and press the "Continue" buttons until you get to the page that has the information you want to change. Delete the old information and type in the current information. Complete the process of filing your form as you did before. Print a copy for your records.

• Understand your rights and the limits on what school officials can demand. Note that near the bottom of the form it says, "Recommendations: It is recommended that a copy of the following be maintained in your home if you are homeschooling children: A school calendar verifying a minimum of 875 hours of instruction. Course outlines verifying that there exists a sequentially progressive curriculum of fundamental instruction."

This statement has appeared on PI-1206 forms since 1984. It is more prominent on the electronic version than on previous paper versions. Remember that the DPI does **not** have the authority to require that you keep either a school calendar or course outlines, and local school district officials do **not** have the authority to ask you for them. (However, officials do have the authority to ask to see your attendance records. See Chapter 10.)

If an official asks to see your school calendar or course outlines, politely respond that they do not have the authority to make such a request. If you need more help, call your Regional Coordinator or email WPA or call the WPA Voice Mail.

Chapter 5

Beginning Under Special Circumstances

Beginning Homeschooling When a Child Turns Six

Wisconsin's compulsory school attendance law covers children from ages 6 to 18. Therefore, homeschoolers need to file form PI-1206 with the Department of Public Instruction (DPI) by October 15 beginning with the school year in which their child is six on or before September 1.

Wisconsin law requires that homeschoolers have a curriculum. However, this does not mean that you have to purchase a curriculum for your children when they turn six (or at any other time). See Chapter 7. Many parents feel there is nothing magic about age six. (In fact, some states do not require school attendance until children are seven or eight.) Many children who have been learning at home since birth simply continue to do so after they turn six.

There is a wide range of normal behavior for six year olds. Boys are often a year or more behind girls in language development. Many homeschooling parents allow their children to develop various skills when they are ready, rather than pressuring them to learn specific things by certain ages. Many children learn well and easily and enjoy it when they can wait until they have the necessary physical, mental, and emotional maturity. Often, all it takes is time. Learning according to one's own timetable, instead of being forced to follow a standardized timetable, is a big advantage of homeschooling.

Beginning Homeschooling a Child For Kindergarten

If you want to homeschool a child who had not turned six on or before September 1 of the current school year and who is not currently enrolled in kindergarten in a public or conventional private school, simply homeschool them using whatever approach you choose. Because your child is not yet covered by the compulsory school attendance law, you are not required to file form PI-1206. In fact, to follow the principle of doing the minimum that the law requires (see Chapter 21), WPA recommends that you not file the form until the school year in which they have turned six on or before September 1. However, if your child had turned six on or before September 1 of the current school year, you need to file form PI-1206 before you begin homeschooling. See Chapter 4. There is no space on the form to report that you are homeschooling a child in kindergarten, but you can use the box labeled "Ungraded 1-8" for kindergarten. Then you can report your child as being in first grade next year or continue to report them as ungraded for as long as you want.

Kindergarten is not legally required in Wisconsin. However, homeschoolers should be aware that because of a law passed in 2009, in order to enroll in first grade in a public school, including a charter school, in Wisconsin, a child must either complete five-year-old kindergarten or be exempted from this requirement. Therefore, if you homeschool your child for kindergarten and then want to enroll them in first grade in a public school or charter school, you will need to work this out with your local school district. If you home-schooled your child for kindergarten and want to homeschool for first grade, simply do so, remembering to file form PI-1206 at the appropriate time.

Beginning Homeschooling a Child Who Is Enrolled in Kindergarten

Sometimes parents decide they want to begin homeschooling a child who is attending kindergarten in a public or conventional private school. Perhaps they're unhappy with the program, there are problems in the classroom, their child is bored and already knows the material being covered, they have decided their child isn't ready for school yet, they don't like the way attending school is disrupting their family life, or there are other reasons.

Before you begin homeschooling, you should to notify the school your child has been attending that you will be homeschooling and ask them to remove your child from their rolls. If you do not notify the school, you may be charged with truancy. This is because a statute passed in 2009 requires children to attend school regularly if they are enrolled in five-year-old kindergarten in a public or conventional private school, even if they are not yet old enough to be covered by the compulsory school attendance statute. (See Chapter 29 and Appendix A.) For information on how to notify the school, see "Notifying Your Local School District" in Chapter 4.

Whether or not you also need to file form PI-1206 depends on your child's biological age, not their grade in school. If they had not turned six by September 1 of the current school year, your child is not covered by the compulsory school attendance law. Therefore, you do not need to file the form, even though they are currently enrolled in a public or conventional school kindergarten and even if they have turned six by the time you want to begin homeschooling them. In fact, to follow the principle of doing the minimum that the law requires (see Chapter 21), WPA recommends that you not file the form until the school year in which they have turned six on or before Septermber 1.

If your child had turned six on or before September 1 of the current school year, you need to file form PI-1206 before you begin homeschooling. See Chapter 4. There is no space on the form to report that you are homeschooling a child in kindergarten, but you can use the box labeled "Ungraded 1-8" for kindergarten. Then you can report your child as being in first grade next year or continue to report them as ungraded for as long as you want.

Kindergarten is not legally required in Wisconsin. However, homeschoolers should be aware that because of a law passed in 2009, in order to enroll in first grade in a public school, including a charter school, in Wisconsin, a child must either complete five-year-old kindergarten or be exempted from this requirement. Therefore, if you homeschool your child for kindergarten and then want to enroll them in first grade in a public school or charter school, you will need to work this out with your local school district. If you home-schooled your child for kindergarten and want to homeschool for first grade, simply do so, remembering to file form PI-1206 at the appropriate time.

Beginning During the High School Years

Many families begin homeschooling during the high school years and find it a reward-ing and satisfying experience. See Chapter 11.

Single Parents

Single parents can and do homeschool. There may be additional challenges such as work-ing out scheduling and providing adequate supervision, but these can be managed. It often helps to develop a support system, perhaps including extended family, neighbors, and friends.

Beginning on Short Notice

Families sometimes need to begin homeschooling on short notice. They may have been considering homeschooling for a while and decide that now is the time. Their children's school situation may have become intolerable. Illness may be a factor. Or there may be other circumstances or concerns.

If a school official has told you that you have to homeschool, stop and think before you decide to begin. Officials cannot force you to homeschool. If you don't want to home-school, or if, despite the information in this handbook, you can't figure out how to home-school given your circumstances, then homeschooling may not be right for your family. There are other approaches to education.

Fortunately, in Wisconsin you can begin homeschooling any time during the school year. You do not have to wait until the beginning of the next academic year or semester, as you would in some other states. However, you do have to file form PI-1206 with the Department of Public Instruction (DPI) before you can legally begin homeschooling. See Chapter 4.

Then stop. Sit down. Take a deep breath. Relax. The more overwhelming your situation seems, the more important it is to take time to figure out what to do next. Homeschooling has worked for thousands of families, and it will work for yours, either as a short term solu-tion or as a new adventure that changes your life. If appropriate, see "When Parents Are Reluctant to Begin Homeschooling" later in this chapter. See Chapter 6 for suggestions on what to do next.

Beginning During the School Year

You can begin homeschooling during the school year. You do not have to wait until the beginning of the next semester or school year. However, you do have to file form PI-1206 with the DPI before you begin. See Chapter 4.

Homeschooling Children With Special Needs

Children who have been diagnosed or labeled autistic, hyperactive, gifted, learning disabled, etc.; who have a physical disability; or who have other special needs often benefit greatly from homeschooling. See Chapter 9.

When Parents Are Reluctant to Begin Homeschooling

Some parents begin homeschooling because they feel their children need the support, opportunities, and flexibility that homeschooling offers. Others cannot find an acceptable alternative. Still others go along with their children's desire to homeschool, even though they themselves have little enthusiasm.

Parents who begin homeschooling reluctantly often find homeschooling is more manageable than they expected. Some even grow to like it. Here are some suggestions:

• Talk with other homeschooling parents. Contact your WPA Regional Coordinator (listed in the WPA newsletter and on the WPA website) or call the WPA Voice Mail. Ask them what they like about homeschooling and what suggestions they have for making homeschooling more manageable.

• Attend a WPA conference. Workshops offer information, encouragement, and support, and it is very helpful to meet other homeschooling parents.

• This handbook offers encouragement and information. Glance through the Contents. See the suggestions in Chapters 6 and 7 and "How Homeschooling Parents Can Find Time for Themselves" in Chapter 15. Look in the Index for topics of special concern.

• See Chapter 15 for reasons why it is easier to parent homeschooling children than people often expect.

• Take a break from worrying about academics. Children have a lifetime to learn. They do not have to learn things in the order conventional schools teach them. They do not have to learn them at the same time as their other children their age. They do not have to learn everything right now. A break is especially important if your children have just left a difficult school situation that has taken its toll on the whole family. Do things that you enjoy. See Chapter 2.

• Include in your homeschooling some activities that you enjoy yourself and some things that you would like to learn. If your children are not interested, do them yourself.

• Watch your children as they relax, learn, and grow. Let some of their energy encourage you.

• Realize that your commitment as a parent is important. With strong parental involvement, children do remarkably well. See Chapter 22 for research that supports the importance of parental involvement.

When a School Situation Has Become Intolerable

Families for whom a school situation has become intolerable often find that homeschooling provides a way to recover and get back to learning. Children who have had a difficult time in a conventional school, for whatever reason, usually benefit from a break from structured or formal academics. Many of the activities in Chapter 6 work well in this situation. Our society puts a lot of pressure on people to correct their weaknesses, but homeschooling parents often find it works better to set aside concerns about academics for a while and give children a chance to develop their strengths and interests. If appropriate, see "When Parents Are Reluctant to Begin Homeschooling" above.

When School Officials Recommend Homeschooling

School officials occasionally recommend homeschooling for children who are having difficulty in a conventional school. However, parents cannot be required to homeschool. In fact, Wisconsin law requires that school boards respond within 90 days to written requests from parents that the school provide their child with program or curriculum modifications. (See s. 118.15[1][d] in Appendix A.) At the same time, if a school situation has gotten to the point that officials are recommending homeschooling, it might be worth considering. If appropriate, see "When Parents Are Reluctant to Begin Homeschooling" above.

When Children Have Had Truancy Problems

Take heart. Many families whose children find school so intolerable that they become truants find that homeschooling works. Truancy is a complex problem that is not necessarily your child's fault. Young people sometimes deserve credit for standing up to a system that may be doing them more harm than good.

People who begin homeschooling are still liable for truancy charges stemming from evidence that they were truant before they started homeschooling. Be sure to file form PI-1206 before you begin homeschooling. See Chapter 4. Read about truancy laws in Chapter 31 and read the text of the truancy statutes in Appendix A. If you think you need an attorney, see Chapter 23.

Parents of children who have been accused of truancy may face three special challenges. First, the children may have been labeled "law breakers" or "criminals" and heard dire predictions about their future. Such a picture of oneself is unsettling, to say the least, and may become a self-fulfilling prophecy unless someone is able to help the children change it. Some parents view truancy as an indication that there is something wrong with the school system, rather than with their children, and are able to convey this to their children and help them make a realistic assessment of their strengths, abilities, and potential.

Second, parents of these children may believe they are being forced into something they don't want to undertake, aren't fully capable of doing, and don't have time to do. Parents who respond positively at this time to their children's genuine needs are often richly rewarded. They discover things they can do with their children that they both enjoy. They sometimes work with their children on learning projects. In addition to the rewards of seeing improvement in their children, these parents frequently end up liking homeschooling better than they expected to.

Third, school officials may scrutinize or harass a family whose children have had truancy problems. Some families deal with this by knowing what the law requires, complying carefully, and standing their ground firmly but politely in contacts with school officials. See Chapter 31 for more information on dealing with school officials. Some families also minimize the opportunities officials have to contact them by appearing as conventional as possible without compromising important principles. For example, they are careful that their children are clearly being supervised during conventional school hours. They explain their homeschooling to neighbors, relatives or others who might be concerned, which reduces the chance that these people will report the family to school officials or social services.

When Children Have Been Expelled

Students are expelled from public schools for a variety of reasons. The position of the DPI and some school officials is that these students still have to attend school, although this position does not seem to be enforced and has not been tested in court. However, on this basis, some people conclude that if these students cannot get into another public school or a conventional private school that they can afford, they have to homeschool. This does not make sense. Students do not have to homeschool simply because they have been expelled.

If your child has been expelled and you want to homeschool, many of the suggestions in "Homeschooling Children Who Have Had Truancy Problems" above may be helpful to you. Also, see Chapter 2 and, if appropriate, "When Parents Are Reluctant to Begin Homeschooling" above.

However, if your child has been expelled and you do not want to comply with Wisconsin's homeschooling law, do not submit form PI-1206 and claim you are homeschooling. Homeschooling is not the solution to the problems you are facing.

PART TWO

LEARNING THROUGH HOMESCHOOLING

Chapter 6

"Where Do I Get the Books?"
Getting Going or Shifting Gears

Here are easy, low cost curriculums that have been life-savers for many homeschooling families. One or more of them may be just what you need if you're in a situation such as:

• You've been considering homeschooling for a while and have just decided you want to start **now**, so you want a curriculum right away.

• Something has happened (maybe a crisis at the school your children are attending or an unexpected event in your family), and you want to begin homeschooling as soon as possible.

• You've been homeschooling for a while. You like many things about it, but it still seems to be so much work. You're tired of struggling, being responsible for planning and directing your kids' learning, and hearing, "So why don't you just send them to school?"

• It's February in Wisconsin: cabin fever time. The kids keep squabbling. You're basically glad you're homeschooling, but you'd sure like to go on a cruise or at least do something different for a while.

• It's early May in Wisconsin. One day is sunny and warm, the next is in the 30's and drizzly. It seems like you've gotten what you're going to get from the curriculum you've been using all year, but it's not time to quit for the summer.

• You've heard other homeschoolers talk about relaxing their approach to homeschooling, and you'd like to try that. But you wonder what would happen. Would the kids learn anything? Would it be pure chaos? What would you do all day?

• You want to try a more structured approach to learning to explore one or more subjects in greater depth and open doors to more opportunities.

• You're facing a complicated situation that has nothing to do with homeschooling. You have a new baby, one of your parents is seriously ill, your husband's business has taken a downturn and you're going to take over the bookkeeping, which will take four hours a day. (In situations like these, you may want to do some of the activities listed here. But more to the point, let this list help you realize that your children will learn invaluable lessons about real life by going through this with you, rather than being shuttled off to school each day and missing much of what is happening. Consider doing a unit study on newborns, or health and disease, or whatever. See "Unit Studies" in Chapter 7.)

> We are all only a slip of the foot away from disaster. Five years I stepped onto black ice, flipped up and landed on my head. Life changed in an instant. Driving, speech, vision, comprehension, and so on and so forth–traumatic brain damage seemed insurmountable. Friends whose children were in conventional schools said, "Aw, now you'll have to enroll your children in school." Homeschooling friends knew better and said, "Thank goodness you're homeschooling." For eight long months, while I slept 12 to 18 hours a day, our curriculum consisted of household management and brain physiology. We slowly resumed our routine. At no time did our yearly commitment to 875 hours of a sequentially progressive curriculum miss its target. Could that have happened in a state where we were tied to some governmental timetable?—From Opening Remarks, WPA Conference, 2000

Starting Homeschooling on Short Notice

Families who begin homeschooling on short notice often assume there's a standard set of textbooks and workbooks that homeschoolers use. This is understandable, since public schools cover certain subjects in each grade and use pretty much the same approach based on textbooks, worksheets, and homework.

However, homeschooling families are responsible for choosing their own materials and deciding how they will approach learning. This may seem overwhelming at first. But once you get used to the idea, it has many advantages. You can choose or develop a curriculum specifically for your children that will work much better than anything a conventional school could offer them. Think of the possibilities! You are working with one child or a small group of children you've known for a long time, not 25 to 30 kids you just met in September. You can focus on their individual strengths and interests and encourage them to learn in their own way and according to their own timetable. (Conventional classrooms would be chaotic if teachers tried that.) You are not limited to what you can bring into a classroom; you have the whole world to explore.

You may want to choose a curriculum similar to those used by conventional schools, or you decide a different approach would work better for your family. (When time allows, see Chapter 7 for more information about some of the possibilities available.) Many parents focus on what their children need to learn to lead effective adult lives, rather than on what they would be doing if they were attending a conventional school. They help their kids learn things like how to learn something new, get a job and keep it, relate to other people, manage money, cook, run a household.

Eight Possibilities for a Curriculum

Here are some suggestions that may help your thinking and planning.

Possibility #1 Follow a low cost or free curriculum similar to those conventional schools use. A book like Rebecca Rupp's *Home Learning Year by Year* outlines what conventional schools cover each year from pre-kindergarten through 12th grade and suggests books and other resources for each subject. Most of the books are available from the library, so you don't have to spend much money. Choose what you think will work best for your children, whether or not it's listed under the grade they're supposed to be in. It's fine to do math from second grade, science from third, and history from sixth. Keep records of topics you study and resources you use so you can develop a transcript at some point if you want or need to.

Possibility #2 Do learning activities you find in library books, on the Internet, at stores that sell learning supplies, and in the list at the end of this chapter. Choose activities that appeal to you and try them. Build on what works. Ignore the ones that you don't like. Don't worry about grade levels; pick things your kids enjoy. They'll learn more, and you won't have to worry about motivating them.

Here are some examples of books.

- *Family Learning: How to Help Your Children Succeed in School by Learning at Home* by William F. Russell
- *Family Math* by Jean Kerr Stenmark, Virginia H. Thompson, and Ruth Cossey
- *Parents Are Teachers, Too: Enriching Your Child's Frist Six Years* by Claudia Jones
- *The Teenage Liberation Handbook: How to Quit School and Get a Real Life and Education* by Grace Llewellyn
- *Trust the Children: An Activity Guide for Homeschooling and Alternative Learning* by Anna Kealoha
- *The Unschooling Handbook: How to Use the Whole World As Your Child's Classroom* by Mary Griffith

Possibility #3 Buy a conventional curriculum and follow it. See the information on purchasing a curriculum in Chapter 7. Some families enjoy having an official-looking curriculum in the house and find that it works well for them. Before you purchase a curriculum, especially an expensive one, it's generally a good idea to try some of the free or inexpensive possibilities listed in this chapter while you explore various possibilities. Look on the Internet, contact curriculum providers, and ask other homeschoolers what they use and what they like and don't like about it. Curriculums can be expensive, so you'll save time, money, and frustration if you do some research before you buy one.

Possibility #4 Encourage your children to pursue their interests and make that your curriculum. You can start with any topic. It doesn't have to sound academic or be a subject conventional schools teach. The more interested your kids are, the easier it will be for them to learn and the less you will have to motivate them. Studying any topic will most likely cover the basic subjects required by Wisconsin law (reading, language arts, mathematics, social studies, science and health). So let them choose music, football, chess, motorcycles, cosmetology, fishing, etc. See "Unit Studies" in Chapter 7 and "Homeschooling Teens Who Don't Like School Work" in Chapter 11 (which includes a curriculum based on motorcycles).

Possibility #5 Do in-depth academic work. For ideas, see "Build a Subject-Specific Purchased Curriculum" in Chapter 7 and websites such as the Well-Trained Mind Forum (http://forums.welltrainedmind.com/). Many homeschoolers find such explorations fascinating and continue to pursue them throughout their lives.

Possibility #6 Use the Internet. Many resources are available, lots of them free. You can find lesson plans, worksheets, sites especially for kids, and much more. Homeschooling websites like A to Z Home's Cool http://homeschooling.gomilpitas.com/ are good places to start. Of course, you can use just plain information that's available at many websites; it doesn't have to be organized as lesson plans or labeled as school work. Or check out MOOCs or enroll in online courses. See "Using the Internet" in Chapter 8.

Possibility #7 Develop a curriculum based on CLEP and AP tests. Young people homeschooling for high school can do high school work and earn college credit inexpensively. See "The Many Uses of CLEP and AP Tests" in Chapter 8.

Possibility #8 Learn from life experience, sometimes referred to as unschooling. A number of activities are listed here to give you some idea of the range of possibilities. Use them in any way that works for your family. Modify them so they fit the ages, needs, personalities, interests, and unique situation of your family. Many families find it helps to involve their kids in the planning and preparation. This may mean less work for parents, and kids (and adults) may be more likely to participate in activities they helped choose. (Parents, of course, eliminate inappropriate or unsafe activities.)

These activities are worthwhile in and of themselves, whether or not you expect to learn from them. But people do learn. Therefore, they can be counted as part of the "875 hours of instruction" and "sequentially progressive curriculum" required by Wisconsin law. To emphasize that point, each activity is followed by the names of some of the conventional academic subjects that could be learned. The claim is not being made that children will learn all the basic subject that they need from these activities. But many parents find it helpful to realize that children can learn the basics from such activities.

If you've been homeschooling for a while and want to take a break and perhaps explore different approaches, you could set aside the curriculum you've been using and just do these activities. Or you could spend less time on your current curriculum. You could do these activities for a week and return to a more conventional curriculum, or do things like this for the rest of your life, learning as you go. At some point, you may want to read Chapter 7 for more ideas about curriculum and learning resources.

Try to find time to listen to your kids' questions and, if they want you to, help them look for answers to some. (Also consider learning to be comfortable with questions that don't have answers. See Michael Ross's *Sandbox Scientist.*) But don't wear yourself (and your kids) out by constantly looking for opportunities to "teach" them something. Focus on their strengths, especially if they have been in a conventional school situation that emphasized their weaknesses.

If your kids complain that they are bored, congratulate yourself: You have managed to help them find some free time that they can decide what to do with. Ask them what they would like to do. List possibilities they can choose from.

Possible Learning Activities

These activities can be used to supplement any curriculum.

• Go to the library. Visit the children's section, no matter how old you are. Many nonfiction children's books provide basic, easy-to-understand explanations of complex topics, like how computers work. Check the adult section for books on other countries, history, and crafts; appropriate magazines and other periodicals; music; etc. Investigate other library resources: DVDs, CDs, recorded books, etc. See Chapter 8. (Learning possibilities: Reading, how to use the library, music, just about any subject)

• Visit a near-by nature area, your own yard or neighborhood, or a park. Take a picnic. Enjoy being outside, looking, and listening. (Science, physical education, esthetics)

• Check out the Wisconsin Department of Tourism. Plan a trip, deciding where you would go, what routes you would take, what you would do, and how much the trip would cost. If possible, take the trip. (Geography, science, math, reading)

• Make baker's clay by mixing together 4 cups of flour, 1 cup salt, and 1 1/2 cups of water (with food coloring, if desired). Knead until smooth. Shape. Bake in a 300 degree oven until dry, about an hour, depending on size and thickness of the pieces. Paint or color with magic markers. (Art, math)

• Choose a craft you know little or nothing about. Ask someone with experience for help getting started, perhaps explaining that this is part of your homeschool. Many people are glad to be asked. Get some supplies and be creative. (Art, problem solving, math)

• Visit a pet store, looking even at animals that do not appeal to you at first. Try to find a clerk who is not too busy to answer questions. If possible, get a new pet or provide foster care for animals from the Humane Society. Observe and keep records. Draw pictures. Do research on the Internet or at the library. (Science, math, reading, writing, art, taking responsibility)

• Color Dover http://store.doverpublications.com/by-subject-coloring-books.html or other detailed coloring books on other countries, history, famous people, designs, animals, anatomy, etc. (Art, subjects the coloring books cover, such as social studies, history, science)

• Use DVDs (perhaps from the library) to learn about science, other countries and history (both fiction and non-fiction), new skills (exercises, cooking, crafts, etc.), and more. Check out MOOCs and sites like Khan Academy (kindergarten through 12th grade) http://www.khanacademy.org/ (Subjects the DVDs or courses cover)

• Reorganize part of your house. Involve as many people as possible in deciding how to store tools and supplies that are most important so they are easy to find and put away. Get rid of things you don't use. Try to provide a large flat surface (besides the kitchen table) where people can work on projects for several days. (Home economics, planning and organizational skills)

• Paint or wallpaper a room. Choose the colors, learn how to prepare the walls, apply the paint or paper, etc. Study design, its history, cultural perspectives, etc. (Art, math, social studies)

• Choose a country. Think of as many ways as possible to learn about it. Read fiction and non-fiction books and watch DVDs. Visit stores with imports from the country. Cook food or eat at a restaurant that offers food from the country. Meet people from the country. Make a traditional costume. Have a party using the country as a theme. Draw a map. Make a book. Visit the country. (Social studies, reading, home economics)

• Plant a garden. Study seed catalogs and gardening websites. Find an experienced gardener. Offer to help in their garden so you can learn from them. Visit a farmers' market for ideas. Learn to sprout seeds. (Science, nutrition, math)

• Buy or build a food dehydrator. Dry different foods and have taste tests. (Science, nutrition, industrial arts if you build it yourself)

• Learn to do something new with the car, like checking fluids, changing the oil and spark plugs, or rotating the tires. (Auto mechanics)

• Fix something that is broken, or do something to improve your home. Put up a shelf or coat hooks, replace a cracked window, or build a bookcase. (Problem solving, reading if you consult books for information, industrial arts, wood working)

• Visit museums. Call the curator, schedule a tour of an area of special interest. Ask if you can use their library. (Science, social studies, language arts)

• Go to a music store and learn about the instruments available and how they sound. If possible, rent or buy one and teach yourself to play, take lessons, or ask someone who plays the instrument to help you get started. (Music)

• Take voice lessons or get recorded lessons. Sing alone or with others, before or after meals, riding in the car, and at other times. Explore songs from other countries. (Music)

• Read aloud. Take turns choosing books. Good books appeal to a wide range of ages. Picture books with attractive art work appeal to all ages, and many young children enjoy listening to books that are supposedly written for older ones, especially while they be part of a cozy family group. Don't insist that children sit still; some people listen better if they can move around. Offer children the opportunity to read aloud if they want to, but don't pressure them. It is more challenging to read aloud than silently, and it's more important that reading be a pleasant activity than that children learn to read aloud well at a young age. (Reading, plus whatever subjects are covered by the books you are reading)

• Interview a person with a job that interests you, an older person, or someone else you want to talk with. Plan questions ahead. Record the interview and take photos, if this is easy and people are comfortable with it. Write about parts of the interview and possibly create a book. (Social studies, writing)

• Put up maps and locate places that come up in reading or conversation. (Geography)

• Do "free writing" as a family. Everyone writes for 10 minutes without stopping. (People who are not yet writing conventional words can draw.) If you can't think of anything to write, just write "I can't think of anything to write" over and over until you think of something. For now, don't worry about spelling or punctuation; it is more important to enjoy writing than to do it perfectly. (Writing)

• Make your own books. Fold paper and cardboard together down the middle and sew along the fold by hand or machine, or find more detailed instructions. Decorate the cover. Draw, write, paste pictures, whatever. Or have books commercially printed with digital photos and your writing. (Art, writing)

• Cook something you've never cooked before. (Home economics)

Chapter 7

Curriculums and Learning Resources

Homeschoolers learn in many different ways. We choose from many different approaches to learning, from unschooling to purchasing a complete curriculum and following an approach similar to conventional schools. Sometimes having so many choices seems overwhelming. But it's also one of the major advantages to homeschooling. We can choose approaches that work well at a given time for our particular family, based on the strengths, needs, and learning styles of each family member; our philosophy and beliefs; and our particular circumstances, including where we live, what resources we have available, and what else is going on in our lives. We can use different approaches for different topics, perhaps using a purchased curriculum for math, and movies and historical fiction for history. We can change approaches that don't work or that used to work but no longer do. We learn now, in the present, what we need to know today. We also prepare for the future because in addition to what we are learning, we are learning how to learn, so we can keep up with a rapidly changing world and add things we missed earlier. A lot of unplanned learning also happens spontaneously. It's exciting and sometimes confusing, gratifying and sometimes frustrating. Homeschooling brings us together as families and enables us to take responsibility for our lives. Wisconsin's homeschooling law allows us to homeschool in the way that works for our family right now, to make changes, without having to get permission from school officials or have our children take standardized tests.

Some Suggestions and Ideas You May Want to Ponder

• There is no one right or best way to homeschool. Many homeschoolers think in terms of developing a homeschool that works for their family rather than choosing one approach and sticking with it. They recognize that learning happens in many different ways. They investigate approaches to homeschooling (like unschooling or developing your own curriculum) that they don't expect to adopt themselves, just to learn what they can from these other approaches. They draw strength from learning about and using different approaches as they consider who they are, and who they could be, as homeschoolers.

If you choose this approach and wonder what to say when another homeschoolers asks you what approach you use, consider the response of the parent who said, "We're eclectic homeschoolers. We do what works." (Note: Various people define the term "eclectic homeschooling" in different ways.)

• Homeschoolers in Wisconsin are not required to do what teachers and students in conventional schools do. Knowing this can be very freeing and open all kinds of possibilities. We can encourage kids to ask questions, all kinds of questions, even when we don't know the answers and can't easily find them. We can learn more broadly and deeply if we don't limit our thinking to conventional schooling. Anyone can do this, of course, but homeschoolers have more time and opportunities than children who put a lot of their time and energy into attending conventional schools. Also, some of what happens in school undermines learning. Bullying, humiliation, competition, fear, strict schedules, and continuous interruptions make it difficult for children to learn. Schools don't do this deliberately. It's partly a result of trying to educate 20 to 30 kids in one room at the same time

This means conventional schools are not good models for homeschools because the situations are so different. Homeschoolers may do what schools do when it makes sense and is consistent with their goals. But it's important to remember that as homeschoolers we don't have to do what conventional schools do.

But conventional schooling is so deeply ingrained in our society and in our own thinking that it can be hard to hold onto this idea and not feel guilty or inadequate when kids spend a day playing or can't do long division when the kid next door can and they're a year younger! Some parents work to deschool themselves so they they're in a better position to take advantage of the opportunities homeschooling offers. Consider the work of John Holt (whose book *Learning All the Time* is a good place to start) and Ivan Illich's classic book *Deschooling Society*. *Growing Without Schooling*, the wonderful homeschooling magazine Holt founded, was published from August 1977 until October 2001. It's now available at http://www.holtgws.com/gwsarchives.html and is a treasure trove of ideas, support, and information.

• Families vary in how they balance guidance from parents and encouraging kids to take responsibility for their own learning. Sometimes there are no easy answers, but it helps to recognize the questions and possible responses and to keep communication channels open as people express themselves and listen to each other.

• Consider involving your kids in the process of planning your homeschool. Pay attention to their interests and the ways they learn. Does one remember what they read while another prefers to listen to information and a third does best with hands-on activities? Do they learn more if they can do gymnastics while you read aloud or take frequent breaks to run around the house and yard? Does one handle numbers easily but have trouble spelling? One major advantage to homeschooling is that people can learn in different ways, following the learning style and timetable that suits them. (Many learning disabilities could be resolved by simply giving kids time to mature.) Parents sometimes find it hard to really believe how different people in the same family can be, but often the more that individual differences can be recognized and respected, the more smoothly homeschooling may go. (For more

information, see the Myers Briggs personality types and books like Susan Cain's *Quiet: The Power of Introverts in a World That Can't Stop Talking.*)
• Ask "What if . . .?" "What if we read this textbook on world history cover to cover?" "What if we didn't even mention grammar for the next month?" "What if we unschooled?"

The conventionally schooled adult followed the directions carefully. One cup warm water, one tablespoon vinegar, three drops of red food coloring, stir, add one hard-boiled egg. Result: a respectable, solid red egg. The homeschooled child asked, "What if we used all vinegar?" He put an egg in the vinegar and added three drops of red and two of blue. "A color explosion."

• Most families use approaches that have varying degrees of structure, some with low structure, some with high, and some in between. Some of this structure is internal, coming from within the family. Some is external, coming from an outside source such as an online course, a teacher-led activity like drama, or a purchased curriculum. Some is in between. For example, learning math at the supermarket is low structure and internal structure. Purchasing a math curriculum and working through it with the kids a few times a week is medium structure and external structure. Purchasing a conventional school math curriculum and following the suggested schedule of lessons, exercises, and reviews so as to finish it according to a conventional school schedule would be high structure and external structure. Some families find that analyzing the levels of structure in various approaches to learning helps them realize that they are already doing activities with varying levels of structure and makes them aware of the possibilities that are available. It also helps keep families from thinking that some options are unavailable to them because they are or are not "highly structured" or "unschoolers" or whatever label might potentially limit their thinking and choices.

The amount of structure a homeschool has is also influenced by other factors. Daily events such as regularly scheduled meals, time for reading aloud, religious practices, playing a musical instrument, and time outside regardless of the weather add structure that many homeschooling families find helpful.
• Homeschooling parents have times when they are convinced that no one is learning anything. It goes with the territory. It's a good time to call another homeschooler for support. (It's a bad time to call your worst critic!) You can also take a break from academics. For support and reassurance, see chapters 17 and 18. Remember that you **can** homeschool, regardless of your own school experience, what degrees you have (or don't have), how challenging your children's school experiences were, and what else is going on in your life. You know your children, you love them, and you can learn with them. You don't have to know everything your kids want or need to learn. They can use the library, learning resources, tutors, mentors, the Internet, and other sources. No matter what approach you are using, your kids will learn in spontaneous, unplanned ways and surprise you with what they know.

A father in our support group years ago said, "It's too bad children don't come with an indicator light, like the ones in your car. Just a little light on their forehead, with a sign saying 'Learning Now in Progress.' We could look at a child playing with blocks or running around the yard with her brother or reading a comic book, see that the light was on, and be reassured."–From Opening Remarks, WPA Conference, 2005

We know that our children are not pieces of clay that we mold or vessels that we fill. Knowledge is not gained in this fashion and development cannot be rushed.

We allow our children to be children, being ever watchful that everything has an appropriate time. And we give them that time to unearth the wonders of their world–to create without criticism–to ponder complex ideas and to draw their own conclusions. We know how difficult it is to trust that our children will learn when the time is right. In our fast-paced society where the trend is to push academics at younger and younger ages, we try to be patient while providing an environment where our children may learn at their own pace. Some years, this creates an inner struggle because we wonder if growth and learning are even happening. During these times, we may even see our children take one step backward before taking two or three forward. Today, we celebrate our ability to look beyond those feelings of doubt and uncertainty that we have from time to time.–From Opening Remarks, WPA Conference, 2004

• Accept the fact that, no matter which approach you choose, how much time you spend, or how hard you try, you and your kids will miss something important. Kids attending conventional schools don't learn everything, or even everything they're supposedly taught. You don't have to include everything conventional schools supposedly cover. Neither you nor your kids nor any professional educator knows specifically what your kids will need to know as adults. But that's okay. Your kids will be able to learn what they need when they need it, as long as they know how to learn and what to do when they don't know something. The more ways you have approached learning as a homeschooler, the more tools they will have at their disposal.

• Keep academics in perspective. We call what we do home**schooling**. We do it instead of sending our children to school. So it's tempting to focus on academics. To be sure, learning is important. But experienced homeschoolers know that academics are not the only part, or even the most important part, of homeschooling. They may consider it more important to be able to manage money wisely than to know how to calculate percentages, or to be a responsible and honest young person than to understand nuclear physics, to be kind and gentle than to be able to solve an equation. Of course, we want our children to learn both academics and the other things that are more important. But sometimes we have to choose. Sometimes too much emphasis on academics undermines our larger goals and takes up time that we need to work on them. Many families use academics to serve their larger goals.

So don't let concerns about academics interfere with your enjoyment of your children or rob them of their childhood. Your kids will want to learn to read, use numbers, figure out how the world works or what happened in the past. They'll ask you and other people for help. Spend a reasonable amount of time on academics. But make sure your kids also have time to play, daydream, make a mess, be bored, exercise, be creative, get to know themselves and each other and you, learn about religion, sleep, do work that matters, decide between right and wrong, and so on. Take time to play in the snow, go bowling, watch a movie, talk about life, clean the garage, go for pizza, share religious and moral values, sing, read aloud, and laugh and cry together. Your kids will learn invaluable lessons, and so will you.

We celebrate those moments that at the time seem so profound–when the light suddenly goes on in our son's mind and long division finally makes sense. We celebrate those moments that at the time seemed so small–when our daughter apologizes for saying something hurtful to a friend. And then suddenly we realize we have it backwards. Academic skills have value but having compassion is priceless.–From Opening Remarks, WPA Conference, 2004

Approaches to Curriculum

Here are some of the many approaches to homeschooling. They are listed roughly from more structured to less just so there's some logical organization. This is not intended to imply that either purchasing a curriculum like conventional schools use or unschooling (or any other approach) is right or best.

Wisconsin's homeschooling law requires that homeschoolers have a "sequentially progressive curriculum," but this does not mean we have to adopt and follow the standardized curriculum that conventional schools use. A curriculum is a plan of study, so each approach in this chapter, including unschooling, is referred to as a curriculum. "Purchased curriculum" means a program that someone else has developed to cover a specific subject or topic, such as third grade math, world history for 10th graders, plant physiology, or auto repair. It can be a textbook; a whole package that includes reading materials, worksheets, instructions for hands-on activities, and supplies; or a live or recorded course. Labels for various approaches, such as "Your Own Curriculum Based on Conventional School Subjects" are designed to be clear and specific but are sometimes rather awkward.

There are a variety of ways to learn about curriculums and learning resources. Read this chapter and other books about homeschooling. Consult websites like A to Z Home's Cool. Talk with other homeschoolers. Join a support group. Attend the WPA conference. Think about how you've learned the things that matter to you. Watch your kids, listen to your kids, think about how your kids learn and what they enjoy.

The approaches explored here overlap and are not crisp, clear-cut programs but rather tools you can use to develop your family's homeschool. The intent is to give you some general ideas about curriculums and learning resources and suggestions for possible ways to learn more about them. The resources cited are examples to help you get started. WPA does not officially recommend or endorse any curriculums or learning resources. Suggestions for ways of choosing approaches to use appear at the end of the chapter.

Purchase a Complete Curriculum Package

This approach is listed first because it's similar to what conventional schools do and therefore familiar, and because it's the most structured.

A number of publishers offer packages that include subjects generally covered in conventional public or private schools for a given grade level. For example, a fifth grade curriculum would probably include textbooks and workbooks for reading, spelling, math, science, social studies, and perhaps also art, music, religion, practical skills like cooking, and more. Some packages also include materials for science experience and art projects, lesson plans, daily schedules, and other teacher resources. Some publishers offer full-service curriculums in which children's work is sent to the publisher for grading. Some award credits for courses completed and perhaps also diplomas.

Among the reasons some homeschoolers purchase a complete curriculum package:

• A complete curriculum package is convenient. The subjects to be covered have been organized, and materials are provided. Parents don't have to plan lessons and gather materials. This may be particularly helpful to families who have decided they need to homeschool (perhaps because the situation in their local public school is unacceptable) but are not sure how.

• Many purchased curriculums are similar to those used in most conventional schools, so homeschoolers can cover the same material in the same grades as students in conventional schools.

• A purchased curriculum can provide the equivalent of material covered in a specialized conventional private school based on a religion or an educational philosophy, such as Montessori or Waldorf.

Before purchasing a curriculum, especially an expensive one, many families learn as much about it as they can. They explore publishers' websites and, when possible, request samples. They read reviews on the Internet and in homeschooling magazines and books. They ask other homeschoolers which curriculums they have used and what they liked and didn't like about them.

Remember that you can use these curriculums flexibly, skipping parts that don't work well for your family, supplementing freely with library and other resources, and following your own schedule if the one provided doesn't serve your needs.

Here are a few examples of curriculum publishers. (Remember that WPA does not endorse or recommend any particular curriculum or approach to education.) These curriculums vary widely in their orientation, content, philosophy of education, approach to learning, and cost.

Religious

A Beka Book http://www.abeka.com/
Accelerated Christian Education http://www.aceministries.com/
Alpha Omega Publications http://www.aop.com/
Bob Jones University Press http://www.bjupresshomeschool.com/
Christian Liberty Academy http://www.homeschools.org/
Christian Light Publications http://www.clp.org/
Clonlara School Home Based Education Program http://www.clonlara.org/home
Covenant Home Curriculum http://www.covenanthome.com/
KONOS http://www.konos.com/www/
Moore Homeschooling http://www.moorefoundation.com/
Seton Home Study School http://www.setonhome.org/
Sonlight Curriculum http://www.sonlight.com/

Secular

Oak Meadow Curriculum and School http://www.oakmeadow.com/
Pearson Homeschool http://www.pearsonhomeschool.com/

Begin with an Outline of a Conventional Curriculum

You can start with an outline of what most conventional schools cover in each subject in each grade. Some are simply a list of topics. (An example is World Book's Typical Course of Study, although there are websites that provide links for the topics listed.) Others include suggested resources. (An example is Rebecca Rupp's *Home Learning Year by Year.*) In either case, you have to find the resources that you want to use, but you don't have to pay for things you don't want. This approach gives you some structural support while freeing you from someone else's ideas about how specifically to go about learning each topic.

An outline is much, much less expensive than a complete curriculum, especially since you can get many of the resources used or from the library. It is easy to modify an outline to meet your children's unique strengths, interests, needs, learning styles, and timetable. You can choose a grade level in each subject area that works for each child. (For example, a child might use reading materials from the second grade level, math from third, and science from fourth, regardless of their age.) You can spend more time on some subjects than others. You can emphasize the types of resources and approaches to learning that work best for you. It often works well to compare several different outlines and pick what you want from each.

Here are a few resources:

Home Learning Year by Year: How to Design a Homeschool Curriculum from Preschool Through High School by Rebecca Rupp

The Three R's: Grades K-3 and *You Can Teach Your Child Successfully: Grades 4-8* by Ruth Beechick.

Typical Courses of Study, Kindergarten through Grade 12 by World Book http://www.worldbook.com

The Well-Trained Mind: A Guide to Classical Education at Home by Jessie Wise and Susan Wise Bauer.

What Your Kindergartner Needs to Know through *What Your Sixth Grader Needs to Know,* edited by E. D. Hirsch

Enroll in Online Courses, Distance Learning, MOOCs, and Others

Computers and the Internet are dramatically changing the field of distance learning. High school, college, and graduate credits and degrees can be earned through online courses, some of which allow students and teachers to interact in real time. MOOCs (massive open online courses) are increasingly available, many at no cost. Many do not grant credit.

Many homeschoolers find this an area worth exploring. A lot of exciting information is readily available. Courses for credit are often relatively expensive, but some families feel it is worth the cost to have someone outside the family supervise and grade students' work and/or to receive a third-party diploma granted by an institution outside their homeschool. Some programs also offer consultation and support for homeschooling parents. In addition, learning is usually through a computer rather than practical, hands-on, real world experience, and the overall approach is based on a conventional school model. Some homeschoolers are fine with this; others question it and work to limit computer time, especially for young children.

For more information, do an Internet search, talk with homeschoolers who have experience in this area, and visit online forums and chat rooms.

Build a Subject-Specific Purchased Curriculum

Many families buy individual curriculums on appropriate grade levels for as many subjects as they want to study in this way. Then they add other subjects that they want to approach in different ways. So a child might use a third grade math curriculum from one publisher; a fourth grade history textbook from another; and learn science by watching documentaries, reading library books, and spending time outdoors.

Here are some suggestions for using this approach.

• Evaluate each possible area of study separately and choose the curriculum that best suits your family. Ways to explore the possibilities for purchased curriculums include the following:

—Ask homeschoolers you know if you can look at curriculums they use. There is nothing like getting your hands on an actual curriculum or textbook for evaluating how well it would work for your own family.

—Post inquiries to Internet-based curriculum-oriented forums, like the Well-Trained Mind Forum http://forums.welltrainedmind.com. (You do not have to agree with the homeschooling approach advocated by a forum to do research on it and gather ideas.) Also, research past threads on Internet-based curriculum-oriented forums. Others parents may have had the same questions you do, even when your questions seem very specific. Large forums have room for all kinds of questions and answers.

—Post inquiries to your local homeschool support group email list or ask at support group get-togethers.

• Be prepared to change curriculums as often as necessary. When one curriculum isn't working for your family, it often pays to research alternatives rather than abandoning formal study of the subject. Curriculums from different publishers on the same subject for same grade level can vary widely. Also, a curriculum that worked great in the past may need to be changed as your kids grow and change. The publisher of the biology curriculum that so excited your child last year may have a physics curriculum that is not nearly as good a match. In addition, a given publisher's textbooks and curriculums covering the same subject may vary from grade to grade, meaning you may really like the ones for the lower grades but are unsatisfied with those for high school or vice versa. Don't assume you can judge a whole series that covers kindergarten through twelfth grade by looking at one or two grade levels.

• Above all, remember that you are in control of how you homeschool. Choosing to use a purchased curriculum does not mean that it can tell you what to do. You can unchoose it or alter it. Impressive schedules and lists of assignments that are often part of such curriculums are merely suggestions from someone who has never met you or your kids. No one, no matter how much formal education they have, how big an institution they work for, how charismatically they speak, or how nice their publicity looks, cares more about your kids than you do or is in a better position than you are to figure out what they need.

Advantages to this approach include the fact that a packaged curriculum or textbook for a specific subject offers kids an introduction to a lot of ideas and information about a topic in an orderly, logical, and relatively efficient way. Parents and kids don't have to start from scratch, find an assortment of resources from various places, and organize them in a way that makes sense. Kids find out what other people think and have thought about the topic. They are exposed to materials similar to those presented in conventional schools, although a homeschooler's experience with the materials is likely to be different from that of kids in conventional schools. Homeschoolers can pursue some areas of interest in greater depth and spend less time on others, skip some areas (as long as they aren't essential background for later material). Homeschoolers can create their own daily schedule, perhaps spending several hours on different subjects on different days rather than 47 minutes on each subject each day. The flexibility available to homeschoolers makes a difference in how and what they learn.

Many homeschoolers using purchased curriculums and textbooks are careful to avoid the negative ways such learning resources are used in conventional schools. In conventional schools, such resources are part of a rigid schedule that requires each student to cover specific material each day, week, and school year, regardless of their individual learning styles, interests, previous knowledge, or readiness to learn the material in question. Conventional schools use curriculums as part of their system of ranking students so a few are on top, most are on the bottom, and no one is too unhappy about their position. Competition and humiliation are also used. Because of the negative ways in which conventional schools often use textbooks, some homeschoolers choose not to use them and sometimes choose not to use any purchased curriculums as well. (Some purchased curriculums are not based on textbooks.) Other homeschoolers enjoy and find value in including some carefully selected and carefully used textbooks and purchased curriculums as part of their learning.

Families who choose this approach may have questions about allocating time between curricular studies and hobbies, passions, social time, and "down" time. Here are some suggestions.

• Decide how important the pace of progress through a curriculum is to you. Do you want to be sure your kids stay at grade level in one or more subjects such as math? Are you unconcerned about how much history they learn as long as they continue to read some historical fiction or narratives?

• Some families love a sense of routine and predictability and like to write up detailed daily and even hourly schedules based on about how many hours each week they want to spend on each subject, or how many math lessons they need to complete, or some other criterion. First efforts at scheduling usually prove far too ambitious. But if you remember that you are in control and no one is forcing you to follow the schedule, you can alter it in good humor until it's realistic. But then as soon as you figure it out, something is likely to change so you'll need to alter it again. Adjustments show that you know how to approach life and learning with flexibility, creativity, sensitivity, good humor, and intelligence.

• Families who follow any kind of schedule often like to take periodic breaks for perhaps a day or a week, leaving more time for unusual pursuits. They generally find this time delightful and rejuvenating and have a new appreciation for the schedule when they return to it.

Some even build several breaks into their yearly schedule, which they see as their schedule, to follow when it's helpful and break from when they want to.

• Other families have little or no interest in a pre-planned schedule. They generally devote some time each day or week to their curricular and other studies. This can be a good option for families who are not particularly concerned about how quickly they work through various resources. It allows them to take advantage of whatever opportunities come along, and kids can work on whatever subjects most interest them at any given time.

Follow a Curriculum Based on a Specific Philosophy of Education

Some homeschoolers base their curriculum on a specific philosophy of education, modifying principles and methods used in brick and mortar alternative schools to suit their homeschools. They either purchase curriculums based on these approaches or develop their own using the basic philosophy for guidance. Among the approaches that could be considered in this general category are Charlotte Mason, Classical Education, Montessori, Thomas Jefferson Education, and Waldorf. A discussion of these philosophies and methods is beyond the scope of this book. However, resources are readily available for each. One place to learn more is the Methods and Styles section of the A to Z Home's Cool website, http://homeschooling.gomilpitas.com/

Develop Your Own Curriculum Based on Conventional School Subjects

Many families begin by choosing conventional school subjects that they want their children to be exposed to. One place to begin is with those required by Wisconsin's homeschooling law: reading, language arts, math, social studies, science and health. Then they add subjects such as arts and crafts, art appreciation, foreign language, music appreciation and performance, religion, and practical skills (homemaking, mechanics, industrial arts, gardening). The 875 hours of instruction required by Wisconsin law can be in any combination of required and added subject areas. See Chapter 3.

Many families using this approach then decide which subjects they want to start with, what the next step is for each, and what resources they want to use. They may also make a "someday/maybe" list for subjects and topics that they want to cover someday and don't want to forget. Such a list may free them to concentrate fully on the next steps. (For more about this approach to list making and organization, see David Allen's *Getting Things Done* and his website.)

> One parent wrote about this approach: "I call this approach 'winging it' in the sense that I have no specific plan or schedule to adhere to (except for a sense of things that everyone should know/be exposed to) and therefore just go day to day with what seems to be working. I also have the sense that we are flying high on an adventure. I don't think of myself as an unschooler, because I do direct what my kids do for large parts of the day ('Time to read Gulliver's Travels, now!'), but my directions do not come from a preconceived plan either."

An **enormous** number of learning resources are available to homeschoolers today. The problem is not finding them; it's avoiding feeling overwhelmed. Here are some suggestions:

• Ask other homeschoolers what has and hasn't worked for them.

• Visit websites such as A to Z Home's Cool at www.homeschooling.gomilpitas.com, Annenberg Learner (teacher resources, lesson plans, etc. for kindergarten through 12th grade), http://www.learner.org/, Rebecca Rupp's website http://www.rebecca-ruppresources.com/, *Home Education Magazine* at www.home-ed-magazine.com, the Well-Trained Mind Forum http://forums.welltrainedmind.com, TED talks http://www.ted.com/

• Investigate websites that offer free online courses such as Khan Academy (kindergarten through 12th grade) http://www.khanacademy.org/ and Coursera https://www.

coursera.org/. This relatively new field is changing and expanding rapidly, so do an Internet search for online courses to find up to date information.

• Read online reviews and comments.

• Attend the WPA Conference where many workshops include suggested resources, and you can talk with other homeschoolers.

• Libraries are a very valuable resource, both when you are looking for material on a specific subject you want to cover and when you are browsing and run into something that looks potentially interesting. See the section on libraries in Chapter 8.

• Many of the best learning resources are not "educational materials" you buy but parts of the real world like kitchen equipment, tools, sewing machines, fishing tackle. Kids are drawn to real things, especially those belonging to people they care about.

Here are a few of the many ways to study a subject. (These examples are not intended to be a year's worth of study in any of the subjects listed.)

Reading and language arts for a younger child: Listen to stories being read aloud. Learn to recognize and write your name. Tell someone about going sledding. Make a phonics notebook with pictures of things that start with a given letter on each page. Play games like "I'm going to Grandmother's house and I'm going to take an alligator, a banana, and a circus tent." (Each person in turn repeats what previous players have said and adds an object that starts with the next letter of the alphabet.)

Reading and language arts for a teen: Read novels from a country and century you choose. Research the authors' lives. Participate in an online group on a topic of interest. Write a letter each week to a friend, relative, legislator, etc. Make a presentation in front of your 4–H group, church group, or other people.

Math for a younger child: Build with Legos. Get an allowance and spend it. Work on the Miquon math series.

Math for a teen: Balance the family checkbook; write checks for your parent to sign. Open your own checking account. Buy the family groceries, staying within a budget. Work on geometry books from Key Curriculum.

Social studies for any age: Choose a country. Read fiction and non-fiction books and watch DVDs. Cook food from the country. Visit import stores. Meet people from the country. Travel to the country.

Books such as those listed above under curriculum outlines can be helpful in developing your own curriculum based on basic subjects. If you want ideas for how to study history, for example, look in the history sections, choosing what appeals to your family, not being limited by grade levels or trying to cover everything.

Create a Curriculum Based on Unit Studies

Unit studies focus on a particular topic rather than an academic subject. They can help you organize the learning you want to do, stay motivated, be flexible so you can meet each individual's needs, keep records, and, if necessary, demonstrate to others that your kids are learning. Individuals can do their own solo unit studies or several siblings can work together on the same topic or project, each working in their own way and at their own level. This is one way to homeschool children of different ages.

A unit study can be any length and depth you want. After half an hour, you may decide you know enough about earthworms. Or what starts as a unit on rocks could lead to a career in geology. When you start a unit, you don't have to know how much time and energy you want to spend. People of any age can do unit studies. Children and parents can plan together. Parents can do units of their own. Kids can learn to take responsibility for their own learning, learn how to learn, and become lifelong learners. Unit studies can be the foundation of your curriculum or you can include them with whatever else you are doing.

You can buy individual unit studies, find websites on unit studies, or purchase curriculums based on them. But many families prefer the ones they create. Here's one way:

• Start with a topic you want to learn about (like butterflies, baking bread, or Bulgaria). It doesn't have to be something most people consider academic. Unit studies can be primarily thinking, such as trigonometry or the philosophy of John Locke, or primarily practical, such as baking cookies, driving a car, or refinishing furniture, or a combination.

• Plan. Consider questions like: What do we already know about this topic? What can we figure out for ourselves? (There are big advantages to getting raw materials and discovering things for yourself.) When can we go to the library? Who do we know who could help us learn more? What field trips or other activities could we do? (Books can be very helpful, but things you and the kids do almost always make a stronger, more lasting impression.)

• Go to the library. See Chapter 8.

• Do what makes sense with the topic you have chosen. Experiment. Talk with others. Read. Do stuff. Take one step at a time.

• Finish. Take five minutes (or more) to make at least a few notes or have your kids make them. Possible things to include: topic, who participated, dates, most helpful resources, a few of the things you learned, academic subjects covered (reading, language arts, math, etc.), things you'd do differently next time, and ideas for future units.

A few practical suggestions: Although it's tempting to demonstrate one's excitement about a new interest or project by buying equipment and supplies, many families fine it works better to spend as little money as possible at first, so they're freer to end units that aren't working. (For example, essential equipment can be cobbled together, borrowed, or bought used.) But on the other hand, relatively high quality equipment and supplies are often required to give a topic a fair trial. Tubes of water color paints that artists use and a good brush are much more satisfying to work with than an inexpensive box of colored squares and a brush that's losing its bristles. Very few people would enjoy playing (or listening to) a piano that's out of tune or a violin that's the wrong size and incapable of producing good sound.

Perhaps most important of all, just plunge in. Don't try to find the beginning. Most subjects don't have a beginning; they're all interconnected. Use common sense and start with the thinner book with larger type and more illustrations or the recipe that has five ingredients and seven steps rather than one that has 29 ingredients and takes two days (that is, unless you're the type who thrives when faced with a real challenge.) But don't worry if you don't understand very much of what you do or read at first, and don't wait to find a book or web page titled *An Introduction to Field Mice.* Just start doing things and reading stuff, understand what you can, and let the rest wash over you. You'll probably be amazed at how soon you'll run into the same words and concepts, understand some of the vocabulary, and find things starting to make sense. Being willing and able to plunge into a new subject is an important life skill. Don't underestimate it!

Don't get overwhelmed by how much one could learn on any given subject. Learn as much as you need or want for now, and let the rest go until later, or forever. Don't try to work all the basic subjects into each unit. If you think you're not doing enough of an important subject (often it's math or spelling), you can either find learning resources to fill the gap, or you can do a unit on multiplication or trigonometry or making words plural or whatever is missing.

Unschool

Unschoolers generally focus on learning from life experience and pursuing their interests and projects at home and in their community. This learning is learner-led and does not rely on textbooks or purchased curriculums. Kids (and adults) learn a great deal in this way, whether they consider themselves "unschoolers" or not. This is not to say that kids will learn everything they need this way, and unschoolers may sometimes add unit studies or learning resources, use a purchased curriculum, or take a live or online course when that makes sense. But kids do learn a lot without formal lessons. If you need to prove to your mother, a prospective employer, a college admissions officer, your kids, or yourself that real learning is happening, you can review your records, photo albums, and memories, and translate what your kids have done into conventional school subjects. See Chapter 10.

Among the advantages to unschooling for all or part of your curriculum are that kids are often highly motivated when they're doing something they're really interested in, especially if they have been involved in choosing it. People discover interests they might not have found in a conventional school curriculum. Many people find it more exciting to discover something for themselves than to be taught. Because this learning is not associated with grade levels, kids have opportunities to work on things that are more challenging than conventional school materials might give them credit for being able to handle. Kids who "don't like school" or have had negative school experiences (including being labeled things like "learning disabled") often thrive and learn a great deal.

So how do you go about unschooling? One approach is to ask what you and your kids want to do—assuming it's not life threatening, or morally threatening, or way too expensive. Can learning really be this easy and this much fun? Yes. Of course, reality helps. Getting hungry motivates you to learn to cook. Wanting to understand squiggles in books encourages kids to learn to read. The vast majority of people throughout history learned this way, devising solutions to problems of daily life and learning from people who had more experience than they did the things that they needed to know, like which plants were poisonous or how to use the Internet. It's also how you have learned most of what you use in your work and daily life. How did you learn about parenting or computers? Even if you studied something in school, think about how much you've learned outside of school: how much more you know about driving than you learned in drivers' ed, or about politics than you learned in civics class. Regardless of what approach to curriculum you choose, this is how your children have learned and will continue to learn a great deal, including how to walk, talk, get along with other people, etc.

All I am saying in this book can be summed up in two words—Trust Children. Nothing could be more simple—or more difficult. Difficult, because to trust children we must trust ourselves—and most of us were taught as children that we could not be trusted. And so we go on treating children as we ourselves were treated, calling this "reality" or saying bitterly, "If I could put up with it, they can too."

What we have to do is break this long downward cycle of fear and distrust, and trust children as we ourselves were not trusted. To do this will take a long leap of faith—but great rewards await any of us who will take that leap. How Children Learn by John Holt

Here are a few suggestions. Spend time in nature, in your own back yard, a near-by nature preserve, or a national park. Volunteer: work at the library, visit a nursing home, deliver Meals On Wheels, clean up a park. The possibilities are endless, the experience valuable. Learn practical skills that will save you money: change the oil in the car, build shelves, make a pair of shorts, wallpaper your bedroom, reupholster a chair, grow tomatoes, make pickles, bake bread, knit a sweater. Get more exercise: walk, run, play tag, swim, organize neighborhood games. Browse through the children's section of the library (no matter how old you are) for attractive books on subjects you know little or nothing about. Do some of the activities in Chapter 6.

The best resource for this approach to curriculum is the world. Simply expose your children to as much of it as you sensibly can without exhausting yourself or them in the process. If you love to travel and do dramatic things, that's great. But don't neglect the opportunities of home, family, free time, and your back yard. The next best resource is your local library. Instead of limiting your search to homeschooling books or educational resources, look for books, magazines, classes, clubs, conferences, etc., on embroidery or China or diesel engines or whatever you're interested in. Kids often prefer "real" books written for adults to watered down versions for kids.

For more information about and support for this approach to learning, consider these:

Learning All the Time and other books by John Holt

Growing Without Schooling (magazine) available online at http://www.holtgws.com/ gwsarchives.html

Teach Your Own: The John Holt Book of Homeschooling by John Holt and Patrick Farenga

The Teenage Liberation Handbook: How to Quit School and Get a Real Life and Education by Grace Llewellyn.

Homeschooling Our Children, Unschooling Ourselves by Alison McKee

Home Education Magazine and website at http://homeedmag.com/

> Looking back, I realize that the most important things our kids learned were from doing real things, many of them unplanned and unscheduled: cooking, hanging out, grieving for dead pets, coping when the pump broke, square dancing in the barn, camping, playing, managing on limited income. This is how they learned to think for themselves, analyze complex situations, earn a living, make responsible decisions, act with integrity, develop healthy relationships, be themselves.–A mother of adults who grew up unschooling

---

A Few Specifics: Math, Music, and Homeschooling Boys

In an attempt to make the choices homeschoolers have clearer and more concrete, here are some specific examples. **First, here's a list of some of the many resources available for learning math.** Remember that you don't have to approach math the way conventional schools do. You don't even have to study math as a subject; you can unschool and learn it from life experience. And if you are going to study the various parts of math (arithmetic, geometry, calculus, etc.), there is no reason to limit your explorations to either the particular topics that a typical school curriculum would include or the order in which topics typically appear. Statistics is a helpful addition, and any order is fine as long as your children seem to be enjoying it. There's no reason to start with little numbers and work toward big. As soon as kids understand "1 + 6 = 7," they can do "100,000,001 + 6 = 100,000,007". Many homeschoolers find that, whatever the subject, there is no reason to limit their kids to what schools or any educational expert thinks "appropriate" for kids, since such people usually grossly underestimate what kids, at least those in a homeschooling setting, are capable of profitably exploring.

There are endless opportunities to explore math both as an academic discipline and as a fascinating part of the world, in nature, as art (especially the branch called fractals) and as part of just about every other human endeavor, including music, poetry, the sciences, and even history. (For example, how did the use of relatively clumsy Roman numerals affect Rome?) Many homeschooling families enjoy the richness that comes from using a variety of approaches and resources, even if they usually identify themselves as unschoolers or people who follow a conventional school curriculum or something in between. Parents who join the exploration with their children sometimes find "I hate math" turning into "Oh, I never knew math could be so interesting." What works well for one year, or one month, or even one day, may need to be changed. What works well for one part of math may be completely different from what works for another. One child's favorite resource may frustrate a sibling or friend. Published programs may change their approach during the years from kindergarten to twelfth grade. A child may enjoy one program in the early grades but be put off by the same company's resources for advanced math.

Here are just a few of the many possibilities.

• Purchased math curriculums that are very similar to what is taught in conventional schools are available as part of a complete curriculum for each grade and also sometimes as individual curriculums. (There's a list of publishers and information on choosing individual curriculums earlier in this chapter.) Since these curriculums include directions on how to proceed, more details are not included here except to remind homeschoolers that they are in charge of the curriculum and can use it in whatever way works for them, regardless of what the instructions say.

• Some online math courses award high school or college credit. Very informative non-credit courses are offered by The Great Courses (formerly The Teaching Company) and recently developed MOOCs (massive open online courses).

• Assorted math programs for various grade levels from sources such as Mortensen Math, Singapore Math, Saxon Math, Teaching Textbooks, and Key Curriculum Press (Miquon Math, which uses Cuisenaire rods, and Key to . . . workbooks).

• Harold Jacobs' books *Mathematics: A Human Endeavor, Elementary Algebra,* and *Geometry,* which many people consider so good that they are in a class by themselves and can be used by kids of various ages (and adults).

• Many, many other books on various aspects of math from picture books such as Anno's imaginative books to Norton Juster's *Phantom Tollbooth,* and Kenn Amdahl and Jim Loat's *Algebra Unplugged,* from Reimer & Reimer's *Mathematicians Are People, Too: Stories from the Lives of Great Mathematicians* to Osen's *Women in Mathematics,* from Charles Seife's *Zero: The Biography of a Dangerous Idea* to David Blatner's *The Joy of Pi.*

• Conventional games from Monopoly to Set provide opportunities for learning math, as do books of activities and games such as Carol Vorderman's *How Math Works* and the Family Math series, or games that you or your kids may make up based on math concepts.

• Books and other resources that inspire budding mathematicians and reveal the beauty of math, such as Richard Phillips' *Numbers: Facts, Figures and Fiction,* Claudia Zaslavsky's *Number Sense and Nonsense,* Hans Enzensberger's *The Number Devil,* Denis Guedj's *The Parrot's Theorem,* or any of Theoni Pappas's books. For even more ideas, see *Read Any Good Math Lately? Children's Books for Mathematical Learning, K-6,* by Sandra Wilde & David Whitin.

• Websites devoted to mathematical ideas or resources and approaches, such as http://www.besthomeschooling.org/articles/lillian_jones_math.html, http://www.kidsites.com/sites-edu/math.htm, http://archives.math.utk.edu/ or http://www.dmoz.org/Science/Math/Chaos_and_Fractals/Software .

• The math that children encounter in everyday life as they earn and spend money, measure, cook, pursue their interests in just about any topic, etc. This is the foundation for some unschoolers' approach to math.

Thus math can be approached in many different ways. Many homeschoolers find it works well to explore a variety of resources such as these, pursue the ones that work well for them, and not worry about the fact that they can't use them all.

Next, what about music? Many families incorporate music into daily rituals (like grace before meals) and special occasions, using traditional music or songs for which they've made up words, music, or both and including performances by any family member who plays an instrument. Any occasion can be made special by putting a song with it. Very young children love singing and musical games, such as those used in classes by KinderMusik or Music Together. These activities can be done as well at home with just a parent and child. Most libraries have books of musical activities to try.

Music lessons are an option, of course. Some families introduce their children to both traditional classical, folk, and rock instruments. They may own, rent, or borrow instruments; introduce their children to people who play them; make their own simple instruments; take their children to an orchestra's "musical zoo" day which allows children to try various instruments before or after a concert; or organize a support group event where children and adults demonstrate their instruments.

A parent can help a child with studying an instrument no matter how little musical training they have. Some parents encourage their children to improvise by asking for a "made-up song" at the end of practice sessions. Some encourage creativity and expression by asking their child to "tell a story" or express an emotion through their performance of a piece and then trying to guess what the story or emotion is. Because parents know their children better than anyone, they can help with technical difficulties by turning the challenge into a game or otherwise fitting its mastery to their child's temperament. For example, one parent helped his son overcome a tense thumb by asking for a "thumb report" now and then during practicing, whereupon the thumb responded like a puppet.

Many children find performing rewarding. Opportunities include support group gatherings, family events for visiting relatives, and visits to nursing homes. Some children find that playing in a group better suits them and team up with a sibling, play with a youth orchestra, start a band, or sing in a choir.

Most children also enjoy and benefit from performances, especially live ones. Many high school, college and amateur groups offer free or low-cost concerts, and professionals present a wide range of music. Recordings are readily available. Some include a story, such as *Beethoven Lives Upstairs* or the DVD of the operetta based on *Where the Wild Things Are*. Many children find performances of adult works completely accessible, such as the DVD of *Pirates of Penzance* directed by Joseph Papp, Tchaikovsky's *Sleeping Beauty* ballet, or Disney's *Fantasia*. Some recordings teach, such as the Lester Family's recordings (lesterfamilymusic.com) or Britten's *Young Person's Guide to the Orchestra*. Many parents enjoy sharing their favorites with their children, from Simon and Garfunkel or Michael Jackson to Beethoven or Hindemith, and many children (especially teenagers) enjoy broadening their parents' musical literacy to include They Might Be Giants or John Corigliano. Some children enjoy drawing a picture of music to which they are listening, which can help especially with music of a type that is new to the child.

Music also ties into to many other subjects. Biographies of composers and performers can be both historically educational and musically revealing. Music has a fascinating connection to physics and mechanics, emotion and the brain. Music theory (the study of music's patterns) shows that even the simplest melody, like *Row, Row, Row Your Boat* has patterns worthy of attention. Why does it work as a round but *Mary Had A Little Lamb* does not?

There are also many options for purchased curriculums that families can use in addition to these suggestions to study many different areas of music.

Finally, homeschooling boys. Many parents find that many boys (and girls) have a lot of energy and benefit from daily physical exercise, outside whenever possible. . . .Many parents find it works much better to work with this energy than to try to stifle it. They allow their sons (and daughters) to move around as much as they need to while they are listening to a read aloud, working on a project, or taking a break from a math lesson. In fact, some families find the fact that kids can move around while learning to be a major advantage to homeschooling.

Resources available on this topic include *Why Gender Matters* by Leonard Sax, *The Minds of Boys: Saving Our Sons From Falling Behind in School and Life* and *The Purpose of Boys* both by Michael Gurian, and http://www.theboysinitiative.org/.

So How Do You Choose a Curriculum?

Given all these possibilities, where do you start? How do you decide which curriculums or approaches would be likely to work for your family now? There's no simple answer. There's no one best curriculum, or, put another way, each of these curriculums works well under the certain circumstances. Most homeschoolers use more than one approach. A family using a complete curriculum package may get interested in ancient Egypt and develop their own unit study. Families focusing on unit studies may take a break and just do "stuff" for a month or so.

A teen learning mostly from life experience may decide to use a purchased curriculum to study algebra or take an American history course online or at a local college. Feel free to mix and match. Try not to label your family as "unschooling," "doing unit studies," or "doing school at home" and restrict yourself to what you think is allowed under that approach. Remember that you don't have to do what conventional schools do or cover the subjects they cover.

The following questions may help you choose a curriculum.

• What do you want your children to learn so they are prepared for adult life?

• How does each member of your family learn best?

• Is your family facing challenges that are more important than academics? Are you dealing with a serious physical illness, recovering from a bad school experience, coping with depression, going through a pregnancy, facing problems at work or the loss of a job, caring for an elderly parent? If so, choose a curriculum that supports the ways you are dealing with the challenges. For example, many children recovering from difficult school experiences, depression, or anxiety choose activities that emphasize their strengths, while their families follow a flexible schedule that allows lots of time for conversation, rest, and reflection. If you end up covering less academic material during this time and feel you are "behind," there will be plenty of time to catch up later. And remember that your children are learning some of life's most important lessons as you work together as a family. When your life has settled down and people are stronger, you may want to think about more challenging curriculums or more emphasis on academics. Or you may choose to unschool so you can continue learning from life experience and pursuing your interests. See Chapter 9 for stories from mothers who have done amazing things while homeschooling children with special needs.

• How much money do you want to spend? You can homeschool well without spending much money by getting most learning materials from the real world, the library, and other free or inexpensive sources. In fact, some learning activities actually save money, like gardening and do-it-yourself projects. Others, like starting your own business, may end up making money. Many homeschoolers who spend very little money find that this approach has many advantages, even if it wasn't their first choice.

Purchasing a complete curriculum package and taking courses are usually the most expensive. Other approaches can be quite inexpensive, depending on your choices. But if your family needs or would benefit from a purchased curriculum or courses (and using curriculum outlines won't work), it may be worth the cost. Used learning materials are available from other homeschoolers, on the Internet, and at the used book sale at the WPA conference.

• Are you or your children fascinated by the larger academic discourse? Do you love learning what others have said and learned without having to design your own curriculum? A complete curriculum package may be a good approach. If your children enjoy knowing what their friends who attend conventional schools are learning and being able to enter that conversation with them, you can start there. Remember that you can use these curriculums flexibly, skipping parts that don't work well for your family, supplementing freely with library and other resources, and following your own schedule if the one provided doesn't serve your needs. Or you can use subject-specific purchased curriculums. Just be sure to carefully research before you buy. Many families find it works well not to spend a lot of money until they're pretty sure about what they're getting, so they don't end up either creating a lot of tension by trying to get kids to follow a curriculum that isn't right for them or having paid a lot of money for something they don't want to use.

• Do you want some general guidance on what conventional or alternative schools expect children to learn at various ages, along with the flexibility to choose how you will study them? Do you want your kids to be able to work at different grade levels for different subjects? A curriculum outline might be a good idea.

• Do you have a pretty good idea of what subjects you want your children to study? Consider any of these options, from carefully choosing a purchased curriculum to partly designing your own to unschooling. You are the world's foremost expert on your own children, and meaningful learning can take place with any of these approaches.

• Do your children have special interests they want to pursue in some depth? Do they do better if they can make some decisions rather than having to do what you tell them to do? Consider any of these approaches. Be glad that your family homeschools, because no matter how you approach learning, your kids can have lots of unstructured time to follow their own interests. Even a complete purchased curriculum is merely a tool that you and your children can use in whatever way is best for you. Don't allow any curriculum, book, or person to dictate what you should be doing or how.

• Do you want to homeschool but also want to make sure that your children get an education that is as close as possible to what children are exposed to in conventional schools? Consider a complete purchased curriculum package, subject-specific purchased curriculums, or a curriculum outline.

• Do you feel you need to homeschool but are overwhelmed? Any of these choices may be your lifeline, depending on why you feel overwhelmed. Purchasing a complete curriculum package means you don't have to design your own curriculum and frees you and your children to learn together, using the curriculum in whatever way works well for you (which is not necessarily the way the publisher intended it to be used). A curriculum outline gives you some structural support without pressuring you to follow someone else's ideas about specifically how to study each topic. Learning primarily (or exclusively) from life experience and pursuing your interests can help you gain confidence in your children's natural abilities to learn vast amounts simply by becoming immersed in areas of interest in the real world. Which of these options sounds good to you? Take that one and give it a try. You have the freedom to find out exactly what works for your family, thanks to Wisconsin's excellent homeschooling law.

• Do you feel overwhelmed with the work involved in homeschooling? Consider purchasing a complete curriculum package with a full-service option or enrolling in live, online, or correspondence courses. Then someone outside of your family will figure out the curriculum, grade papers, and perhaps award credits. This is expensive but may be worth it.

• Are you homeschooling several children of different ages? You can choose a curriculum package or a curriculum outline and have each child do their own work, but remember that curriculums aimed at one age group can often be used fruitfully and pleasurably with a range of ages. A younger sibling might enjoy helping set up and observe a lab project related to a science textbook an older sibling is studying. Younger siblings often learn math from older ones who are working on assignments. Older siblings sometimes help younger ones with their lessons, too. Unit studies and/or unschooling also work well because kids can work on the same topic or project, each learning in their own way and at their own level. Whichever approach you choose, the kids will learn a lot from each other. So ask yourself which option sounds most rewarding and least stressful, and use it with confidence.

• Do you want to make sure your children have time to play, express themselves, be creative, and explore their interests? Aren't you glad that you homeschool! Except in rare cases, even the most academically-oriented homeschooling families have far more unstructured free time during which children can play, direct themselves, and explore their own interests than do families whose children attend conventional schools. If you want them to have maximum time for this, consider using unit studies or unschooling. But whichever method you choose, you can leave significant time every day for these other important pursuits.

• Do you want to make sure your children have the best chance of getting into college? Choose the approach that appeals most to you and keep records of what you do.

• Does your family want to explore the world freely, unhampered by the expectations and constraints of conventional schools, taking on new projects, plunging into new areas and new questions and pursuing familiar ones in greater depth, taking one step at a time, embracing the temporary uncertainty, gradually sorting things out, seeing where the quest leads you? Many families with this perspective find unschooling or unit studies work well.

Once you've chosen a curriculum, how well it works is determined in part by how you use it. Any curriculum works better if you are flexible: take breaks when the going gets tough, spend extra time on parts that really interest you, move quickly through sections that aren't particularly interesting or that the kids already know, and have fun whenever you can. If what you have chosen doesn't work well for one or more of your children, consider making a change.

Choosing and using curriculums gets easier as you gain experience homeschooling. Remember that you only need to take the next step. Right now, you don't need to figure out how to homeschool for the next 12 years, or even for the rest of this year. Build on what works. Don't forget that finding out what doesn't work is part of the learning process. Many experienced homeschoolers think the key is to watch your kids, listen to them, and help them find the ways of learning that work well for them.

We value the freedom to set our own schedules and determine priorities. This results in allowing our children to immerse themselves in a chosen interest whether it is snakes, skyscrapers, or scuba diving. They not only have time but we help them find resources, and we rejoice as they strive to learn everything they can about a topic. However, this is not always easy. Some of us are squeamish when it comes to snakes and would find it hard to embrace one as a pet. For others this may mean supporting a daughter as she develops an interest in rabbits. Soon you are building cages for 100 rabbits, raising baby bunnies in the house and getting up at 4:00 on a cold Saturday morning, traveling to a show clear across the state. For other parents it may mean building a new garage for a son who has a passion for everything that has a motor–from weed trimmers to tractors. You soon get used to tripping over engine parts, housing broken 4-wheelers, and eventually seeing wrecked cars in your driveway, awaiting some body work.

As a homeschooling parent, you value that learning process. It's not the end result or the finished product that is most important. It doesn't matter that your daughter who raised rabbits for eight years no longer wants to become a veterinarian. We understand that was never the goal. We supported her interest so she could learn to be responsible while discovering something about herself. She learned to deal with competition and that life isn't always fair. She learned that success comes with a lot of hard work, a little luck, and some help from your friends. She experienced the thrill of winning and an ache in her heart when she mourned the loss of an animal she raised from birth. We serve our children well by standing by them, by speaking words of encouragement and by comforting them. And we honor each other for the energy it takes to do this for them, each and every day.–From Opening Remarks, WPA Conference, 2004

As our children experience learning as part of daily life, they come to know that work, family and community, the natural world, religious or spiritual life, play, and learning are all part of one whole. Life cannot be compartmentalized into separate realms of work, family, faith, society. They are all connected.

One word for this sense of the wholeness of our lives is integrity–and it is one of the greatest gifts we give our children. It is something many people in our culture are hungry for, and I think they recognize and appreciate it when they see it. So as we celebrate and honor these young people who are moving out into the world, we can know that this gift of integrity is one that they will pass on to the larger society, simply by the way they live their lives.–From Opening Remarks, WPA Conference, 2005

Chapter 8

Using Libraries, the Internet, Local Communities, and CLEP and AP Tests

Looking for resources? Finding them is easy. The challenge is choosing among them. Questions you may want to ask when considering a resource include: Will family members be able to use it easily? Is it consistent with our family's beliefs? Can we afford it? Experienced homeschoolers know they will miss some great resources. Some are too general or too specialized or at the wrong level for their family. Some are too expensive. But mostly they don't have time for everything. It really is okay, though. We have time to learn enough. So, do a reasonable amount of research; choose what your family is interested in, enjoys, and needs or wants to learn about; and don't worry about the rest.

Using the Library

Ah! The key to affordable homeschooling. Libraries hold more resources than you could ever use, all of them free. Add in the advantage that the library wants everything back, so you don't have to add on to the house to make room. Let the library store them, let others use them, and when (or if) you need them again, you can check them out. Libraries carry trade books and rarely have textbooks in their collections. Many homeschoolers find that this means they can get into greater depth in the areas that interest them.

How do you make effective use of the library?

• Contact a nearby public library and explain that you are homeschooling. Call, email or walk in, but make an appointment for a personalized tour on how to use the library. Explain that you want to use the library yourself; you are not asking the librarian to do the work. Ask questions like:

   —Who would be the best person on staff to help me find materials for homeschooling?

   —How do we use the library's online catalog?

   —How can we log onto the online library catalog from our home computer?

   —Can we renew books from home?

   —Can we consult the catalogs of other libraries, request materials from them, and pick them up and return them here?

—How can we find materials in magazines, newspapers, and other periodicals?

—What can we do to make it easier for you to help us?

—How can our family volunteer to help the library?

—Is there a space where our children could display a project?

—Could our family/ homeschool group present a class or workshop on _____(subject) for other families/children?

—If we have suggestions for book purchases, how should we share those with you?

• If you want special privileges, pick a good time to talk calmly with a librarian, perhaps requesting an appointment.

• Don't limit yourself to what is on the shelves of your library. Consult lists of recommended reading in books you like, mail order book catalogs, websites, and other sources for titles of books and other materials. If your local library or library system doesn't have the item you want, ask how to borrow it through interlibrary loan. This service allows libraries to borrow from public and university libraries throughout Wisconsin and sometimes from other states. To determine if material is available in a Wisconsin library, go to WISCAT at www.wiscat.net. For materials outside Wisconsin, see WorldCat, which calls itself the world's largest bibliographic database, at www.oclc.org/worldcat. Be extra careful to return interlibrary loan materials on time, since your library has to get them back to the library that owns them.

• The Children's Department of your public library may host a variety of educational opportunities. Reading programs, arts and crafts, artist and author talks, presenters and more might all be featured (for free) at your local library. To find out when events will be held, check their website calendar or bulletin boards, or sign up for any newsletters they might offer.

• Check the bulletin boards at your public library for announcements about educational events that will be held in your community by other organizations. You may find programs or program series on subjects such as art, music, and nature.

• Consider choosing a specific day and time to visit the library on a regular basis. This makes it easier not to miss due dates for checked out books and pick-up dates for requested materials.

• Make good use of the library's on-line search, request and renewal features to locate titles and call numbers to make better use of your time at the library.

• Keep track of books that your family has read by using the website Goodreads [http://www.goodreads.com/]. "Goodreads users recommend books, compare what they are reading, keep track of what they've read and would like to read, find their next favorite book, form book clubs and much more."

• Check out the services that are available on libraries' websites in addition to BadgerLink. (See "Using the Internet" below for more on BadgerLink.) They may include topics such as investments, health and wellness, and genealogy and can be accessed from your home.

• The Internet Public Library (IPL) [http://www.ipl.org/] is a public service organization and learning/teaching environment founded at the University of Michigan School of Information and hosted by Drexel University's College of Information Science & Technology. "We will provide library services to Internet users." Activities include: finding, evaluating, selecting, organizing, describing, and creating information resources plus direct assistance to individuals.

• Treat your library as the valuable community resource that it is and your librarian as a colleague. Express your appreciation. Help your children learn to behave appropriately and respect other people using the library. Do not leave young children alone in the library. Return materials on time and in good condition. Cooperate with library rules and policies concerning computer use and other matters. Allow plenty of time to check out all your materials before the library closes. Don't act as if it's the librarian's fault if specific material you want is unavailable; consider their suggestions for substitutions. Join the Friends of the Library group if one exists; if not, consider starting one. Participate in library book sales and other fundraisers. Donate books and/or money to the library. Take the library staff occasional treats that can be shared by the whole staff (they are not allowed to accept individual gifts): strawberries, tomatoes, or flowers in the summer; cookies or festive bread at holiday time.

Support your library in your community and in the Wisconsin legislature. Ask if there are library board meetings that are open to the public and visit at least once a year to express your appreciation for the library. Write letters to the editor of your local paper describing how important the library is to you and encouraging others to support it. Offer to testify at county, city, or town board meetings. Let your legislators know that you strongly support funding for libraries. Respond when WPA notifies its members about pending legislation concerning libraries.

Visit other libraries in your region for fun and variety. You may find a library that suits your needs better than the closest one and decide it is worth the drive. Some university libraries allow the general public to use their materials in the library; others permit them to be checked out.

> One of my favorite things about the library is that it offers free, unfettered access to information with no conditions, except that we treat each other and the library's resources with respect. No one there will grade you or your children or have any expectations about what you get out of the information you take from the library.

> I remember cruising the library aisles many, many times just looking for books. Sometimes I was looking for something specific, such as another book on volcanoes when my kids were really interested in those, and sometimes I was just looking for something interesting. In either case, though, I often serendipitously came across something I was not looking for that turned out to be very interesting to us all. As I recall, that is how my kids got interested in Egypt—I was looking for something else and found a fictionalized account of Queen Hatshepsut. That led to an interest in Egypt that lasted for years. I think that it is good to know how to find what one wants very efficiently, but there is also something to be said for the serendipity of browsing in a library.

> And, as always, when you need to know: remember to ask a librarian!—From a homeschooling parent who is also a librarian.

Using the Internet

Homeschoolers use the Internet in many ways.
- To search for information. How do you make a kite that really flies? What is the population of the capital of Brazil? See below for suggestions for doing searches.
- To connect with other homeschoolers through social media, online groups, blogs, etc.
- To take online courses for credit on various levels, including college and beyond. Do a search for "online courses" or "online degree programs."
- To learn from online, non-credit courses, including MOOCs (massive open online courses).
- To get articles from many magazines, newspapers, and other periodicals without subscribing to them. BadgerLink allows Wisconsin residents to read, print, and email articles from a wide variety of magazines, newspapers, and other periodicals. Consult with your local reference librarian about using BadgerLink or go to the BadgerLink website. Many publications normally charge for this service; BadgerLink is available at no cost

as a part of Wisconsin's public library service. While you are at the BadgerLink site, check out some of the other offerings, including Searchasaurus, their search engine for kids. You can also access the WISCAT catalog discussed above through BadgerLink.

However, remember that the vast majority of humanity has learned a lot throughout history without a computer. Some homeschooling families limit computer time, preferring hands on interactions with people and the real world.

Netiquette (Internet etiquette) and online safety are important skills in today's world. Many parents make sure their kids have them before they allow their kids to use the Internet by themselves.

Searching the Internet

Things to keep in mind when choosing the words to type into a search engine such as Google, Yahoo, or Bing.

- Keep your entry simple. Describe what you want in as few terms as possible, using descriptive, specific words, and avoiding general or common words. Imagine how the webpage you want to find will be written, and use words that are likely to appear on your ideal page.
- Every word matters. Searches for [who], [the who], and [a who] lead to different results.
- Order matters. A search for [blue sky] turns up different results than one for [sky blue].
- Capitalization does not matter. You get the same results whether you use [George Washington] or [george washington].
- Punctuation does not matter-except when it does. [Red: delicious! apple?] and [red delicious apple] give the same results, but [nikon 400] and [nikon $400] don't.
- For advanced and specialized searches, try Google Advanced Search, Google Images, Google Scholar, Google Books, etc. Useful tools are available at Google Search Features.

Suggestions for dealing with search results:

- Remember that different search engines rank pages according to different systems, but you usually get useful results toward the top of the list.
- In your search results list, the first line of each entry is usually the title of the webpage. Below that is the web address (URL). Below the URL is a description of the webpage that may include an actual excerpt of text from the page. Your search terms are often highlighted to help you decide if the page has what you want.
- You need to decide for yourself if the results are any good. Consider these factors:
  1. Accuracy: Almost anyone can publish on the web. Most web resources are not verified by editors and/or fact checkers.
  2. Authority: It is often difficult to determine who wrote a webpage. Even if the author's name is listed, their qualifications frequently are absent. Publisher responsibility is often not indicated.
  3. Objectivity: The goals and aims of persons or groups presenting material are often not clearly stated. The web often functions as a virtual soapbox.
  4. Currency: Dates are not always included on web pages. When they are, they could indicate when the information was first written, or when it was placed on the web, or when it was last revised.
  5. Coverage: Does the information seem to be complete and comprehensive? Are there links to other sources of information on the same topic?

Fortunately, there are wonderful people who search the web for the very best stuff which they collect into guides that are browsable and searchable. Thus the resources in these guides have been chosen by actual people who have looked at the sites and decided they're worth another look.

- Internet Public Library: "Information you can trust." IPL includes tens of thousands of entries, maintained by librarians and library school students.

- Scout Archive: More than 24,000 "critical annotations of carefully selected Internet sites" mostly from the weekly "Scout Report."
- APL QuickRef: A big list of selected resources from the Appleton Public Library. Many libraries or library systems have lists like this, but few are as thorough.
- Wikipedia: "The free encyclopedia that anyone can edit." And that means anyone...
- BadgerLink: This provides "access to quality online information resources for Wisconsin residents in cooperation with the state's public, school, academic, and special libraries and Internet Service Providers."
- Museums (for example, the Exploratorium Museum in San Francisco) and teachers' professional organizations (such the National Council of Teachers of Mathematics) are other good sources of kid-friendly sites, information, and lesson plans. You can also ask people you know about their favorite sites; click on links on sites you trust, including blogs; and check your local public library's website.

If you need to make reference to a web resource in a formal way, the Online Writing Lab (OWL) at Purdue University is very helpful.

Note: Few websites are listed in this handbook. WPA does not endorse or recommend specific learning resources. Each family is in the best position to decide which are consistent with their needs, values, and interests. Also, websites sometimes change abruptly or disappear, making it unwise to include a list in a book that will outlast some of the sites.

Becoming Involved in Your Local Community

We celebrate that learning happens all day long, 365 days a year. It happens in the sandbox, at the theater, on vacation, in the barn, on the soccer field, in the car, at the neighbors, in the grocery store, and at the junk yard. Wherever life takes us, whoever we meet, whatever situation we encounter, there is a lesson. It doesn't matter if we homeschool using conventional methods or we consider ourselves unschoolers. Everyone here understands that our community is our "classroom" and our community is wherever we are. Rich environments surround us providing infinite learning opportunities.—From Opening Remarks, WPA Conference, 2004

Many homeschoolers are active in youth organizations such as 4-H, scouts, youth orchestras and choruses, theater programs, community sports teams, and religious youth groups. These activities provide homeschoolers with social opportunities.

Homeschoolers also participate in organizations and activities that are for people of all ages or primarily for adults. Young people can learn a lot and find mentors by joining groups that match their interests in gardening, knitting, flying model airplanes, cooking, etc. If the group is accustomed to having only adult members, it may help to have a parent accompany the young person. Even adults who are prejudiced against children often change their minds when they have the opportunity to share their interests with respectful young people. It may take time for a group to warm up to young people, but it's often worth the effort.

If you can't find an appropriate group in your area, consider starting one. Find people who share your interest by posting a notice in the library or local stores. Starting small and growing by word of mouth often works well. Share the work; ask other people to take responsibility for specific jobs if they don't volunteer.

Many homeschoolers volunteer at nursing homes, libraries, community centers, and places of worship in their local communities. Some join existing volunteer programs. Where programs do not exist, homeschooling families meet with people in places that interest them, determine what is needed that they could help with, and make adjustments as they learn from the experience.

Some homeschoolers volunteer in small businesses such as pet stores, repair shops, and bakeries while they are too young to hold jobs there. They learn about work in general and about the specifics of the place they have chosen. Such experience can be invaluable when they are deciding what kind of work they do (and don't) want to do and when they need references and experience in applying for jobs when they get older. Sometimes volunteer work leads to paid employment.

Consider exploring opportunities in your local community and learning something you hadn't even considered. Every community has its own unique groups and individuals who are surprisingly passionate about something. See if your library has a list of local groups. Check with the local paper for information about "famous citizens." Don't be afraid to call people you haven't met, explain that you are homeschooling, and ask if they would be willing to tell you about their interest in model railroads, decorative painting, raising parakeets, or whatever. Some people may decline, but most people enjoy talking about their special interests and appreciate an audience.

The Many Uses of CLEP and AP Tests

College Level Examination Program (CLEP) tests and Advanced Placement (AP) tests both provide a way to earn college credit without taking a college course. CLEP tests are designed so adults can document what they have learned outside conventional classrooms (through independent study, on-the-job training, life experience, etc.) and receive college credit for it. However, people of any age can take CLEP tests. AP tests are designed for students who have taken an AP course in a conventional high school, but you can take the exams without taking the courses. Both series of tests are created and administered by the College Board, the same corporation that produces the SAT. They can be invaluable to homeschoolers.

How You Can Use CLEP and AP Tests

• As a homeschooling teen, you can develop a high school curriculum directed in part or almost entirely by CLEP and AP tests. Choose the tests you are interested in, study, and take them. The time you spend can be counted toward the 875 hours of instruction required by Wisconsin's homeschooling law. Many of the tests will help you cover the required subject areas of reading, language arts, math, social studies, science and health. In addition, when you have completed high school, you will have an impressive and well-documented transcript and credits that will be accepted by many colleges.

• If you find it easier to study when you have a specific goal to work toward, CLEP and AP tests can give you an outline of what to study and a sense of accomplishment when you pass.

• CLEP and AP tests often save time. You get credit for what you already know and what you learn on your own, working at your own pace, without needing to spend time in a classroom or doing assignments for a correspondence or Internet course.

• CLEP and AP tests are by far the least expensive way to earn college credit. CLEP tests cost $80 for three to six (and, for foreign languages, up to 12) college credits. AP tests cost $89. Compare this to Internet and correspondence courses which usually cost $200 to $500 or more for three or four credits. Tuition at selective colleges can be $30,000 or more per year, during which students typically earn 30 credits, which averages out to be $3,000 for three credits and $6,000 for six.

Important: Not all colleges and universities give students credit for CLEP and AP tests. If you want credit from a college, be sure to find out directly from the college which exams they give credit for, what score you need to get credit, and how many credits you will get. (Don't rely on the CLEP and AP websites for this information.) Some colleges that do not give credit for CLEP and AP tests will allow you to use them to meet basic requirements, so you can take more advanced (and often more interesting) courses and get more from the time and money you put into college.

• Credits from CLEP and AP tests can often be used to meet requirements for a college degree, so you can reduce the amount of time and money you need to spend on college. In fact, you can earn an associate degree, a bachelor's degree, and some graduate degrees using only examinations. (You will need to earn some credits for upper level courses by taking examinations from other sources such as DSST http://getcollegecredit.com/ and Excelsior College http://www.excelsior.edu/. You can also earn necessary credits by taking live, online, and correspondence courses.) Fully accredited colleges that grant degrees like this include Excelsior College and Thomas Edison State College http://www.tesc.edu/.

• College credits from CLEP and AP tests are very useful even if you are not working toward a college degree. They can be used to convince a conventional school, a potential employer, and others that you have learned a significant amount about a specific subject. For example, if you are creating a high school transcript based on your homeschooling, you can include CLEP and AP credits and explain that since you have earned college credit in a subject such as American history, you have met and surpassed high school requirements in that subject.

Differences Between CLEP and AP Tests

• CLEP tests are offered year round; AP tests are given only in May. To take an AP test, you must contact AP Services by March 1 to get the names of local AP coordinators, and then contact a coordinator by March 15.

• CLEP tests are 90 minutes long and primarily multiple choice, although some tests require the test taker to type a few words or a number for some questions and four tests include optional essays. For more details, go to the CLEP website at http://clep.collegeboard.org/exam.

AP tests include multiple choice questions plus "free response" questions that require test takers to write an essay, solve a problem, etc. Each test is two to three hours long. For more details, go to the AP website at https://apstudent.collegeboard.org/home.

• Some colleges will give credit or advanced standing for AP tests but not for CLEP tests.

• Thirty-three introductory-level college subject CLEP exams are available. Thirty-four AP courses and exams are available across 22 subject areas. Both programs offer tests in subjects like US history and biology, but some subjects are available from only one or the other.

• You get CLEP scores as soon as you complete a test (unless you have done the optional essay that is available for a few CLEP tests) along with official documentation that you can copy and give to other people. You can also arrange to have your scores sent to one or more colleges, if you want. This means that no one knows your scores unless you tell them. You can retake a test after six months if you want to try to improve your score.

AP scores are available several months after you take the test. You can take an AP test over to try to improve your score, but you have to wait a year, and your grade report will include all the AP tests you have taken.

Suggestions for Studying for CLEP Tests

• Because CLEP tests concentrate on general principles, you can focus on understanding the most important parts of a subject, things you're more likely to remember, and avoid getting bogged down in memorizing insignificant details that you may quickly forget. In preparing for a CLEP test, focus on basic principles and basic vocabulary. CLEP tests generally stick to the big picture and don't try to trip people up on picky details. Math questions cover basic operations and understanding of fundamentals and do not require complicated arithmetic to answer questions.

• Learn at your own pace. You can take CLEP tests when you are ready, as long as you allow time for scheduling with the testing center.

• Helpful test preparation materials are available for CLEP tests from the College Board and commercial publishers. Unfortunately, some commercial material is inaccurate and misleading; some includes detailed material that is not covered on the exams. Make sure the guides you choose are appropriate to and match the tests you are planning to take.

• A good place to start is with the *CLEP Official Study Guide* and guides for tests you want. Review the introductory material. If you think you might know enough already, take the practice test. Determine your score. (Hint: If you don't look up the correct answers to the questions, you can use the practice test again later. If you do study the correct answers, you might remember the answers the next time you take the test, which means you won't get useful information about how well prepared you are for the test.)

Decide whether your score is high enough for you to meet your goals. If you get 55 to 60% of the questions right, you can probably get a 50 on the test (scores range from 20 to 80). If you just want to pass the test and move on with what you really want to do, or if the college you are planning to attend will give credit for a score around 50, you may want to take the test right away. But if you want a higher score than you got on the practice test, you may want to study before taking the test.

One very important point: The official CLEP materials suggest studying college textbooks. This works for some people, but others find that college textbooks have too much detail and are more likely to be confusing than helpful. These people prefer materials such as the following:

—Guides to CLEP tests that are not published by the College Board. Guides vary in how well they cover the material that is on CLEP tests. Some, like *Cracking the CLEP* by Tom Meltzer and Paul Foglino, published by the Princeton Review, are very helpful. Before you choose a guide, compare it with the official CLEP list of topics covered by the test.

—Good books (not textbooks) written for middle schoolers and high schoolers. This material is often well-illustrated, fun to read, much easier to understand, and more in line with what you'll need to know. Check websites and the children's section of the library. For example, if you want to take CLEP tests in American History I and II, consider Joy Hakim's series *A History of US*, which many people find more appealing and readable than a college textbook and which provides the needed information.

—For tests in more advanced subjects like introductory business law, you can check the adult section of the library for popular works written on the topic. Such books are often 200-300 pages, so they're shorter and more manageable than college texts. Since they do not have the guaranteed market that college texts do, they generally have to be clear and appealing or people won't buy them.

—Consider using resources available on the Internet. However, as with printed study guides, be sure the material you are using actually corresponds to the tests you are planning to take.

• If you decide to use a college textbook, try to visit a college library or bookstore where you can compare several. Choose one that's attractively laid out and appeals to you. Ideally, it will have a one to two page summary for every chapter. Compare the table of contents to the list of topics on the CLEP test to make sure most, if not all, are covered.

Once you have selected a textbook, don't begin at the beginning and work your way through all 450-600 pages, one page at a time, unless that's what you want to do. If your goal is to learn basic principles, pass the CLEP, and move on to what you really want to do, try just reading the summaries for the chapters covering topics that will be on the test. (Don't spend your time on the other chapters unless, of course, you want to learn more than is required because you're interested in the subject.) If you think you have a pretty good grasp of basic principles and vocabulary, take the CLEP practice test to decide if you need to study more and what kinds of things you need to learn.

Suggestions for Studying for AP Tests

AP tests were developed for students who have taken AP courses in a conventional high school, but you can take the tests without taking the courses. Some homeschooling parents and other people create a syllabus, have it approved by AP, and teach an AP course for homeschoolers. Helpful test preparation materials are available from AP. Materials from commercial publishers are another possibility, but these vary in quality and appropriateness, so investigate carefully and make sure the guides you choose are appropriate to and match the tests you are planning to take. The suggestions above for finding materials to study for CLEP tests may also be helpful for teens preparing for AP exams.

Strategies for Taking CLEP, AP, and Other Tests

• Don't cram. Study what you want to cover in the days, weeks, or months before the test. Then get a good night's sleep.

• Stay calm. Remind yourself that you have nothing to lose except about $80 if you don't score as well as you want. If you get so nervous taking a test that it interferes with your ability to answer the questions, find a book or website on test-taking strategies and choose the suggestions that appeal to you.

• Learn how the test is structured, and take at least one practice test before taking the actual test. The CLEP website at http://clep.collegeboard.org/exam has helpful tips.

• Plan your time carefully. If you don't know enough about a question to make an educated guess, go on to the next one without wasting any time. You can come back to the more difficult questions if you have time after you answer the ones you know right away.

• If you're taking a CLEP test, answer every question; CLEP does not penalize for guessing. For other exams, find out before you take the exam whether they penalize for guessing and plan accordingly.

• Don't worry about how well you are doing while you are taking the test. Focus on answering the questions. Remember that some of the questions on the test are being tried out for future tests and won't count in your score. If you encounter a confusing question, assume it's a poorly written trial question and go to the next question. Don't let it shake your confidence.

Chapter 9

Homeschooling Children With Special Needs

This chapter is about children who have been diagnosed and/or labeled as learning disabled (LD), attention deficit hyperactivity disorder (ADHD), on the autism spectrum, gifted; who have other special needs or syndromes such as Down; or who are blind, deaf, or have other physical disabilities. It discusses advantages to homeschooling and general suggestions for dealing with any of these diagnoses and labels. But the stories from mothers who have homeschooled their special children are the most powerful part of this chapter.

Advantages to Homeschooling

• Children get individualized attention and care from someone who knows them well, loves them, and can focus on meeting their needs. Parents can choose or develop a unique program that meets the needs of their children.

• Homeschooling provides continuity and stability for children so they can focus their energy on developing their potential.

• Homeschooling gives parents much more control over what happens to their children. Parents know what happens each day; can avoid having their children treated in ways they don't want; and don't have to worry about inappropriate or harmful treatment from a teacher, staff member, or other children. Also, a homeschool can provide many, many things a conventional school may not be able to offer, such as fresh air, special diets, background music, and pleasant surroundings. The flexible schedule allows children to eat, rest, sleep, and be active when it suits them best, instead of having to follow a rigid school schedule.

• Parents can spend time and energy working with their child instead of having to meet with school officials and trying to convince them to treat their children the way the parents want.

Suggestions for Parents

• Trust what you know about your child, even when experts disagree. The stories below show how often parents are right and experts are wrong. This is not surprising, since parents have known their children well for most or all of their lives, have seen them in a variety of settings, and have a lot more information about them as individuals than experts who only see them once or occasionally. Experts often say that parents can't be trusted and aren't objective about their own children. However, many parents feel that their knowledge of and love for their children enables them to see realities and possibilities that experts who are "objective" often miss. To be sure, an expert probably has more details about the specific condition your child has, but you have much more information about your child. If you think an expert is wrong about your child, stick to what you know and tell the experts you don't agree with them (but don't be surprised if they overlook what you are trying to say).

• But at the same time, there may be times when you would benefit from information from professionals and others who have more experience with children similar to yours. Learn from other people's experiences and information, but choose your sources carefully, stick to what you know about your child, and don't be afraid to disagree with experts. Their experience may help you make decisions, although it may only help you decide what not to do. For example, experts are likely to have only seen children who attended conventional schools and may be unaware of the possibilities that homeschooling offers. Think carefully about what you hear and read before you accept it.

• One way to get experts to listen to you and take you more seriously is to learn some technical vocabulary associated with your child's condition. When you use scientific names for parts of the body, diagnostic tests, test results, medications, etc., experts realize they are talking with a knowledgeable person. Information about various conditions is available at the library, on the Internet, from other parents, and from other sources. Ask people to spell the names of technical terms they use and to explain things to you. Write down, print off the Internet, or make copies of information that might be helpful. Also keep records of your child's behavior, what experts tell you, test results, and related information. You may feel overwhelmed at first, but gradually you'll begin running into more words you recognize, and the information will start making more sense.

• If appropriate, question the diagnosis. Some are clear-cut, such as obvious physical disabilities. But many children who have been labeled have shown that they can learn well given a good learning environment, the support they need, and the opportunity to learn in their own way and according to their own timetable. Consider getting a second opinion.

• Many parents choose to focus on their child as a person rather than on the label someone has given them.

• Be open to alternative approaches to your situation and seek information from a range of sources. Some people have found that acupuncture, homeopathy, and other alternatives can help in some situations.

• Your decision to homeschool your child may be questioned and challenged by school officials, experts, and others. You may be told that you should not or cannot homeschool your child because you do not have special training. It takes extra strength to stand up against such challenges. However, there are many advantages to homeschooling children such as yours, and many parents have homeschooled children in similar circumstances and been very glad they did.

　　When talking with school officials who are trying to convince you not to homeschool, it may help to remember two things. First, they may want you to send your child to school partly because school districts receive extra money for each child with special needs. Also, without enough special students, special education teachers may lose their jobs. Second, despite the extra funds they receive, school districts often do not have the teachers, equipment, facilities, or time to deal well with children with special needs. Some teachers really want to help children but simply have too many students to give them what they need.

• If you choose to use services provided by public schools, be careful what you sign. If you give permission to have your child evaluated for learning disabilities, you may have to also agree to psychological testing, which you may or may not want. Parents of children in special education lost some ground late in 2005 when the US Supreme Court ruled that parents have to prove that an Individualized Education Plan (IEP) is not the right plan; school districts do not have to show that it is. Know your rights. For example, you can get out from under an IEP you are unhappy with by withdrawing your child from a public school. An IEP cannot follow your child into a private school, including a homeschool.

• All homeschooling parents need support; parents who are homeschooling special children need extra support. Think about what kind of support you need (someone to talk with, help with household tasks, a break from your daily routine, time with your spouse, etc.) and where you can find it. You may find some parents of children similar to yours are supportive while others have different approaches to the situation and may even challenge your decision to homeschool. You may find you have more in common with parents who understand and are committed to homeschooling even though their children are different from yours than you do with parents whose children are similar but who send them to a conventional school. If you need household help, teens (including homeschooling teens) sometimes work out well. Internet groups offer support, but again, you may come into contact with people whose perspectives are different from yours.

• You may want to work especially hard to protect your family's privacy in light of the records that exist about your child. See Chapter 33.

Children Who Have Been Labeled

Some children are given subjective, sometimes controversial labels such as "learning disabled," "ADHD," "high functioning autistic," and "on the autism spectrum." Children who have been labeled have often had such negative school experiences that beginning homeschooling is both a relief and a special challenge. However, many parents have found that homeschooling solves many problems and allows the children to grow and learn in amazing ways.

The first step in resolving such a situation is often the parents' realization that labels are frequently wrong. Sometimes children are misdiagnosed. The tests and techniques used to label children have been shown to be highly questionable. Although extensive research has been done, there is no clear evidence that children labeled "learning disabled" actually have neurological or other physiological problems. It seems much more likely that difficulties in learning are caused by a combination of factors, including the stress and tension of school, pressure on children to learn before they are ready, not allowing children to use the learning style or approach that suits them best, trying to teach children material they find boring or irrelevant, children's lack of experiences their teacher assumes they've had, lack of time with their parents, problems of poverty and lack of resources, and so forth.

We all have difficulties in learning at times. Some children have more difficulty than others in learning what is expected in a school setting. But having difficulty in learning does not mean people have a "learning disability."

Many parents make it clear to their children and to other people they know that the school was wrong. They express confidence in their children and their abilities. They deal with their feelings but don't waste a lot of time on anger or guilt, moving on instead. Many find it works well to begin homeschooling with activities different from the conventional school assignments, workbooks, and tests that may have been part of the problem.

After homeschooling for a while, many children relax and regain their natural curiosity and desire to learn. It is encouraging to see how many problems resolve themselves, once a child is no longer under pressure to perform at a certain level. Parents are amazed at how much children learn easily and happily. Many parents also take advantage of this opportunity to help their children see how much ability they have and to boost their self-confidence.

Gifted Children

What is giftedness? Gifted children can be very different from one another, but they usually share several characteristics and traits. They learn rapidly and with little effort; they might teach themselves to read at a very young age or seem to understand math concepts almost instinctively. They have excellent memories, especially for topics in which they are most interested. Their interests can be extremely wide or very narrow, or they might have serial interests as they move from one area of obsession to the next. They are driven and self-motivated to learn, but not necessarily what adults want them to learn. They ask more questions than other children and with more persistence, even to the point of exhausting or annoying others around them. They are often very sensitive, both emotionally and physically. They can be excitable and might be seen as "too much": too curious, too talkative (or too quiet and too much in their own heads), too driven, too argumentative, too emotional.

Gifted learners do not always excel at standardized tests. They can be very creative and divergent in their thinking, which can impede their ability to answer convergent questions quickly, or they simply might not care about getting good grades or scores. Gifted learners can be easily misdiagnosed with learning disabilities, because of the overlap of characteristics of giftedness and learning disabilities. At the same time, it is possible for gifted children also to have learning differences such as ADD/ADHD, dyslexia, or autism.

Many parents of gifted children find that homeschooling works well because they are not constrained by the pace of classroom learning. Their children might have interests and talents in areas that are not part of the standard curriculum, such as economics for a ten-year-old or a focused interest in photography. Children who learn in creative or intense ways can find freedom of movement, both mental and physical, in homeschooling. Sometimes children who would benefit from a faster or more flexible approach to education are not formally identified as gifted, so they do not qualify for special classroom programming. Even when children are identified as gifted, some parents find that gifted and talented school programs do not provide the answer. Still other families wish to avoid unnecessary labeling of their children, whether the label is "gifted" or "learning disabled."

Parents who homeschool gifted children usually need to modify or even ignore traditional lists of what needs to be learned when. These children may be ready to learn not just one grade level ahead, but several, depending on their areas of greatest strength. These children are often difficult to identify as being in a single grade, since they may learn unevenly (for example, they might be reading at a pace expected for their age but doing math at a much more advanced level). As gifted children enter their teenage years, they often benefit from being able to dip into college level learning while still at home. They might find a mentor, use books or free online courses to learn on their own, take online college classes, audit classes at a community college or take classes for credit, or even enroll part-time in a local college or university.

Homeschooling offers parents the chance to address their gifted children's social and emotional needs, as well as their academic needs. Children who are highly sensitive can benefit from a slower entry into large groups, both for learning and social activities, than classroom education provides. Young introverts may benefit from more time to learn independently or one-on-one with family members as opposed to daily group settings. Parents often find that meeting the needs of their gifted children also helps them to learn about themselves, as they rediscover their own passion for learning and individual strengths.

Some resources that address the specific needs of homeschooling gifted children are the online Hoagies' Gifted Education Home Schooling Page (http://www.hoagiesgifted.org/home_school.htm),the Gifted Homeschoolers Forum website (http://giftedhomeschoolers.org/), and these books: *Making the Choice: When Typical School Doesn't Fit Your Atypical Child* by Corin Barsily Goodwin and Mika Gustavson; *From School to Homeschool: Should*

You Homeschool Your Gifted Child? by Suki Wessling; and *Creative Homeschooling,* 2nd edition, by Lisa Rivero.

Mothers' Stories

The following stories have been shortened to fit in this book. The complete stories are on the WPA website. To protect the children's privacy, their real names have not been used.

It was a difficult decision to take John out of the mainstream. We began to be worried in January when John began to cry daily before school, not wanting to go. Of course, I told him he had to go. I spoke with his teachers and principal, who offered no help but sympathy. He was labeled a low self-esteem child, and the school social worker worked with him with little improvement. By summer, I began reading anything I could on helping him with school. I also read some about homeschooling and talked with a homeschooler I knew.

In second grade, John's problem was worse. His teacher thought he was slow, he could not get his paperwork done, and he couldn't concentrate on the day's activities. He was a wreck at home. Asking him to eat his dinner or brush his teeth was too much-let alone any chores. It was a constant battle of nagging and punishment from after school until bed.

We still weren't confident to take John out, so we took him to a psychiatrist for more information. He felt John was hyperactive with an attention deficit. He offered a behavior modification program and advised us to prohibit TV action and violence. We were in favor of TV limitation. I was doubtful that the original program could do anything for John's depression and anger, and I knew the changes his teacher made in it would be more harmful than helpful.

We took John out in November, and by the following January, we were pleased to have a happy, cooperative child again. He soon realized he could read just about anything he wanted to read and is continually finding more to read, including some books from the adult section of the library. His judging of a book by the size of the print and number of pictures disappeared shortly after he was away from his reading program. It took nearly a year for John to be able to write papers such as math problems without great stress, but he is improving daily. The best improvement is that John has become interested in life's work and life's choices. He's become responsible for developing (with us) his curriculum and better at carrying it through.

Just looking at the improvement in John's behavior, attitude toward life, and ability to be cooperative and positive is enough to judge our program as successful. A great added plus is that he is also learning a great many things, some of which he might get in school but many not necessarily.

Before I begin, I want my readers to know that both of my daughters have given me permission to share parts of their stories. Because of space constraints, this article focuses on our older daughter, Esme. Both of our girls, ages 12 and 14, are on the autism spectrum. They have needs that can't be met in public schools.

We seriously considered homeschooling Esme when she was in kindergarten. But we decided to send Esme to half-day kindergarten. After a week, Esme came home with a stress rash on her face. Her teacher told us that she was "hysterical" much of the day. Our family doctor suggested a school team evaluation. I decided we would benefit from the results, but I intended to resume my plans to homeschool. However, the school psychologist suggested that Esme would benefit from daily exposure to other kids. The evaluation team recommended a compassionate teacher and gradual inclusion starting at 20 minutes a day so Esme could adjust to school. The schools did provide the therapy Esme needed in sensory integration, adaptation, help with motor planning, and physical education. Esme and her teacher formed a close bond and keep in touch.

Esme was schooled in the public school system until sixth grade. While Esme excelled academically, she struggled, as most children with autism spectrum disorder do, in multiple areas, including making friendships, working in small groups, distractibility, following multi-step directions, and organization. We found it was often hard to get school personnel, including many exceptional and highly respected teachers, to listen to our concerns or to respond. Teachers were stressed with too many kids, an increasing number of them with special needs.

There's a myth that children on the autism spectrum want to be alone because they're happier that way. But the fact is they choose to be alone because they don't know how to be with others.

School became increasingly challenging for Esme as the demands for self-organization and the complexity of instructions and social interactions increased. Her teachers handled this improperly, trying a behavioral approach that made the problem worse. I'll never forget the day I picked Esme up from school when she was crying and saying she did not want to return the next day, that she felt like killing herself.

When I approached the teachers, they were downright rude, insinuating that somehow I was causing Esme's stress. It took two weeks of letter writing to get the school principal, who initially sided with the teachers, to take the problem seriously and listen to our suggestions for helping Esme. I realized I was spending my time working with school people, not with my daughter, and it was negative time. I felt emotionally drained and sapped of all my energy. I decided to take responsibility for Esme, but I had to change my work schedule first. We decided to sell some property we used as a getaway to help us afford my reduced income, and I devoted myself to helping my daughter.

Since she was already academically strong, I decided we should focus on helping her participate in new experiences, tolerate frustration, compensate when she missed information, and communicate with her peers more effectively. Doing less academic work was hard for Esme at first. It was a bit of a culture shock when she began homeschooling. But she met all of the goals I set for her within a year, with individualized attention to her specific needs.

I have the freedom to support her as needed. For example, I can foreshadow with Esme what to expect during an upcoming activity, ensure that she does not miss any directions, or allow her to move to another area where there is less background noise and confusion. It makes a big difference that I know my daughter. I can review events with her afterward, which has helped her comprehend situations as a whole, rather than stressing about one detail or another.

Teaching what kids need to know in a way that revolves around their interests is key for any child, but especially for those on the autism spectrum. Without the burden of homework, Esme has been able to develop an array of gifts and talents, including poetry, photography, and public speaking. She is able to stay with a task despite frustrations for a longer period of time. Esme is generally more comfortable around homeschooled kids because they rarely tease and are more likely to share her interests.

Esme has days when she just needs to unwind with a book or indulge in a spontaneous writing project. We have the flexibility to allow this. With homeschooling, you have the power to prioritize. I cannot overemphasize the importance of this in our lives.

Based on our family's experiences, my reading, and my conversations with other parents, I have come to the following conclusions:

- It is very important for parents to be able to have the flexibility to make decisions that will work for their own unique children. This is especially true for kids who have special needs.
- It is a myth that children on the autism spectrum will learn how to socialize simply by being thrown into large groups of children without any support or guidance. Homeschooling allows parents the opportunity to teach social communication skills gradually, at whatever level the child is ready for.
- An advantage to homeschooling is more time for children to participate in activities in their communities and develop talents and areas of interest.
- I feel extremely fortunate that Wisconsin's homeschooling law allows parents the flexibility to do whatever it takes to meet the individual needs of their children.

An update: Recently Esme told me, "Mom, it used to be that I didn't like change and would do anything to avoid it. Now, I look forward to the unexpected...it's what makes life interesting." This was a monumental statement coming from a person with autism, since a hallmark of the condition is to have great difficulty with change. Since life is full of changes, you can imagine how learning to cope, and even enjoy, change would be "life changing" for the whole family. I would not have been able to help Esme develop this ability if I had not had the opportunity to gradually expose her to small changes in a safe environment, without the additional social and homework pressures of public school.

A few weeks ago, my 10-year-old daughter read a short chapter book.

That may not be too impressive to you. But for me, it was an exciting breakthrough that brought tears to my eyes. It was another proof that homeschooling works, as well as proof that our current Wisconsin law gives us the freedom necessary to achieve great things.

You see, we'd already been homeschooling for many years when my youngest child came along. Her first years were full of doctor visits and surgeries. Her next hurdle was learning to talk. When Liesl was five, a specialist diagnosed a particular genetic abnormality that manifests itself in physical defects, speech difficulties, and learning disabilities. We were told that Liesl would need special education classes and would probably never live independently. Although many doctors and nurses were supportive of our intentions to homeschool Liesl, some "experts" were vehement in their opposition. Some said we just didn't have the expertise needed to provide specialized education.

One of the many sad prognoses was that Liesl would not be able to read. Yes, they said, she could learn phonics and be able to decipher a job application at McDonald's. But her comprehension would be minimal, and she would never enjoy the pleasures of curling up with a story book. Even worse, this wasn't just a doctor's worst-case-scenario prediction; it was commonly acknowledged by other parents of kids with this syndrome.

Because we were "lacking in expertise," we proceeded to educate her in a way that was NOT in accord with standard operating procedure. Had we lived in a state that required standardized testing or portfolio review or curriculum oversight by the local superintendent, it's very unlikely that we would've been allowed to continue homeschooling the way we did in Wisconsin.

A year or so ago, we rejoiced when Liesl began to read easy chapter books. She was not capable of reading a book unless she had previously heard it read aloud more than once. Still, it was progress. And most importantly, she was enjoying these books. I wished she would be able to read new material, too, but it seemed that was not to be. She would try and then give up because the words were senseless. Maybe the experts were right. Maybe her reading comprehension would always be seriously limited.

Then a couple of weeks ago, I read aloud a "Russell" book. It wasn't long, only 1.5 hours for the whole story. She wanted more. But I had work to do, and my voice box was wearing out. An hour later, I discovered that Liesl was two-thirds of the way through a different "Russell" book. She read it. With no bribes from me. She read it. And understood it. She read it. And enjoyed the funny parts. Not only that, but on our next library trip she also wanted to find the series so that she could continue reading these chapter books. Books that the experts said she could never read. What joy that brings to a mommy's heart!

As homeschooling has become more mainstream, many people have become aware of its positive results with regard to academics. Many of us are proud to tout the academic record of homeschoolers. And that's okay. But we must never become so confident in our academic success that we're willing to request favors from the government (be it tax credits or sports in the public schools or something else) based on homeschoolers' ability to measure up academically. "Oh, we don't have to worry if the state checks up on homeschoolers because, after all, we're doing so well anyway!" Please remember that there are homeschoolers who cannot compete in the academic contests. Those children are very likely doing better academically in homeschool than they would in conventional school, but they still wouldn't measure up if the government increased its regulation of homeschoolers. All of us, because we are their parents, have the right and the authority to homeschool our children. It is not a privilege parceled out by the state only to those who measure up. It is critical for homeschoolers to recognize this and never to ask for "help" from the government which will come with strings attached. Those strings may be something you're willing to live with, but those just might be strings which strangle another family out of the homeschooling lifestyle, a family which may be desperate for an alternative to conventional schools.

I wish to share the story of our son, Tom. My husband and I have three children. Mark is presently 13, Tom, 9, and Mary, age 6. We have always homeschooled our children.

From the time Tom was two years old, I could see that he was a more challenging child. He was frequently in trouble, and experience didn't always prevent him from getting into the same trouble again and again. We have had to be very consistent disciplinarians with him. We were also very loving, and he is a sweet, loving child in return. By the time he was in first grade, I had learned some about Attention Deficit Disorder and elected to have him tested by our family pediatrician. He was a difficult child to teach as he couldn't sit still and was not really learning to read. The pediatrician diagnosed him as ADD. I know that, had he been in school, he would have also been diagnosed.

We were given a prescription for Ritalin, and I discussed with the pediatrician how I planned to use it. Dr. Smith completely supported me. I never gave Ritalin to Tom when we were at home, only when we were on field trips. Tom is a tactile learner but is so highly distractible that it was hard for him to learn in his best learning environment! Thus, the Ritalin really helped him when we were on field trips. Also, he used it for soccer games, as otherwise he was unable to concentrate on where the ball was!

At home, I was able to be patient with him and didn't mind if he was standing on his head when we were doing a reading lesson. I understood that was how he operated. Had he been in a classroom situation, I know he would have been on Ritalin daily, as a teacher could not tolerate his behavior with an entire classroom as I could at home—he would distract everyone.

Although he did well in math, his reading progress was very slow. I tried a number of different approaches to teach him and ended up with a combination of A Beka phonics and library books as ideal for him—a different approach than I used with his older brother. He made very slow progress until the third week of January in his second grade year. That week, a "light" went on for him, and he has been reading well ever since!

I've been so thankful that I was teaching him at home because he was never really frustrated. He had no idea that everyone else his age was reading and he wasn't. His self-esteem stayed intact because I always let him know he was doing well. Most ADD children really struggle with self-esteem; Tom doesn't very much.

Now in fourth grade, Tom is doing well with reading. He is a little slower now in math. His fine motor skills are terrible, as his hand writing quickly illustrates. But he is much more independent now and enjoys reading and learning. We have worked very hard with him and been very patient, and our efforts are paying off well. He still doesn't "think before he acts" and will probably always have some struggles in life his brother and sister won't have. But I feel that he is working at his potential and is a happy, loving child. Further, he has not had Ritalin in over half a year now. We travel a lot, and I still take it with me, but he has been successful without it.

I especially wanted to tell Tom's story because I am a special education teacher. I am certified in elementary education K to 6 and special education Learning Disabled, Mentally Retarded and Physically Handicapped K to 12. I taught special education for seven years. I am presently a substitute teacher at a small Christian school. To me, the important part of my story with Tom is that my teaching background really did not help me a lot with Tom. I didn't do anything any differently than any other conscientious mom would have. Perhaps I am a little more confident in my abilities or have an easier time locating materials, but I am not a better teacher to my children than any other mom.

The entire key to working with Tom was patience. I worked at his pace. I kept trying different materials until I found what worked for him. I prayed for him. I loved him as only a mom loves her child—which kept me motivated to work with him even when it seemed difficult. Any caring mom could do this.

This was the same approach I used when I was teaching brain-injured children who were six to nine years old. I worked at their pace and kept trying materials until I found what worked for them. I also worked hard on social skills and teaching general information. I wanted my students to learn to be polite and respect people, to be socially acceptable in public, and to be able to hold a friendly conversation—to be interesting to talk to. I knew they would never succeed academically, but I wanted them to be the best people they could be.

When we get down to it, that is a lot of what I want for my own children. If they go far academically, that's great. But it is more important that they love God, are happily married, are conscientious parents, and contribute back to their communities. I want them to enjoy learning all their lives. I want them to be responsible for their actions. I want the world to be a little better place because they were here. By homeschooling, I'm not teaching to a test, or teaching to someone else's values. We are teaching what we believe. We are teaching because we completely accept the responsibility for the children we brought into this world. Some day, when they are grown, I believe we will look back and say, "We did the best job we could." I believe we will be pleased.

Our second son, Todd, was born with Down Syndrome. We were a bit overwhelmed and figured we needed all the help we could get. Our doctor referred us to the Early Education program in our school district. To be honest, we appreciated the information we received about Down Syndrome from the early education teacher. What we could not stand was someone telling us how to raise our children and what was best for their growth.

Our first of many battles came when Todd turned two. It was strongly recommended that we send him to school to learn daily living skills with other children with disabilities. The idea of sending our child to school to learn how to function with and from other children who were dysfunctional seemed a little ridiculous to us. We chose to keep Todd home to learn from his big brother, who was more then happy to play, interact, and teach his little brother how to be a normal kid. It never occurred to our then four-year-old normal child that there was anything different or slow about his little brother. The boys developed a loving respect for each other and a solid friendship that still exists today. This experience was something school could not provide. We knew we were doing the right thing, but our decision did not endear us with the school system. They felt we were depriving Todd of a greatly needed education that by law he had a right to. Talk about a guilt trip! It was a good thing we decided early on to stand up for what we believed was right for our kids, because intimidation was the name of the game!

At six Todd started school. He had a mind of his own and was very determined. We had taught him the alphabet by phonetic sound only. We were hopeful that in school with a real teacher, he could make great strides. So we sent the little boy we were so proud of off to school.

After one week, we realized school was going to be a struggle. The teacher explained, "Todd is not listening to directions. He sits where he wants to sit, not in a circle like all the other children who have been in school for four years. Let's be reasonable, Mom. You only think he knows his alphabet; don't be surprised if reading is a skill he won't be able to learn because he can't talk after all. Besides children with Down usually aren't capable of learning to read." Imagine the teacher's surprise when a month later she noticed that instead of sitting in the circle, Todd was actually sitting on the carpet square with the letter of the day. She finally agreed he did know his letters. This little episode made us realize the necessity of staying involved in Todd's learning.

Armed with knowledge of our son, a firm belief in our child's ability, and an unbeatable determination, we stood our ground and said, "Let the battle begin." After all, Todd had a right (by law) to a good education, and we were willing to fight for that right. Year after year we attended every Individualized Educational Program (IEP) meeting as a couple and submitted our own list of expectations to be covered with Todd for the following year. When the school didn't have the necessary materials, we found them and took them in.

We started to realize we were winning some short-term battles, but basically we were losing the war. Todd was becoming more and more frustrated and unruly. All our time and energy were being spent on fighting for education. We finally decided to use that time and energy to teach him ourselves.

At age twelve, we pulled our frustrated, angry son out of school and started homeschooling. We gave him time to learn what he wanted to learn. He spelled words and read everything from cereal boxes to children's dictionaries. He became very handy with a calculator and loved playing educational games on the computer. And much to our surprise, Todd started to play the piano. He taught himself, with a little help from Dad, to read music. Todd started to enjoy learning, and rather than just doing what was expected of him, he was always doing more. Our angry, withdrawn son again became a happy, relaxed child with a great sense of humor. Todd started reaching out to others outside of the family. We were so excited with the changes in Todd because of homeschooling, we also pulled his two younger brothers out of school.

In June, we had a graduation celebration for Todd. He has become a confident, loving, happy, and independent young adult. In the last year, Todd and his dad sang a duet at the Very Special Arts Choir concert. He also played the piano for the audience while his dad sang a solo. Todd reads at a third to fourth grade level, has started writing simple sentences, and if he says a word we can't understand, he just spells it out for us. And much to our surprise, he has turned out to be a good photographer. We gave him a Polaroid camera as a graduation gift, and he took nicely posed, perfectly centered pictures of everyone at his party. Must be time to enjoy another talent!

It's true; every child has the right to a good education. It's their God-given right, which has nothing to do with the "law." Homeschooling has been an answer to our prayers. Through this wonderful experience, we have come to realize that, not only do we love our four boys, we also recognize and appreciate who they are and the responsible men they are becoming. We certainly have been blessed. Life is good!

When we began homeschooling at the end of our son's second grade year, he had been in both a public school gifted program and a private school for gifted learners. We knew that he needed something different, but when we decided "to try homeschooling for a year" while we figured it out, we had no idea we would continue all the way through high school. Now, as he is getting ready to graduate from college, I cannot imagine having spent those ten years at home any other way.

So many of our initial worries were unfounded, especially the perennial socialization question. Homeschooling allowed him to develop empathy and interpersonal skills at a pace that adjusted to his needs and in group settings that were varied and multi-age. Even more important, as an introvert—someone who gets energy from oneself and who is exhausted by extended social interaction—he was able to find the right balance between alone time and group time. In fact, I was surprised at how few outside activities he needed or wanted in the early years of homeschooling, and because he wasn't forced to fit into an extroverted mold, he came to a self-knowledge that allows him now to continue to make choices to honor his need for time to recharge.

By the time he got to high school, homeschooling was such a natural part of our life that I often forgot that his education or daily life was any different from that of any other teenager. He still spent a lot of time learning on his own, but he also took some online courses in subjects he was interested in, was part of a homeschooling group that put on yearly Shakespeare performances, took classes from and acted in plays produced by a local children's theater academy, and began to take classes at Marquette University as a part-time, non-degree student, entering as a full-time degree student when he was 17.

Like so many other homeschoolers I know, his homeschooling approach didn't fit neatly into a category, although we always used unschooling as a base. The only grades he got were in his online and university classes, and he took the SAT only once, at age 14. Our son has said that he feels homeschooling prepared him for college better than a traditional or even college-prep high school would have, in part because he wasn't already burned out by the time he was a college freshman. He also has said that he felt better prepared than many of his classmates for the long-term planning and personal responsibility required by university education, and the skills he didn't get from homeschooling—such as learning to take notes in a large lecture course—he picked up when he needed them.

This year, he was accepted at all 11 law schools he applied to, including half of the U.S. News and World Report's list of top 14 law schools, and will attend Harvard Law in the fall. While I hesitate to mention his academic achievements, as they are his own and not the reason we homeschooled, they do show that homeschooling does not necessarily close doors to traditional or rigorous educational careers.

Our decision to homeschool was by far the best decision we ever made as a family. My only regret is that we can't do it all over again.

Chapter 10

Recognizing and Evaluating Learning and Keeping Records

The information on record keeping in the second part of this chapter applies to all homeschoolers in Wisconsin, regardless of their approach to curriculum and learning. The first section on ways of translating learning into conventional school language applies to primarily to what kids learn without using purchased curriculums or approaches to learning similar to those used in conventional schools. Purchased curriculums usually focus on conventional school subjects and can easily be included on a transcript. (See Chapter 7 for more about using purchased curriculums and other approaches to homeschooling.)

Translating Learning Into Conventional School Language

Many homeschooling parents are very aware, just from watching their children and interacting with them, that they are learning many important things. However, at times, their activities and experiences that are less obviously "educational" than using a purchased curriculum need to be translated into conventional school language. For example:

• Homeschoolers applying for employment, college, and other opportunities need to demonstrate their qualifications. Often their experiences differ from those of people who have attended conventional schools and from what potential employers and others generally expect. Homeschoolers increase their chances of being accepted and given credit for what they know when they do the work of helping other people understand their qualifications instead of expecting non-homeschoolers to figure this out. See Chapter 12.

• Translating can help prepare homeschooled children to respond to questions from other children and from adults. Our society is strongly dominated by conventional schools. Even children who have not attended a conventional school often try to compare what they know with what they think other children their age have learned in conventional schools. Because our society has such a strong bias toward conventional schools, some home-schooled children may feel they are behind their contemporaries and know less. Many homeschooling parents try to help their children realize the wide range of things they are learning, some of which are not even included in conventional schools. But translating can be a way of helping homeschooled children realize how much they are doing and learning that is like what children learn in conventional schools, so they feel more confident and comfortable with themselves and so they can respond to challenges from other children. "Can you read?" "What's 9 times 12?" "What's the capital of Brazil?" Some homeschoolers respond to such challenges by saying, "I don't really like those kinds of school games. Do you? Let's do something that's more fun instead."

• It often helps non-homeschoolers relax and maybe even become supportive of homeschool-ing if they can see that conventional school subjects can be learned through hands-on activi-ties and what may first appear to be "play." For example, when children set up a pretend store, weigh food, and wait on customers, they are learning math and social skills.

• Translating helps parents who usually have confidence in homeschooling but who occa-sionally have doubts. They realize how much their children are doing that even non-home-schoolers would recognize and give them credit for.

• If homeschoolers are questioned about truancy, they might find it helpful to include some examples in which they translate what they have been doing in their homeschools into conventional school language.

At the same time, however, many homeschoolers work very hard to remember that they are only doing this translating to help other people understand homeschooling, to bridge a gap that exists because our society is so dominated by conventional schools. When homeschoolers translate, they are not saying that conventional schools are the standard for education and learning that homeschools have to measure up to. Homeschoolers are not saying that the only learning that really matters is what can be shown to be like the learning that goes on in conventional schools, that the only subjects worth studying are those that are included in conventional schools, or that the only way that homeschools can be legitimate is by showing that they are really a lot like conventional schools after all. Homeschoolers know that homeschooling has a legitimacy and value all its own, just by virtue of being what it is, learning together as families. Homeschooling does not need to earn legitimacy by showing that it is like conventional schooling.

Here are some specific examples of translating experiences and activities into the lan-guage used in conventional schools. This is a responsibility that homeschoolers have to take themselves, because no one else will do it for them.

• Children playing with blocks or Legos are learning arithmetic and geometry as they dis-cover from direct experience important concepts such as how various shapes fit together, how smaller units can be added together to form larger ones, and how numbers as repre-sented by blocks relate to each other.

• Children talking with older relatives and friends about times past or with people from other countries about their cultures are learning history and social studies as they learn about the past, changes that have brought us to the present, and how other people live.

• Children who know something about Wisconsin's homeschooling law and the way in which homeschoolers have worked to protect their rights know about government, civics, law, and reclaiming and maintaining rights.

• Children listening to someone reading aloud and recognizing stop signs are learning to read as they understand how words fit together to make a story and how symbols are used to represent words and ideas.

The list goes on. (See Chapter 6 for more examples.) The possibilities are endless. Experienced homeschoolers have many examples of their own to add.

This translation process makes it possible for us as parents, for our children, and for others who are concerned about our homeschooling to see that real and important learning is taking place even when our children are not necessarily doing the same things that children do in conventional schools. When we recognize some of the basic differences between a homeschool and a conventional school, we can provide our children with many more learning opportunities than a conventional school can. We can encourage them to learn in many more ways than children in conventional schools do.

Evaluating the Learning of Homeschooled Children

Parents need to evaluate the progress their children are making toward their goals. Fortunately homeschooling provides many opportunities for parents to observe what their children are capable of doing and what they have learned. For example:

• Parents observe and evaluate their children without needing to plan or think about it. They do this naturally and automatically because they love their children, are interested in what they say and do, and want them to have opportunities to learn about the world. Parents then make adjustments as a result of these observations. They may do extra reading with children who are having trouble recognizing words, write notes to children who need encouragement to write, or talk about the price of groceries with children who say they don't like math.

• Many parents also make deliberate and self-conscious observations of their children. These observations are guided by the family's goals and curriculum. Parents ask themselves questions like: What interests my children? What skills have they mastered or made progress on? What do they do with their free time? What kinds of questions do they ask? (Someone once said that the real measure of intelligence is not the ability to answer questions but the ability to ask them.)

• Evaluating children's learning environment can also be helpful. Many parents ask themselves what more they could do to encourage learning. Do the children have a variety of things to look at, listen to, and work on? Are there enough of the right kind of reference books? Maps on the wall? Are there other learning aids that would be intriguing to the children? Many parents find that some of the best learning aids are the tools and materials that adults use. Children learn a great deal from using their parents' sewing machines, wood working equipment, computers, garden tools, and other equipment.

• Many parents find it helpful to review their homeschool records (see below), comparing what children were able to do in the past with their present abilities.

• Some parents use standardized tests and other assessments as part of their evaluation of their children's learning. If you want to use them, it is a good idea to have testing privately done and make sure the results are reported only to you and not made part of any government agencies' records on your children. For up-to-date information on having your children tested, search for "testing services" on a site like A to Z Home's Cool http://homeschooling. gomilpitas.com/ However, many homeschoolers avoid standardized tests and assessments, since they know their children well from working with them. They are also concerned because standardized tests and assessments have been shown to be biased, unfair, and inaccurate. They undermine children's confidence and interfere with the learning process. Their results can have far-reaching negative effects on children. See Chapter 24 for information on testing and Chapter 31 for problems with preschool screening.

> For me, the questions that Dan and Ben ask say a lot about what they understand. When one asks, "How many words are there in English?" or the other asks, "Why are all the Noble elements gases?" I get a pretty good idea of how they are relating that knowledge to their understanding of the rest of the world.
>
> The questions I want my children to be able to answer are the questions they raise themselves. Can they determine that they know enough for their own needs? Can they trust their own assessments without having to call in some outside expert? Do they know how and where to find more information if they need it? And can they learn that ignorance is not the same as stupidity?
>
> Maybe, somewhere along the way, they'll learn wisdom.—From Opening Remarks, WPA Conference, 2000

Record Keeping

To decide what records to keep, many families ask two separate questions. First, "What records should we keep to be in compliance with Wisconsin's homeschooling law?" Second, "What additional records do we want to keep for ourselves?"

Although there may be some overlap, generally different records are needed for these two purposes. Each family needs to decide what kinds of personal records will best serve their approach to education and their unique situation. Personal records may have a strong impact on a individual family, but they generally have little effect on other homeschooling families. However, the records we submit in response to a legal challenge can affect other homeschoolers and our homeschooling freedoms. When we are careful to give to the state only the minimum records and reports needed, we are making an important contribution to maintaining homeschooling freedoms for our families and others. Conversely, when we submit more records and reports than are necessary to deal with a legal challenge, we threaten the homeschooling freedoms of our family and others.

Records Required by Wisconsin Law

According to Wisconsin law, homeschools should keep attendance records as other private schools do.

WPA recommends keeping a daily attendance record that shows that children attend their homeschool each day. Such records document that children are complying with the compulsory school attendance law. Homeschooled children can be marked "present" when they are learning away from home, such as on field trips or more extended excursions. Some parents indicate as "sick" days when children are not feeling well, although many children who are not seriously ill learn a great deal on these days. It makes sense to comply with a clear-cut requirement of what is basically a reasonable homeschooling law.

If a truant officer comes to the door, show the official your attendance record and/or offer to send in a copy of it; keep the original. Often officials simply need a piece of paper to put in their files, and your attendance record will suffice, especially if you remind them that the law requires compulsory attendance but not compulsory education. See Chapter 22. Your attendance records document attendance. Unless you are called into court because a prosecutor has convinced a district attorney that there is substantial evidence that you are not obeying the homeschooling law, you are not required to show your curriculum or evidence that your children are learning.

Having shown the official your attendance record, you can then explain that you are busy working with your kids. If the official has additional questions, ask that they be sent to you in writing or that an appointment be made for a convenient time. See Chapter 31.

Attendance records are simple and easy to keep. When families begin homeschooling, they establish a calendar that will provide at least 875 hours of instruction. Some families adopt their local school district calendar so they are on the same schedule as the rest of the neighborhood. Others feel that children learn every day, so they mark attendance every day.

In addition to keeping attendance records, many families save samples of their children's learning so that in the unlikely event they were called into court on a truancy charge, this material would support their claim that they have complied with the requirements of Wisconsin's homeschooling law. The materials might also be used to document a transcript or an application for a job or college admission. Use common sense; don't go to extremes. Even without such samples, homeschoolers are very good at figuring out ways to show officials that they have been complying with the law and to convince potential employers that they are capable and have learned important things. Most homeschoolers' records are not in the form or detail that is sometimes required in a conventional school. But if necessary, homeschoolers can use notes, examples, and memories to make their case.

Occasionally a family finds its homeschooling challenged by a public official. These challenges may arise because we are unlucky enough to live in a school district where officials are suspicious of homeschoolers and are threatening and intimidating them. Or perhaps someone we know has told school authorities or social service workers that they are worried about our children and think our homeschool should be investigated. Or we may be involved in a custody dispute. A reasonable goal in responding to such challenges is to provide enough information to minimize or resolve the challenge without providing so much that we set precedents that will be difficult for other families or us to meet in the future.

Personal Records Not Required by Law

Homeschoolers who keep attendance records are in compliance with the record keeping portions of Wisconsin's homeschooling law. It does not require that homeschoolers keep records of their educational activities or accomplishments. It is written to be consistent with the principle of "innocent until proven guilty" by requiring that the state show that a family is not complying with the law.

Each homeschooling family decides what kind of personal records will work best for them. Some have extensive records; others have few. It is obviously more important to enjoy spending time together as a family and to have a wide variety of experiences than it is to worry about trying to record them all, especially if the record keeping interrupts the activity or becomes a chore that takes the fun out of it.

Reasons to Keep Personal Records

• Records highlight and celebrate what we have done and help us remember. Putting together some kind of presentation can be a way of making part of learning visible, tangible, and appreciable. The presentation may be a recital or show, a collection of pieces of work assembled on the dining room table, a scrapbook, a video, a written report, or whatever else we choose. The presentation itself can be recorded through photos.

• Personal records boost confidence. Assuming so much responsibility for our children's learning is a serious undertaking. It can be difficult to feel sure about what we are doing, especially when so many non-homeschoolers assume children should attend conventional schools. Records help us recognize and appreciate the learning our children are doing. They also help our children realize how much they are learning and prepare them to respond to challenges from others.

• Personal records also promote long-range perspective. They provide an overview and show us patterns in learning and development that we might otherwise miss. They demonstrate that more learning is taking place than we might otherwise recognize. They are a wonderful support at times when we doubt ourselves, our children, or the very idea of homeschooling. They help us learn to trust our children and ourselves.

Many families include in their records areas of special concern. For example, if a parent, a young person, or someone outside the family is concerned about socialization, the family can simply note each time they interact with other people, including visits, outings, phone conversations, emails, and letters. Similarly, if there are concerns about math, the family can record each time they work with numbers, spatial relationships, and other aspects of math. In most cases, the records are very reassuring; if not, they provide additional information on problems to be addressed.

• Personal records help families set their own goals and move toward them. Deciding what to record is an exercise in goal setting. Knowing an activity will be recorded gives extra incentive to do it and makes us more likely to notice and remember it.

• Personal records can be useful for explaining homeschooling to others (except for school officials and truant officers). They provide valuable raw material for applications and credentials. As homeschoolers we often have the opportunity and the responsibility to develop our own diplomas, transcripts, and other credentials and to convince employers that they should hire us and colleges and volunteer programs that they should accept us. Records are invaluable in stimulating our thinking, creativity, and confidence at such times. See Chapter 12.

• Some families feel more comfortable and secure knowing that they have records available if they ever need to show them.

• The process of keeping records can be a good learning experience, especially when kids are involved in record keeping.

Choosing a Focus That Supports Learning

Record keeping works best if the personal records we keep are consistent with and support the approach to learning we are following.

Families who choose an approach to learning similar to that used in conventional schools often organize their personal records according to conventional school subjects such as reading, writing, math, and social studies. This shows parents, children, and others that homeschooling includes the kind of academic work that people assume children do in conventional schools.

However, organizing records by academic subjects also keeps families somewhat tied to the school model, and some families are homeschooling because they want a different approach to life and learning. They often simply record children's activities without labeling them as conventional school subjects.

Actually most families use a combination of these two approaches. Families using purchased curriculums include ways in which children learn in addition to the planned academic studies, such as things they learn from hobbies, travel, involvement in religious and volunteer organizations, and other activities. Families that emphasize alternative approaches to learning find that some of their activities include conventional academic subjects such as

	Sun.	Mon.	Tues.	Wed.	Thurs.	Fri.	Sat.
Reading							
Language Arts							
Mathematics							
Etc.							

reading and writing about all sorts of topics, using math to figure out how to build something, or using science resources to help understand phenomena they have observed. The kind of translating discussed at the beginning of this chapter is an important part of record keeping because it sometimes helps us to record as much of the learning that our children are doing as possible.

If keeping personal records feels overwhelming, it makes more sense to change or reduce the record keeping than to give up homeschooling.

Ways to Keep Personal Records

Possibilities for personal homeschooling records are limited only by homeschoolers' creativity and imagination. They don't need to be modeled on conventional school records. Conventional schools keep records to track of students who encounter new teachers each year, store information on students that few if any people in the school may know well, convince legislators and voters that the schools are doing a good job and that problems arise from students and their families, determine who is the valedictorian and who is eligible to play on the school's sports teams, be covered in case someone takes legal action against them, etc. Homeschoolers seldom if ever need records for such reasons; homeschooling records can be very different from conventional school records.

Flexibility is a key to keeping homeschooling records. Many families try different approaches, building on what works and discarding what doesn't. If record keeping is interfering with a family's enjoyment or bogging them down, they can try a different approach or simply stop keeping the records that are causing them problems.

Some examples of the kinds of records that homeschoolers find helpful:

• A daily or weekly journal can record children's activities. It can be a narrative, a brief list of activities, or some other format. Some families make a "to do" list each morning, check off what they do, add unplanned events that occurred, and use this as a record.

• A monthly or quarterly summary that reviews what has been done and summarizes important developments. "Our son is now paying more attention to words on cereal boxes and pointing to the ones he recognizes." "Our daughter has made two blouses and a dress in the past three months and obviously feels more confident in her sewing abilities."

• Some families who want records by subject area use a chart such as the one shown here. Any subject can be listed. In the boxes notes are made about activities and perhaps the amount of time spent on each. For example, the rectangle for reading on Tuesday might say, "Little House in the Big Woods, 1 1/2 hours." Language arts on Thursday might say "Wrote to Grandma, 3/4 hour." Not every subject needs to be covered every day. Families select the subjects they want to include and need not limit themselves to subjects their children would be studying in a conventional school. This chart is quick and easy to fill in, and it shows whether any subjects are being overlooked.

• Some families using purchased curriculums record when they do the parts of the curriculum they choose to do and add other learning activities that supplement the curriculum, such as reading aloud for pleasure, cooking, and going on nature walks and other field trips.

• A quick and easy approach is to simply collect, in a file folder or box for each child, some samples of their written work and art, lists of books read, snapshots of projects in progress or completed, brochures from places visited, and similar materials with dates on them. They can be kept as is or used to make a scrapbook or portfolio.

• A scrapbook or portfolio can be made with samples of children's work. Many families include more than paperwork. They write a description, include drawings, or take photographs of accomplishments like cooking dinner, raising an animal, producing a play, or building an elaborate block structure.

• Photo albums provide rich and easy records and can include pictures of typical activities, special projects, children working with adults, places you visit, people who visit you, etc.

• Parents' and children's memories are an important part of record keeping, even though they are informal and require little conscious effort. Memories can be the mainstay of personal homeschooling records; some families have few if any other personal records. Memories are richer and more detailed than tangible records. In fact, sometimes photographs and written records interfere with our memories, as we either subconsciously decide we no longer need to remember an event or a scene because a photograph has been taken, or we remember the photograph but have trouble calling to mind the actual event or scene itself.

For information on developing credentials, see Chapter 12. For recording unit studies, see Chapter 7.

Responding to Officials' Requests for Our Records

A frustrating irony of record keeping is that, in a sense, the more complete and extensive our records are, the more careful we need to be about when and to whom we show them. WPA strongly urges homeschoolers to give careful and serious consideration to any request for our records and to show them to officials only after we have clearly established that it is essential that we do so and in the best interests of our own family and other homeschoolers in Wisconsin.

If you are contacted by letter, phone, or in person by a school official who asks to see your records, see Chapter 31.

Chapter 11

Homeschooling for High School

> ***From a 16-year-old homeschooler:*** For me, homeschooling is a way of life. It is about learning what kind of person I am, what I want to know, and what I can do to make a difference in the world.
>
> I'm not exactly certain of how my future will unfold, but whatever I do, I believe I will be ready for it. I don't feel that I could be better prepared for my future. I will never "graduate" from home-schooling because there is so much to know and so many ways to learn it. After all, the world is my classroom.

Can you really homeschool for high school? Questions abound. Some teens wonder about missing the social life at school, getting into college, being prepared for the "real world," being bored, getting tired of younger siblings, and so on. Some parents worry about helping kids learn things they don't know themselves, getting enough equipment for chemistry without blowing up the house, having to spend so much time with a volatile teen, getting teens to learn math and spelling, and helping them get into college.

Questions and doubts are to be expected, especially given the unfairly and undeservedly negative attitude our society has toward teens. But families who have homeschooled for high school can tell you that it's possible to answer these questions positively. In fact, homeschooling for high school is better than attending a conventional school. You can have friends your own age and older and younger. You can learn at your own pace and explore what interests you. Spending more time together as a family reduces tensions, strengthens bonds, and paves the way for interacting as adults. Your flexible schedule makes it easier to find part-time jobs. There's time for music, art, sports, and community service. Colleges increasingly are seeking homeschoolers. You have more control over your life.

Here are ideas for new and continuing homeschoolers. The information is for both teens and parents. But since it had to be addressed to one or the other, it's mostly directed to teens, assuming that parents are reading, too. Many families also find that workshops for teens and parents at the WPA conference provide important information, support, and encouragement that are difficult to find elsewhere.

A few years ago, I was asked to speak to a workshop in our local community on "simple living" about some of the choices our family has made over the years. When I mentioned how much I'd been enjoying my sons' teenage years, one of the participants commented "You're the first person I've ever heard say they enjoyed their teenagers!" He was completely amazed. That brought home to me just how unusual good connections between parents and young people are in our society today—and it made me feel sad for the people who are missing them. I'm guessing there are a lot of parents in this room who are enjoying your teenagers. Don't take that connection for granted—it is something valuable.—From Opening Remarks, WPA Conference, 2005

Choosing an Approach to Curriculum and Learning

Having so many choices for curriculum and learning can be both exciting and overwhelming. You may find it helpful to think about or even list things such as:

- Current interests, including topics you know a lot about; things you want to learn more about (areas of special interest to you and conventional academic subjects like math, philosophy and economics); hobbies, sports, and other activities you enjoy; skills you want to acquire or improve; and anything else that's important to you.
- Short-term goals and plans, including things you'd like to do or learn this week and this month.
- Long-range goals, including major projects, trips to take, work and careers to explore, college plans, and other alternatives for after high school.
- Your strengths, talents, abilities, what you're good at and enjoy.
- Ways of learning that work well for you.
- Resources, including purchased curriculums you might use, courses you might take, people you know who might serve as mentors in various areas, and opportunities for part-time work, volunteer service, travel, etc.

For information about approaches to curriculum, see Chapter 7, which applies to homeschoolers of all ages. Here are ideas particularly for teens.

• Many homeschooling teens pursue their interests and passions in greater depth than conventional schools allow time for, whether learning advanced math, studying classical languages, playing violin or drums, visiting American Civil War battlefields, swimming, hosting websites, serving others, or something else.

• Teens are usually more interested in and motivated to use a curriculum they have helped select or develop, whether this is purchased curriculums, courses they are taking, or projects and interests they are pursuing. Many parents involve their teens and give them as much responsibility as possible for their own learning. Teens who know how to learn and enjoy it are likely to keep learning long after their parents and Wisconsin law require that they do.

• Some teens find that it works well for them to emphasize serious, conventional kinds of academic work in one or more subjects, perhaps by using purchased curriculums or taking live, online, or correspondence courses. (See Chapter 7.) Some teens find the intellectual challenges stimulating; some pursue more conventional study in order to keep certain college or career choices open to them a few years down the road; some simply enjoy this way of learning. Whether teens have used more structured approaches to homeschooling in the past or newly adopt them during the high school years, this can be a rewarding approach for some people.

• Some families use CLEP, AP, and other tests to direct or structure part of their curriculum. It can be satisfying and rewarding to choose a subject area, study for the test, take it, receive college credit, and save a great deal of time and money in the process. See Chapter 8.

• Most of the curriculum packages, outlines, and correspondence schools listed in Chapter 7 offer materials for high school.

• Some homeschooling teens take classes at a community college or technical school before they are 18. They gain college experience and earn college credits. Transcripts from these courses can strengthen applications to other colleges. A note of caution: whatever grade is earned at a community college or technical school will be reported on any future college applications, so make sure that the class is a good match for the student.

• Some families find Grace Llewellyn's *Teenage Liberation Handbook: How to Quit School and Get a Real Life and Education* useful for teens who want to plan their own curriculum.

• Homeschooling for high school takes balance. There is a lot of pressure to prepare for adult life. No matter how you choose to homeschool for your teen years, remember to enjoy the fun, excitement, and wonder that life can bring all of us.

Starting Homeschooling During the High School Years

Many families begin homeschooling during high school and find it rewarding and satisfying. If you are beginning during high school, you have good reason to feel encouraged about the prospect, even if it's because of health concerns, a difficult conventional school experience, truancy, failing grades, or other less than ideal circumstances.

Experienced homeschoolers recommend taking a break from academics, especially if you've had a difficult experience in school. This is especially important for teens. Plan a week, a month, or more to rest, recover, and reconnect with your parents, your siblings, and others. Don't be surprised if you sleep a lot. Most students in conventional high schools don't get enough sleep, and fatigue contributes to whatever problems they face. Many parents find they need a balance: giving teens some space and letting them make some choices while at the same time offering support, making suggestions, guiding their decisions when necessary, and listening when they want to talk.

Activities that work well for this time include: physical exercise, spending time in nature (sitting in the back yard, hiking in a nearby park, camping at the Grand Canyon), creative work (taking photos, doodling, doing counted cross stitch, building a doghouse). Discovering that you're capable, needed, and appreciated does wonders, whether it's driving an elderly neighbor to the doctor, painting the garage, walking the dog, or organizing a game of tag for neighborhood kids. Taking a trip is a great way to make the transition from school to homeschooling. Could the whole family manage a weekend away, or even just a day trip to a nearby park or activity? Do you know someone who supports homeschooling who you could visit? Getting away is a relief, offers new perspectives, and opens the door for a fresh start.

Don't feel pressured or hurry to get into academics, and don't buy a curriculum, especially an expensive one, until you've considered the options. You'll quickly realize that you are learning by doing the activities listed above, and you may want to add some from Chapter 6. To meet Wisconsin's requirement for 875 hours of instruction each school year, you can start counting what you are learning now. For ideas on how to do this, see the section on translating what kids do into school language in Chapter 10. If you attended a conventional school for part of the year, you can count those hours toward the 875.

When the time is right, read Chapter 7 and decide which approach to a curriculum you want to start with. If you're not interested in "school work," see "Homeschooling Teens Who Don't Like School Work" below.

For information on diplomas and other credentials, see Chapter 12.

Homeschooling Teens Who Don't Like School Work

Lots of teens don't like school work. Some had negative school experiences and are convinced they don't like studying or are no good at it. Others think school work is dull and boring. Fortunately, there are many ways to learn, and the approach used by conventional schools is only one. For many people, it's not the best. As a homeschooling teen, you can learn very important things in ways that work well for you. Some people learn well by working with their hands and have amazing abilities to build, fix things, and keep things running. Some learn and work best on projects that involve people working together for a good cause. Some rise to the occasion when given the opportunity to serve those in need, including children, the sick, and the elderly. Artists and other creative types learn by creating and make important contributions through their work. Teens benefit from having the opportunity to do real work that matters.

So don't despair if you didn't do well in school or don't like to do school work at home. It's good that you know that this isn't the best way for you to learn and that you have the courage to say so. (Think how many people know school doesn't work for them but are afraid to say anything, so they just put in their time.) You can discover and develop the important gifts and talents you have and use them to do important work that will make a contribution, whatever it may be.

Consider developing your own curriculum. Developing a curriculum is much easier than it sounds. A curriculum is a plan for learning what you want to learn the way you want to learn it. Suggestions for homeschoolers who don't like school work include:

• Concentrate on your strengths. People have abilities in different areas. Unfortunately, our society tends to overemphasize reading, writing, math, and doing well in school. Much less credit is given to people who have mechanical, musical, physical, or artistic abilities; social skills; problem solving skills; common sense; or other abilities, even though these are at least as important and valuable as doing well in school. (Thomas Armstrong's book *In Their Own Way: Discovering and Encouraging Your Child's Personal Learning Style* discusses the different types of intelligence that people have and the variety of ways in which they learn.) Find the non-school things you're good at (if you don't already know what they are), emphasize them, and worry a lot less about the school stuff. On the other hand, if you really like school stuff but don't like being treated the way schools treat people, now that you're homeschooling you have a chance to learn the way you want to learn, concentrating on the areas that excite you and worrying less about things that don't. If you work on what is important to you, you'll learn the math, spelling, or whatever you need along the way, or you'll discover that you really need them and be motivated to study them.

• Many families start with what interests their teens. Homeschooling lets you build on what you are doing now that works well, on activities that you enjoy and want to do. Don't worry if your interest is motorcycles or photography or baking or something else that isn't usually covered in conventional schools and that doesn't sound like school work. Teens who pursue their interests usually cover the subject areas required by Wisconsin law (reading, language arts, mathematics, social studies, science and health).

• Instead of thinking about what you would be doing if you were going to a conventional school, think about what you need to learn to be an effective adult. Some families build a curriculum based on life skills: learn to get a job and keep it, learn new skills, deal confidently with change, run a household, manage money, buy a car or truck and keep it running, etc. They find that this prepares their kids for life more effectively than a conventional high school curriculum would.

• Every subject offers learning opportunities. Don't limit your homeschooling to things that sound like school subjects. You can learn an amazing amount from baseball, motorcycles, chess, cooking, gardening, caring for animals, repairing equipment, etc.

• Think in terms of learning by doing. We all learn this way. Ask your parents how they learned to do a lot of what they do each day: driving, cooking, things they do at work, parenting, etc. Most people spend most of their lives doing things, not studying.

• Find someone who knows what you want to learn and ask if you can work with them. It could be one of your parents, a sibling, a relative, a neighbor, a friend, or someone you don't know yet. Tell them what you want to learn. Ask them if they will answer questions, share tools and equipment, and things like that. Ask how you can help them, too, maybe by doing easy tasks, cleaning up, or answering the phone for them.

• Include learning to make money in your curriculum. (Conventional schools call this work-study or vocational education.) Call some places that sound interesting and ask if you can visit and find out what people actually do there. Look for part-time jobs that you'll learn from. If a paying job is not available at a place you'd like to work, see if you can be an apprentice or an intern and not get paid. You'll still learn a lot, and it will help you get your next job, since employers want to know what experience you've had. Another possibility is starting your own businesses. Lots of teens baby-sit, mow lawns, and shovel snow. Think about other possibilities: selling homemade specialty breads, making cloth dolls, walking dogs, reading to nursing home patients, setting up and troubleshooting computers, and repairing bicycles. Look for things that need to be done and figure out ways to do them.

• Life skills can be included in any curriculum, offering learning opportunities and practical benefits. Consider cooking, cleaning, laundry, keeping a car running, balancing the family check book, gardening, sewing, home repair, interior decorating, and learning how to work cooperatively with other people (your family or others you know) to get work done so everyone benefits. Conventional schools call this learning "home economics," "industrial arts," and/or "financial management." But these activities also include the basic subjects of reading, language arts, mathematics, social studies, science and health, and learning how to work cooperatively with others.

• Many teens find it helps to spend time on their health. If you already like playing sports and doing other physical activity, count that as part of your curriculum. If not, now is a good time to get more exercise. Consider learning or improving your skills in sports and activities that you can do for years to come: swimming, volleyball, yoga, walking, jogging, whatever appeals to you. Learn about nutrition and improve your diet. Grow a garden. Learn about alternative approaches to health and healing, like acupuncture or herbs.

As an example of how you could develop a curriculum, suppose you're interested in motorcycles. Your curriculum could include some or all of the following, plus other things you think of.

- Visit motorcycle shops. Learn about different cycles. Ask questions. Look at brochures, manuals, etc.
- Buy an old motorcycle or get one from a junk yard. Take it apart and put it back together. If it doesn't run, try to fix it or at least figure out what's wrong with it.
- Start with some money and figure out how you want to spend it: buy a motorcycle, buy gas for the cycle you already have, buy tools, whatever. Keep track of what you spend.
- Visit a motorcycle repair shop. Ask if you can watch the mechanics work. Consider asking if you can work there part-time or help without getting paid.
- Subscribe to motorcycle magazines. Get catalogs of motorcycles and gear. Find websites about motorcycles. Consider joining an online forum.
- Read the history of how motorcycles have been manufactured and used throughout the world.
- Learn how and why Japanese companies have become the major manufacturers, leaving the US with only one significant manufacturer, Harley-Davidson, in Milwaukee.
- Design a motorcycle, making the drawings as detailed as you want.
- If you have your own motorcycle, keep track of how much you spend on gas, repairs, etc.

With a curriculum like this, you learn by doing. You cover the basic subjects required by law. Activities such as reading instruction manuals and magazines, using the Internet, and talking with others about motorcycles are reading and language arts. Figuring the cost of motorcycles and parts and miles per gallon of gas and using metric measurements are math. Talking with older cyclists about how motorcycles have changed, studying the history of the manufacturing and use of motorcycles, and understanding laws governing motorcycle riding are social studies. Science and health are studied by learning how motorcycles run, safety measures, first aid in case of a mishap.

Finally, try not to get stuck thinking of yourself as someone who doesn't like school work or isn't any good at it. Some teens find that once they are working on a topic that interests them or makes sense to them, they are better at reading, writing, and math than they ever thought they would be. Leave the door open to discover this about yourself.

Note to parents: It may be hard to give up the idea that your teens really should be learning school stuff in conventional school ways and to trust that they will be all right if they learn and do what interests them in ways that work for them. However, many families have found that this approach works. Some very famous people, like Thomas Edison and Albert Einstein, did not do well in school. And if school stuff clearly isn't working for your teen, isn't it time to try a different approach?

Enriching Experiences

Whatever approach to learning you have chosen, it is often helpful to think seriously about including practical experience. Here are some possibilities:

• **Apprenticeships and internships**. Some homeschooling teens participate in formal, conventional apprenticeships that are widely recognized, such as those in the building trades, although most require at least a high school diploma. Others design their own informal apprenticeships that involve working, perhaps as a volunteer, with a person or an organization in an area that interests them. Many organizations offer internships in which they hire young people to work with them in exchange for practical experience. (There is considerable overlap between internships and apprenticeships.)

Figure out creative ways to meet the requirements for schooling. For example, if an internship requires "one or two years of college," you can explain that as a homeschooler, you study and learn independently. Describe some of the things you have done that are related to the internship. If you have college credit from CLEP and AP tests, technical school, Internet courses, or other sources, mention that. (See Chapter 12 on diplomas and other credentials.)

If you want to do an internship with an organization that does not offer internships, you may be able to set one up yourself, perhaps modeling it on internships you have heard or read about. You will have a better chance of working something out if you are as flexible as possible about what hours you are available, how many weeks or months you are willing to work, what you are willing to do, etc. However, be clear about your goals and expectations. You will probably be asked to do some routine tasks, like data entry or photocopying, but indicate while you are making arrangements that you only want to spend a quarter of your time (or whatever amount you choose) doing this type of work. Then if you are asked to spend most of your time this way, you can refer to the agreement that was made.

An internship in an area of interest can give you good experience, impressive credentials, and a clearer idea of whether you want to explore the area further. Some organizations frequently offer interns full-time jobs at the end of the internship. But if you decide you do not want to pursue this area, realize you saved yourself time and possibly money by finding that out now instead of after you'd invested in a degree or training in the area. On the other hand, an internship in an area you have no intention of pursuing can be an interesting learning experience and a chance to do something different before you settle down.

You can do an internship in your home town or in another place, giving you a good opportunity to learn about another part of the country or the world. Organizations are often willing to help interns from out of town find housing.

In short, internships are a good way to learn and gain practical experience at much lower cost and sometimes in more interesting ways than enrolling in a technical school, college, or university. Some interns actually earn money; some get a large enough stipend from the sponsoring organization to break even.

• **Employment.** Many approaches are possible. Visit websites like *The Whole Work Catalog* http://www.newcareerscenter.com/

Usually, people under 18 need a work permit. For specific information about who needs one and what hours people under 18 are allowed to work, see the brochure titled *Wisconsin Employment of Minors Guide http://dwd.wisconsin.gov/dwd/publications/erd/pdf/erd_4758_pweb.pdf*

To get a work permit:

1. Get a job.
2. Get the following:
   –A note or form from your employer stating your duties and the hours you will be working.
   –A note (or sometimes a portion of the employer's form) signed by your parent stating that they understand and agree to your duties and hours of work.
   –A copy of either your birth certificate or your baptismal certificate with your birth date on it.
   –Your social security card.
   –Money to cover the small fee. (This will be repaid to you by your employer, often in your first paycheck.)
3. Submit these items. Most public high schools have someone who gives work permits to students in public and private schools, including homeschools. In some places you need to go to a county office instead.

• **Volunteer work.** Volunteering often gives teens the opportunity to serve and to gain valuable experience in areas where jobs are not available or teens are not yet qualified. Teens have volunteered in places that do not usually have conventional volunteers, such as veterinarians' offices, bakeries, pet stores, and other small businesses. Often such work eventually leads to paid employment.

• **Travel.** Again, possibilities and sources of information abound.

Teens and Their Families

Many families who homeschool for high school discover that homeschooling makes the teen years even better. Teens who do not have to cope with the problems and tensions of conventional schools are more confident and easier to get along with. Families who spend significant time together get stronger.

For parents: Many parents find ideas like these helpful.

• Many parents try to concentrate on the positive characteristics of teens, like their energy, enthusiasm, courage, and sense of humor. At the same time, they try to minimize the strong messages from the mainstream culture that teens are difficult and that the teen years are a time of trouble, conflict, and heartache. Generally, this isn't true. Worse, this message tends to become a self-fulfilling prophecy because people (including teens) tend to act in ways they think others expect them to act and because people (including parents) tend to interpret what others say and do on the basis of what they are expecting. Positive expectations really help.

• Work to develop and maintain a strong relationship with your teens. Make time for activities that you enjoy doing together. Go for walks, go shopping, watch movies, read aloud, listen to music, cook favorite foods, and share household tasks. Make communication a priority. It takes a lot of time and energy, but try to be available to listen when teens want to talk and try to see their perspective, remembering that sometimes teens make statements to test out an idea or start a discussion and not because they firmly believe what they are saying. It helps to make eye contact, hug them, and make sure they know you're on their side and you love them.

• Encourage sibling interactions. The strong relationships that can develop among siblings are one of the biggest advantages of homeschooling.

• Ups and downs are an inevitable part of the teen years. One minute a teen may be so mature, thoughtful, and cooperative that their parents are congratulating themselves on what a good job they have done in raising them. A few minutes later, the very same teen may have lost it and have, from the parents' perspective, blown some minor detail totally out of proportion and turned it into a crisis. Understanding that these ups and downs happen to teens, and remembering that they will happen less as teens get older, can help parents stay calm and offer their teens support and love.

• Respect teens' privacy. Don't read notes, journals, or mail unless they ask you to. Treat what they tell you as confidential, even if they haven't said, "Promise you won't tell," with the understanding that you may have to share information they give you with their other parent. Many parents feel that teens' triumphs, worries, experiences, and ideas are for the teens to share, not the parents.

• Ask your teens before you make commitments for them, even if you're sure they'd like to go to the movies with the Browns or you really want them to shovel Mrs. White's sidewalk. Simply say, "I've learned not to make commitments for other people without checking with them. I'll ask John and call you back." Or better: "I'll ask John to call you."

• Many parents learn to care but not to worry. Obviously, they want their teens to be safe, so they discuss concerns they have with their teens, perhaps asking, "What are you doing to make this safe?" They point out that knowing where someone is going and when they expect to be back is a safety issue, not an attempt by parents to control or ruin their teens' lives. (After all, parents don't just disappear without telling anyone where they are going and when they expect to be back.) Once an agreement has been reached, try to relax and trust that all will be well. Worrying takes a lot of energy and is hard on the person who's worrying. It can also undermine the confidence of the person who's being worried about. Keeping their worries under control is one of the most important things parents can do to strengthen their relationship with their teens. Parents can do things like setting an alarm clock for the time teens are supposed to be home at night and then going to sleep. If the teens get home on time, they turn the alarm off. If not, the alarm wakes the parents, and they can decide what to do next. An arrangement like this gives teens a vote of confidence, a reasonable amount of responsibility, and a safety net while parents get more sleep and avoid pacing the floor and then getting upset with returning teens because the parents are so tired and so relieved.

For teens: Teens play a very important role in how well parent-teen relationships work out. Here are some ideas. Again, use what works for you and ignore the rest.

• Sometimes teens have to remind their parents just how mature and capable they are. For years, parents were responsible for keeping their young kids safe, warm, fed, clothed, and all. It's understandable that they occasionally benefit from a gentle reminder that teens can handle parts of their lives now. If your parents aren't giving you as much independence and responsibility as you want, ask yourself and them what you could do to change this.

• Try to see things from your parents' perspective as well as your own. They may be worried about their job, money, their parents, grey hair, new tires for the car, you name it. They could probably use some support and encouragement from you.

• Let your parents know what you appreciate about them.

Teens and parents who spend time together working, playing, learning, and living daily life, who respect each other, and who take time to listen to each other, develop strong, mature relationships that are an enormous help to everyone involved throughout their adult lives.

Social Life

"What about the prom?" Homeschooling teens are often asked about social life, the assumption being that theirs is lacking. Many homeschooling teens enjoy their social lives, and some do attend proms-either those held by conventional schools or events planned especially for homeschoolers. Here are some ideas:

• Homeschooling offers people, including teens, great opportunities for wholesome inter-actions with people of all ages. Therefore, many families consider the social life of home-schooling teens better than that available in conventional schools.

• Homeschooling teens usually develop strong relationships with their parents, siblings, and extended family. It's a big advantage to have a flexible schedule and time to spend with these important people. Many teens feel these relationships more than compensate for any posi-tive social opportunities they might miss by not attending a conventional school.

• Many families help their teens find groups that focus on things they enjoy, like playing sports, producing a play, making music, gardening, learning to spin, or playing chess. If groups do not already exist, consider starting one, which is easier than most people think. Some teens and their families find it works well to plan events that can include the whole family in dif-ferent ways. For example, everyone could share in a potluck. Then the teens could play active sports, board games, music, or other such activities. Parents could organize informal discus-sions or just chat. Younger children could do crafts, active play, or other things.

• When teens want to attend a conventional school for the social life but homeschooling really may be a better alternative, some parents conclude that this decision is too important to be left to teens who do not have the life experience necessary to realize the many ways in which public schools impact people. Some parents ask their teens questions such as: Looking realistically at what conventional high school is like, would your social life really be better? What are you missing that's positive? What are you glad you don't have to deal with? If you went to school, how would you handle the negative? What are the positive and negative aspects of homeschooling that you would lose by going to school? How could you improve your social life other than by going to school, and how could we help you?

Obtaining Good Student Discounts on Auto Insurance: A Model for Getting Homeschooling Credential Accepted

Most automobile insurance companies offer discounts for teen drivers who qualify as a "good student" according to the company's criteria for good students. Homeschoolers have succeeded in getting discounts, setting a helpful precedent.

To get a discount, ask your insurance agent what your company requires and how most people demonstrate that they qualify. Submit a homeschooling equivalent, formatting it so it looks as much like those from a conventional school as possible. Under Wisconsin law, parents or guardians are the official administrators of homeschools, so you have the right and authority to create a report card, assign letter grades, create and sign transcripts, etc. If you purchase a complete curriculum or curriculums for individual subjects, you can use this information to create documents. If you can develop your own curriculum (see Chapter 7), you can translate learning into conventional school language (see Chapter 10). Insurance companies are more likely to understand that you qualify for a discount if most courses are similar to conventional high school courses.

To help convince your agent and the insurance company that you deserve a discount, write a cover letter with information, perhaps on official stationery you have created for your school. Mention points such as:

• Many insurance companies grant good student discounts to homeschoolers.

• Under s. 115.30 (3) of Wisconsin statutes, you as the parent or guardian are the administrator of your homeschool and are qualified to sign the enclosed transcript.

• Many other organizations accept transcripts from homeschoolers. For example, colleges and universities accept them as part of applications for admissions.

If your initial request is denied, you will probably need to write to the management of the insurance company, since agents cannot change company policy. Write to the person who made the policy that is denying you equal and fair treatment. Include a copy of your original letter and your transcript or report card. Send a copy to your insurance agent.

• Homeschools are private schools. There is no basis for thinking that homeschoolers' grades and transcripts are less reliable than those issued by other schools.

• It is discriminatory for insurance companies to refuse to grant homeschoolers the same discounts they offer students in public and other private schools, unless they have compelling evidence that homeschoolers who receive discounts result in more claims at greater expense to insurance companies than non-homeschooling students who receive such discounts.

• Studies have shown that the single most important factor in influencing students' grades is the involvement of parents in their education. Since homeschooling requires strong involvement of parents, it is not surprising that homeschooled students generally receive high grades.

You may want to include a statement indicating you are considering switching to an insurance company that gives good student discounts to homeschoolers who qualify.

Chapter 12

Diplomas, Other Credentials, and Opportunities After High School

Because homeschooling offers opportunities to learn in more ways than conventional schools offer and to gain practical experience in the real world, credentials that homeschoolers develop are different from (and, dare we say, often superior to) conventional transcripts, diplomas, and resumes. Homeschoolers' credentials help make possible a range of exciting opportunities after high school. As a homeschooler, you can feel good about the opportunities that credentials give you to present your experiences and qualifications. You don't need to apologize or worry about not having conventional credentials. Of course, it takes some effort to develop your own credentials. But learning to present yourself well is a valuable skill that will help you gain access to opportunities discussed later in this chapter.

Although homeschooling parents may find this chapter helpful and want to work with their teens in the ways suggested, this chapter is primarily addressed to homeschooling young people.

General Perspectives on Credentials

• Be realistic and positive. Homeschoolers are a minority, different from the dominant culture. Therefore, you need to take responsibility for demonstrating that you are qualified. You won't be handed a widely recognized high school diploma and transcript. You have to translate what you have done into terms that people with conventional backgrounds and experience understand. See Chapter 10. You need to show them that your experiences and knowledge fit their categories and requirements. When you realize that this is inevitably your responsibility simply because you are a member of a minority, when you expect to have to do these things, and when you realize you can do them, you may see this process as an interesting challenge and an opportunity to exercise your creativity.

• Realize that **you** are your most important credential. You as a capable, experienced, energetic person are far more important and impressive than any diploma, transcript, or test score. You can get the credit you deserve by submitting documents that are clear, neat, and direct. When you are meeting someone in person, dress appropriately, make eye contact, shake hands firmly, and speak clearly and directly. If you'd like more information about how to present yourself, ask a parent, family friend, someone you know in business, or another supportive and experienced person, or check the library or the Internet for information on resumes and job interviews.

• Whenever possible, tell the person you are contacting what you can do for them rather than asking them to do something for you. "Think how your business would benefit from having a responsible, energetic teen to serve your customers" is more likely to get the attention of a potential employer than "I'd like to work in your hardware store because I've always liked tools."

• Emphasize your strengths. For example, if you feel your age is an asset, put it near the top of your resume. On the other hand, if it's likely to be a handicap, place it at the bottom or omit it altogether unless you're specifically asked.

• Think outside the box. Don't limit yourself to the style, format, or content of conventional credentials. Submit samples of work you have done, letters of recommendation, and anything else that shows how qualified you are. Show how past activities have prepared you for what you want to do now. For example, point out that you have taken responsibility for a daily paper route, done child care, and organized a neighborhood softball tournament as evidence that you have the skills, responsibility, and experience to work in a city recreation program. Include ways homeschooling has prepared you for whatever you are applying for. (Since many people are not very familiar with homeschooling, they will not realize this unless you tell them.) For example, "As a homeschooler, I am used to taking some responsibility for my own learning. I have been able to spend extra time studying science, which strongly interests me."

• Start keeping records if you're not already. List what you can remember from the past. It is easy to forget or overlook activities and accomplishments. Include as many activities as possible that show yourself acting responsibly, taking initiative, exercising good judgment: hobbies, employment, volunteer work, internships, special projects, presentations, and performances. It is impossible to predict now what might be helpful in establishing qualifications in the future.

• Request letters of recommendation, addressed "To Whom It May Concern," from people who know from experience what you can do. This can include youth group leaders, employers, neighbors, pastors, and others. Request the letters when the activity or connection ends, before you lose track of them or their memory fades.

• Develop ways to meet requests and requirements. Try to show how your experiences fit conventional categories, rather than claiming you're so different that you just don't fit. For example, if a college application requires a recommendation from a high school guidance counselor, rather than writing, "Homeschooler—no guidance counselor," your mother could write something like, "As John's mother, I have also functioned as his guidance counselor. I have observed that he is generally..." Or, better yet, ask someone who has seen you in a learning situation, such as a 4-H or scout leader or a mentor you have worked with, to write a letter to fill the requirement. This is legitimate to do. Remember that administrators who are responsible for getting credentials from applicants, especially in large organizations or institutions, are often more concerned about filling in blanks than they are about what is actually written on them. Once you have filled in the blanks, you can be considered for the next step in the process.

• Consider arranging a personal interview, even if it is not part of the normal selection process. Many people are somewhat surprised to discover how "normal" and qualified homeschoolers are in person.

High School Diplomas

Homeschool diplomas are widely recognized and accepted, partly as a result of the hard work and impressive achievements of thousands of homeschool graduates and their families plus the work WPA has done to interpret Wisconsin's homeschooling law and educate homeschoolers and others. However, there are still times when homeschoolers run into obstacles when they present their diplomas in response to a requirement of a college or university, an employer, a military recruiter, or others.

Basic Information About High School Diplomas in Wisconsin

• Homeschools in Wisconsin are required by statute to meet the same criteria as any other private school and are able to award diplomas just like any other private school. Wisconsin statute 118.165(1) states that "An institution is a private school if its educational program meets all of the following criteria" and then lists the criteria homeschools are required to meet. In other words, homeschooling families can grant their own diplomas as long as they have homeschooled in accordance with Wisconsin's private school/homeschool law and the person receiving the diploma has completed the graduation requirements established by their homeschool. These diplomas are as valid as those from other schools.

• To give your diploma more credibility, print and save a copy of your PI-1206 form each year. Copies of forms filed online during previous school years can be downloaded and printed from the DPI website.

• High school diplomas issued by the administrator of a Wisconsin homeschool (that is, the student's parent or guardian) are recognized and accepted by colleges and universities throughout the US, including all the University of Wisconsin campuses; federal financial aid programs for college and university students, including Pell grants, student loans, etc.; the Wisconsin Attorney General's Office; employers; and the US military.

• Some accredited schools (including some of those listed in Chapter 7) award official third-party diplomas to homeschoolers who have met their graduation requirements. These diplomas are widely recognized, but meeting the requirements costs time and money and may mean that you have to do things you wouldn't otherwise do.

• You can include passing scores on CLEP and AP tests (see Chapter 8) in a number of subjects as part of the basis for a diploma, pointing out that if you have earned college credit, you clearly have more than the equivalent of a high school education.

• Don't assume that you can homeschool for part of high school and then enter or re-enter a public high school and graduate with your class. While a few high schools and school districts are reasonable about giving homeschoolers high school credits for work they did while homeschooling, many others are unreasonable. If you want to homeschool for part of high school and then get a public high school diploma, discuss this with your local high school in advance.

• Earning a General Educational Development (GED) certificate or a High School Equivalency Diploma (HSED) is one way of obtaining "an official diploma." However,

GEDs and HSEDs are widely regarded as an indication that the holder is a quitter, a high school dropout, or someone who was unable to perform well in high school. Because of this social stigma, many homeschoolers understandably resist having a GED on their resume or college application.

Responding to Requests for a Diploma

• Potential employers frequently ask whether an applicant is a high school graduate, but few ask to see a physical diploma. If they do, provide a copy of your diploma along with a cover letter explaining why a homeschool diploma is legitimate.

• Most colleges and universities have experience dealing with homeschoolers and either don't ask for a diploma or accept a homeschool diploma and pay more attention to transcripts, test scores, interviews, etc. However, colleges or programs that haven't had experience with homeschoolers can be quite insistent and among the most difficult institutions to deal with.

• The Federal Government accepts homeschool diplomas as part of applications for student loans and other student aid. To avoid getting involved in a potentially long bureaucratic hassle, WPA recommends that homeschoolers filing a Free Application for Federal Student Aid (FAFSA) check "Homeschooled" only and not "High school diploma" (even if the student expects to receive a diploma) for question 26 on page 3.

• The US military: See the section at the end of this chapter.

• If you need a physical diploma, begin by giving your school a serious name, if you haven't already done so. Possibilities include place names such as Prairie View Academy or River Bend School. Using your last name may emphasize the fact that it's a homeschool, sometimes working to your disadvantage. Then create your own diploma, perhaps adapting the format and wording from a friend's or relative's from a conventional school. Or purchase a blank form online and fill it out. Or hire a calligrapher to letter one in fancy script or learn enough calligraphy to make one yourself. There are also companies that create diplomas, including fold-out versions with padded covers.

Consider including a cover letter with your diploma. Explain that according to Wisconsin laws, the administrator of a homeschool (in other words, the student's parent or guardian) has the authority to grant a diploma to a student who has met the homeschool's graduation requirements. List the individuals and institutions that accept homeschool diplomas. Mention that homeschool graduates have done very well in a wide range of jobs, colleges, universities, technical colleges, the military, etc.

If Your Diploma is Questioned or Rejected

• Don't give up. Diplomas are accepted as widely as they are today because homeschoolers before you worked hard to convince individuals and institutions that homeschool diplomas are legitimate and should be accepted. Now it's your turn to do your part for yourself and those who follow.

• Remember that what you do will affect demands made on others. Work to educate people about homeschooling and diplomas. Don't comply with unreasonable demands that will set precedents and make things more difficult for you and for others in the future.

• Accept that you have to take responsibility for educating the people you are working with. Dealing with homeschoolers is undoubtedly only a small fraction of their job, so you may well know more than they do about homeschooling, Wisconsin statutes governing homeschooling, rules and procedures followed by other institutions concerning diplomas, etc. The officials you are dealing with may have been misinformed. They often see themselves and are seen by others as authority figures, so they don't expect to have their pronouncements challenged. They may not have much experience working out alternative approaches. It's up to you to educate them and suggest other ways to meet requirements. Think outside the box and encourage them to do the same.

• Make sure that a diploma is actually required. Officials are sometimes misinformed and give you inaccurate information. If you are told that a diploma is required by law, ask them to show you the statute, read it yourself, and make sure that it does in fact require a diploma and does not offer alternatives. If you are told that an organization's or institution's rules require a diploma, request a copy of the rules and see if they offer an alternative.

• Explain (perhaps for the second or third time) that homeschool diplomas are legitimate and widely accepted. Use the information above, explaining that homeschools are private schools and you are the legally recognized administrator of your homeschool. Convey this information in person, by phone, in an email, or in a postal letter. If you have already explained all this, try stating it again, perhaps in a different format. For example, if you have already told the official during a phone conversation, send a postal letter this time.

• Sometimes an individual or an institution questions or rejects a homeschool diploma because of information they have read on the DPI's website or have been told by an employee of the DPI or a local school official. When this is the case, you can explain that statements made by the DPI, including those made on its website, are the DPI's opinion. They have not been made into a rule or code and approved by the Legislature, so they do not have the force of law. When the Wisconsin Legislature passed the current homeschooling law in 1984, it did not grant the DPI rulemaking authority with regard to private schools, including homeschools. This is logical since the DPI is responsible for public instruction, not private. In fact, the DPI has no authority to define or regulate homeschools. Instead, homeschools are required to comply with the statutory requirements for private schools, to report their enrollment to the DPI just as other private schools do, and to meet the requirements of the compulsory school attendance law.

Because of the drawbacks to a GED or HSED discussed above, WPA recommends that they only be used as a last resort.

• If you need more help, email WPA or call the WPA Voice Mail.

Developing a Transcript

A transcript is a one-page summary of subjects studied, grades received, and credits earned. Developing your own transcript can be a challenge, especially if you are unschooling or using unit studies. Suddenly you are asked to condense years of learning onto a one-page form that was developed to summarize what students in conventional schools do. How can you give yourself credit without appearing to claim to have done something you haven't done, especially when the brevity of the form doesn't give you a chance to explain?

Let's put transcripts into perspective. A transcript is a quick summary that assures an employer, college admissions officer, or some such person that you have worked on a number of general subjects. It is not ideal for homeschoolers. But when one is required or requested, you are likely to handicap yourself if you don't provide it, so it's a good idea to translate what you have done into categories on a form. Anyone who really wants to know about you will ask for more: samples of your work, a portfolio, a personal interview. A transcript is a quick overview to meet a formal requirement; don't worry about trying to make it more than that.

If you have used a complete curriculum package, it may include a transcript or you can create one by listing the courses covered. If not, list them yourself. If you have used purchased curriculums for individual subjects or created your own, list them. Scores from PSAT, SAT, ACT, CLEP, AP, and other tests can also be included. However, remember that such tests are voluntary, not required.

You can develop your own transcript based on either (1) the number of hours you spent studying a subject (also called "time on task") or (2) what you have learned.

(1) Many conventional schools give one semester credit for 90 hours of class work plus homework. Some homeschoolers use this guideline to develop a conventional transcript with something like 8 semesters of English; 4 to 8 semesters of science; 4 to 8 semesters of math; 2 semesters of American history; 2 semesters of world history; 1 semester of American government; and electives such as art, music, religion, foreign language, industrial arts, home economics, sociology, psychology. Some homeschoolers keep records while they are doing the work, perhaps jotting down things like two hours of English literature right after they spent two hours reading *A Tale of Two Cities,* etc. But you can also look back and estimate the time you spent; creating transcripts is not an exact science. (2) You can develop a transcript that lists general subject areas you have learned about. (If you have been doing unit studies, unschooling, or using some other approach, your transcript is more likely to be accepted if you translate what you have studied into conventional school subjects.) Since conventional transcripts are organized by year, it's a good idea to do that. If you did unit studies, you can group the units under their major subject areas. (For example, frogs and dogs would go under biology, Ancient Egypt and the Civil War under history.) If you read a reasonable number of novels, short stories, and/or poetry, you can list American, British, or world literature. If you learned about political developments in the U.S. and abroad by reading newspapers or other periodicals and perhaps working on a political campaign or opposing legislation that undermined homeschooling freedoms, you can include political science. You can use terms like "General Math" or "General Science" if you didn't focus on specific areas such as geometry or chemistry. If the place where you are applying requires trigonometry or physics, you can study those subjects to fill in gaps you may have.

Or you can explain that you used an interdisciplinary approach that covered basic subjects by focusing on . . . (the major units you studied). If your curriculum was based on learning from living a worthwhile life and pursuing your interests, either translate what you did into conventional school language or explain that you used an interdisciplinary approach and list your major projects.

Since reading, language arts, mathematics, social studies, science and health are required by Wisconsin statutes, be sure to include them. For high school, reading and language arts can be combined as English. Mathematics can be divided into algebra, geometry, etc. or can be one or more years of General Math. Social studies can be divided into American and world history, American government, economics, etc. Science and Health can be divided into Biology, Chemistry, Physical Education, etc. or listed as General Science and Physical Education. Add electives if you want to. Possibilities include Art, Music, Home Economics, Industrial Arts, Bible, Computer Science, etc.

If you will be having a personal interview based on your transcript, it would be wise to think ahead about how you would answer questions like, "How did you study science?"

Conventional transcripts include letter grades for each subject, and families can give grades. People who have taken responsibility for education, worked hard, and learned a lot deserve credit.

Remember that public school students are required to have a certain number of credits in specific subject areas, but private school students, including homeschoolers, do not have to meet such requirements. On the other hand, your transcript is more likely to be understood and accepted if it's not too different from the typical high school course of study. For an overview of what students study at various grades in conventional schools, see a book like Becky Rupp's *Home Learning Year by Year* or a website like World Book Encyclopedia's *Typical Course of Study* http://www.worldbook.com/typical-course-of-study. (Just don't feel overwhelmed when you see what's listed. Students in conventional schools don't learn everything that's listed.)

Developing Portfolios

Although portfolios are longer than transcripts, they may be easier to develop because you have flexibility to include what you want and to explain what you have done. Feel free to be creative and present whatever you think will best communicate your strengths and experiences to your audience.

Letters of Recommendation

Request letters of recommendation, addressed "To Whom It May Concern," from people who know from experience what you can do. This can include youth group leaders, employers, neighbors, pastors, and others. Request the letters when the activity or connection ends, before you lose track of them or their memory fades.

Graduation Ceremonies

Some families participate in the recognition of graduates during the General Session at the WPA conference. Some celebrate the completion of high school with their own graduation ceremony. This can be done for one student and can include a rented cap and gown, guest speakers, musical performances, special awards for younger children in the family, photographs, a reception for friends and relatives, and newspaper coverage. Some choose alternative celebrations and have a family outing, a trip, or whatever they prefer. And some pay little attention to graduation, emphasizing instead the continuity that comes from viewing learning as a life-long process.

Opportunities Available After High School

Although many people expect teens to either go to college, get a full-time job, or join the military after they turn 18, a small but increasing number of young people are choosing to continue homeschooling during the "college" years. Some homeschoolers who could easily go to college decide to continue learning in other ways. Some of them are so good at learning in their own way at their own pace that the idea of college does not appeal to them. Some decide they would rather spend the time and money that college requires to learn in other ways. Since they are saving so much money by not going to college, they feel they can afford to do volunteer work, travel, or continue learning at home rather than needing to find a job immediately. If they need credentials, they consider using CLEP and AP tests (see Chapter 8) or other non-traditional approaches to college or find other ways to meet requirements.

If you decide to postpone college or skip it altogether, there are many possibilities: independent study, internships, apprenticeships, volunteer service, travel, etc. You can take advantage of opportunities you may not have again to explore the world and pursue your special interests before you're tied down by serious responsibilities. You can learn more about what interests you without incurring college debt.

One of the biggest challenges of continuing homeschooling is dealing with the seemingly ceaseless questions people ask you. Say you're going to college, and warm smiles and nods appear. Say you're not, and brows furrow. Such responses can be discouraging, especially if you're not a hundred percent sure of what you're doing yourself. It helps to have a few pat answers ready to hand. Try to use language that sounds familiar to questioners. Say you're studying independently. If you've taken CLEP tests, you can say you're earning college credits independently. If you're mowing lawns or selling handmade dolls or specialty breads, you can say you're running your own business. You can be disarmingly honest: "I haven't figured that out yet," or "I don't know." Or try humor: "I'm getting my mid-life crisis over with now." Really, it's not fair that our society accepts people in their 30's and 40's and 50's deciding to change jobs and careers but expects 18 year olds to know exactly what they plan to do with the rest of their lives. But that injustice will not prevent people from asking you what you're doing. Some mean well and want to be supportive; some are just plain nosy. You can guess what's motivating them and respond accordingly.

Sometimes young adults continue to live at home, or to use home as a base between trips and other explorations or while they attend college. In such cases, everyone needs to make adjustments as a family of parents and children turns into a community of adults. But family members can continue to learn from and support each other; parents and adult children can develop mature relationships; and siblings can stay in close touch. It often takes continuing effort to devise good ways to share household chores. There's no one right way to handle finances, but families make arrangements based on the needs and incomes of each person. Some have a family fund that people contribute to in various ways and that covers shared expenses such as food, rent or house payments, and car expenses. The rewards of continuing to learn, work, and play as a family are great.

A few examples of helpful websites and books for more information on this section include the University of Waterloo's *Career Development eManual/* https://emanual.uwaterloo.ca/, Richard Bolles' classic book *What Color Is Your Parachute? A Practical Manual for Job-Hunters and Career-Changers* www.jobhuntersbible.com/ or a newer approach to the topic, and Barbara Sher's *Wishcraft: How to Get What You Really Want* wishcraft.com/.

Selecting and Applying to Colleges

Admission to college is not a problem for homeschoolers. Although there are a lot of pieces to the college search, many homeschooling families jump in and embrace it as a learning process. Ultimately, it comes down to doing research, visiting campuses, looking at the facts and finances, getting the feel for the personality of each college, and finding a school that is a good overall fit; you're unlikely to find there is only one school that is right for you.

Begin by considering what you're looking for. Small vs. large? Public vs. private? Co-ed vs. single sex? Secular vs. religious? Research institution vs. teaching institution? Highly selective vs. selective vs. open enrollment? Urban vs. rural? Distance from home? Specific majors, sports, or programs? Liberal arts vs. technical?

Do the research and do it early!

• Use the Internet. College admission websites are a great source of information about individual colleges and their programs. Consider college search tools like CollegeBoard's College Matchmaker and the College Navigator http://nces.ed.gov/collegenavigator/.

• The mail you get after you take the PSAT, ACT, and/or SAT tests may introduce you to schools you haven't considered.

• Talk to friends and family. Ask current students and recent graduates about their experiences—what they like, don't like, and wish they had known. The school that's perfect for one person might not be the best fit for another, but talking to these "inside sources" and getting closer to the college experience can help you decide what's important to you.

Reflect on yourself and make a checklist. Write down what's important: academic major, campus setting, distance from home, residence life, study abroad, diversity, activities, etc. This is an ongoing process, but the more you know about yourself and your goals, the easier it will become to find a good match.

When your list of schools is under 10, find a contact person at each school…and keep in contact with them! Your admission rep will be a great source of information on that college, the admission and financial aid processes, deadlines, visits, and so much more. E-mail or call to get more information, find your contact online, or meet them in person at a college fair or a campus visit. Ask if there is someone who works with homeschoolers—there probably is.

Consider attending a college fair. For information, see Wisconsin Education Fairs (WEF) www.wefs.org and NACAC National College Fairs http://www.nacacnet.org/

college-fairs/Pages/default.aspx. Plan ahead. Get a list of participating schools, and mark the ones you definitely want to talk to. List questions to ask. Consider making name labels with information for inquiry cards. During the fair, collect information from schools, share your contact info with them to join mailing lists, meet your admission rep, introduce yourself and show interest in your top schools. Most important, ask lots of questions.

A campus visit program is another possibility. For example, see Wisconsin Private College Week at http://www.waicu.org/students/.

Visit campuses. Make an appointment. Take a tour, eat in the cafeteria, meet as many students as you can. Visit a class and notice class size, how the professor interacts with students, how students act in class, and how engaging it is for students. Talk with a professor, advisor, coach, or someone from Admission or Financial Aid. Stay overnight if possible; this is one of the best ways to get to know a school. Pay attention to everything. Read posters about upcoming events. Notice what the student body is like, how they interact, whether the buildings and grounds are taken care of, and even what's being served in the dining areas. You can find out a lot about a college's personality by visiting the campus and meeting the people who live and study there.

Find a good "fit." Use all of these tools to learn as much as you can about each school and how it matches what you want to explore and accomplish in college. Also, find "target schools" that fit you academically, though you might want to apply to a few "reach" and "safety" schools as well.

Stay organized. Keep a folder for each of your top schools, including notes and questions you need to ask. Set up a calendar to track all the scholarship and admission deadlines. Plan ahead. Start brainstorming for your college application essay and extracurricular list. To save time, find out which schools are on the Common Application.

College Applications

As a homeschooler, your education and experience are different and unique, so you will need to build an application that shows the strength of your experience in a slightly different format. You may want to go into greater depth to explain your transcript, classes, and co-curricular activities to show how they've made you uniquely prepared for college.

• Colleges may have their own application or use a universal one like the Common Application (www.commonapp.org) which allows you to submit the same form to several schools. Applications may be online or by mail. Application fees may vary. Be neat and follow directions; simple things but important.

• The essay shows how well you can write and communicate and gives you an opportunity to let the college get to know you more in depth as an individual, not just a collection of forms and details. Follow the specific topic for colleges that have one, but remember to be creative and show who you are and what's important to you.

• Your transcript is often the most important part since it shows your curriculum, accomplishments, and how well you are prepared academically for college. Wisconsin homeschoolers can create their own transcripts, which should include a list of courses, duration (credits), and a mark of performance (grades). (See the section on transcripts above.) Feel free to also include an annotated transcript that gives a more substantive account of books you used, what and how you learned, and/or a portfolio of writings or projects.

• Letters of recommendation are outside sources that back up your transcript and the strengths of your application. Submit 1-3 letters from teachers, supervisors, coaches, youth group leaders: adults who know you well and can comment on character, strengths, personal interactions, and academic capability. Ask them to briefly describe their relationship and then give a brief account of you in that setting. Parents can submit a "counselor" recommendation but shouldn't be the main recommender.

• Most selective schools require either the ACT or SAT test; most will take either. Take these tests in fall or spring of your junior year. Review books and practice tests are extremely helpful preparation. The PSAT, the early version of the SAT, qualifies you to apply for a National Merit Scholarship (http://www.nationalmerit.org/). You can take the ACT or SAT multiple times, but check with your colleges to see whether they take the best composite score, average all the scores, or take the best of each of the individual scores to make a "superscore."

• You are probably involved in more activities than you realize, so start building your extracurricular activities list early. It's helpful to make one long activity list or resume and attach it to all applications. It can include 4-H, Scouts, homeschool groups, clubs, religious activities, youth groups, volunteering, theater/music, sports, work experience, travel, public speaking, awards, and more. Give yourself credit for everything you've done. Go into detail and show leadership positions and particular projects. Extracurriculars are not usually the deciding factor in an application, but they can be significant for scholarships.

• If you use the Common Application, you can include their homeschool supplement which gives you an opportunity to explain your philosophy of homeschooling, curriculum, grading system, and any outside classes or programs. It can make it easier for colleges and admission reps to understand your educational background.

College Search Timeline

Sophomore/Junior Year

Begin thinking about colleges.

Do some initial research and start setting your parameters for colleges.

Attend a college fair.

Junior Year

Prepare for and take the PSAT test in October.

Prepare for and take the ACT or SAT in the fall or spring.

Read your college mail.

Start making some campus visits.

Find a contact person at your top schools.

Senior Year

Apply to colleges in the fall. (Most teens apply to 4-5 schools, often including a "back-up.")

Retake ACT or SAT in the fall, if necessary.

Apply for scholarships from colleges and outside organizations.

Follow timelines for scholarship interview days, housing deposits, etc.

Visit or revisit top schools.

File FAFSA and financial aid paperwork by March 15.

Enroll by May 1, the National Response Date for all colleges and universities.

Instead of attending a conventional college or university, college credit and a college degree can be earned from recognized and accredited colleges on the basis of live, online, and correspondence courses; tests such as CLEP, AP, and DSST; and learning from life experience that is documented in a variety of ways. Although these programs were originally developed for adults, they are adaptable to homeschoolers and are an excellent alternative for teens who prefer independent study and/or learning from experience. The significant savings of time and money makes them worth considering. (See Chapter 8.)

Writing Successful Scholarship Applications

The total costs of college include tuition and fees, room and board, books and supplies, transportation, and other personal expenses. College websites are now required to have a Net Price Calculator online where students can enter academic and financial information and get an estimate of what the net cost of attending might be, once aid is factored in. This can be very helpful, but keep in mind it is just an estimate.

Costs of many private colleges look higher than those of public ones initially, but private schools often have more to offer in scholarships and financial aid. Also, research each school's four-year graduation rate. While many public universities are less expensive per year than most private colleges, many students find that it takes a fifth or sixth year to graduate. Additional years may be doubly expensive, considering the cost of tuition plus the missed opportunity for income. However, students who begin at a public university with credits from CLEP, AP, etc., have a better chance of graduating in four years.

Scholarships and need-based financial aid are two separate things. Scholarships are based only on merit of the student: academics, leadership, extracurriculars, and skill in the arts or athletics. Need-based financial aid is based on your family's ability to pay for college and includes grants, different types of loans, and student employment.

Almost all financial aid for college students is handled by the institution you attend. Colleges and technical schools usually require that parents submit the Free Application for Federal Student Aid (FAFSA) http://www.fafsa.ed.gov/. It requires private information about your family and its finances, based on information submitted to the IRS. The federal government calculates your family's contribution based upon family and student income and assets, with income more heavily weighted. This amount is nearly constant no matter where you go to college. For example, if the FAFSA determines that your family should pay $6,000 a year, a state college and an Ivy League university will both expect your family to pay that much of the total cost per year, whether it's $7,500 or $43,000. Schools usually offer financial aid to cover the rest. However, the proportions of loans to grants (scholarships) may vary. Obviously, the larger the loans and the smaller the grants, the more debt you'll end up with.

You can estimate your family's Expected Family Contribution (EFC) by using the EFC calculator at www.finaid.org. This site also has other calculators and many valuable resources for understanding the financial aid process, as do www.collegeboard.com and Financial Aid for Students http://www.studentaid.ed.gov. See http://heab.state.wi.us/index.html for financial aid programs offered by the state of Wisconsin.

Most scholarships come directly from colleges, so check for separate applications and deadlines and ask if they are renewable each year and require a minimum grade point average.

Private scholarships and grants are offered by organizations and individuals that are not connected to a specific school. These awards are not based on how much money your family has. Many fewer students apply for them than request financial aid from a given college, so they are a very good option to consider. However, they are subtracted from the financial aid the school is giving you, not from the amount your family is expected to contribute, until the private scholarships and grants you have gotten total more than the school's financial aid.

Here are suggestions for applying for these private scholarships and grants.

• Start early. Two years before you plan to go to college is a good time to begin. Writing essays and collecting information always take more time than expected. To be eligible for some scholarships, you have to take the PSAT or the National Merit Student Qualifying Test (NMSQT) in the fall of your junior year. Students who score well on the NMSQT are awarded grants based on their scores, but the test results are also used by others.

• Look widely. No one place lists all the scholarship opportunities, but one reliable site is FastWeb: http://fastweb.com. Scholarship offers may also be posted on the bulletin board at the bank or your grandmother's place of work. The public library has books at 378.3. Free Internet screeners abound. (Places that charge a fee are likely to be a scam or to do the same service offered for free elsewhere.) The free Internet sites do require you to reveal personal information, especially about your abilities, background, and interests, to identify possible matches. Each year scholarships go unused because the left-handed piccolo-playing descendant of an Italian chef can't be found.

• Check out the sponsors. Does the scholarship or its sponsor have a website? How much money do they give out? Are there multiple scholarships or just one? How many people applied last year? Being one of twenty applicants gives you a better chance than being one of twelve hundred. You may even see essays from last year's winners and get a better idea of what the sponsor is looking for.

• Apply for scholarships that match your strengths. You have unique qualities, talents, and heritage. The largest scholarships ($10,000 to $100,000) are awarded to those who have completed some special project. The grand prize of them all, the Siemens-Westinghouse Science Competition at www.siemens-foundation.org may not be your cup of tea, but perhaps the citizenship-oriented Ronald Reagan Future Leaders Scholarship is.

• On applications, neatness counts. Do not have Mom fill it in even though her handwriting is better. The gender and generation of the writer are fairly easy to figure out. Typed applications are even easier to read and make it look as if the applicant is taking time and care.

• Be complete. Think of applications as a way for the people giving scholarships to get to know you. Of course, most applications are oriented to conventional schools and ask about after-school clubs, student government, and team sports. Think creatively about how you can introduce yourself, fit your experiences into their categories, and show them why you are so wonderfully deserving of their scholarship. Put something in every section; incomplete applications get eliminated early in the process.

Well-rounded students always look good. Even if you love nothing but baseball, you can demonstrate how much you've covered. Statistics are math as a hobby, running the fundraiser for your team demonstrates leadership, making announcements at the game is public speaking, photographing the team qualifies as art, and sports is easy, just say baseball. Suddenly a narrowly focused individual has a finger in every pie.

Letters of recommendation are opportunities to present additional perspectives on who you are to people reviewing scholarship applications. No matter how disinterested they try to be, parents' letters are easily discounted. Students who attend conventional schools may use no one but teachers for letters of recommendations, but homeschoolers need more variety. Your pastor, choir director, and Sunday school teacher look like one recommendation to the scholarship reader since they come from the same place. Try to have a set of recommendations from people who know you from different viewpoints, perhaps one from someone from church, one from an employer or volunteer supervisor, and one from someone who has experience with you as a learner, such as a 4-H or scout leader or a teacher from a class you took. Ask them for reflections on you as a motivated and mature person.

Essays can make up for great weaknesses in the rest of an application, but only if they are great essays. Write, wait a day, and then reread and rewrite. Get comments from others. Rewrite again. Check out examples of good essays online and in the public library in the section on essays and applications, 378.1. Reread those winning essays from years past at the scholarship sponsor's website. And rewrite again.

Remember you are trying to earn money here. If you regularly earn $10 an hour, a $5,000 scholarship is equivalent to 500 hours of work. Doing a thorough job, putting in 25 hours on an application, means you could be reaping $200 an hour, and you can use the information you have gathered again and again. You may be able to use the same letters of recommendation, different versions of the same information, perhaps even variations of the same essays on other scholarship applications and even college or apprenticeship applications. Opportunities are there if you look hard enough.

Attending Technical College

The Wisconsin Technical Colleges System consists of 16 colleges with 47 campuses throughout the state. Here are general admissions policies. Because each college has some control over its own policies, you may find that the campus you contact has different policies that work in your favor or against you.

You can take individual courses as a special student when you are 16 years old (or younger if the dean of the college determines that you can handle the course). These can be counted as part of the 875 hours of instruction required for homeschooling. To enroll in a certificate or degree program, private school students, including homeschoolers, must have a high school diploma. (Public school students can enroll in a certificate or degree program and take courses before they have graduated from high school through the Youth Options program, but that opportunity is not available to private school students.) A homeschool diploma awarded by a parent or guardian is acceptable if it is accompanied by a transcript that identifies the subject areas and explains the grading system and by a statement that the high school course of study was completed and a diploma awarded. Some high school courses that are prerequisites must be taught in specific ways. For example, some science courses must include lab work. An additional, unusual, and unnecessary rule states that homeschoolers who are still in high school cannot take courses during hours that public schools are in session.

Since some technical colleges may not have much experience with homeschoolers, they may not have firm policies or may initially say no to your requests simply because they are uncomfortable dealing with uncertainty and change. If so, it often works well to keep things somewhat open and fluid, ask who else you could talk with, and keep going until you reach someone with the authority and flexibility to give you a better answer. Feel free to suggest alternatives and solutions to problems. You are, after all, a creative and experienced homeschooler who will get farther if you take responsibility for yourself rather than just accepting what other people tell you.

If you are considering attending a technical college, contact them and ask questions like those suggested below. Make detailed notes that include the name of the person you spoke with, their title, the date, and their responses. If their answers are definite enough and what you were hoping to hear, you may also want to write them a letter in which you state your understanding of what they told you and ask them to respond within 10 days if anything you have stated is incorrect.

1. What are the admissions requirements for the following courses or degree or certificate programs? (List the ones you are interested in.)
2. May I take individual courses as a special student before I graduate from high school and count them toward a degree or certificate program once I have graduated?
3. If there are high school courses I must take before I enroll in courses I want to take, are there special requirements for how they are taught?
4. What type of high school diploma is required for the degree or certificate program I am interested in?
5. Can credits from CLEP, AP, or DSST tests be used to meet the degree or certification program I am interested it? (See "The Many Uses of CLEP and AP Tests" in Chapter 8.)
6. Is there anything else I should know?

A note of caution: whatever grade is earned at a community college or technical school will be reported on any future college applications, so make sure that the class is a good match for the student.

For more information, go to Wisconsin Technical Colleges http://www.witechcolleges.org/.

Military Service

Tier I recruits have more opportunities in the military than Tier II or III. The military will now accept homeschool diplomas. Specifically, the most recent Department of Defense policy memorandum regarding educational credentials for recruits, dated June 6, 2012, implements Section 532 of the National Defense Authorization Act for 2012 and states that diplomas issued by homeschools are to be treated the same as diplomas issued by public and conventional private schools, provided that the candidate for enlistment scores 50 or higher on the Armed Forces Qualification Test. Your homeschooling diploma and a score of 50 or more on the AFQT qualifies you for Tier 1 status. (Recruits with diplomas from public and conventional private schools are automatically classified as Tier 1.) Another option is that one semester (fifteen hours) of college credit can be used by recruits, including homeschoolers, to gain Tier I status.

Here are suggestions for those who are interested in military service:

• Keep copies of your PI-1206 forms, especially during the high school years. (See Chapter 4.) They will give you something official to give to a recruiter.

• Provide your homeschooling diploma. You can submit a transcript and "third party diploma" from a correspondence school or homeschool program from which you graduated. Or you and your parents can create your own diploma, following suggestions earlier in this chapter. Include any "third party" certification you have, such as transcripts from courses you have taken in college, technical school, or through distance learning or scores from ACT, SAT, CLEP, AP, or DSST tests. (For information about these tests, see Chapter 8.)

• If the first recruiter with whom you talk will not grant what you want, find another recruiter.

• Check recent WPA newsletters and the WPA website to see if there have been further developments on this topic.

Chapter 13

Socialization

"What about socialization?" Homeschoolers are frequently asked this question. Many non-homeschoolers can understand that children could learn basic subjects at home, perhaps even better than in conventional schools. But what about socialization? Aren't homeschoolers too isolated? How do homeschooled children learn to get along with other people, especially those with backgrounds different from theirs? How do they learn to hold a job?

In response to such questions, homeschooling parents explain that actually homeschooling is a big advantage when it comes to socialization, for reasons such as the following.

• Homeschooled children have many opportunities to interact with their peers. Homeschoolers are often active in youth organizations such as 4-H and scouts, church groups, and sports teams. They interact with children in their neighborhoods and in homeschool support groups.

• Homeschooled children interact with people of all different ages, benefiting from the rich experience and perspective this provides. They play with and baby-sit for younger children and participate in activities that include children of different ages. They get to know adults through jobs, apprenticeships, community organizations, neighborhoods, volunteer work, shared interests, and in other ways. They may volunteer in nursing homes, visit senior citizen centers, and get to know older relatives.

Many homeschooling parents feel that it is better for their children to grow up surrounded by people of different ages than to be limited to children their own age. School and army boot camp are about the only places people spend time limited to people their own age. It helps a lot to have older, more mature people around as role models. It is usually difficult to find strong role models in a classroom of children who are close to the same age.

• Homeschooled children learn a great deal from interacting with members of their immediate family and often their extended family as well. They have more opportunities to spend time with their families, get to know them well, and develop strong bonds. They learn how to maintain relationships over time and work out long-term solutions to problems rather than moving on to a new set of friends.

• Homeschooled children have good opportunities to develop a strong sense of identity and a commitment to their values and beliefs. People with this kind of inner strength are often better able to get along with others, including people who have ideas and beliefs very different from theirs, than are people who are less sure of themselves and more easily confused and threatened.

• Homeschooled children have more opportunities to see and participate in real life on a daily basis. They are home while a plumber makes repairs and the neighbors' house is built. They have a clearer and more realistic sense of what grownups do in their jobs and in other interactions. They observe their parents solving problems, managing the household, and pursuing their own interests. They have opportunities to participate in things that happen in the real world, to balance the family checkbook, change a flat tire, help redecorate the family room. They watch younger siblings and friends' babies grow, and they have a clearer sense of the responsibilities of parenthood.

• Many homeschooling parents feel that the social interactions that take place in conventional schools are negative often enough that they are glad their children do not have to have these experiences at such a young age. As John Holt put it, "If there were no other reason for wanting to keep kids out of school, the social life would be reason enough." Homeschooled children learn to resolve conflicts, deal with difficult people and challenging situations, speak up for themselves, and work well in groups, even though they are not forced to deal with challenging situations in classrooms and on playgrounds and school busses. Many homeschooling parents feel that because their children have the opportunity to grow up in a secure family environment, with many positive role models to follow within their family and outside it, they become strong individuals who are capable of dealing with challenges as adults. They are not limited because they did not grow up facing difficult situations in conventional schools. Rather they are stronger because they had a chance to grow in a more supportive environment.

• Colleges and employers have discovered that grown homeschoolers are strong people who can take responsibility, exercise initiative, cooperate with others, participate in team efforts, and function well as young adults.

How many of you have ever had someone comment on how unusual your child is because he or she can carry on a conversation with an adult, or play with children of a different age?

As our children grow up, at some point we see that they are ready for experiences beyond the home. For homeschoolers, this will probably be in a family-to-family context—a church or community group, homeschool support group, 4-H club—where we interact with people of all ages and generations. This is very different from the kinds of interactions that happen in institutional settings where people are segregated by age or ability or interest. I believe these family-based relationships are healthier for children—and for adults. . . .

In addition, every child is learning about his or her place in the family and community, about responsibility, respect for others, communication, interdependence. This kind of "socialization" is far more valuable than the hierarchical, age-segregated institutional social life kids get in school.—From Opening Remarks, WPA Conference, 2005

From a homeschooled teen: I still keep in touch with friends that I've known since I was two. I still keep in touch with friends that I've known since **they** were two. I've made lasting relationships with interesting people of all ages.

Chapter 14

Support Groups

Participating in Support Groups

Homeschooling support groups serve several important functions.

• Many homeschoolers value the opportunity to share experiences, concerns, and resources. It can be affirming and strengthening to talk with others about common values and concerns. Hearing about other families' homeschooling experiences can help new homeschoolers get off to a good start. It can also be reassuring to experienced homeschoolers and give them fresh perspectives, new ideas, and strong support. It's nice to be with a group of people who celebrate a family's decision to homeschool and don't question it.

• Children often benefit from a chance to meet and interact with other children. They enjoy finding other children who are also homeschooling, which helps them deal with being different from conventionally schooled children.

• Support groups also provide a means by which homeschoolers can coordinate their efforts and work together to promote a favorable climate for homeschooling and solve problems on the local and state level. Groups can plan ways in which they will deal with local schools and school boards, share experiences they have had, meet their state legislators, decide who is in the best position to meet with a reporter requesting information about homeschooling, and work together in other ways so that their actions are more effective. Sometimes people who feel they are being forced into homeschooling by threats of prosecution for truancy, or who are headed for legal difficulties for some reason, are able to avoid problems because of what they learn from support group members and meetings.

Support groups come in all sizes, have a variety of purposes, and choose their activities from a wide range of possibilities.

• Some groups rely on emails; members share experiences, resources, concerns, information about local events, etc. They seldom have face-to-face meetings of the whole group.

• Some groups have primarily activities for children and the whole family. Field trips are popular. If parents take turns making arrangements, the planning and organizing take less time than if each family planned its own outings. Parents, older children, or outside resource people can lead craft activities, science experiments, folk dancing, singing, and sports activities. Guest speakers can cover a wide variety of topics. Activities in which many people participate also work well, such as talent shows or events that focus on a historical period or another culture.

• Some groups emphasize meetings for parents that may cover legal and political issues, approaches to learning, curriculums and resources, or provide opportunities to share experiences and concerns.

Many homeschoolers belong to both WPA and a local support group, since each of these provides different kinds of assistance. WPA works with support groups in a number of ways. Homeschoolers can support their local group and WPA at the same time by joining WPA through their support group. The group keeps part of the membership fee and sends the rest to WPA. The homeschoolers have the benefits of full membership in WPA. It works best if as many people as possible from a support group are also members of WPA. Then each family receives its own copy of the newsletter and special bulletins, and WPA is better able to continue its work. When a support group counts on receiving important information from just a few people who are members of WPA, communication and effectiveness are much more limited.

For information about support groups in your area, contact your WPA Regional Coordinator listed on the WPA website and in newsletters. Since groups differ, consider visiting more than one, if possible.

Starting a Support Group

If there is not a support group in your area, consider starting one, even if you have not done this kind of thing before. Here are some suggestions:

• Talk with other support group leaders. Your WPA Regional Coordinator can give you the names of leaders in the surrounding area.

• Support groups often work best if they meet the needs and desires of the families involved, so feel free to plan your support group so it suits the people participating. You may want to have the first meeting be a potluck of snacks, brunch, lunch, or supper, since food brings people together and breaks the ice. Then there could be a general discussion of what kinds of activities the people in the group would like. Many groups find it pays to be flexible and willing to make changes as the group grows and develops. Remember that getting started is often the hardest part. Once the group has some experience, it can build on events and activities that have worked well in the past.

• Decide how the group will be oriented. Some groups focus on homeschooling in general and welcome anyone interested in homeschooling, regardless of their approach to education, life style, religion, etc. Other groups prefer the support that comes from being with a group that has more in common, so they limit the group to people with a particular perspective on homeschooling or religion. Each of these approaches has advantages and disadvantages.

• Keep the organization of the group as simple as possible, but share the work as much as possible so one person or a few people do not have all the responsibility and work. It often works well to start by having the person who is most interested in a given activity (like a field trip) be its coordinator.

• Feel free to start small. Two or three families is enough to start a group. Small groups are often easier to manage than larger ones. If a group starts small and grows, members have a chance to learn a lot while the group is still small and be prepared for the challenges of a larger size.

• Register with WPA using the form on the WPA website. Also, inform your WPA Regional Coordinator. If you want new members, ask them to mention the group to people who call for information about homeschooling.

• Many groups grow by word of mouth. Most homeschoolers know at least a few other homeschooling families. Other approaches to publicity include an article or ad in a local newspaper and posters in your library, place of worship, natural foods store or co-op, and children's book store or resale shop.

Years ago, homeschoolers belonged to support groups because the law was difficult, materials were difficult to find, homeschoolers were scarce. We joined in mutual support no matter why or how each family chose to learn.

We belong to Wisconsin Parents Association because we still need to keep abreast of those legal concerns. But why are we in a local support group after more than a decade of homeschooling?

There are the easily seen advantages of activities and field trips. Those new to homeschooling find somewhere to start to find information. There are opinions on books and materials, some even available for your use. And if you are moving to another state, someone in the group is sure to have some sort of contact there to find out about the legal situation. But what besides potlucks does a group offer to those who've been around for a while?

Support. Perspective. It is really quite simple. Thank goodness that on the day when it seems that little Elroy will never learn to read (and the kids squabble, dinner burns, the dog runs away, and you have the flu), someone else can listen and remind you of the day when Elroy figured out the tax on the Christmas tree. And you can help the someone else on his or her bad day.

Further, we can see examples of the variation in styles and aptitudes of our family members. My child may sink his teeth into specialized subjects and never come up for air, and I fear that he'll never master basics like spelling. Your child may have a thorough grasp on all those essentials but hasn't ever been passionately interested in something, anything. Or it may be that Elroy's brother Eddie learns only through music, a fact unimagined by mother Edwina until she saw Beauford's daughter Beatrix memorize, in one afternoon, four pages of her role in a play by singing it to herself. Or it may be that your way of explaining how to divide numbers with decimals is easier to understand than mine.

Group members whose children are older can give us some idea of what to expect in days to come. I remember being so envious of Martha when she described the many things George was doing at twelve. He was so capable, mature, so independent! It sounded so far away from what our son, then ten, would or could do. Now I have a twelve year old, and he is so capable, so mature (usually), so independent. And so am I.

And younger children remind those with older children that some skills have been learned that were previous challenges. Tying those shoelaces may have seemed like climbing Everest until figured out. Then it was as forgotten as was the process of learning to walk.

From those ahead, I see that there will always be something to worry about. Reading and arithmetic, then spelling, then to: Are they getting enough challenge in science? Do they need more foreign language? And I realize I will always have something to be concerned about in a conventional school or at home. A speaker said at a WPA Conference a few years ago that after 17 years of homeschooling, she felt she was finally getting the hang of it. Her message reminded me that although I often tell my children that mistakes are part of life and learning, I still expect my parenting and my homeschooling to be perfect.

When your friend with children in conventional school complains, you are the safe listener—uninvolved, unlikely to cause a problem with the status quo. Yet were you to have a conversation where you mentioned some problem with homeschooling, your schooling friend immediately suggests that putting your child into a conventional setting is the answer. You won't have to hear that in a support group!

Support and perspective. And friends whose values of family are similar to our own. Our family still belongs in our local support group.

Chapter 15

Being a Homeschooling Family

We understand that homeschooling is not just a form of education, it is a lifestyle. As families we immerse ourselves in the rhythm of life and relish each and every moment.
~We share our child's joy as they discover the quiet magic of a butterfly.
~We witness our child's pride when they master a new skill such as tying their shoes.
~We dry their tears when the family dog dies and are surprised when they comfort us in return.
~We worry when our newly-licensed teenager drives off alone for the very first time.
~We experience those bittersweet feelings when a child moves away from home, and we wish them all the luck in the world as they take the next step on their journey.
~We hope our adult children will find a soul mate with whom they can share life's adventure.
~And, we stand by as they struggle to overcome defeat for that is what life hands all of us at times.

Some may say these experiences are not unique to homeschooling families, and indeed they are not. What makes us different is that we simply experience more of these events. We not only spend a lot of time with our children, we embrace the opportunity. And as a result, our lives are enriched and we are forever changed.—From Opening Remarks, WPA Conference, 2004

From an at-home father trained as a corporate lawyer: When I think back on this half-finished journey, and ponder alternative paths I could have taken, I am convinced that nothing I could have done in this wide world would have been more important or fulfilling than what I have done and am doing. I feel incredibly fortunate to be so fully involved in the lives of my two children and to enjoy a closeness to them that sadly seems all too rare.—From Opening Remarks, WPA Conference, 2002

Without question the single most significant and important thing that homeschooling has given our family is . . . our family. When I reflect on our family's experience during these "school" years, what stands out are the relationships (including those with extended family and close friends) that we have been able to build and strengthen, the times we have spent together in activity, long conversation (or companionable silence), and the trust between us that has allowed our son to pursue rewarding and challenging activities on his own. I can't imagine it would've been possible if we had given over the care and raising of our child to the state for eight hours out of every "school" day.

Now that he is on the cusp of the next stage of life – as an adult – I treasure even more the opportunity that I have had to really come to know him and the privilege I have enjoyed to witness and participate in all the stages of his development into the compassionate, caring, and competent person that he is. And it's not any less important that we have had **fun**!

Many homeschooling parents find it's helpful to think about how they will parent as homeschoolers. The more confident and comfortable they are with the approach to parenting they have chosen, the more smoothly their homeschooling goes. In fact, some homeschooling parents feel that parenting is the most important part of homeschooling. When parenting is going well, learning seems to go well, too.

Of course, parenting homeschooled children does not always go smoothly. But it is much more manageable than it may seem at first. Homeschoolers find that the time they have together as families is very different from the time that is left over after children attend a conventional school. It is more even, more manageable, more enjoyable (most of the time), and more satisfying.

Homeschooling parents often find it is easier to parent children when they are home-schooled than when they attend conventional schools. Among the reasons:

• Homeschooled children are often more relaxed and easier to get along with than those who are dealing with the tension and stress that result from being with a large group of people for long periods of time in a big and impersonal institution.

• Homeschooled children and their parents spend more time together and share more experiences than they would if the children attended a conventional school. They generally know and understand each other and get along better. Homeschooled children also have more opportunities to develop strong relationships with their siblings.

• Homeschools have more flexible schedules than conventional schools. Homeschoolers can reduce tension by doing things at a more reasonable pace. They can take time to deal with challenges and conflicts when they arise. They can get enough rest.

• Homeschooling parents can support and encourage their children more through home-schooling than can parents of conventional school students. Homeschoolers can choose the curriculum and schedule they want to follow, the food they will eat, the physical setting in which they will work, and other important things. Many parents find that even with the work and responsibility involved in homeschooling, it is easier than trying to work with conventional schools to provide learning environments, curriculums, social interactions, safety, and other things they want for their children.

Homeschooling also nurtures connections between siblings. When we first started homeschooling, a neighbor told me that during the school year, her children, though only a year or so apart in age, would have nothing to do with one another. It was not "cool" to like one's brother or to spend time with someone in a different class or age. During the summer, the siblings would gradually come to enjoy one another's company. "They're just getting to be friends with each other about the end of August," she said, "and then school starts again and that is all lost." I really value the deep connections my children have with one another—and I often forget to appreciate how out-of-the-ordinary that is in our culture.—From Opening Remarks, WPA Conference, 2005

Learning More About Parenting

Learning to parent can be challenging. Many people do not want to simply follow in their parents' footsteps. Our society has multiple approaches to parenting, not one "right" way. However, the choices that are available give parents the opportunity to parent in ways that they feel work for them and their children. WPA is committed to working to reclaim and maintain parents' and families' rights and responsibilities. WPA does not recommend any particular approach to parenting. Each family needs to make its own decisions.

Here are some ways many parents learn more about parenting:

• Parents talk with other parents. They find it helps to spend time with parents who are parenting the way they want to and learn from their examples and experiences. Some form support groups in which parents meet regularly to share their concerns. (See Chapter 14.)

• Reading is another option. Given the wide range of books available, they choose carefully, concentrating on books that make sense to them and support their ideas and beliefs and ignoring books that they disagree with. They may rely on a source they trust for suggestions, such as friends, an author they like, or an organization or website that recommends and sells carefully selected books on parenting.

• Many parents gain knowledge and direction about parenting from their religious and moral beliefs and practices.

• Many learn from their own experience and from watching and interacting with their children. They build on what is going well and work to solve problems that arise.

Some Ideas About Parenting Homeschooled Kids

Many parents find that ideas like these make parenting homeschooled kids more manageable and enjoyable.

• Many families work hard to develop and maintain respect for each other as unique and important individuals who have important things to contribute to the family, depending on their age and talents. They develop and maintain patterns of communication that demonstrate this respect in many ways, such as by listening to each other and emphasizing the positive.

• Many families make communication a high priority, reasoning that if they can communicate effectively, they can handle challenges. Good communication takes a lot of time and effort.

• Being careful about labels can be important. Negative labels limit people's ideas about themselves. They tend to become self-fulfilling prophecies, because people often do what's expected of them and observers tend to interpret what they see so it fits what they're expecting, thereby confirming the negative label. People often get stuck living up to a negative label. Even positive labels cause confusion and problems. How can someone who is "the musical one" have trouble understanding sharps and flats? What are people who have been labeled "always cheerful" supposed to do when they're feeling down?

• Discovering and developing ways of working and relaxing together strengthen family bonds and give children good opportunities to grow. With the rapid pace of today's society, it often takes extra effort to ensure that family members have time together. Families share household tasks, attend religious services, play active and quiet games, read aloud, cook special meals, go on short and long trips, play music, and do other activities. These shared experiences make it easier to get along.

• Some families find it helps to give children opportunities to make some of their own decisions, in ways that work within the family structure. Young children can be asked whether they want to wear the red shirt or the blue one. Older children may participate in the family decision making process in a variety of ways, depending on how the family functions. Children who have the opportunity to make decisions are often more cooperative, feel they have a part in what is happening, gain valuable experience, and are more prepared for adult life.

Opportunities for Homeschooling Parents

Finding time for everything that needs to be done is a challenge for parents, including homeschoolers. Parents' time for themselves often gets sacrificed first. Here are some ideas:

•Decide what **you** want to do when you have free time: journal, finish your skirt, plant lettuce, order prints of recent photos, wash the kitchen floor that's bugging you, sleep, daydream. It's your choice, not up to someone else. Some parents make a list so they don't waste time thinking up things. Some only do things they can't do when the kids are around.

• Include yourself in the ways your family meets everyone's needs for rest, nourishing food, exercise, a chance to relax, and attention to whatever special needs they have as individuals.

• Plan family activities you enjoy. Read some of your favorite picture books and novels. If nature nurtures you, go outside as much as possible. Share crafts you enjoy with your kids, making adjustments for their abilities, expecting a slower pace and bigger mess, and reserving some supplies for yourself. Cook your favorite foods and encourage others to try them. Play music, sing, and dance together. Meeting several people's needs simultaneously pays big dividends, and you may end up with kids who share your interests and passions.

• Include yourself in your family's curriculum. Consider studying some of the same topics as your kids, perhaps reviewing American history or learning Japanese. Or explore your own topic while they're studying independently. Parents who are enjoying learning set outstanding examples for their kids. Keep a project of your own going, such as knitting. Simple projects that can easily be interrupted and do not require lots of equipment or big blocks of time often work best. Some families have times when everyone reads silently or writes. Some parents get so much enjoyment from working with their children and exploring and learning new things themselves, that they count homeschooling as time for themselves.

• Often a change of pace, a break from daily routine, helps. Play music, spend several hours reading aloud, go on a field trip, or get together with another homeschooling family. Sometimes just getting out of the house is enough to ease tensions and change moods.

• Be realistic. If you expect to be interrupted, you're less likely to be surprised or annoyed and more able to calmly do what's needed and return to what you were doing.

• Evaluate your approach to household management. Declutter. Consult websites and books like David Allen's *Getting Things Done* and Julia Morgenstern's *Organizing From the Inside Out* for ideas. Investigate efficient approaches like "once a month cleaning." Simplify meals.

• Remember that having children in school takes a lot of time and energy, parents have much less control, and the results may be far less satisfactory than homeschooling. The peace of mind that comes from knowing one is giving one's children a very important opportunity keeps a lot of parents going even when they have little time for themselves. Many feel that, demanding as homeschooling is, they end up getting more than they give.

When you start homeschooling, **no one** tells you how much you learn about yourself and your kids and everyone else in the world by making slime, baking bread, digging a 4 foot deep hole, building with Legos, fishing, shooting arrows, reading thousands of books over and over and over again, lying on your back looking up at the clouds, making a world history time line, talking, discussing, arguing, volunteering at the food bank, listening to audio books, and traveling all over the country to skate.

In the beginning, we are all so focused on our anxieties about whether our kids will learn to read, do math, and interact well enough with others to satisfy the rest of the world, that we completely ignore that **we** get to be participants! That this whole exercise benefits not only our kids, but **us** in a profound way which leaves us changed for the better; forever to be more knowledgeable, skilled, compassionate, patient, and loving human beings. And this, of course, is why homeschooling **works**—it creates a continuous loop of learning, interest, and love that nourishes not only our children but ourselves.

Chapter 16

Handling Challenges

Homeschooling works and is exciting. But sometimes homeschools don't run smoothly. Conscientious parents may worry, question what they are doing, and get discouraged. Here are observations that may help. In addition, the WPA conference offers workshops on preventing and solving problems.

Many parents put homeschooling "problems" in perspective by considering their size and cause. Was it really a bad day, a whole day? Or was it a difficult 15 minutes, or maybe two challenging half hours? Should a whole day be labeled and sacrificed because one or two things went wrong? How much difference will these "catastrophes" make an hour from now? A week? A month? By any chance do they have a funny side?

Is this a homeschooling problem? Or is the real problem perhaps worries about money, a serious illness, difficulties with a parent's job, or rude comments a neighbor keeps making? Pressure and stress that have nothing to do with homeschooling can create tensions that interfere with learning, but these are not homeschooling problems. Some that could be called homeschooling problems are:

It seems like no one's learning.

To whom have you been listening? Comparisons can be dangerous. Of course, they are tempting and may even seem necessary. Homeschooling is a big responsibility. Don't we need comparisons so we know we're on the right track and our children are doing all right?

To be sure, some reassurance is helpful. But it seldom comes from comparisons. All of us, parents and children, are unique. It doesn't work to compare ourselves to other homeschoolers and try to become like them. We can learn from and be inspired by others. But homeschooling based on comparisons rarely works.

Another problem with comparisons among homeschoolers is that we tend to combine things inappropriately. We listen to several parents and conclude we should be learning fractions the way the Smiths are, and studying astronomy like the Joneses, and working on

Spanish like the Browns, and playing music like the Greens. We may forget that even if it made sense for us to try to follow one example, it would be way too much for us to try to do them all. Probably none of these families is doing everything the other families are. Instead, we can concentrate on deciding what would work well for us.

Okay, but what can we do on those dark days when it still seems like no one is learning anything? Maybe this would be a good time to think back to what we were doing a month ago, six months ago, a year ago. We can review records we are keeping, remember what it was like before we started homeschooling. It becomes clear that everybody (parents included) has learned a lot recently–maybe not this morning or last week, but recently.

Remember that children learn all kinds of things in all kinds of ways. It isn't just a question of whether John has memorized the multiplication tables. Is he developing a sense of the way numbers work together and how he can use them in his projects? Many parents also review their non-academic goals, which may be more important, anyway. People who are ready and motivated can learn basic math with a fairly short period of concentrated study. But spiritual and moral values, ways of getting along with other people, and social responsibility cannot be learned this way. They are the result of years of thinking and doing. Parents also find it helpful to understand that they can't always see what their children are learning, but learning is taking place nonetheless.

Our children are having trouble with reading (or math or whatever).

Learning is exciting and satisfying, but it can also be hard work. Everyone who is trying to learn is challenged in some ways, but having difficulty does not mean they have a "learning disability." It helps to be calm, patient, and positive. It may help to ask the children what they think the problems are and what they would like to do, not to let children just do anything they please, but to get their perspectives and insights. Sometimes there's a surprisingly simple solution that perhaps the parents hadn't thought of.

There are various ways to handle difficulties while learning, including the following.
• Try a different approach. Written material that is incomprehensible when you are trying to read it silently to yourself can become much clearer if someone else reads it to you, even if you are an experienced reader. Or if you are having trouble with cursive, maybe a different style of handwriting or keyboarding would work.
• Change your curriculum. Trying a purchased curriculum for the first time or switching to a different one may clarify material. Or consider the other possibilities outlined in chapter 7.
• Hands-on experience sometimes works well. Math manipulatives make concepts concrete and real. An ethnic meal can help another culture come alive. Museums, nature centers, parks, and the back yard offer opportunities. Balancing the family checkbook demonstrates the importance of math while one is learning a valuable skill.
• Consider taking a break from material causing difficulty. Things may go more smoothly with a fresh start. The material may be more manageable when children are older. Children having trouble with fractions could work on percents or graphs instead. Some homeschoolers set aside a whole subject area for a while. Some problems even seem to resolve themselves. Spelling may improve when kids stop trying to memorize word lists and instead concentrated on reading widely and writing for fun.

Our children won't settle down and study.

Some parents talk with the kids. What's the problem? What might help? Would studying be easier if they worked in a different place? At a different time of day?

Some families try a different approach to one or more subjects, as described above.

Some parents' main goal is to help their children learn how to learn and start on a path of lifelong learning. These parents reason that it is more important that their children generally enjoy learning than that they learn today or this week to read or add or locate Spain. Many learning opportunities appear when children discover and pursue activities they enjoy, whether these be arts and crafts, wood working, gardening, visiting an elderly neighbor, or raising an animal. The desire to learn more about a special interest leads many reluctant children into academics.

Taking a break often allows children to discover new interests that lead them back to studying in a new way or with less resistance.

The children seem to squabble so much.

Having one or more siblings provides learning opportunities along with conflict. Many parents feel that, on balance, siblings learn much that is positive by interacting with each other, so they try to take a reasonable amount of squabbling in stride.

It often helps to give everyone their own space where their privacy and possessions are respected. A whole room for each person is great, but many children manage well with a clearly marked part of a shared bedroom, or even a corner or desk.

Comparing siblings can contribute antagonism. When parents value kids' uniqueness, it encourages siblings to accept each other and get along. It may help to remind kids that learning is available to everyone. Mary's learning to multiply does not reduce John's chance to learn it, too.

Sometimes siblings squabble because they are bored.

Some families develop a list of relaxing activities, such as reading aloud, listening to music, or going for a family walk, for times when tension starts building.

Friends, relatives, and neighbors sometimes criticize our homeschooling.

See Chapter 26.

As homeschooling parents, we don't have enough time for ourselves.

See Chapter 15.

Solving family problems

We are in the best position to solve our family's problems. We understand the underlying issues and available resources. Solutions often grow out of the fabric of our own families, the unique strengths, abilities, and talents of each member and the group as a whole. Some families seem to solve problems without actually concentrating on them. Others use a model and step-by-step suggestions. Here's one possibility. Parents can use it themselves, but it's often even better to include others in the process.

1. Identify the problem. Write it down. Sometimes we assume the problem is one thing only to discover, when we focus on it, that it's really something else. Sometimes we have a vague sense something is wrong for a while before we figure out what's the matter. Ask what you can learn from the problem, what it has to teach you.

2. Ask what you're doing now in this area or a related area that's working. It may take a little while to think of something, but there's almost always at least a little bit that's going right.

3. Write down as many possible solutions as you can. Don't try to decide yet whether something will work. If more than one person is involved, listen to everyone.

4. Review the alternatives and cross out the unacceptable or impossible ones. Again, make sure everyone is heard.

5. Choose a solution and decide specifically how it will work. If more than one person is involved, this step isn't finished until you've figured out something everyone agrees on.

6. After an appropriate length of time, review the situation. Was the problem correctly identified? Is the solution working? If not, what changes or alternatives should be tried?

Problems provide opportunities to learn and grow. They give us strong incentive and get us going on things we might not get around to otherwise, some of which are important. If this sounds too unrealistically positive, think about the most important things you've learned in your life. How many of them did you learn in response to a problem?

Dealing with discouragement

Here are suggestions for parents who want to continue homeschooling but are feeling overwhelmed, tired, or confused.

• Try to enjoy your children as they are, without comparing them to others. Expect your house to look more lived in than those of families who are away from home all day. Remember that homeschools are different from conventional schools and don't need to duplicate them.

• Try a different curriculum or a different approach to learning. See Chapters 6 and 7.

• Consider taking a break from academics, or at least the part that is frustrating you or your children. Take off a day, a week, a month, or more. After all, you may be homeschooling for years, and your children can continue learning throughout their lives, so you can certainly afford some time off. Or, if taking a break for a week or longer sounds too risky, try taking off every Friday. Start by doing the day's household tasks, then decide what you most want to do for the rest of the day. Try some of the activities in Chapter 6 or invent your own. At the end of the break, look around. What have the kids learned? What have you learned? Many families are amazed at how much they learn during breaks.

• For ideas about parenting homeschooling children, including finding time for yourself, see Chapter 15.

• Join a support group or start your own. One possibility is to invite one or more families for a brown bag lunch or a potluck. Parents can talk informally or discuss a specific topic while the children play or use simple materials you have provided like paper and magic markers, board games, play dough, ingredients to make cookies, or ideas for outdoor active games and activities. It helps if the kids can interrupt you whenever they need you. If the gathering works well, plan the next one, perhaps asking someone else to plan and host. If it doesn't work, try again with a different group of people.

• Remember that many problems are "life problems" or "kid problems" and not "homeschooling problems." Some would be even more difficult to deal with if the children were attending conventional schools.

• Think about the alternatives to homeschooling. Many homeschoolers feel that even at difficult times, they are still better off than they would be if the children were attending conventional schools.

• Include topics and activities that you enjoy in your family's curriculum. Homeschooling provides many opportunities for parents to grow, explore new areas, learn things that we were told in school we did not have the ability to learn, and express ourselves creatively. By setting an example, we are doing important things for our children and our communities, as well as ourselves.

• Attend the WPA conference. Many parents find information, encouragement, and support that help prevent and overcome discouragement.

Custody cases

Homeschooling sometimes becomes an issue for a divorced homeschooling parent whose ex-spouse opposes it. Many parents recognize the advantages to resolving conflicts without going to court. Most attorneys and judges know little about homeschooling; many are biased against it. Judges often rule that parents can only homeschool if they agree to do more than the law requires. Parents have more flexibility, freedom, and choice if they make their own agreements instead of being restricted by court rulings they have to continue to obey even if both parents later agree the rulings are a mistake. Staying out of court also saves a lot of time and money and avoids the tensions surrounding court appearances.

Testing is a complicated question in custody cases. Wisconsin law does not require that homeschoolers take tests, and the vast majority of homeschoolers oppose state-mandated tests. Test results do not automatically resolve conflicts and can lead to more testing, including psychological testing. But sometimes parents feel having their children tested is worth the risks if it's enough to convince their ex-spouse to drop their opposition to homeschooling or to avoid having the guardian ad litem argue that the homeschooling parent should no longer have primary or joint custody of the children. Also, judges often want testing done. Many parents who agree to testing work to get the minimum number of the least objectionable academic tests and refuse to allow psychological testing.

If a court case is unavoidable, you are much more likely to get a favorable outcome if you work closely with your attorney rather than turning your case over to them. Tell them to prepare your case based on laws, educating judges about them if necessary and preventing judges from making decisions based on their opinion of what would be in the best interests of the child. As a parent, you have the right, recognized by Wisconsin statutes, to homeschool your children, regardless of whether the judge or guardian ad litem thinks homeschooling is a good idea. Make sure you and your attorney are very familiar with what Wisconsin's homeschooling law requires. See Chapters 3 and 28 and Appendix A. In addition, your attorney can point out that the compulsory school attendance law requires attendance; it does not require compulsory education. (See Chapter 22.) This should limit judges' ability to insist that homeschoolers prove that their children are learning by submitting test scores, evaluations done by public school teachers, etc.

Guardians ad litem appointed by the court have enormous power and can turn a case you and your attorney have carefully prepared against you. They are very much a part of the conventional educational, judicial, and social service systems. Their job is to uphold these systems. It's not surprising that most of them are at least skeptical of homeschooling, and many are opposed to it. Their reports can displace statutes concerning education, the strong wishes and desires of children and their parents, and other important factors. However, there are some guardians ad litem who can be convinced to support homeschooling. Therefore, begin by presenting homeschooling in the most reassuring and conventional terms you can. If the guardian ad litem objects to homeschooling, see if you can reach a better understanding about it.

If your guardian ad litem continues to oppose homeschooling, find out as much as you can about what they are likely to report. Any time after 120 days following the appointment of a guardian ad litem, you may request that the court schedule a status hearing related to the guardian ad litem's actions and work. This can be repeated 120 days after each status hearing. WPA strongly suggests that you request such status hearings unless you are very certain that the guardian ad litem supports your position concerning custody and homeschooling.

Often the only way to counter a biased or unfavorable custody evaluation presented by a guardian ad litem is to have a private evaluation performed by an independent professional. This can cost as much as $10,000, but in some cases, it may be necessary.

Chapter 17

Secrets of Experienced Homeschooling Families

To help new homeschoolers get started and experienced homeschoolers keep going, some long-term homeschoolers share what helps them homeschool. As with the rest of this book, take what you can use and ignore what doesn't work for your family.

• **Take time to enjoy your children.** Homeschooling is about relationships. Each child is a miracle. Homeschooling gives us extra opportunities to appreciate them. One of the most important things we can do for our children is let them know how much we love them and enjoy being with them. Our enjoyment of them as people helps them develop the confidence they need. The heart of homeschooling is families spending time together and learning together. Don't miss it!

• **Create your own version of homeschooling.** There's no one right way to homeschool. There's room for every approach to education, every learning style, every special interest, every individual's unique timetable. You can learn from the experiences of other home-schoolers, but don't try to duplicate what they have done. Instead, do what's right for your family, based on your principles and beliefs.

• **Don't compare your family to other homeschoolers.** Every family is unique and has its own strengths. Some families may have gotten very involved in a special interest. One may have formed a band and made an album; another may have built their own house. Don't be intimidated; celebrate the uniqueness of your family.

• **Slow down and take your time.** Learning is a life-long process. Your relationships with your children and their self-confidence are much more important than whether they learn to add fractions today. Also, many things are easier to learn at a later age, when you have more context for them and more experience living and learning.

• **Homeschooling gives the answers when kids have the questions.** By contrast, conventional schools often give the answers before kids have the questions, when they're not yet ready to learn.

• **Encourage your children to pursue their passions.** Learning is easier when we're pursuing something we love. We have more energy and motivation. We don't need someone else to set goals for us or keep us going. Sometimes this leads us to discover our life's work.

• **Focus on learning rather than teaching.** Trust that your kids will learn. Some parents say, "I don't teach; we learn together." Or "I'm just one more resource for our kids." Don't draw lines between living and learning. People learn all the time.

• **Help your kids learn how to learn.** One approach: First, admit that you don't know something. (How many adults can do that?!) Then try to figure it out yourself, ask someone, look it up on the Internet, research it at the library, find a tutor, or take a class. As long as your kids know how to learn, they'll be able to learn things they missed.

• **Take a break from topics that kids can't seem to understand right now.** If parts of speech aren't making sense today, set them aside for a day, a week, a month, or longer. "First, do no harm." It's better for kids to know very little about a subject than to become convinced that they hate it or are no good at it. If you let go of things that they're not ready for today, there's a greater chance they'll be interested, want to learn them, and be able to learn them later.

• **Often the way you use a curriculum is as important as which one you choose.** Many homeschoolers make their curriculum fit their kids, instead of trying to get their kids to fit the curriculum.

• **Homeschooling isn't "hard," like school is.** Sometimes homeschooled kids think they're not learning because they haven't gotten to "the hard part" yet.

• **Don't try to find the beginning of what you're learning.** Wherever you start **is** the beginning.

• **Learn, yourself.** Learn things your kids are interested in, even if you've never cared how a car runs or always thought bugs were disgusting. Learn things that you want to know, even if your kids aren't enthusiastic when you announce that you're going to learn Spanish or grow zinnias or bake whole wheat bread.

• **Realize the importance of what you are doing.** One homeschooling mother observed, "Homeschooling is the most wonderfully difficult job I've ever had."

• **Find things to do with your children that nurture you as well as them.** And learn to be nurtured by things they love to do. If you love to be outside, spend hours outdoors with them and marvel at what they learn without lesson plans or textbooks. If you love crafts, share your enthusiasm, give them their own supplies, and accept the fact that you'll get a lot less accomplished while you are working with them, but you may end up with children who share your passion or at least understand how important it is to you. Choose books to read aloud that you love, from picture books on up. Play in the snow, build sand castles, rake a pile of leaves and jump in it. Do what you loved to do as a child and what you always wanted to do but never did. Sing (even if you think you can't carry a tune). Dance (even if you never learned how). Write your own stories. Paint with water colors.

• **Consider limiting the use of TV, computers, and other electronic devices.** Some families eliminate some of them. Families who limit TV are freer from advertising, violence, and values they object to. They have more time and incentive to do real things together. Other families prefer to own one small TV and carefully limit its use. Some families use computers in public libraries. Others limit their use. One can get an outstanding education without any online resources, some of which are misleading and inaccurate.

• **Some children need to be encouraged to read less and do more.**

• **Understand the value of our homeschooling freedoms.** Wisconsin has one of the best homeschooling laws in the nation only because many homeschoolers worked hard through WPA to get and maintain it. (See Chapter 20.) If we don't continue to work to maintain our freedoms, we will lose them. Chapter 21 explains what we can do. What we do or don't do will affect the future of homeschooling for us and others. The wonderful possibilities homeschooling offers will be lost if homeschools are unnecessarily regulated by the state, and many ideas in this chapter will no longer be possibilities.

• **Develop a support system that works for you.** Possibilities include joining an existing local support group or starting your own, getting together with one or a few other homeschooling families, keeping a few favorite homeschooling books nearby to reread when you need reassurance, having a few people who you can call when you need to. (continued)

• **Attend the WPA conference.** Besides the stimulating, helpful workshops, the conference offers the chance to meet and interact with lots of other homeschoolers, an experience you and your family may find energizing and encouraging.

• **Expect to be discouraged sometimes.** Not every day is a good day (although sometimes it's a "bad 15 minutes" or "bad hour" rather than a whole "bad day"). Homeschooling is great, but it's also intense and tends to change your life. Then there are the times you wake up in a panic, thinking, "Our kids haven't learned how to add fractions." Talking to someone about your discouragement can be a big help, but don't complain to people who are critical of homeschooling. Their response is likely to be, "Why don't you just put the kids in school?" Instead, call another homeschooler who can say, "Yes, I know. I've felt that way, too. You'll feel better soon." Then be prepared to say this to them when they get discouraged and call you.

• **Take a break when you need one.** Set aside "school work" for an hour, a day, a week, or more. Do things you really want to do. Then look back, see how much you've learned when you weren't even trying to, and perhaps ask if you could spend less time on "school work."

• **Accept the fact that your kids will miss some things**, quite possibly some big important things that they will need later in life. (Kids who attend conventional schools certainly do.) Learning doesn't end at age 18. If your kids need to know something, they'll learn it, no matter how old they are. Think how much of the knowledge you use today you have learned **since** you finished school.

• **Remember that you can homeschool.** You can give your children much better learning opportunities than any conventional school can, simply because you are not confined to a school building or to conventional "school work," because you have only a few young people to work with so you can be more flexible and offer them more opportunities than you would be able to if you had 20 or 30, because you know them better than classroom teachers can possibly get to know their students, and because you love them.

• **Don't be overwhelmed by the number of homeschooling resources.** There are far more good, even excellent, resources than anyone could possibly use. The problem is not finding resources; it's keeping yourself from being overwhelmed by the resources that seem to find you. There's no magical set of resources that every homeschooler should use, and a search for resources that are so good that no homeschooler should miss them is more likely to lead to frustration than the perfect education. Really, you don't have to buy anything to homeschool.

• **Spend as little money as possible.** The library is free and you have to take back what you borrow, which keeps the amount of stuff you have to deal with more manageable. Just because you bought something doesn't mean you have to use it. In fact, expect to buy some resources that won't work for your family. This isn't a waste; it's a valuable lesson in learning what won't work. You can decide at any point that something is not for you, perhaps selling it. It may be just what another family is looking for.

• **Make your relationship with your spouse a priority.** It is one of the foundations of your homeschool and your family life. You can do small things in the midst of daily life, like a note, a quick phone call, a flower. When the kids are playing outside or asleep, do things that strengthen your relationship. Sometimes this means tackling a major family decision or working together, maybe paying bills or doing the dishes. But often it means relaxing and spending time together, having fun, reminiscing, talking about how amazing the kids are, playing a game, watching a movie, sharing a special dessert, or whatever you choose. You can also get time together by taking the family to a place like a playground, where you can talk while the kids play, although it helps to expect to be interrupted.

• **Keep your sense of humor.** Convince your kids (and yourself) that some things that don't go as planned are great bonding experiences. What seems like a disaster today, if it's not too serious, will make a great story and a wonderful memory!

PART THREE

HOMESCHOOLING WORKS!

Chapter 18

Why Homeschooling Works

Experienced homeschoolers know that homeschooling works. But conventional schooling plays such a prominent role in the lives of the vast majority of children that many people assume such schooling is essential and are surprised to hear that homeschooling works. Let's consider some reasons why it works. This list is only a beginning, the tip of the iceberg. Readers are encouraged to add to it.

The richness and diversity of approaches to learning and living that are available to homeschoolers allow them to try different approaches, to what works and what doesn't, and to discover or create ways of homeschooling that work for them. There is no one right or best way to homeschool. Each family has to decide for itself which approaches to learning and living work well for the individuals in their family and for their family as a whole, in light of the circumstances in which they live.

Most families use a variety of different approaches, depending on the children's ages and other circumstances, making changes as children's (and parents') ages, interests, needs, and skills change. See Chapter 7.

The flexibility of homeschooling is also one of the main reasons homeschooling should not be unnecessarily regulated by the state. Such regulation would diminish the freedom and flexibility that are essential parts of homeschooling as an approach to education that works well.

Homeschooling offers many different ways of learning. Children learn from reading books, hands-on experience, talking with other people, technology, and in other ways. Children can move around as they are learning, which makes it easier for some children to process information. Children can concentrate on something they find particularly fascinating for several hours or longer. This flexibility means that children who had (or would probably have) difficulty learning in a conventional school setting often do very well at home. If our society is really committed to meeting the needs of all children and helping each child become educated, homeschools are a critical part of the alternatives that should be available so families can choose an approach to education that works for each child.

Homeschooling works because it is based on one of the most highly respected and recommended approaches to learning: tutorial or one-on-one learning. This allows children to work at their own pace, moving rapidly ahead when they are ready, taking time when they need or want to, and setting things aside until later if they're not ready to handle them yet. Children have a chance to discover what interests them and to pursue their special interests.

Homeschooling works because it gives people opportunities to discover things for themselves and to understand why things work. People usually remember what they understand, especially if they have discovered it themselves, because it makes sense. There is much less need to memorize isolated facts that may be hard to remember because they don't make sense.

Homeschooling works because children learn how to learn. No one can learn everything. But people who learn how to learn can learn what they need to know at any age. It's a matter of recognizing that you don't know something, being willing to admit it, and then finding out by figuring it out yourself, asking someone, looking in the library or on the Internet, working with a mentor, taking a class, or some other approach.

Homeschooling emphasizes and builds on people's strengths. It starts with what people already know and are interested in and encourages them to learn more by using approaches to learning that work well for them. When people are given a chance to learn in ways that work well for them, at their own pace, they can learn instead of being labeled "learning disabled." But what about subjects that people need to learn that are difficult for them, perhaps reading or math? Homeschoolers find that when people are given opportunities to learn what interests them, using a variety of approaches including lots of hands-on experiences, and are allowed to work at their own pace, they often increase their ability to learn and also develop enough confidence and physical, mental, and neurological maturity that they can then learn at least some of the things that were challenging them before. Emphasizing strengths rather than weaknesses really works, and it builds strong people.

Homeschooling works because it's fun. Homeschoolers can spend extra time on the subjects and learning activities that they enjoy most. People who are happy about what they're doing are well motivated, have an easier time learning, and absorb and remember more of the ideas and information they're exposed to.

Homeschooling works because people and families are better than institutions at raising children, giving them the love and support they need, and providing a place where they can learn. People are social creatures who do better in small groups than in large institutions. The family is the basic unit of society and provides a safe, secure, supportive place for people to learn. Throughout history, most people have learned at home. It is still the place where most people in our society learn two of the most complex skills, walking and talking.

Children are eager to learn about the world around them, especially when they feel safe and do not have to deal with excessive competition, ridicule, and bullying.

Homeschooling strengthens families. They have more time together, to share activities and work, to get to know each other better, and to develop strong bonds and meaningful relationships. They also get to be even better at homeschooling.

In a way, every family homeschools. Families whose children attend conventional schools do homeschooling kinds of activities when their children are out of school. Families who decide to homeschool do these things more of the time.

Parents are good at helping their children learn. Parents have the opportunity to work with one child or a small group of children they know well and to whom they are strongly committed. They love their children and are willing to work hard and make sacrifices for them. Parents are consciously and subconsciously tuned in to their children's strengths and the ways they learn well. They understand why their children do some of the things they do. Love gives them extra patience and commitment.

Homeschoolers have time. When homeschooling parents make mistakes, either in helping their children learn or in interacting with them, they have time to think, apologize and make amends if necessary, and move on.

Homeschooling families have more control over their lives. They can eat foods that they prefer, create living and learning spaces that work well for them, and live according to their principles and beliefs.

Homeschooling gives parents opportunities and encouragement to learn what interests them. When parents are unsure of something themselves (how to multiply fractions, for example), they often can learn with their children and make sense of something they didn't understand when they were in school. Homeschooling encourages whole families, not just children, to learn.

Homeschoolers learn about the world by being it, in their homes where a lot happens and in their communities where even more is going on. They are not limited to what can be brought into a classroom. They have lots of opportunities to develop common sense.

Homeschooled children develop the social skills they need to function well in the real world. They form strong bonds with family members. They learn from and befriend people of all ages, from babies to the elderly. They can make choices and are not forced to spend long hours in relatively large groups of people who are all the same age, an artificial situation that exists only in schools and army boot camp.

Homeschools work because they have one child or a small group of children of different ages. Therefore, homeschools don't need extensive rules for maintaining order or bureaucratic procedures that often don't respect children and their needs. Homeschools have more flexible schedules, so children can continue working on something they're excited about or take a break to take advantage of an unexpected opportunity.

Homeschooling works because by deciding to homeschool, parents have had the courage to follow their convictions and do something that they feel is right, even though this means choosing something different from what most people do. Homeschooling parents are able to take responsibility for their families and to exercise more control over their time, space, and lives. Their example helps their children become strong, confident, and responsible.

Homeschooling works because it has sensible and meaningful goals. Compare homeschoolers' goals with those of most conventional schools, which include things like: keep the taxpayers happy so they will continue to pass bond issues; make sure that 25 students all try to learn the same list of spelling words at the same time; respond to pressure from big business for schools to prepare students to work at boring and routine jobs for low pay; rank and label kids so a few are on the top, most are on the bottom, and no one is too unhappy about where they are; keep kids out of adults' way and make sure they don't do work that adults could do for pay.

Homeschooling works because it provides a means by which parents can reclaim some of the rights and responsibilities that have been taken from them by institutions.

Homeschooling families have their own reasons to add. The point is that homeschooling is an approach to learning and living that works. We can trust the process and proceed with confidence.

Chapter 19

Stories from Homeschooling Families

Note: Names have been changed to protect families' privacy. For additional stories, see Chapter 9 and Stories in the Index.

We have three children ages four, six and seven. Our homeschooling journey began a few years ago when, after checking out various preschools, we discovered that we were accomplishing the same activities at home. In the meantime, I began researching homeschooling at our library and was so thankful to read the WPA handbook and many other helpful resources. The decision to homeschool liberated us from many of our concerns. Our children did not want to be separated from the family to go to school. As parents, we wanted a more active role in educating our children than volunteering weekly in the classroom or chaperoning field trips. We felt that homeschooling was a natural extension of our family values.

At the time we began homeschooling, we did not know any other homeschoolers. So our first hurdle was explaining our decision to well-intentioned extended family and friends, who were not familiar with Wisconsin's homeschooling law. Library resources were very helpful in this respect. As time progressed, there was little room for discussion as they could see our children's natural curiosities led to a positive learning environment. We still answer a lot of questions about homeschooling, but as our confidence increases, our answers come easier.

Our next decision was to become WPA members. The first WPA Conference that we attended was informational and inspirational. I'll never forget the emotional graduation ceremony where the graduates could thank their families for their support throughout their homeschooling experience. Each workshop offered us important information that we could use at home. At the second WPA conference that we attended, I met a fellow homeschooler located in my community. Our friendship has provided a wonderful resource for my children so that they know they are not alone on this homeschooling journey. My friend also introduced me to a homeschooling support group in our area that has been a wealth of support for parents as well as children.

Homeschooling has provided us with so many benefits. We have made many Wisconsin, out-of-state (and one international) educational trips, including children's, historical, aviation and science museums, orchards, bakeries, confectioneries, nature trails, insectariums, biodomes, zoos, plays, concerts, art shows, and all kinds of interesting adventures. The library has continued to be a precious resource, and we make regular trips there. It has been an exciting and rewarding experience to work with our children to make learning experiences available to them in all subject areas. Listening to our children read their first book out loud, enjoying their pride as they write their first alphabet, watching their eyes light up after making a scientific discovery, and observing them making healthy nutritional choices have been joyful experiences.

Homeschooling gives us the flexibility to maximize time with their grandparents, who have been natural teachers for the children. With their grandparents, the children have enjoyed building everything from birdhouses and gingerbread houses to an electrical circuit, as well as visiting our state capitol, museums, and zoos. Our children enjoy relationships with a group of friends that span a range of ages, which richly enhances their educational experience and daily life. Homeschooling also provides us an opportunity to focus on each child's specific interests, learning style and preferences so that their learning is a natural, flowing process.

We are thankful for the support we have on this journey through WPA's annual conference, newsletter, and handbook, as well as our community homeschooling support group. Homeschooling has been a rewarding experience for our family.

A mother who was homeschooling before the Wisconsin homeschooling law was passed in 1984 wrote:

In 1979 my husband and I had three small daughters, a newborn, a two year old, and a four year old. We got a letter from our school district inviting our oldest daughter, Theresa, to come for a kindergarten screening. My maternal instincts kicked in 100%. I couldn't bear the thought of trusting my child to total stranger, even if only for a half day. My husband assured me that every mother goes through these feelings and that I'd get over it. I broke the news to him that I wasn't going to send her to school. I had it all figured out—I would teach her everything she needed to know right at home! After I spent a summer of arguing my point and not being willing to accept "no" for an answer, my husband humored me and told me that since our Theresa was only four years old, and since she wasn't required by law to attend school that year, he would allow me to teach her kindergarten at home. He would decide after the year was up if she actually learned anything.

We purchased a structured curriculum from Christian Liberty Academy. All I had to do was present the materials to Theresa, have her do the work, and return it to CLA for grading. They issued report cards showing that our child had straight A's. My husband became a little more supportive of my belief in educating our children at home and gave me the go-ahead to homeschool the following year. First and second grades came and went, again with all A's on Theresa's report card. Our next daughter, Elizabeth, was ready for kindergarten. How would I manage? Two children in school, a toddler, my husband's blind grandmother came to live with us, and I discovered our fourth baby would be due in September.

We forged ahead. Our second daughter was as brilliant as the first and our first few weeks of school held a lot of promise for a great school year. By this time our local school district decided we were truant. We weren't complying with the law! We were served truancy notices and were told that we had three school days to have our girls in school or they would be taken from us and placed in foster care. My sister, who had children the same ages as mine, was sent truancy notices also. Together we hired an attorney from Madison who assured us that our children wouldn't be taken away. But there were a lot of problems we had to deal with.

Our school district had no experience in dealing with anyone who wanted to homeschool their children. They didn't know how to deal with us. They didn't seem to know what, if any, authority they had over us, and all WE knew was that we wanted to continue building our strong family bonds and teach our children at home.

After a year, Grandma went to live with her son. Shortly after, we had our fourth child, a boy. Because there was no specific homeschool law, our attorney did his best to keep the truancy problem very low-key. He told us to continue homeschooling, but we weren't to tell anyone what we were doing. We kept our curtains closed and were as quiet about homeschooling as possible so as not to arouse curiosities. Our children were not to be seen if anyone came to the door. They had their designated hiding spots when the door bell rang. If we had to go somewhere during regular school hours, they sat on the floor of the car so no one would see them.

Then we got a notice from our fire department notifying us that if we felt we were a school we had to have fire drills once a month. I had to record how long it took my students to vacate the building and get to the meeting place and send them monthly reports. We complied.

The fire chief declined my invitation to come to our house during fire prevention week to talk to my students about fire safety, but he did let me know that the street commissioner wanted school zone signs posted a block from our house. When I wrote to the commissioner asking that the signs be placed, he refused saying that he couldn't put school zone signs in a residential neighborhood, even though our property adjoined the elementary school a block away.

The Department of Public Instruction sent us a copy of building codes that apply to private schools. Our lawyer advised us to humor the DPI and comply as much as possible. We were "required" to have two bathrooms, one for boys and one for girls. We had to have **exit** signs over each door leading outside. We had to provide sufficient water bubblers to accommodate our number of students. We were given a "**list of specific laws of Wisconsin relevant to non public schools**" that we were expected to follow, from displaying a flag, to certifying teachers, to teaching a class called "dairy products," to pledging allegiance once a week. Each employee of our school was required to submit results of a physical exam to the Department of Health and Social Services each year. We complied.

Each September we were served truancy notices. The truant officer and the local sheriff would come to the door (the children were hiding) and read the truancy notice as though I was illiterate. I would quietly accept it. The lawyer advised us that any time public officials asked us questions, we were to ask that their questions be put in writing so we could submit them to our lawyer. We complied.

About this time I was beginning to doubt my sanity. We were informed of a hearing in Madison that had something to do with legalizing homeschooling in Wisconsin. We couldn't believe it! We HAD to go and see that there were really other people out there who had the same ideas as we. If this was true, then other families must be going through the same purgatory of red tape with the public system. We knew that we must attend this hearing and become active with the group fighting for their God-given right to educate their children in the sanctuary of their own home.

We learned that a group of about 80 "secret" homeschoolers had met in Stevens Point a few weeks before the hearing to come up with a strategy of dealing with the upcoming legislation. This group realized a few basic principles, namely, that homeschoolers must become and remain united. All agreed on the basic principle that each family must be free to teach their own beliefs. This was the very beginning of Wisconsin Parents Association. This infant organization busied itself during the next three weeks to inform small Christian schools of their work on Act 512. They circulated written information and sent articles to newspapers informing people of the hearing.

On January 25, 1984, about 2,500 homeschoolers attended the hearing in Madison. Act 512 was passed and homeschooling as you know it became legal in Wisconsin. We answered people's questions. We explained our positions. We listened patiently to verbal attacks on how we were abusing our poor, unsocialized children. We did what we could to help people understand that homeschooling is an acceptable alternative to public education. But mostly, we thanked God for answering our prayers—that WE could educate the children HE gave us according to our consciences.

Many of you didn't have to work for your right to homeschool. For some, all you had to do was fill out form PI-1206 and begin your 875 hours per year. I cannot stress it enough—please do not abuse this right. If you aren't a member, join Wisconsin Parents Association and help maintain the law we have. We don't want anyone to have to go through what we did prior to the passage of ACT 512. Support WPA and do what you can to preserve Wisconsin's homeschool law. Help us to resist the efforts of DPI and society to erode our rights as parents.—From Opening Remarks, WPA Conference, 1999.

A year ago, just before Christmas, we decided to give in to our discomfort regarding our children's education. Over the years, we had many reasons to be dissatisfied with our children's experiences in school: too little challenge, too much TV ("Popeye"—at school!!), teachers who used *Interview with a Vampire* rather than *The Three Bears* to show a class of first graders how stories have a beginning, a middle and an end. (As Dave Barry would say, I am not making this up!) I was even once accused by a pair of well-meaning and well-qualified teachers of being overprotective of my second-grader: this because, although I never set foot in their classrooms, I spent many days at the school editing the school newsletter, developing a parent volunteer program, running a school-wide recycling program, and serving on the PTA board! I had the nerve to suggest to these teachers that my son, though capable of the challenging work they were giving him, was also frightened by the challenge, and in need of nurturing. They knew all the signs.

We drew the line, however, when our children's elementary school teachers would not come for dinner at our house. Perhaps other parents invite their kids' teachers to butter them up, but we had every confidence that ours didn't need "buttering." We simply felt it was essential to get to know the strangers who had custody of our offspring for the majority of their waking hours. We wanted to have one evening's casual conversation with the people for whom we sent our children to bed early each night, the people into whose care we chastened and hastened them out the door each morning. We were informed that such a meal might jeopardize the teachers' "perspective of [sic] your children as our students." Clearly, gaining perspective on our children, or us, as human beings was not a priority.

So, a year ago, our kids came home, to "school." Yesterday, my husband took our two daughters, ages six and eight, to tell Santa Claus of their Christmas gift wishes. Poor elf: each girl climbed on his lap and told him she wanted a teddy bear. Santa waited politely, and then asked, "What else?" Nothing, especially, just a bear apiece, thanks. Side effects: no TV advertising, no school-based peer pressure for the latest junk, and they find they are mostly happy with just what they have.

Sure, their acquaintances in our immediate neighborhood are fewer, now that they're out of the preselected, intensive society of the classroom, but their current friendships cut across generations and geography. At a recent party for my husband's colleagues at our home, almost all of our guests stopped on their way out the door, especially to comment on their pleasure in holding genuine conversations with our youngsters, who have "never met a stranger," and who would never consider the possibility that they wouldn't be taken seriously by an adult. A novel side effect, as good for the adults as the children.

Yesterday also included a ride snuggled with Dad on the mall carousel, and a visit to a science store at the same mall, where each child was allowed to purchase one special, polished rock. Then all came home to inquire quietly of various resource books about the specific heritage and characteristics of the rocks, and to read E.T.A. Hoffman's Nutcracker in front of the fire with Mom. A mile-long walk in the falling snow, at about 9:00 pm, ended the day. The remarkable thing about these events is that they took place on a Wednesday—a "school day," a "school night." (No other children were encountered on our magical hike in the pristine, glittering snow!) I found myself grateful that we could share so many of these joyous family moments, in a day and age when magazines and the newspapers seem daily obliged to coach parents in the value of a shared meal, oh, once a week or so.

Another unanticipated side effect of our increased time with our children is a kind of return to comfort in knowing them: Remember when you could tell by the first whimper from your infant's crib whether it was a wet cry or a hungry or an angry or a frightened? I know my kids again, and I can increasingly trust my understanding of them. This means, among other things, that we can trust each other more and experiment with how to express ourselves completely and peacefully to each other, even in angry or otherwise uncomfortable times. It also means that we can be together A LOT (as homeschooling very young children more or less requires) and still give each other plenty of room. I marvel when friends throw up their hands, learning of our choice, and say, "I could never spend that kind of time with my kids—we'd all go crazy!" Surely being apart so much has taught us this false and dangerous thing; for most of history, families have depended on each other, and no one else, for survival! And the children's relationships to each other have taken several more quantum leaps in quality: they know each other better and need each other more.

Our youngest benefited from a side effect of homeschool that completely surprised us: from the age of five months to the month she left kindergarten for home, at age five and a half, she was never without an ear or sinus infection for more than (if we were lucky) a month or two in the summer. Suddenly, within a few weeks, we noticed that her raspy breathing had disappeared. I thought it a fluke, at first, but her health has held steady. True, homeschooling has added various expenses to our lives—but it has saved us on medical bills and the fear and heartache of having a chronically ill child.

Each day that we slow down to find time to make and do our own work, together, we find more that is sacred in everyday living. We have become more of a family, more blessed and alive, and we find we crave increasingly more of the experience.

I, too, have grown, and have "learned to learn" again by watching my brave children. I have learned new crafts, learned and remembered much about history that had little or no meaning to me in earlier situations, and I, who had few prior political interests, have begun asking questions and speaking up about how to secure our freedoms to homeschool.

Certainly the most central and amazing side effect, though, has been a kind of awakening to the value of our own children as young intellects and human beings. How many questions did we once respond to with a half-hearted grunt? We can no longer afford that complacency, with the result that we feel as if we had only just discovered parenthood. Our children come to us as their guides, and if we cannot help them ourselves, we are obliged to clear a path to those who will pull and push them onward to their self-crafted goals—goals which, we have learned, have as much meaning as any adults'. Taking children seriously—as learners and human beings—was not a goal when we began homeschooling, any more than was the view of the ocean to the first explorers pushing west to the Pacific Coast. But the rewards of our adventure have been, similarly, breathtaking.

We are in our second year of homeschooling. Our children are presently in the sixth and eight grade. We also have a six-month-old baby.

We are so excited about what homeschooling has done for our family.

Our reason for starting homeschooling was to help our oldest child who seemed to be lost in the public school setting. He needed more of a one-on-one way to learn at his own pace. So with the encouragement and blessing of his principal at the time, we decided to try homeschooling.

We have seen such a change in his learning and comprehension. He has gone from reading three books in a school year to one to two books a week. We now have children who watch about one to two hours of TV a week and actually look forward to going to bed because they are allowed to read for one hour before lights out!

As a family we've become a team at getting projects completed, each of us pitching in whatever way we can. Homeschooling has become a learning experience for all of us. Mom and Dad learn things they've forgotten, and baby is watching all of us and learning, too.

As for the social issue, interaction with people of many different backgrounds and ages rather than isolation with age-mates provides our children with adult role models and lessens stress and problems of peer pressure and dependence.

Just last week our oldest was a little long on his paper route. He was stopped by one of his retired customers to hear a few of his poems from a book which will be published soon. The poems tell of his life and military experience. Our son is first on his list for a book, and he's become interested in learning more about World War II and the process of writing and publishing a book.

This is just one example of the daily social and educational experiences our children go through with neighbors, friends, relatives, and other homeschooling families.

Our other child loves working on her own and has advanced greatly in all subjects. She loves to learn, and now there is no stopping her or holding her back.

Our home has become an environment in which our children feel safe and secure, and this fosters exploration, discovery, and independent learning. For this reason, we have accepted homeschooling as a part of our life and love it.

Homeschooling is a big responsibility and a lot of work which we have chosen to do. The state should continue to make it possible for families to homeschool in Wisconsin by not changing the reasonable and workable law which we now have and not adding further regulation which would be restrictive and unnecessary and prevent homeschoolers from doing their best.

Parents who began homeschooling their 15-year-old son after 10 years of conventional schooling wrote:

"What did you consider the most serious problem your child was having in school?"

He was receiving straight A's with very little effort, while really not knowing how to study. Because he was a good student, treated his teachers with respect, and was not an athletic "star," he experienced rejection and ridicule by peers.

"What changes did you notice in your child after you began homeschooling?"

In his years in public school, he went from a talkative, outgoing child to a shy, withdrawn teenager. Upon homeschooling, he gradually began to come out of his shell. He has assumed leadership in our local support group and has been praised by parents as a good role model for the younger ones. His communication, writing, and studying skills have vastly improved. He is **happier!!**

"What have you done while homeschooling that seemed most helpful to your child?"

Removal from negative peers has been the most positive thing for him. We have encouraged him to develop leadership and many outside interests to replace those he had in school. He is learning self-discipline in scheduling his own time.

As a homeschooling parent, I'm convinced that homeschooling is providing our children with the best preparation for their lives as adults. But given my own upbringing and the years I spent in conventional schools, there's a part of my brain that keeps whispering,

"People who went to good schools and have prestigious, high-paying jobs are qualified, know what they are doing, and can handle complicated situations." I certainly counted Jane as one of these people. She's a well-paid attorney with a prestigious job while I'm an unpaid mother-at-home.

When a problem came up in an organization Jane and I belong to, I was surprised that she called me to ask what to do. As she was describing her confusion and distress over the situation, I couldn't help wondering, "Why is Jane calling me? Haven't her training and experience prepared her to deal with this?" But the more I listened, the more I realized that she simply didn't know what to do.

I found myself forgetting about Jane's credentials and shifting to the "homemade" approach to solving problems that our family has developed as we've homeschooled together. First I listened to her and responded with brief, empathetic comments like, "That must have been hard." Experience has taught me again and again that it pays big dividends to close my mouth and listen to other people.

Then I used my common sense and described to Jane the situation as I saw it, pointing out some of the reasons the problem had arisen. Yes, she agreed. So far so good; on to the next step. I said, "It seems to me there are two questions we have to deal with: First, what do we need to do to get through the current situation? Second, what can we do to prevent this kind of situation from developing again?" Once I had come up with these questions, Jane was able to respond.

Then I proposed that a few of us meet to talk about how to prevent this problem from developing again. Jane objected, explaining that she did not think a small group should be tackling the problem, that more people should be involved. I explained to her how I view communication and how I think groups work, beginning with the idea that communication has the best chance of happening without misunderstanding when the fewest number of people are involved. (For example, I wouldn't try to solve a tricky problem with one of our children while their sibling was listening.) I couldn't help thinking, "Here I am explaining communication and group process to a prominent attorney, and I'm using what I've learned as a homeschooling mother to do it." Jane soon agreed with me, and then it was easy to figure out the next steps.

Jane thanked me for talking with her. "I knew you'd have good ideas," she said. Interesting—Jane recognizes and acknowledges my "homemade" credentials, even though she may not realize that they come from homeschooling. This is not to say that I'm prepared to take over Jane's job—something I wouldn't want to do anyway. I'm much happier with my family work, which has prepared me to deal with people, communication, and other things that matter to me. I just hope that, as a result of this experience, I'm a step closer to letting go of my school experience and my automatic respect for conventional credentials and a step closer to fully accepting the value of homemade credentials, for parents as well as for children who are homeschooling.

Our family consists of four daughters born in three and a half years, with a son fourteen years later. The girls all went through the public school system. They were excellent students academically, but our family values were disregarded and our relationship with them made distant.

Therefore, the day I heard about the homeschool movement, I pulled our son out of school. He was in his second month of kindergarten. We were living in Minnesota where you need to test your children every year, which basically means you will be bringing "school" home. Of course, I would eliminate the social pressures of the public system, but we weren't free to expand in whatever direction my child wanted to go or learn at our own pace. Therefore, we chose to move to Wisconsin following his first grade year.

Once we were semi-settled in Wisconsin, we found a whole new world opened up to us. Now we could pursue the things that really interested him and have fun doing it. We could attend plays and concerts or spend a day at the nature centers. He became a member of our local 4-H group and there could pursue many of his interests to see what he might enjoy. This was worked in with our book work.

Presently, our son has completed his second full year at UW River Falls, receiving scholastic honors for both years. Technically, he is in his junior year, however, as he began his studies there as a junior in high school. When I spoke to the Dean of Admissions concerning his early start, the dean said he had no problems with homeschool students starting early, because he knew they were self-motivated and serious about their studies. However, he did not have the same confidence in public school students. Our son has upheld the dean's expectations and then some.

The one thing I was privileged to experience with this child that I didn't get to with the girls was that I could actually see him blossom. Because he was free to expand into the directions he felt comfortable going, he was able to define his own talents and desires. The girls, on the other hand, were limited by the public system, and are still struggling with who they really are and where can their talents best be used. They're now in their late thirties and he is twenty. What a difference a child's foundation makes!!

The one thing that astounded me all the years I was home educating my son, was the question concerning socialization others seemed so concerned about. All the while I thought it was education that my children were in school for and now I realize that isn't the case at all. When you focus on the total picture, socialization is, indeed, the main theme of our present public education system. What else could it be? Since the public system isn't geared toward each child's unique learning abilities or needs, socialization is all that they can accomplish, isn't it? And it was the socialization that I was unhappy with! Our son is quite comfortable with people of all ages and is a teacher's dream student. He can change diapers for an infant, chat freely with an elderly person, or be a leader among his peers. His sisters, on the other hand, still look to their peers for their leadership and guidance, whereas our son values our wisdom.

Wisconsin Parents Association has made so much of this possible here. **A huge thank you** for all your hard work on our behalf!! Your vision is truly toward a better tomorrow, with a younger generation fully ready for their responsibilities.

Our youngest of three has started college this fall. A landmark in our family history, signaling the official end of our homeschooling days, yet with John living at home, it is emotionally satisfying for me, A.K.A. Mom, not having to leave him to fend for himself away at college in a strange place. We also have another son living at home, which is okay with us for the time being. The oldest is at work on a career in the Navy using his talents working on the electrical systems of jet fighters.

John intends to pursue majoring in electrical engineering. This is not surprising since from about the age of three, we saw he was very interested in how things worked, especially plumbing and electrical systems of houses. All the boys came to prefer real tools to most toys, so John grew up in an enriched environment. As our sons grew, they found it was okay to take things apart; fortunately, they left the telephone and cars alone! Much later I found out this is referred to as "reverse engineering." I often mentioned our "junk curriculum" to fellow homeschoolers, who gave me a blank look and possibly concluded I was one of those "fringe" elements they would occasionally read about. No problem: what we were doing seemed to be what the boys were born to do. My job was to see how we could help nurture their special talents as well as learn the core curriculum through a more loosely scheduled and child-centered plan. I had the opportunity to do a lot of reading research in the last few months before our first son was born, and John Holt (author of *How Children Learn* and others) was a large influence in developing my educational philosophy. After John came along four and a half years later, I was sure I wanted to homeschool. My husband was a bit unsure, but we agreed to take it year by year and see how things developed.

Books and the public library were an important part of our homeschooling life, although for reading material, the boys tended to prefer technical manuals and catalogs rather than fiction. I have memories of bedtime reading to John from a Do-It-Yourself book on making concrete upon his request at three years of age. One of the boys' requests for shopping was to be taken to the local secondhand stores to spend their birthday money on electronic castoffs. Sometimes they even managed to get them working again. One book I was ecstatic to find was the Usborne book, *Introduction to Electronics*. I ended up buying a copy for each child. It was really the only book written to help a child understand how electricity and electronic components work. As my (and my husband's) higher education was in music, I was learning right along with them. Our dining table was often given over to serve as their workbench, laden with exposed parts of radios, VCR's and circuit boards.

One of the WPA conferences I attended helped reassure me that our kids were indeed using the gifts they were given. One of the presenters said that, as a child, his parents thought he was crazy when he kept taking things apart. They were just about at their wit's end when he took apart the grandfather's clock in the front hall. He ended up having a career in a mechanical field and was teaching his sons how to weld in their basement. He also wanted us to know that if any of our children couldn't help themselves from taking things apart and always wanted to know how everything worked, they weren't crazy, just mechanically gifted. I smiled knowingly as he told about his childhood antics and decided to continue as we had been, although the consequences are having to live with a certain amount of messiness and trusting the children with tools. I'm pleased to say we have a nearly perfect safety record with no major injuries.

Another advantage was my husband bringing home cast-off computers from work. This allowed the boys to learn programming and, when a new model came along, they got to see the insides of the old ones. These kids have never known a world without computers. I must say it's nice to have a live-in techie when I have problems!

John continues to be involved in our church choir, of which he has been a member since age nine. He has joined the ceramics club at college and continues his interest in listening to pop music and video gaming. While I know I haven't been entirely 'successful' by my own standards in getting him to know all I wanted him to learn during the homeschooling years, he continues to grow and learn. We all have gaps, no matter what method of education we use or have grown up with. The best part is, we can continue to learn new things and expand on what we already know for the rest of our lives.

Chapter 20

History of Homeschooling In Wisconsin

Working together through WPA, homeschoolers in Wisconsin have reclaimed and maintained basic freedoms in education and family life. We have worked to get and maintain the reasonable homeschooling law that was passed in 1984. Our work makes it possible for our families and thousands of other families to choose an approach to homeschooling that works for them and to follow it without unreasonable interference from the state.

Often knowing the history of something helps us understand it and support it. It is easier to understand homeschooling in Wisconsin today and how we can act to maintain our rights and freedoms if we know how we got here. Here is our story.

Note: This chapter is a brief overview. For more details, see *Kitchen Tables and Marble Halls: WPA and Homeschooling in Wisconsin*, a free download available on the WPA website.

We face obstacles as individual families, but protecting our homeschooling law is a challenge our entire homeschooling community must endure. In the spirit of celebrating our common goal, it is appropriate to dedicate some of our time today in recognition of the people who, 20 years ago, worked so diligently to "get it right."

I am humbled by the unwavering dedication of the few people who started this movement. Regardless of their personal philosophies, economic status, educational approach, or spiritual beliefs, they came together with a vision and a universal passion. Over the course of just a few weeks and through countless phone calls and meetings during the winter of 1984, this small group swelled to over 2,500 homeschooling supporters who went to the Capitol sending a very important message to the legislature. These visionaries focused on a common goal and did not allow their differences to pull them apart. Furthermore, they understood it was their diversity that made their voice strong and their message clear. —From Opening Remarks, WPA Conference, 2004

As you read this, think about where we would be now, what homeschooling rules and regulations we would have to obey, if homeschoolers had not worked together through WPA and stood up to challenges and unreasonable demands, time after time, as individuals and in groups. Remember that when homeschooling laws and regulations are reasonable, homeschoolers have the chance they need to do a good job of homeschooling. On the other hand, when homeschoolers have to deal with unreasonable and unnecessary laws and regulations, homeschooling itself becomes more difficult. Remember, too, that the work described here has been done by Wisconsin homeschoolers, not by "outside experts" coming into the state. In fact, we have worked hard to discourage such people from coming into Wisconsin, realizing that much of our strength comes from working together on the grassroots level in our own state to build a solid foundation for homeschooling here.

Let's begin with some general observations. As homeschoolers, we have a lot going for us and a lot at stake.

• Homeschooling is not an isolated activity that we do for only five hours a day, 175 days a year. Homeschooling is part and parcel of the way we view our families, the value and importance of our children, and our roles and responsibilities as parents. It is central to the way in which we live our lives. At stake is more than how our children will learn to do long division or locate Japan on a map. We are fighting for a way of life, for recognition of the primary importance of the family (the basic unit of every known society), for the right to educate our children without unnecessary regulation from the state, for the right to exist as an alternative to conventional schools, for the right of our children to learn in ways that work best for them and according to their own schedules. With so much at stake, we are a determined, committed group of people.

• We are people of vision. We have learned that most major changes, for good or for ill, take place one small step at a time. We know that our children do not go to bed one night having never looked seriously at a written word and wake up the next morning able to read. We know that reading is a lifelong process that is accomplished one tiny step at a time. Similarly, we know that our basic responsibility for our children and our right to educate them can be taken away from us in the same way, one tiny step at a time. This is why we bother to take the time from our busy lives to work to reclaim and maintain our rights and freedoms.

If we were living in a society that accepted and respected homeschoolers, that viewed parents as the people with primary responsibility for their children, and that trusted parents, then we would not have to be as concerned about small infringements on our rights.

But we don't live in a society that trusts parents and families. Instead the government, corporations, and professionals are taking increasing control of people's lives. Sometimes not in big, earth-shaking ways. In little bits, just one small piece at a time. So we oppose changes in the homeschooling law that will give others control over our children's educations and then over our families' lives, a little bit at a time.

Homeschooling in Wisconsin Before the Current Law Was Passed

Homeschooling is the way the vast majority of people have been educated throughout history. By the 1970s and early 1980s, although homeschooling was not illegal (parents have the right to choose an education for their children that is consistent with their principles and beliefs and no state had laws that forbid homeschooling), there were very few homeschoolers in the United States.

Homeschooling pioneers in the 1970s and early 1980s were often asked, "Is homeschooling legal?" Homeschoolers in Wisconsin chose one of three possibilities. (1) Some requested official permission from the Department of Public Instruction (DPI). (2) Others incorporated their home as a private school.

3) Most families recognized and acted on the fact that families have a right to choose for their members an education consistent with their principles and beliefs. Parents do not need permission from the DPI or any other government agency. They don't need a statute saying that homeschooling is legal because the right to homeschool comes from nature or

God, not from the state, especially since there has never been a statute stating that home-schooling is illegal. At that time, Wisconsin's statute defining a private school was vague. Families who recognized their right to homeschool also understood that their home met the vague requirements for a private school, so their children were, in fact, attending a private school.

Although most homeschoolers were convinced that homeschooling was legal, they were pretty sure officials disagreed. Concluding that it was better to stay out of trouble than to have to get out of trouble, they maintained a very low profile, mentioning homeschooling as little as possible. Often this required staying indoors at home during "school hours," which put pressure on families and decreased opportunities to learn in the community. Many children (and parents) found it stressful to be asked common, seemingly simple questions like "What school do you go to?" "What grade are you in?" "Who is your teacher?" In addition, it was difficult to find other homeschooling families, partly because most home-schoolers were so cautious about identifying themselves. There were no homeschooling support groups, no state-wide grassroots organizations, no homeschooling conferences. In an attempt to gain a more secure position, some homeschoolers went to the work and expense of incorporating as a private school, wondering whether this would protect them or simply expose them to school authorities. Vague feelings of not being quite legal and fears of getting caught and taken to court were not uncommon among homeschoolers.

> Our family was not one of the "pioneering" homeschooling families. We began homeschool-ing in 1985, when our oldest son turned six. But as I met homeschoolers with older children and began to hear some of their stories, I started to see how fortunate we were.
> One of those stories that gave me a real feeling for what it had been like to homeschool before the current law was in place comes from my friend Jan, whose children are just a few years older than mine. She was a member of a food-buying club, and once a month she and half-a-dozen other women met to unload the truck from the warehouse and divide up 50-pound bags of flour, five-gallon buckets of peanut butter, etc. She was working with another woman in one room of the old schoolhouse where they met, and told her that they were homeschooling. "Oh!" said the other mother, "So are we!" Within a few minutes, five or six other people had heard the word "homeschooling" and come into the room to say "You are homeschoolers? So are we!" These were people who had been working together as part of the buying club for months or years-and none of them knew that any of the others were homeschooling. "At that time you just didn't tell people about it," Jan said.-From Opening Remarks, WPA Conference, 2005

The few homeschoolers who applied to the DPI under the "home tutorial" program often found themselves in even more difficulty. The DPI officials were very difficult to deal with and made ridiculous and impossible demands. Consider some of the experiences pre-sented as part of a hearing on proposed homeschooling legislation held by the Wisconsin Senate Health, Education, Corrections and Human Services Committee on March 13, 1984.

• A mother, who happened also to be a certified teacher, felt that the approval process took a long time and the DPI was unreasonable. For example, if at any time during the school day she and her children needed to leave home, she had to notify her local school district. Also, the DPI told her they could visit her home at any time, unannounced, and they did.

• A boy who was having problems in school had a chronic health condition that caused him to miss the equivalent of one year of school over a period of several years. Once he began homeschooling, both his health and his academic work improved. When he was then tested (at the DPI's request) for learning disabilities, the results showed that he did not have a learning disability. Previous school problems were determined to have been the result of his poor health and resulting absences rather than learning disabilities. However, the DPI ignored this evidence and flatly refused to approve his homeschooling on the grounds that the public school could better provide for him.

• One family was required to hire a certified teacher from five to eight hours a week to work with their children. They were told that their children would have to be tested at the end of the year, and if the test results were satisfactory, they would have no problem being approved the following year. Although the children had had certain remedial problems prior to being homeschooled, all three school-age children tested two years above their respective grade levels at the end of the first year of homeschooling. However, the family was denied approval the following fall because now the DPI was concerned about their physical education, music, and art programs. They were informed that guitar lessons were an unacceptable alternative to owning a piano. When the family agreed to rent a piano, they were told that this was not sufficient even though the mother had studied piano for several years. She was asked if she had ever played in her high school band. She felt that nothing she could say or do would please the DPI.

The testimony presented at the hearing included the experiences of a total of 17 families identified by name who had been harassed or treated unfairly by the DPI during their attempts to get information about homeschooling and/or gain approval of their homeschool from the DPI. A summary was also presented of information from 25 additional families who did not want their names or specific stories included in the testimony because they feared further harassment or denial of approval. Several of these families were required to send the DPI a picture of their children, copies of the floor plan of their house, and the daily personal schedules of both parents from the time they arose in the morning until they retired in the evening, seven days a week. There were even more families who were not contacted due to lack of time before the hearing was held. Wisconsin homeschoolers continue to be grateful to the families who were willing to speak up at a time when homeschoolers were regarded with derision and threatened with truancy charges.

For a personal account of the difficulties facing homeschoolers before 1984, see the second story in Chapter 19.

Passage of the Current Homeschooling Law in 1984

The situation changed in 1983. A homeschooling family named Popanz had been charged with truancy on the grounds that their home was not a private school. The Wisconsin Supreme Court heard the case and on April 26, 1983, declared that Wisconsin's compulsory school attendance law was "...void for vagueness since it fails to define 'private school.'" (*State v. Popanz*) In other words, the Court ruled that if prosecution of individuals for failure to attend a private school were to be constitutional, the statutes first needed to be changed so people had a clear definition of a private school. Homeschools were included in this process and definition.

1983 Assembly Bill 887 was drafted by a committee dominated by the educational establishment; no homeschoolers were included. It was introduced in December 1983. It defined home-based private educational programs (homeschools) as instruction elsewhere than at school and required that such programs be approved by the DPI as substantially equivalent to a public or private school. It prevented homeschools from qualifying as private schools and made homeschooling unreasonably difficult.

On January 6, 1984, a group of homeschooling parents met in Stevens Point and organized WPA to oppose AB 887 and work for the passage of a more appropriate bill. The group included people with different backgrounds, incomes, lifestyles, and approaches to education and philosophy and religion. There were conservatives and liberals, Republicans and Democrats. The name Wisconsin Parents Association was chosen because the organization included such a diverse group of people. But people at the meeting that day agreed on one very important principle: They were going to insist that the legislature recognize parents' right to choose for their children an education consistent with their principles and beliefs. They were not going to compromise by agreeing to state regulation of homeschooling. Parents who were trained teachers would not agree to submit their curriculums for review and approval. Those whose children scored well on standardized tests would not agree to requirements for state-mandated testing. Those with high school or college degrees would not agree to requirements that parents have diplomas. Everyone would stand together in opposition to state control of homeschooling.

Homeschoolers worked hard through this new organization to educate legislators and the general public about homeschooling, supply information sheets to people who attended public hearings on the bill, find allies (including small private schools), and build a network of homeschoolers throughout the state who worked together to reclaim their right to homeschool. Since email and the Internet were not yet widely available, this work was done by phone (oh, the phone bills!), postal mail, and face-to-face meetings.

The seriousness of the legislation and the strength of public reaction against it were demonstrated to the Legislature on January 25, 1984, when 2,500 people, the vast majority opposed to the bill, converged on the capitol for the first public hearing. Testimony presented the advantages and importance of homeschooling. Further testimony collected by members of WPA was presented before the Wisconsin Senate Health, Education, Corrections and Human Services Committee on March 13, 1984. This testimony clearly showed that having the DPI review and approve homeschools was unacceptable because of the arbitrary and unfair way in which the DPI had dealt with homeschools, as described above.

Several important amendments to AB 887 changed it into a reasonable and workable bill. It was passed by the Legislature and was enacted as 1983 Act 512 on May 10, 1984, at a time when the Governor's office and the Wisconsin Senate and Assembly were all controlled by Democrats who in turn were supported by the educational establishment including strong teachers unions. This showed the importance of WPA's being an inclusive organization that could speak effectively to both Democrats and Republicans.

How Homeschoolers Have Worked Since 1984 to Maintain the Law and Develop a Favorable Climate for Homeschooling

Homeschoolers working through WPA soon discovered that the passage of the law was only the first step in a long fight to maintain their homeschooling freedoms and their right to homeschool without unnecessary state regulation. Challenges came from many different parts of the educational establishment. New proposals for increased state regulation of homeschooling were presented; some were introduced as legislation. Teachers unions and organizations of school administrators and school boards considered and sometimes passed resolutions calling for increased regulation.

Responding to such challenges required a clear vision; a commitment to working on the grassroots level with people with different approaches to education, religion, and life in general; a thorough understanding of the new homeschooling law and other relevant statutes; an ability to find and work with unlikely allies; a commitment to working with legislators from both political parties; and the creative thinking to devise a wide range of strategies and tactics that would allow a small, often misunderstood minority to prevail against the powerful educational establishment and the general public's suspicion of homeschooling. It also required (and continues to require) countless phone calls, letters, and emails to legislators; attendance by hundreds of homeschoolers at legislative hearings; researching and writing about complex issues; anticipating and forewarning homeschoolers of developing issues; writing fact sheets and testimony for legislative hearings; and working to keep homeschoolers alert to key topics of concern, often educating homeschoolers to see past the superficial attractions of money and "favors" that would cost us our freedoms.

Here are some of the challenges faced and victories won so far. Our work to maintain homeschooling freedoms continues.

The DPI's Power Grab: August through November 1984—Wisconsin's homeschooling law requires homeschoolers to file a form with the DPI each year. The DPI's first version of form PI-1206 exceeded the law by requiring that homeschoolers have available for review by the local school district attendance officer "materials verifying 875 hours of instruction" and "a course outline listing such items as goals, objectives, instructional activities, printed materials and audiovisuals to document a sequentially progressive curriculum." These requirements clearly are not authorized by the law. WPA alerted its members and encouraged homeschoolers to modify their forms before filing them with the DPI. In November 1984, WPA initiated and coordinated a meeting among key legislators who supported homeschooling, a representative of small private schools, the State Superintendent of Public Instruction, and a representative of WPA. As a result of this meeting, the illegal requirements were dropped from the form, making it consistent with the law.

The Lufler Report: January 1987—The DPI released a report on homeschooling written by Henry Lufler that it had contracted for. The report was an inaccurate and misleading document intended to discredit homeschoolers. WPA representatives defused the report through radio and TV appearances and press releases. An Associated Press story quoted a University of Wisconsin professor as saying that the Lufler study was flawed and biased against homeschoolers. WPA requested that the Wisconsin Legislature audit the report to see whether the researcher followed reasonable management guidelines for oversight and research procedures. Once the Legislature had the audit done, the Lufler report seemed to disappear.

Anti-Homeschooling Resolutions: From January 1986 onward—Resolutions calling for increased regulation of homeschooling were taken up by a number of organizations, including the Wisconsin Association of School Boards (WASB). WPA successfully countered a number of them; others passed.

Legislative Council Study of Homeschooling: May 1990 through February 1991—The continuing attempts to increase state regulation of homeschooling were escalated, despite the fact that the law was working well, there was no evidence that it needed to be changed, and thousands of families were successfully homeschooling. This time it was suggested that the Legislative Council form a special committee to study homeschooling. WPA strongly opposed this by demonstrating that there was no evidence that such a study was needed and by pointing out that such studies almost automatically lead to the introduction of legislation. Nevertheless, a special committee was formed and spent five months and $100,000 studying homeschooling in Wisconsin. WPA refused to give the committee credibility by sending a WPA representative to serve on it, although WPA did provide testimony and information to the committee. Homeschoolers also circulated WPA petitions which over 5,000 people signed to show their support for homeschooling and their opposition to further regulation of private schools, including homeschools. The committee unanimously voted to make no recommendations for changing the homeschooling law, which was highly unusual, since Legislative Council committees such as this almost always recommend legislation. In response, WPA organized a Day at the Capitol (February 6, 1991), attended by over 2,000 homeschoolers and their supporters, to emphasize this important decision and promote communication between homeschoolers and their legislators.

The outcome of the Legislative Council study was especially significant because, at that time, various members of the educational establishment were trying very hard to find evidence of problems with homeschooling. Homeschoolers working through WPA exposed these attempts by knowing their rights and using Wisconsin's Open Records Law. (See Chapter 29.) Among the documents received through the Open Records Law was a letter that Herbert Grover, State Superintendent of Public Instruction, wrote June 19, 1990, stating that he was continuing "to do battle with those folks who think that home schooling is a satisfactory alternative to the public schools." Another was an August 8, 1990, letter in which the President of the Wisconsin Education Association Council (WEAC), Wisconsin's largest teachers union, with over 75,000 members, solicited evidence of "problems that we have seen with home schooling in Wisconsin. What is needed are concrete examples of students who had a home schooling experience and came back to the public schools with problems that we then had to correct." (Copies of both these letters are included in this chapter.)

Misleading Information From the DPI: July 1992—The DPI published a misleading and inaccurate document titled "Frequently Posed Questions and Responses Relating to Home-Based Private Educational Programs" that it sent to local school officials and people who contact the DPI for information about homeschooling. (A similar document is now on the DPI website.) WPA exposed the inaccuracies in its newsletter. WPA also sent a letter to school officials clarifying information about entry/re-entry, shared services, dual enrollment, and the fact that homeschools are private schools according to Wisconsin statutes.

Preventing Habitual Truants from Homeschooling: March through April, 1997—WPA informed members that SB 106, a bill to prohibit habitual truants from homeschooling, would undermine homeschooling freedoms by allowing the government to decide who would be permitted to homeschool. About 400 people attended a hearing on April 9. Sixty people registered to testify against the bill while only the sponsoring senator and one of his constituents spoke in favor. The committee decided not to vote on the bill, which eventually died in committee.

Tax Credits for Homeschoolers: Since 1998—WPA has been educating its members and others about the problems with tax credits, informing legislators that most homeschoolers don't want them, and opposing legislation that would give homeschoolers tax credits.

Legislation on Sports: January through September 1999—Homeschoolers worked through WPA to oppose AB 129, a bill that would have supposedly increased opportunities for the few homeschoolers who want to participate in public school activities, including sports, but that actually would have undermined homeschooling freedoms. A hearing in September was attended by 300 people. Only five people registered in favor of the bill, including its sponsor. AB 129 eventually died. (See "Sports" in Chapter 32.)

One Family Unit: February 2001—A national homeschooling organization suggested that homeschoolers in Wisconsin disobey the provision of Wisconsin's homeschooling law that limits homeschools to "one family unit" by including children from other families in their homeschools. WPA corrected this misinformation by explaining what the law requires. See Chapter 28.

Virtual Charter Schools: Since 2002—January 2002—WPA led a statewide drive to educate homeschoolers and the general public about the problems with virtual charter schools and to ensure that virtual charter schools were not called homeschools. WPA representatives attended meetings and testified at a legislative information hearing. Hundreds of homeschoolers attended virtual charter open houses to distribute fact sheets, correct misinformation, and report on open houses. Homeschoolers working through WPA have convinced people not to call these schools homeschools.

In 2008, WPA wrote a detailed memorandum in response to a request from the Wisconsin Audit Bureau for input prior to their audit of Wisconsin virtual charter schools. In 2010, WPA identified serious flaws in the audit. (Both WPA's memo and the critique are on the WPA website.)

Federal Legislation Concerning Homeschooling: Since 2003—In August 2003 and again in December 2005, WPA opposed the federal Home School Non-Discrimination Act (HoNDA), legislation that would have given the federal government authority over homeschoolers by allowing it to define homeschooling. The legislation did not pass either time.

School Districts Marketing to Homeschoolers: June 2005—Working to help homeschoolers maintain their privacy, WPA gathered resource information and provided a sample letter homeschoolers could send to their local school district administrator explaining that

Street Address:
125 South Webster Street
Madison, WI 53702
Phone: (608) 266-3390

Mailing Address:
Post Office Box 7841
Madison, WI 53707-7841

Herbert J. Grover
Superintendent of Public Instruction

June 19, 1990

        , Administrator
School District of
Route #1
      WI

Dear

Thank you very much for submitting the information relative to
your experience with home schooled students and home schoolers.
I also appreciate you contacting your state representatives so
that they will become apprised of the seriousness of this matter.
I will use the information you have forwarded to me as I continue
to do battle with those folks who think that home schooling is a
satisfactory alternative to the public schools.

Any additional information you have gathered, I would appreciate
receiving. Thanks again for your help.

Sincerely,

Herbert J. Grover
State Superintendent

HJG:jmh

WISCONSIN EDUCATION ASSOCIATION COUNCIL

Richard W. Collins, President
33 Nob Hill Drive
P.O. Box 8003
Madison, WI 53708-8003
(608) 276-7711 • (800) 362-8034

M E M O

TO: WEAC Board of Directors   DATE: August 8, 1990
        Local Presidents
        UniServ Presidents

FROM: Richard Collins *Dick*

Superintendent Grover has, in the last few months, raised the issue of the lack of requirements in the area of home schooling. Bert and other Department of Public Instruction (DPI) employees have received much criticism from home schoolers and their supporters because of the Department's concerns.

It would be helpful if we could provide some examples of problems that we have seen with home schooling in Wisconsin. What is needed are concrete examples of students who had a home schooling experience and came back to the public schools with problems that we then had to correct.

We are also looking for examples of students who are still in a home schooling situation and not receiving the educational services that every child should expect.

Please share this request for information with your members and forward any examples of home schooling problems to me as soon as possible. We will consolidate these examples and share them with legislators and the Department of Public Instruction.

Please feel free to contact me if you have any questions or concerns.

RC:ml

cc: UniServ Directors

it is illegal for districts to release information about homeschooling students or parents or to use information from homeschoolers' PI-1206 forms, without the parents' written permission, to contact them to gather information or to encourage students to enroll in public school programs.

Mandatory Five-Year Old Kindergarten: 2009—WPA provided the only testimony in opposition to Wisconsin legislation to make successful completion of five-year-old kindergarten a prerequisite for enrolling in first grade in a public school. Although the bill passed, WPA worked for two amendments that minimized the damage. First, school boards are required (rather than just authorized) to allow qualified students to be exempted. Second, the requirement was removed that children demonstrate "the social, emotional, and cognitive skills necessary for admission to the first grade" to gain an exemption.

After the amended bill passed, WPA provided information in its newsletter and on its website explaining that, thanks to WPA's work and the amendments to the bill, the new law does not directly affect homeschoolers.

Online Version of Form PI-1206: Since 2010—To save money, the DPI switched from a paper form to an online Form PI-1206 in August 2010. WPA convinced the DPI to respect homeschoolers' privacy by not requiring their phone numbers or email addresses, which the DPI had originally planned to do. WPA then posted on its website detailed instruction on how to file the form. When a national homeschooling organization suggested that homeschoolers file a paper form instead of the online version, WPA pointed out that the online version is the same as the paper version was and is consistent with the law. WPA also explained that many government agencies require online filing. Other Wisconsin homeschooling organizations agreed with WPA.

How WPA Has Informed Homeschoolers and Others About Issues

Since its founding in 1984, WPA has informed its members and others, including non-homeschoolers, about important issues that are not directly related to homeschooling but that do affect homeschoolers indirectly and are important to families in general. WPA has researched, written about, and often taken action on topics such as these. (For more information on these issues, see Chapters 31 and 34 and the WPA website.)

Preschool Screening: Since 1986—WPA has encouraged parents to seriously question the effects of preschool screening and to refuse to have their children screened. (See Chapter 31.) As pressure to have children screened increases, WPA is continuing its efforts to inform and support parents.

Education Reform Legislation: November 1991 through March 1992—Through many communications with legislators and a hearing attended by about 300 homeschoolers, WPA convinced legislators not to include homeschooling in proposed education reform legislation. Then WPA informed homeschoolers and others about problems with education reform legislation. Hearings in nine cities were attended by over a thousand people, the vast majority opposed to the legislation. WPA was influential in slowing the passage of the legislation and in having some of the worst provisions removed, including the requirement for portfolios for three year olds.

Outcome Based Education: April 1993—WPA published a fact sheet that outlined problems with outcome-based education (OBE), state goals in education, state-mandated standardized testing, and collaboration. After WPA members and others expressed strong opposition to state goals, the Governor and the State Superintendent of Public Instruction decided not to push to have the goals enacted into law. WPA members and other parents registered opposition to OBE with the Legislature and at the local level.

Exemptions for Public School Students from Required Testing: June 1993 through 1994—WPA supported legislation that allows parents of public school students in Wisconsin to have their children exempted from the new state-mandated standardized tests and assessments for fourth, eighth, and tenth graders. Although homeschoolers are not required to take standardized tests, this exemption is consistent with WPA's commitment to reclaiming and maintaining parental rights in education. Also, if testing were ever proposed for homeschoolers, this exemption would be very valuable as a precedent that could be used in claiming that homeschooling parents should be able to have their children exempted from tests as well. The legislation became law in 1994. See s. 118.30 in Appendix A.

UN Convention: December 1994—A paper titled "Perspectives on the UN Convention on the Rights of the Child" was written and published by WPA, explaining that although this Convention would not become the supreme law of the land in the US, the Convention could still displace families, and it contained other problems.

Parental Rights Amendment: Since 1994—As WPA has repeatedly explained, the government is not the source of parental rights and it is dangerous to ask the government to guarantee these rights through state or federal legislation or constitutional amendments. In March 1998, homeschoolers working through WPA helped defeat a proposed parental rights amendment to the Wisconsin constitution that would have undermined parental rights by asking the government to protect them. In June 2012, WPA informed members and other of problems with a federal parental rights amendment.

Juvenile Justice Code: January through May 1995—WPA brought to light some unreasonable provisions in the Juvenile Justice Code being established by the Wisconsin Legislature and in the recommendations of a Legislative Council special committee studying legislation relating to Children In Need of Protection or Services (CHIPS). WPA held a "Families First" rally at the capitol in March that drew 400 people.

Library Funding: Since 1999—In June 1999, May 2001, and March 2002, WPA worked with other library supporters to increase state funding for public libraries.

Public School Student ID System: Since March 2004—WPA has alerted home-schoolers and others to problems with the new public school student identification system that the DPI devised so it could comply with the complex reporting requirements of federal programs such as No Child Left Behind. WPA also explained that homeschoolers should not be included in the database and told them how to stay out.

Mental Health Screening: Since December 2004—WPA has researched and informed its members and others about risks from the increase in mental health screening that is being promoted by drug companies and others and about ways to avoid or minimize such screening. See Chapter 31.

WPA's Work on the Local Level and With Individuals

• Since Wisconsin's homeschooling law was passed in 1984, WPA has interpreted it and informed homeschoolers about what is and is not required. (See Chapters 3 and 28.) This has made it possible for families to homeschool without being restricted by more state regulation than the law requires. It also means that homeschoolers comply with Wisconsin's reasonable homeschooling law and in that way demonstrate strongly and clearly that parents can be trusted and that a reasonable homeschooling law works.

• WPA has helped hundreds of individual homeschoolers solve problems they faced in situations such as dealing with school officials threatening truancy charges, getting work permits and good student discounts on automobile insurance, responding to calls or visits from social services. The people involved have benefitted, and, in addition, a wide range of challenges have been resolved without claims being made that new homeschooling legislation was needed and without cases being taken to court, both of which could have threatened our homeschooling freedoms. See Chapters 21 and 23.

• Numerous local school officials have sent homeschoolers threatening letters inaccurately claiming that they have the right to review homeschool curriculums, visit homeschools, or collect personal information from homeschoolers in addition to the information on form

PI-1206. WPA has worked with many homeschoolers who have received these threats, resolving issues in favor of homeschoolers and preventing serious problems.

• Entry/re-entry policies initiated at the local level have often discriminated against homeschoolers. Homeschoolers have worked through WPA to make policies more reasonable.

• Since 1997, WPA has worked with homeschoolers throughout the state to oppose local curfew ordinances and truancy sweeps.

• WPA continues to remind homeschoolers not to comply with demands from officials that exceed the law. This includes not completing surveys, not providing more information about their family than is on form PI-1206, not reporting to school officials about their homeschool, not providing more information than is required of other private or public school students when entering or re-entering a public school.

• Although homeschool diplomas are now widely accepted, this has not always been the case, and there are still institutions that reject them occasionally. WPA has helped many individuals negotiate with various employers, colleges and universities, the Wisconsin Department of Justice, and the US military to get their diplomas accepted. In 2012, WPA convinced the DPI to change the statement on its website to indicate the widespread acceptance of homeschool diplomas. See Chapter 12.

• Homeschooling sometimes becomes an issue in divorces and custody cases, and WPA provides assistance when asked.

PART FOUR

MAINTAINING RIGHTS AND RESPONSIBILITIES

Chapter 21

Ten Principles for Keeping Our Homeschooling Freedoms

> The essence of homeschooling is in the freedom to make our own choices, the freedom from any state regulation telling us when, where, how, or what in particular we must learn. Protecting this freedom is absolutely essential for us to realize the full benefits of homeschooling. Anything that diminishes that freedom, however slightly, turns me, to that extent, into an unpaid agent of the state, carrying out someone else's directives as to how my children should learn. From Opening Remarks, WPA Conference, 2002

Why Homeschooling Freedoms Matter

Wisconsin has one of the most reasonable homeschooling laws in the country. Since January 1984, homeschoolers have worked hard through WPA to gain and maintain it. (See Chapter 20.) As a result, every day of our lives is freer, easier, more under our control than are the days of homeschoolers in most other states. (See "Homeschooling Laws in Other States" at the end of this chapter.) We can choose whatever curriculum we want and change it whenever we decide to. We can give our children tests we have chosen, that agree with our values, whenever we choose, and share the results with whoever we want, or with no one. We can also decide not to test our children. We can set our own daily, weekly, and yearly schedule. As long as we include "reading, language arts, mathematics, social studies, science and health," we can decide what to include in our curriculum and what to leave out. We can travel near and far, study indoors or out.

Consider what we don't have to do, things that are required of homeschoolers in other states. We don't have to present our curriculum to school officials and hope they will approve it. We don't have to prepare our children for state mandated tests or worry about whether they are at grade level or how they compare with others their age. We don't have to send periodic reports to school officials. We don't need to be concerned about a school official visiting our homeschool to check on what we are doing. We don't need formal education ourselves or other parent qualifications. Any of these requirements would limit what we can do as homeschoolers and curtail our freedoms. Any of them would pressure us to make our homeschools more like the public schools that many of us are homeschooling to avoid. Any of them would cause us to think less about what we want our children to learn and more about how to prepare them for state tests or how to describe what we did today so a school official would approve. They would lead us to worry about children whose major strengths are not academic, or who are learning at their own (slower) pace, or who have a unique way of learning.

Some parents feel they are so busy homeschooling their children that they don't have time to work to maintain homeschooling freedoms. But imagine the burden if the law were changed and we had to comply with increased state regulation. Think how much less time we would have for homeschooling itself. Fortunately, if we work together and each do our part, WPA will continue to be a strong force for maintaining homeschooling freedoms.

Raising a child is a huge responsibility, and we all look for assurances that we are doing the right thing. One way to achieve peace of mind is to hire acknowledged experts to take over some of this task. When it comes to education, these experts are called teachers, administrators, and counselors. But in the name of efficiency, a large group of children is assigned only a few of these experts, so the school's mission is seriously compromised right from the start. The school is like a large and efficient greenhouse, with rows and rows of pots and a carefully set schedule of light, warmth, water, and just the right kind of fertilizer. The problem is that the whole setup assumes that only one kind of plant will be put in all the pots-all tomatoes. So all the pots are the same size and shape and the amount and timing of everything needed for growth has been designed to be optimum for just this one kind of plant. Now some of the plants do turn out to be tomatoes, so they thrive. But others are different: they are daisies or roses, broccoli or watermelon. These are all plants, so they all grow to some extent, but not as much as they could, and some are left permanently stunted.

The homeschooling greenhouse, by contrast, is small and has just a few plants, so each can receive exactly what it needs, when and how it needs it, and so the homeschooled plants grow and flourish and .... But wait a minute, isn't this analogy getting a bit ridiculous? It's too cute and convenient, and applying labels is the mistake schools make. My daughter is not a daisy and my son is not a watermelon. (Sometimes I wish they were, because then I would know exactly what to do to help them grow.) But no, they are much more complicated and interesting. They are mystery plants, unfolding to become something unique in all of history, a one-specimen species never seen before that will never be seen again. And therein lies the challenge: how do I guide the growth of a plant that has no label, does not come with a tag telling its requirements, and, moreover, sometimes changes its requirements without any notice? To properly guide my children, I must be wholly open to their unique set of talents and interests as those grow and change day by day, guiding, responding, suggesting, and even demanding in the ways that will help them realize their potential. . . .

For me, homeschooling is one of life's great truths, the kind of truth that everyone should rejoice in knowing but most seem unable to risk opening their eyes to see. I know that the freedom it gives us, while often daunting, is also a spur to supremely satisfying achievements, both for my children and for me.

But like most valuable freedoms, the freedom to homeschool is fragile and under nearly constant siege. I have not always appreciated this fact. When I first joined the WPA, about 9 years ago, I remember receiving my first issue of the WPA newsletter with excitement. As a neophyte homeschooler, I was hungry for guidance, advice, and reassurance. To my dismay, the newsletter had little of that. Instead it had articles with exciting titles like "Impact of DPI's Inaccurate Document on Home Schooling" and "Effects of Collaboration Plans on Families, Schools, and Society." At that time I knew nothing about the WPA's role in creating our current homeschooling law, and I remember thinking that the WPA seemed practically paranoid in the way it saw threats to homeschooling around every corner.

Over time, my ignorance has turned to appreciation. Gradually, I came to realize that the defining characteristic of homeschooling is not that our children are at home when others are at school, or that our children can study nuclear physics at age 9, or learn to read at age 11, or study creationism, atheism or any other topic that seems worthy and interesting. The essence of homeschooling is not in these particular choices, important though they may be to some families. The essence of homeschooling is in the freedom to make our own choices, the freedom from any state regulation telling us when, where, how, or what in particular we must learn. Protecting this freedom is absolutely essential for us to realize the full benefits of homeschooling. Anything that diminishes that freedom, however slightly, turns me, to that extent, into an unpaid agent of the state, carrying out someone else's directives as to how my children should learn. For example, if I want to have my children take a standardized test, I can do so. But if the state requires me to do so, our freedom is diminished. If the state then labels my son a watermelon based on his test score, our freedom is significantly undermined. If the state then specifies what exactly I must do to turn him back into a tomato, then our precious freedom is largely gone.

So I now see that the WPA's vigilance, which is to say, our vigilance, in protecting this freedom is the most important work it-and we-can do. And, yes, unfortunately, threats to that freedom are around every corner. Having worked as a lawyer, I know how quickly a law, even a seemingly well-established one, can change or even disappear if the powerful are against it and those who rely on it stay silent. I also have seen how an apparently unrelated or innocuous law can be twisted and put to quite different purposes if that suits those who have the power to enforce it. We are fortunate to have this great freedom called homeschooling, but we must keep in mind that we are not lucky to have it. Luck has nothing to do with it. This freedom was won by hard work on the part of many, and it can only be maintained with help from all of us.—From Opening Remarks, WPA Conference, 2002

Ten Essential Principles for Maintaining Homeschooling Freedoms

Here are things we can do to maintain our freedoms. They require understanding and a strong commitment, but except in the time of a crisis, they do not require much time or money. They provide important learning opportunities for us and our children. And they help us discover how to maintain freedoms in other areas of our lives as well.

1. Know what is required of homeschoolers in Wisconsin. Read the explanations of the law in Chapters 3 and 28 so you clearly understand what the law requires and, perhaps more importantly, what it doesn't require. If you don't understand, you are likely to put yourself, your family, and others at risk. If you don't know your rights and exercise them, you will not have them. No one else, including lawyers, will make sure your rights are respected and protected; you have to take responsibility for them. If you don't know what the law does and does not require, you will not be able to follow some of the other principles.

Have a copy of the homeschooling statute available for reference when you need it. (See Appendix A.) Don't ask school officials or the Department of Public Instruction (DPI) for information about statutes, regulations, or what is required. They often do not know, misunderstand, have been misinformed, or have purposely misconstrued what the statutes or regulations say. Be careful about information from books or websites that cover the laws in all 50 states. They sometimes provide only the text of the statutes without essential information about how they are interpreted and enforced.

2. Comply with the law, but do ONLY the minimum required by statute or regulation. Homeschoolers who don't comply with the law provide a golden opportunity for opponents and critics who want to increase state regulation of homeschooling to claim that more regulation of homeschooling is needed. As a result, Wisconsin's reasonable homeschooling law could be changed. For example, file form PI-1206 online at the appropriate time for your circumstances. (See Chapter 4.) Under Wisconsin law, homeschoolers are required to have a curriculum. Since a curriculum is basically an educational plan, even the most determined unschoolers can (and should) say "Yes" when asked if they have a curriculum.

However, do **only** the minimum the law requires. When people do more, they voluntarily and unnecessarily increase the power and authority that public officials have over homeschoolers. They set precedents that limit their freedoms and those of other homeschoolers. Therefore, if a school official asks or tells you to do more than is required, politely refuse and explain what is and is not required. If they persist, ask them to show you the statute or regulation that gives them the authority to make such a request. See Chapter 31.

Occasionally, it may be tempting to take what seems like the easy way out and do more than the minimum by showing officials our curriculum, samples of our children's work, test scores, etc. even though these are not required by statute in Wisconsin. Perhaps we are proud of our children's accomplishments or want to educate officials about homeschooling or show them how well it works. But any action that exceeds statutes or regulations sets a precedent and is likely to increase demands officials make of us and other homeschoolers in the future. It may also increase the questions, doubts, concerns, and criticisms that officials have about our homeschooling.

3. Maintain the distinction between homeschools and public school programs, including virtual charter schools. Homeschooling parents take direct responsibility for their children's education. By contrast, parents of public school students (including those who enroll in a virtual charter school or other public school program that allows them to study in their homes) turn the responsibility for their children's education over to the public schools. Unless a clear distinction is made between virtual charter schools and homeschools, homeschoolers are likely to be expected to comply with these standards and requirements. See "Virtual Charter Schools" in Chapter 24.

4. Don't ignore violations of your rights, even if they seem too small to matter. Major freedoms are often lost one small step at a time. Our failure to respond also encourages those who are limiting our freedoms to continue. For example, suppose a school district requires that homeschoolers submit their curriculums for review and approval, something not required by Wisconsin statutes. If homeschoolers do not object, before long the district may also ask for periodic reports. On the other hand, if homeschoolers object strongly the first time the district exceeds its authority (either by mistake or deliberately), school officials will probably be more reluctant to take on homeschoolers in the future. It also reduces future, perhaps more serious, challenges. Some people think that homeschoolers shouldn't complain about requirements like review and approval of curriculums, reporting, or testing as long as no one declares that homeschooling is illegal. Such people greatly underestimate the importance of choosing an approach to education and a curriculum, allowing children to pursue their interests and learn at their own pace, and offering our children an education consistent with our principles and beliefs rather than those of the public school system.

5. Learn to work with your legislators, regardless of their political party. Communicate with your federal and state legislators at the beginning of each new legislative session. Establish a working relationship before there is a crisis. Remember that homeschooling is not a partisan issue. We need to work with members of both parties to avoid problems when control of the Legislature changes from one party to the other. Start with an issue you and your legislator agree about, no matter how minor. Share information with them that they are most likely to find convincing given their overall perspectives. (Note: In 1984, Wisconsin's reasonable homeschooling law was passed by a Senate and Assembly that were both controlled by Democrats, and signed by a Democratic governor.) See Chapter 30.

6. Do not seek or accept favors from the government that are connected to education, including public funds for homeschooling, tax deductions, or tax credits, and permission to play on public school sports teams. It is tempting to think about benefits for children or money for more homeschooling resources, especially since most homeschoolers give up income and make a financial sacrifice so parents can spend more time with their children.

However, there is no such thing as a free lunch. Such benefits are likely to be followed by increased regulation, especially since the government is accountable for how tax dollars are spent. Even benefits that seem quite safe, like homeschoolers playing on public school sports teams, open the door for increased regulation of homeschooling. (Athletes who are public school students need to meet eligibility requirements such as grade point average. Surely requirements would be placed on homeschoolers as well.)

Regulation stemming from favors or benefits would undoubtedly apply to all home-schoolers, not just those accepting the benefits. Families would not have the option of refusing the benefit and avoiding the increased regulation.

It's important for homeschoolers to resist the temptation to seek benefits or favors from the government, to refuse such benefits if they are offered, to make it clear to legislators that they do not want such benefits, and to encourage other homeschoolers to do these things as well. See Chapter 24.

7. Do not push for new homeschooling legislation. Small minorities generally have difficulty getting legislation passed. In addition, once a bill has been introduced, it is very difficult to control. It can be changed so much through amendments that it actually ends up working against the minority that introduced it rather than in their favor. (For example, Wisconsin's good homeschooling law resulted from legislation that was introduced by opponents of homeschooling and then changed through amendments so it ended up supporting homeschooling.) It is easier for a small minority like homeschoolers to gain support from non-homeschoolers when we are a beleaguered minority being put upon by a large interest group like a teachers union than to find support for legislation we initiated ourselves. (This is why we would be unlikely to succeed in getting favorable homeschooling legislation passed if we initiated it, even though we were successful in turning harmful legislation around in 1984.) In addition, since we have one of best laws in the county, we don't need legislation.

8. Stay out of court if at all possible. It is almost always better for homeschoolers to try to reach settlements through negotiation or arbitration than to take cases to court. Rulings in court cases having to do with any topic, not just homeschooling, generally uphold the status quo and support the dominant culture. This means that rulings concerning small minorities such as homeschoolers tend to be biased in favor of conventional education rather than alternatives. We are much better off without any court rulings than with rulings that go against us. Evidence to support this idea can be found in a 1990 report by Jane Henkel of the Wisconsin Legislative Council titled *Recent Court Cases Examining the Constitutionality of Other States' Laws Regulating Home Schools.* (Available on the WPA website.) Her report showed that court cases uphold the constitutionality of increased state regulation of home-schooling. The report states, "Special care was taken to attempt to find reported cases striking down state regulations. With the limited exception of cases which found regulations to be unconstitutionally vague, that effort was unsuccessful, which tends to indicate that there are few, if any, such cases." The cases having to do with the most substantive aspects of regulation, namely review and approval of curriculum, required testing, and periodic reporting, have not been overturned in courts and still hold true as regulatory constraints on homeschooling liberties in the states where the cases were heard and more generally in most states.

9. Understand and apply the distinction between compulsory school attendance and compulsory education. Basically, remember and remind school officials and others that the law requires that young people attend school, but it does not require that they receive an education while doing so. Therefore, it is discriminatory for school officials, judges, court commissioners, and others to insist that homeschoolers demonstrate that their children are receiving an education that is equivalent to the education that children supposedly receive in public schools, or that they are at grade level, or to penalize them for failing to achieve specific educational goals. For more information, see Chapter 22.

Remember that your actions affect other homeschoolers' freedoms.

10. Share these principles with other homeschoolers. Some of homeschooling's greatest strengths come from the fact that it is a grassroots movement. It becomes even stronger as we communicate with each other, share information and experiences, support each other, and work together to maintain our freedoms. On the other hand, our freedoms are at risk when individual homeschoolers or homeschooling organizations fail to understand what Wisconsin's homeschooling law does and does not require, do more than the minimum the law requires, blur the distinction between homeschoolers and public school students studying in their homes, seek homeschooling legislation and money and other favors from the government, and take cases to court when there are other ways to resolve the issues.

Joining WPA is an excellent way to work with other homeschoolers. WPA is strong because it includes all homeschoolers, regardless of their approach to learning, homeschooling, lifestyle, religion, etc. WPA is strong because it relies on people like you knowing their rights and responsibilities. Our homeschooling freedoms depend on our working together. Renew your membership; tell others about WPA; donate; buy copies of this handbook for others, including your library; and attend the conference each spring. Also consider joining a local homeschooling support group. If none exists in your area, start one. See Chapter 14.

> My homeschooling friend Miranda wrote at age eleven: "Freedom means you can have your own thoughts without having to tell anyone what they are . . . But freedom also means that every choice you make has a consequence . . ."—From Opening Remarks, WPA Conference, 2000

Homeschooling Laws in Other States

Homeschoolers in almost all the other states have to deal with more state regulation than those in Wisconsin. Approximately half the states require testing of homeschooled children. In some states, homeschoolers have to submit their curriculums to school officials for review and approval before they can begin each school year. In some, homeschoolers have to submit yearly, or even quarterly, reports on their children's progress. Many states have multiple requirements. Requirements in some states vary depending on how much formal education parents have. Each of these requirements limits homeschoolers' freedom to homeschool and conduct their daily lives according to their principles and beliefs.

> You know, if I had to submit our curriculum or report on our homeschool, I'd rather deal with firefighters or park rangers than school officials. At least firefighters and rangers would understand the importance of practical skills and hands-on learning, setting priorities, understanding principles (not just memorizing facts for a test and then forgetting them), learning how to think clearly, and teamwork. And they wouldn't insist that we do what they do every day, the way school officials would. Public schools just aren't a good standard for judging homeschools.

Many homeschoolers find that knowing what laws in other states require helps them appreciate Wisconsin's homeschooling law and understand why it is important to work to maintain it. Here are some examples.

> *From a Wisconsin Homeschooler:*
> When my son was very young, we thought about relocating to Portland, Oregon. My husband had a job offer; we had lined up housing and made a reservation for a moving truck. We purchased a non-refundable airplane ticket for my father, who would be driving our truck to Portland. We had everything in place.
> I knew that I wanted to have homeschooling as an option, so on a whim, I looked up the Oregon homeschooling laws. They were rather restrictive with assessments required at grades 3, 5, 8, and 10. You had to pay for the testing by "qualified" testers. If your children didn't test high enough in these assessments, they were tested again the next year. If they still didn't meet the standards set, they might be allowed to continue homeschooling, or the state might decide their education had to be overseen by a licensed teacher with continuing testing, or the state might remand them to school.
> The state could "remand" my child to school. Hmmm...
> Well, we thought, Portland is close to the Washington border. Maybe we could live there. Washington was worse. You could only homeschool if you had earned 45 units of college credit

or attended a "parent qualifying course" or if you worked with a certified teacher or were "deemed sufficiently qualified to provide home-based instruction by the superintendent of your local school district." Wow! In addition to all of that, you would have to have your children tested annually. If you planned to send your children to public school at some point in the future, you had to provide annual test scores (or assessment records) and immunization records.

None of this seemed as appealing as the Wisconsin homeschooling laws. I started reading about the history of homeschooling in Wisconsin. We realized that if we wanted the freedom to homeschool the way we wanted to, Wisconsin would be where our children would grow up. We cancelled our housing arrangement. My husband turned down the job offer. We cancelled the moving truck. We forfeited the money for the plane ticket.

That was over a decade ago. We are happily homeschooling our three children and are incredibly appreciative of the homeschooling laws and history here in Wisconsin.

From a Wisconsin Homeschooler:

The Green Mountains of Vermont call me. They whisper in my ear with watery voices like the mermaids who call sailors to the sea. I am enchanted and cannot resist following. Yet, as I consider answering their chorus, I realize that Vermont poses formidable challenges for me.

Trying to find some practicality, some tangible reason to go to Vermont, I decided to research the homeschooling laws. The Department of Education sent me a 47-page packet entitled "Guidelines for Home Study in Vermont," which included four forms to fill out and an enrollment checklist. Under General Information, the page begins with this paragraph:

During the 1999-2000 school year, over 1,700 Vermont children received their education at home. Parents or guardians who decide to educate their children at home assume a great responsibility. In effect, they take on the roles of teacher, administrator, resource coordinator, librarian, curriculum supervisor and performance evaluator. All this, combined with the everyday tasks of good parenting, presents a formidable challenge, which can be successfully met only by dedicated, concerned parents, willing and able to devote the time and effort necessary to make home schooling work well. [bold in original]

I am utterly dumbfounded. How dare the government use such a patronizing, and suspicious, tone to describe what I do? But the affront does not stop there. Page after page describes the rules. A homeschooling family must fill out forms. If this is their first year filing, they must fill out a Pre-assessment on which their child is screened to determine whether the child has a disability that would affect the child's learning. They file a Minimum Course of Study describing how they intend to have learning experiences in six fields. Later in the year, the family submits a Progress Assessment on which a child's progress in the six fields is documented in one of six ways. The options include submitting a portfolio of work to the Department of Education, having a certified Vermont teacher assess your child, or completing a standardized achievement test which tests skills in all six fields. Vermont is vigilant for its children!

Next, the packet continues with the consequences and threats. If the Commissioner has significant doubt about whether the Minimum Course of Study is comprehensive enough, s/he may call a hearing. During this time, if your child is not already enrolled in a home study program, enrollment will not occur until after the hearing. This means that your child may be required to enroll in a public or private school.

All of this is shocking to those of us who live in a state with a wonderful homeschooling law. Yet, when I spoke to Vermont homeschooling families, they often told me what a good law they had. Good compared to what? Good compared to having a Department of Education officer visiting once a week to observe?!

Through my research, I feel deep admiration and gratitude for the people who worked so hard to pass this law (and have continued to work to maintain it). These visionaries had wisdom which has benefited me, years later. Their work makes a wonderful environment for homeschooling families, no judges or evaluations or tedious paperwork, only the free joy of growing. I am very, very thankful.

The Vermont mountain nymphs continue to call, but the sensible freedom of Wisconsin's rolling corn fields also has its appeal. As homeschoolers, Wisconsin is the only choice.

From a Wisconsin Homeschooler:

We were living in Minnesota when I learned about homeschooling. In Minnesota you need to test your children every year, which basically means you will be bringing "school" home. Of course, I would eliminate the social pressures of the public system, but we weren't free to expand in whatever direction my child wanted to go or learn at our own pace. Therefore, we chose to move to Wisconsin following his first grade year.

From a Wisconsin Homeschooler:

Meeting families from other states, I am continually struck when people speak of having evaluators look over portfolios as "not much interference" or having to test "only" every other year.

The mother that has made the deepest impression is from New York state. That state has some of the most intrusive laws in the US, AND the county AND the local school district can add to these. The NY family has to supply quarterly reports in each of up to 12 subject areas for each child. Testing is mandatory at certain grades. Detailed descriptions of curriculum and lesson plans must to be submitted for approval-approval that has been withheld for such infractions as not including her telephone number. Tears welled up as she explained that she spent more energy complying than she did working with her children. The decision to submit to such a drain made each year's decision to homeschool a struggle. To think that I frequently grumble about our official attendance record!

My children were not yet born when the fight for Wisconsin's laws was fought in 1984. I thank each of the families who forged a group that could work together no matter why or how each family chose to homeschool. I greatly appreciate the patient hours they spent enabling our homeschooling law to pass. The legacy given my family allows us to proceed in the ways most meaningful to our needs and beliefs. Thank you.

But we cannot rest on their laurels. The New York law replaced an older and now easier law. We need to continue to monitor our local school boards and our legislature. Each of us is able to contribute information about our local situations to the WPA newsletter: articles from our local newspapers about truancy or copies of letters the local officials send to homeschoolers in their districts. Meeting with our state senators and assembly members to explain how well the law serves us is best done when there are no fires raging. We can always take the easiest way out and contribute money so that WPA can work up to a budget on a shoestring.

We must never forget: "Eternal vigilance is the price of freedom."—From Opening Remarks, WPA Conference, 2000

Chapter 22

Foundations of Homeschooling Rights and Responsibilities

The following list of foundations of homeschooling rights and responsibilities is based on principles that support reasonable homeschooling laws and oppose unreasonable ones. Many of these ideas also support other important family rights, and the list itself provides a model for ways in which rights can be maintained. A wide range of ideas is presented so that the most appropriate and compelling ones can be selected for a given situation. It is important to understand that we have inalienable rights. These rights are not given to us by the state. We should not look to the state as the source of these rights, we should not give them over to the state, and we should not ask the state to protect them for us through laws or constitutional amendments.

Many of these ideas are based on common sense and a willingness to question assumptions and practices that are widely accepted. They are organized into categories for convenience, but in reality they overlap and interrelate. Some basic ideas are repeated so each category is nearly self-contained and so subtle points can be included.

Legal foundations are listed first because homeschoolers and other parents must deal with them so often. However, legal arguments are often not the most compelling or effective way to support and maintain family rights and responsibilities and should not be heavily relied on. See Chapter 23.

Legal Foundations

(1) Constitutional provisions. The U.S. Constitution does not specifically mention education. This was not an oversight. The idea of including education was discussed and rejected.

However, the several amendments to the Constitution guarantee rights that are important to homeschoolers and others.

• **The First Amendment** covers freedom of religion, speech, and the press, and the rights of assembly and petition.

• **The Fourth Amendment** states, "The right of the people to be secure in their persons, houses, papers, and effects, against unreasonable searches and seizures, shall not be violated, but upon probable cause." In other words, the state must have reasonable cause or evidence before officials can enter the houses of citizens or threaten their persons or insist that they answer questions.

• **The Fifth Amendment** protects citizens from being compelled to testify against themselves. It guarantees the right to trial by jury and the right not to "be deprived of life, liberty, or property, without due process of law." The right to due process has been used to protect personal liberties. It is strengthened and given more authority under the Fourteenth Amendment.

• **The Ninth Amendment** says that there are some rights that are retained by the people even though they are not listed in the Constitution. This amendment is important for people who want to reclaim rights that the state has usurped by custom and even by statute, since they can argue that the state had no constitutional basis for taking away these rights in the first place. On the basis of this amendment, courts have recently upheld parental rights in education and rights to privacy.

• **Section 1 of the Fourteenth Amendment** provides civil rights that are very important to individuals, especially minorities.

> **First,** "no state shall make or enforce any law which shall abridge the privileges or immunities of citizens of the United States." In other words, state laws may not take away fundamental privileges (rights and liberties) guaranteed by the U.S. Constitution.
> **Second,** "nor shall any state deprive any person of life, liberty, or property, without due process of law." While this provision seems to repeat the language of the Fifth Amendment, here it is establishing that a state government may not do this. For example, a state may not pass laws that deny parents' constitutional rights to choose for their children an education consistent with their principles and beliefs.
> **Third,** the section continues, "nor deny to any person within its jurisdiction the equal protection of the laws." Each individual has equal rights and liberties under the law. Homeschoolers can use this in dealings with public school officials. For example, officials cannot legally deny homeschoolers the opportunity to participate in public school programs and activities merely because they are homeschoolers. They cannot legally require more of former homeschoolers who are entering public schools than of students transferring from other schools.

(2) Case law. Rulings by the U.S. Supreme Court and federal, state, and local courts interpret and expand on the Constitution. Important for homeschoolers are the U.S. Supreme Court cases *Pierce v. Society of Sisters* (268 U.S. 510 [1925]) and *Farrington v. Tokushige* (273 U.S. 284 [1927]) in which the court ruled that parents have a right to secure for their children an education consistent with their principles and beliefs and that the state may not have a monopoly in education.

Homeschoolers involved in serious legislative or court battles are strongly encouraged to study the Constitution and case law in greater depth. More detailed information is in John Holt and Patrick Farenga's *Teach Your Own* and John W. Whitehead and Wendell R. Bird's *Home Education and Constitutional Liberties*. Of course there is no substitute for reading the original documents themselves.

(3) Common law. This is a system based on practice, court decisions, and customs and usage rather than on statutes. Some of the legal maxims or principles that are so widely accepted that they do not need to be written down and that can be applied to homeschooling in the United States are:

• **"Innocent until proven guilty."** In other words, the state must prove an individual is guilty; individuals do not have to prove they are innocent. Although the state has an interest in ensuring that children do not grow up to be a burden on the state, courts have confirmed that parents have rights in education which the state may not violate. Homeschooling parents should not need to prove themselves innocent (by meeting certification requirements or showing that their curriculum is substantially equivalent to that of a public school or having their children tested) as a condition for exercising their parental rights in education.

• **Rights of minorities.** People cannot be prosecuted or forced to abandon their principles or practices just because the majority of the people do not agree with them or choose their approach. Homeschoolers should not be prosecuted simply because they have chosen an approach to education that is different from that of the majority of Americans today.

• **Civil liberties**. Everyone, including homeschoolers, is entitled to fundamental civil liberties, some of which are described in the Bill of Rights.

• **"Hard cases make bad law."** In other words, a law designed to take care of the worst possible hypothetical case is almost certain to be long, difficult to enforce, and more likely to prevent good people from doing good than bad people from doing bad. It is unfair and solves nothing to punish conscientious homeschoolers by passing an unnecessarily restrictive law that does not solve the problem of high risk children anyway. Such a law would damage the effectiveness of good homeschools.

(4) Limits of the compulsory school attendance law. Homeschooling laws are based on compulsory school attendance laws. (If there were no attendance laws, the state would have no basis for regulating homeschooling. People who wanted to homeschool would simply not attend school.) However, it is extremely important to realize that compulsory school attendance laws require attendance, not education. See below.

Compulsory Attendance, Not Compulsory Education

Compulsory school attendance laws require that children of certain ages attend school. Wisconsin's law (s. 118.15) reads in part: "Any person having under control a child who is between the ages of 6 and 18 years shall cause the child to attend school regularly." Other laws define what schools must do that is educational (such as having a curriculum that covers basic subjects), but they do not require that students become educated. Additional requirements are placed on public schools that want to receive state tax dollars (which, of course, all public schools do). They often include ensuring that curriculums meet state standards and students take standardized tests. In addition, schools in states that want to receive federal tax dollars for education (which virtually all states do) are required to meet additional criteria that have recently been greatly increased under federal laws such as No Child Left Behind. Private schools that accept state or federal tax dollars or both are also required to meet extra criteria. These extra requirements are not part of the basic definition of a school. Private schools (including homeschools) that do not accept tax dollars do not have to meet them.

The fact that laws require attendance can also be seen in the definition of truancy, which is clearly understood as failure to attend school and is independent of education. Laws don't say, "If you can come up with a better way to learn what you need to know than attending classes, you may be excused today." Laws do say, "If you're not in school and don't have what school officials consider a 'good excuse,' which pretty much means a serious illness, YOU ARE TRUANT, regardless of how smart you are, how much you already know about what's being taught, how meaningless or irrelevant or wrong it is, or how much more you could be learning some place else."

Generally speaking, laws do not require compulsory education. Among the reasons:

• There's no common agreement about what it means to be "educated." Can you dislike math and still be considered educated? What if you have outstanding mechanical or musical abilities but are not drawn to the printed word? Or what if you're smart enough to see through the phoniness and artificiality of school and strong enough to protest?

• Even if we could agree on what one needs to know to be "educated," we lack the means to determine what people know. Tests can only cover a tiny fraction of a subject. They measure how well a person performed on a given test on a given day, not how much a person knows. Some know a lot more than tests show; in fact, they know so much that they realize many questions oversimplify and distort things, and they have difficulty choosing a "right" answer because, really, all the possible choices are usually at least a little bit wrong. Some people have different perspectives and life experiences from the test makers, so the questions don't make sense to them. Some excel at things that are not covered on tests (such as creativity, mechanical ability, musical ability, compassion, justice) but not on the things that are included. Some have good test-taking skills even though they don't know much about the material being covered, so they score "too high."

• Perhaps most important, schools apparently aren't capable of educating many students. Obviously, many people don't learn what they need or want to know in school. Assuming schools would educate people if they could, we have to conclude that they can't. Passing compulsory education laws that require education would not change this. Instead, such laws would show schools' failings without providing realistic solutions.

So laws wisely require attendance, not education. If you don't measure up to the schools' idea of what education should be, you and your parents don't have to pay a fine or go to jail. The worst that can happen is that you're not allowed to move on to the next grade, although many, many children keep moving along even though they haven't learned what they were supposed to. Further evidence that laws do not require education appears when parents get really fed up and sue schools for failing to educate their children. In such cases, courts rule in favor of the schools. This is not surprising; in fact, the courts have to rule that way. Think of the chaos and the number of lawsuits that would result if courts allowed parents to sue schools for failing to educate their children!

It is important to note that the lack of laws requiring education plays a major role in maintaining freedom of education for everyone, not just homeschoolers, and thus in maintaining freedom of thought. If laws did require education, the government would directly control education and indirectly control people's thinking, since education has a strong influence on thought and belief.

At this point, the distinction between compulsory attendance and compulsory education may seem obvious. After all, people generally refer to the laws under discussion as "compulsory attendance laws" or "compulsory school attendance laws." Why then aren't these points obvious to legislators, judges, the general public, and even some homeschoolers? Why don't legislators and the general public realize that it is inappropriate to require compulsory education of homeschoolers (or anyone else)? One reason is the wide acceptance of the notions that "real learning" takes place in a conventional school and that the most important things people learn are what they study in school between the ages of 6 or 5 or 4 and 18 or 22 or 26. We homeschoolers have done a lot to reclaim learning, but the task is far from complete.

In addition, our society gives moral authority to people who have important positions in education, such as teachers, principals, school superintendents, etc. Many people look to such officials for the answers to questions about education and trust their responses. However, we need to remember and explain to others that, although these school officials may have moral authority, they do not have legal authority either to define education or to require compulsory education. We can ensure our freedoms by not confusing the moral authority ascribed to them by the larger society with legal authority.

As homeschoolers, we can use the distinction between compulsory attendance and compulsory education in a variety of situations.

• When legislators or others claim that laws are needed to ensure that homeschoolers are being educated, we can explain that compulsory education is not required of students who attend conventional schools, so it would be discriminatory to require it of homeschoolers. We can also explain that requiring compulsory education of homeschoolers would set a dangerous precedent for students in conventional schools and for our society as a whole.

• In situations where social workers, judges, or court commissioners insist that homeschoolers demonstrate that they are being educated and/or are at grade level, homeschoolers can oppose such compulsory education on principle. If authorities threaten to require that homeschoolers attend conventional schools because they are not learning enough or may not learn enough through homeschooling, a similar argument can be used.

• When someone challenges our homeschooling on the basis of our children's failure to learn something important, we can point out that, although we want very much for our children to be educated, the laws do not require education, people don't agree on what it means to be educated, and we don't have a good way to determine what people know. These points may seem formal and stilted, but using them in this way reminds us of their importance and helps other people understand them.

Logical Foundations

1. Laws regulating homeschools are basically unnecessary. The experiences of hundreds of thousands of parents and children have shown that parents are very capable of educating their children at home. In addition, thousands of formerly homeschooled children have entered or re-entered conventional schools without problems, showing that their homeschooling experience did not handicap them or make them unable to handle the work done in conventional schools.

2. Homeschooling laws and regulations do not improve homeschools. Homeschooling works because children and adults are good at learning if given a chance. Homeschools are small enough and flexible enough to meet the needs of individual children and allow them to use their strengths. They work because parents care about their children and want what is best for them. People do not become loving and caring parents or conscientious homeschoolers because there are laws that require them to do this. (See Chapter 18.)

3. Regulations can be harmful to homeschools and limit their effectiveness. Regulations frequently interfere with the alternative nature of homeschools, limit their flexibility, and make it more difficult for homeschools to be effective and meet the needs of families.

4. It is commonly understood and widely accepted by people who think seriously about it that decisions about children's educations should be made by parents. Some parents choose to delegate part of the responsibility for their children's education to a conventional school while others (called homeschoolers) decide to fulfill this responsibility directly themselves.

5. Some proposed homeschooling laws and regulations imply that parents cannot be trusted to homeschool their children. However, parents can be trusted because:

• Homeschooling is a big responsibility and a lot of work. It is not something parents undertake lightly. Free public schools are a readily available alternative for parents who do not want to be strongly involved with their children through homeschooling.

• Children and adults are good at learning if given a chance.

• Homeschooling families regularly interact with other people. Some critics of homeschooling argue that homeschooled children are too isolated and too strongly influenced by their parents. However, rather than being isolated, homeschoolers are active in their neighborhoods, communities, and other groups. Homeschooled children interact with a wide variety of people of differing ages and backgrounds. Also, children are strongly influenced by their parents whether they are homeschooled or not.

6. It is widely held that parents have a stronger influence on children who attend schools than do the schools. For example, when schools are criticized for not educating children, school officials often defend themselves by saying that they are unable to overcome the influence of the children's families and home life.

Writing in the *Journal of Economic Literature* (September, 1986), Eric A. Hanushek critiques 147 studies that sought to correlate student achievement with a wide variety of school-related factors including teacher certification and advanced degrees, curriculum, time on task, quality of the facility, expenditures, class size, etc. The single variable that consistently correlated positively with student achievement was family background. (Most if not all of such research is highly questionable, especially since it relies on standardized tests to measure achievement and equates achievement with learning. However, it is worth noting that much of what passes for the soundest educational research indicates that the family rather than the school correlates positively with academic achievement.)

Historical Foundations

Throughout history, most people have been educated at home. In fact, many people, unfortunately labeled "primitives," have had the good fortune to live rich and full lives without anyone telling them they were being "educated." The first compulsory school attendance laws in the United States were not passed until after 1850, and it was not until after World War II that all states required people of high school age to attend school. Although homeschooling is often labeled "new and different," it is really a very old, traditional, tried-and-true approach to education that works very well.

Some people argue that "times have changed" and that formal education is required in today's highly technological society. However, times are changing so fast that it is most important that people learn how to learn, how to be flexible and handle change, and how to solve problems. Homeschools are especially good environments for this learning.

Unfortunately, the historical foundations of homeschoolers were undermined by a paper by Scott Somerville, an attorney for the Home School Legal Defense Association (HSLDA), a national organization claiming to represent homeschoolers. Somerville presented a paper titled "The Politics of Survival: Home Schoolers and the Law" before the American Educational Research Association on April 11, 2001. The opening sentence was "Twenty years ago, home education was a crime in almost every state." (In response to strong criticism, Somerville has since changed this statement so that the current version on the Internet reads, "…home education was treated as a crime…")

Among the serious problems with this statement:

• The statement is incorrect. Actions are crimes when laws prohibit them. No state had a law outlawing homeschooling. Some had strict requirements for homeschooling, but that did not make it illegal. Most did not have homeschooling laws. An activity is not a crime just because no law specifically gives citizens permission to do it. If that were the case, most of what we do everyday would be a crime, because there are no laws that give us permission to do most of what we do.

• Saying homeschooling was a crime before the 1980s gives the government too much power and weakens our position as homeschoolers. It implies that the right to homeschool comes from the government when it is based on the sources discussed in this chapter. They give homeschooling a much broader and more solid foundation than laws giving parents permission to homeschool.

• Various media pieces on homeschooling have picked up the catchy idea that "homeschooling was illegal," spreading misinformation and undermining the true foundations of our homeschooling freedoms.

Practical Foundations

1. Homeschooling works. See Chapter 18.

2. Homeschooling provides a wide range of learning opportunities and ways of learning. Because of this, homeschools prevent the development of learning difficulties in many children and are good places for children who learn better by doing than through reading and writing, the main approaches to learning offered by conventional schools.

3. Homeschools provide an excellent opportunity to learn about how children learn. By their nature, homeschools can focus on learning and do not need to deal with classroom management and discipline, often the first concerns of conventional teachers. (If teachers cannot control a class, how can they teach?) The flexible, many-faceted, alternative character of homeschools means that they offer a rich opportunity for children to learn in many different ways, and for professional educators to learn from homeschoolers' experiences.

4. Homeschools save taxpayers money. Children who do not attend public schools reduce the schools' expenses.

5. Parents learn a great deal from homeschooling, which is an educational experience for the whole family.

6. Neither lay persons nor professional educators can agree on the best way to educate a child. In the absence of such agreement, a range of alternatives, including homeschooling, must be permitted and ought to be encouraged.

Moral Foundations

1. Our society has an obligation to provide children the education best suited to them as individuals. Since children vary widely in their needs, abilities, interests, and talents, a wide range of alternative approaches to education, including homeschooling, should be available. Families should be able to choose the best alternative for each child. For homeschools to function as true alternatives, they should be free from unreasonable restrictions, some of which would force them to become similar to conventional schools. They would then cease to be alternatives, and children who have difficulty learning in conventional schools would not have as good an alternative.

2. A society that believes in freedom of thought and freedom of belief should allow parents to choose for their children an education consistent with their principles and beliefs and should allow people to choose alternative approaches to education without unreasonable regulation.

3. The family is the fundamental unit of any society. Homeschooling strengthens families. Opposition to homeschooling and unreasonable regulation of homeschooling weaken families. Parents who choose to homeschool are choosing one way of taking seriously their responsibilities for their children. They deserve the support of the larger community.

Religious Foundations

Religious beliefs and arguments are important to many homeschoolers and provide strong support for homeschooling. Under our federal and state constitutions, the state may not pass any law or engage in practices that would either establish a religion or interfere with the free exercise of religion, including parents instructing their children in religion.

Specific religious arguments that support homeschooling are not presented here because they are understandably personal and vary widely.

Chapter 23

The Role and Limitations of Laws in Maintaining Rights

> **Note:** Nothing in this handbook is intended or should be taken as the giving of legal advice. This handbook is not intended to substitute for privately retained legal counsel.

Laws matter to us as homeschoolers. Reasonable laws can make homeschooling much more manageable; unreasonable laws can make life more complicated and difficult. Homeschoolers worked hard through WPA in 1984 to gain a good homeschooling law and have worked hard since to maintain it. (See Chapter 20.) As a result, homeschooling in Wisconsin is in a much better position than it would be if the law were less reasonable.

However, it is important to realize that any law, including Wisconsin's homeschooling law, is less than ideal, a compromise, perhaps even a last resort. Ideally our communities and our society as a whole would give families the support they need and would trust parents and children to learn together. Then homeschooling laws would not be needed. Families who chose to homeschool would simply do so, without even filing a form with the state. In addition, having a reasonable law is not enough to maintain homeschooling freedoms.

Understanding these points is important, not so we will feel overwhelmed or pessimistic or paranoid, but so we can be realistic about what we need to do to maintain our rights and responsibilities. We need to understand the limitations of laws, even reasonable laws like Wisconsin's homeschooling law. We need to realize that a good homeschooling law is not enough to maintain our rights and responsibilities. It would be nice if we could simply concentrate on our families and our homeschooling activities and assume that Wisconsin's law is all we need. But if we do that, we will lose our rights and responsibilities.

The more we understand about laws in general, as well as the specifics of Wisconsin's homeschooling law, the better prepared we will be to use laws in ways that benefit our families and our communities and that minimize the chances of our losing our rights and responsibilities or getting into legal difficulties. Therefore, this chapter will present general information about how laws work followed by suggestions for ways in which we can deal with the law.

Understanding the Role and Limitations of Law

Laws can occasionally be helpful tools, but they are not an effective way to protect our rights and freedoms, and they can get us into trouble. To retain our rights and freedoms, two things are required. First, we need to recognize the strength we have through homeschooling and communicate to others in our communities how well homeschooling works. (This represents most of the work that needs to be done to keep homeschooling alive, healthy, dynamic, and secure.) Second, we need to work to prevent laws that would increase regulation of homeschooling from being passed in Wisconsin.

Here are some perspectives on how laws work and what limitations they have:

• **Laws do not give us anything we did not already have in nature or under God.** Laws are merely a way of trying to shore up what otherwise might become worse. For example, the homeschooling movement has developed not because of laws but in spite of them. In general homeschoolers have more freedom in states that have not changed their education laws to include homeschooling and in states that have merely clarified their laws to include homeschools with other private schools. Homeschoolers have less freedom in states that have specific laws that supposedly give parents the right to homeschool and at the same time require that parents have their curriculum approved, have their children tested, or submit portfolios or other evidence that their children are learning. Homeschoolers in these states have not gained homeschooling freedoms as a result of these laws. They have lost freedoms and rights that should be theirs as parents. Similarly, the strength of the homeschooling movement does not depend on homeschooling laws. It rests on the rights and responsibilities inherent in being parents.

• Laws give order to a society, but they represent a compromise rather than the best way for people to organize themselves and get along. Ideally people figure out a way to interact based on communication, consensus, cooperation, and trust. However, when a society becomes too large or takes wrong turns, laws become necessary. Therefore, **laws are not a sign of strength, although they can be a protection for those who would have even less standing without them.**

• **The law is a process, not a finished product.** A law sets a direction, but it does not make a once-and-for-all final decision. It is not "set in stone." In a very real sense, a law is only worth the value of the paper it is printed on, because the way a society interprets and enforces a law determines its real meaning and value. A law does not have much effect until someone enforces it or exercises the rights it guarantees. There are laws which are meaningless because they are not enforced. On the other hand, sometimes a law is passed which is unconstitutional or violates a basic right. If no one objects, this law can be enforced and become accepted practice. It is part of our responsibility as citizens to make sure that laws that are passed are fair and consistent with basic rights. The law can be a great ally, but it is just a tool which cannot do anything for us unless we use it.

• Laws are limited in what they can achieve. **Laws can only govern behaviors that can be described, observed, and evaluated.** Laws do not simply state that people should "drive safely." Such a law would require continual subjective judgments on the part of drivers, and enforcing it would require similar judgments by the police. However, determining the right of way at intersections can help prevent accidents. Therefore, signs and signals are used to increase safety, and violations are punished.

However, some things that cannot be controlled by law can definitely be encouraged and made easier by passing supporting laws. For example, it would not make sense to pass a law requiring that homeschooling parents "do a good job." But it is much easier for parents to do a good job when homeschooling laws allow them the flexibility they need to meet their children's needs, and allow children to learn at their own pace and in their own way. It is harder for parents to do a good job when laws require that they have their children tested.

• **Laws cannot protect parental rights.** Parental rights do not come from the state. But if a law were passed in which the state supposedly protected parental rights, it would inevitably imply that those rights came from the state. In other words, parents have to surrender their parental rights to the state before the state can pass a law that supposedly protects them. In the process, parents lose more than they gain. See Chapter 34.

• **Laws are made by the most powerful segments of a society and reflect their values and goals.** It is very difficult for a small minority that does not have much money or power (like homeschoolers) to get favorable laws passed, especially if that minority is seen as a threat to a larger, more powerful group (like the educational establishment). The few laws that guarantee the rights and freedoms of minorities and less powerful people come about only because these people get fed up. Then they work together to secure such laws.

Therefore, it is better to work not to have laws that seem to benefit homeschoolers introduced in the legislature. It is difficult to get enough support to pass such laws, and they often backfire because additional homeschooling requirements are added to the bills. Homeschoolers in Wisconsin have maintained our freedom since the reasonable homeschooling law was passed in 1984 by resisting any change in that law and by resisting the temptation to seek legislation that would give us supposed benefits like vouchers and tax credits at the cost of our freedom. See Chapter 24.

Reading and Interpreting Laws Ourselves

One of the best ways to increase our ability to use laws in ways that are as positive and constructive as possible is to read and interpret the texts of laws. Among the reasons this is important:

• **Usually the best way to understand a law is to read it ourselves.** Then we can present ourselves, and if necessary defend ourselves, with greater confidence. If we are in a conflict, our confidence makes a big difference in how we act and how our adversary reacts.

• **We may be in a better position to find the most important parts of a law than anyone we could hire or turn to.** Self-interest is an excellent motivator. It takes time, careful attention to detail, and creative thinking to interpret a law. The people most directly affected may be the most willing and strongly motivated to do this. Also, doing at least part of our own research may be the only affordable option, given the cost of attorneys' time. Experience and legal training may sometimes be useful. But in reading homeschooling laws, for example, our experience with and commitment to homeschooling may be as valuable as (or perhaps even more valuable than) the experience of an attorney who has read a lot of other laws. (If you are considering working with an attorney, see "Working with an Attorney" below.)

• **If we don't know what our rights are, we cannot be sure we are getting the protection we are entitled to.** We are literally "at the mercy of the court." For example, the Wisconsin law that requires that children have certain immunizations before entering school, also specifies that this requirement can be waived if parents object to immunizations "for reasons of health, religion or personal conviction." However, schools often do not tell parents this.

If parents are not familiar with the law, that right does not exist for them. The phrase "exercise one's rights" is very appropriate. Like muscles, rights must be exercised or they become weaker. Before we can exercise our rights, we have to know what they are.

• Few laws are so simple that there is no question as to their intent or application. Most laws need to be interpreted before they can be obeyed or enforced. (This is more often a result of the inherent complexity of life, including political compromises made in passing laws, than a reflection on the verbal skills of those who draft laws.) Our familiarity with issues, details, and nuances increases our ability to apply a law to our particular circumstances. **To ensure that the interpretation given to a law will be most beneficial to us, we must read and interpret it ourselves.**

In short, in a government based on law, citizens are the custodians of the law. If we simply accept legal experts' interpretations of laws or if we allow school officials to enforce their interpretations (which undoubtedly will be different from ours), we will lose our rights and responsibilities.

In reading laws, it helps to accept the fact that laws are not designed to be as accessible as possible to ordinary citizens. They are not written in the vocabulary that most people use for casual conversation, but they are written in English. A good place to start reading laws is in Appendix A to this book, which contains Wisconsin statutes that are important to homeschoolers. It is also good to read proposed legislation (see Chapter 30) and court cases that have interpreted and thus shaped laws. Because statutes are numbered and classified using a logical system, a lay person can do more detailed and extensive legal research without being a trained lawyer.

Two books on locating and reading laws are Stephen Elias's *Legal Research: How to Find and Understand the Law* (Berkeley, CA: Nolo Press, 1982) and *Using a Law Library*, published in 1983 by HALT, Inc. Two books that have excellent information on homeschooling laws and their foundations are John Holt and Patrick Farenga's *Teach Your Own* and John W. Whitehead and Wendell R. Bird's *Home Education and Constitutional Liberties: The Historical and Constitutional Arguments in Support of Home Instruction*.

A word of caution: Don't use your confidence in working with the law to jump into a court case. See "Avoiding Court Cases" below.

Participating in a Grassroots Organization

Developing and maintaining a strong grassroots organization like WPA is one of the most effective ways for a minority to deal with laws. Through such an organization, a variety of people can come together to work toward their common goal of maintaining rights and responsibilities. By making it clear that the organization is based on the work and commitment of its members, and not on the actions of a few key leaders, a grassroots organization has a solid foundation. Sometimes the presence of a strong grassroots organization that is recognized and respected by the legislature is enough to discourage the introduction of unfavorable legislation that might otherwise be introduced.

Members can watch for developing legislation that would affect them negatively and work to defeat or change it. They can develop interpretations of laws that are as favorable to them as possible and work together to have their interpretations accepted by others. Members can anticipate upcoming issues and problems and stay one or two steps ahead of the opposition by having an effective network of active grassroots members who pick up issues long before they become widely known in the state capitol or in the media. Members can support each other, exchange information, plan strategies, and work to foster a positive climate of opinion in their state.

Watching Developing Legislation and Acting When Appropriate

The more favorable laws are in the first place, the easier they are to work with. Therefore, it makes sense to review legislation being considered by the legislature and work when appropriate to support, change, or oppose it. One of the most effective ways to monitor legislation is through a grassroots organization. For example, WPA tracks legislation in Wisconsin that will affect homeschoolers and reports to members in its quarterly newsletter. Minorities like homeschoolers are also more likely to be effective when they work together through an inclusive statewide organization like WPA.

Using Our Own Abilities Instead of Relying on Outside Experts

It is important to realize that we homeschoolers are our own best experts. We rely on our own knowledge and abilities, which are considerable. We do our own careful ground work, we watch for new developments, we fight our own battles, and we live with the results.

Of course this kind of "stubborn independence" can be carried too far. We can learn from the ideas and experiences of other homeschoolers around the country. This kind of communication is positive and helpful and benefits us all. But we need to be careful not to become dependent on people (or organizations) working on the national level who would come in and "solve" our problems for us. Such reliance would be unwise and would not work in Wisconsin because:

• Using outside experts decreases the commitment and energy that members of a grassroots organization put into the work that must be done, thus weakening the organization.

• Much of WPA's success depends on the reputation we have established in Wisconsin. We are seen as a responsible, informed, and committed group of people. We have many contacts throughout the state with whom we can work on a personal basis. Outside experts simply don't have the time or ability to do this kind of careful groundwork.

• We can sometimes work with legislators who strongly disagree with us because, underneath our differences, we all live in Wisconsin and we all care about its future. (Of course our commitment to Wisconsin is not our highest commitment, but it is important.) Obviously outside experts cannot have this kind of a bond with legislators, simply because they don't live here.

• Legislators view outside experts differently than they view us, their constituents. Once experts are called in, a legislator's role shifts from that of a champion of minority-interest constituents to a judge of claims made by experts in response to other experts.

• Outside experts who emphasize one particular perspective or belief can seriously divide a movement. Once a minority grassroots movement has been divided, it loses the best chance it had to achieve and maintain its goals.

• Sometimes outside experts' personal experiences (such as the way they handled a similar problem in another state), training, or self-interest give them a perspective that may be inappropriate to another state.

• When outside experts come into a state, the result is generally more restrictive laws than when outside experts are kept out of a state. Experts often have a vested interest in creating controversy and restrictive laws because then they will have more clients and more business.

Avoiding Court Cases

WPA strongly recommends that homeschoolers stay out of court whenever possible for several reasons:

• Court cases are often long, very costly, usually require trained legal help to handle logistics and technicalities, and can have very serious outcomes. People involved in court cases are in vulnerable positions and are open to attack by adversaries. It is better not to initiate a court case than to present one poorly and lose. Before voluntarily getting involved in a court case, homeschoolers should take a long hard look at questions such as: Do we have the resources necessary to undertake this case and handle it well? Is there any other way this question or difficulty could be resolved? Is the case worth the time, energy, and stress involved? Is there a reasonable chance of success? Similarly, if we find ourselves in a situation in which we may be taken to court, we may want to work for an out-of-court settlement (unless, of course, this would require compromising important principles).

• It is unrealistic to expect courts to make clear-cut, black and white, once-and-for-all decisions that will resolve complicated issues and be fair to everyone involved. To be sure, courts can sometimes be helpful in protecting innocent people and resolving conflicts without bloodshed. But we cannot protect homeschooling from unnecessary and unreasonable regulation by the state by working through the courts or through the legislature when the courts fail us. This leads to the mistaken idea that lawyers and other professional experts can solve our problems and protect our rights.

A much better approach is for citizens to take responsibility for solving their own problems in ways other than by taking cases to court. Citizens understand clearly what is at stake, are strongly committed to getting the best possible outcome, and will be in a position to do the necessary work to follow up and maintain the gains that have been made and the positive agreements that have been worked out. In other words, informed citizens can do a much better job of protecting their rights and freedoms than can lawyers working for pay.

Lawyers and courts have an adversarial approach to resolving conflicts. Sometimes it works well, but the vast majority of conflicts that arise in our lives are resolved outside of courts. People explain their positions to each other and reach a consensus or work out a compromise or agree to disagree. We need to move homeschooling issues out of the courts and work harder to deal with them in other ways such as through grassroots organizations and educating the general public about homeschooling.

• Courts reflect the prevailing opinion of the community, which often is not supportive of homeschooling. Because the idea of homeschooling is not well understood and is still not something that most people view favorably, homeschoolers often encounter prejudice and misunderstanding when their case is heard.

• Courts operate to protect the status quo and the power structure in our country, as well as protecting the innocent. Since homeschoolers are not part of the current power structure and in fact are often seen as a threat to it, we cannot expect many court cases to be decided in our favor.

• The consistency with which homeschooling court cases have been lost during the past 25 years should serve as a strong indicator that the courts are not the place to win or maintain basic homeschooling freedoms. (Note: Some lawyers have claimed "victory" in cases which many homeschoolers feel have clearly been lost. Some claim victory in nearly any case in which the court does not jail the parents and/or strictly forbid the family's homeschooling, while many homeschoolers consider a case lost if it upholds unreasonable and unnecessary state regulation of homeschooling.) Except for a few state supreme court cases around 1980-86 that ruled that state laws were too vague, federal district courts, federal courts of appeals, and state courts of appeals (including state supreme courts) have all upheld the constitutionality of state laws regulating homeschooling. Arguments concerning the right of free exercise of religion, the right of equal protection and due process, and against self-incrimination and unreasonable searches have all been unsuccessful in convincing the courts to rule against state laws regulating homeschools.

As a result, we now have a body of precedent-setting case law that says that it is constitutional for the state to review and approve homeschooling programs or to require instructor qualifications and/or standardized testing. This collection of cases does not help the cause of homeschooling in the courts, legislatures, the media, or the general public.

(**Note:** More information about court cases involving homeschooling is available in a 62-page document *Recent Court Cases Examining the Constitutionality of Other States' Laws*

Regulating Home Schools, by Jane R. Henkel, Senior Staff Attorney for the Wisconsin Legislative Council, November 21, 1990. [This document is available on the WPA website.] This report states: "Special care was taken to attempt to find reported cases striking down state regulations. With the limited exception of cases which found regulations to be unconstitutionally vague, that effort was unsuccessful, which tends to indicate that there are few, if any, such cases." [page 2].)

In addition, it generally does not work to try to overcome the negative effects of unfavorable court decisions by introducing new legislation. In states such as Pennsylvania, New York, and New Hampshire, this strategy backfired, resulting in very demanding state laws that regulate homeschooling unreasonably. This strategy seldom advances homeschooling freedoms and often leads to further restrictions, more court cases, and more business for lawyers.

• States that have unfavorable homeschooling laws are those that also tend to have more court cases, and so the vicious circle continues. The way to stop it is to work at the grassroots level, avoid going to court, avoid introducing legislation, learn to live with ambiguity, and find quiet and effective ways of maximizing freedom by interpreting the laws ourselves and helping other homeschoolers do the same.

• An individual or a court case may become a pawn of more powerful individuals or institutions that have a very different agenda than ours. This is a risk especially for people who have gotten involved in a case to prove a point. Sometime their efforts backfire as the issue for which they were fighting is lost or becomes distorted or is used to support an end very different from the one they envisioned.

Civil Disobedience

People who find that their principles and consciences will not allow them to comply with a given law and who therefore choose to practice civil disobedience can greatly reduce the change that they will end up in court. Some people get others to also practice civil disobedience. In this way, they show that their action is not that of a single misguided individual and that if the state is going to prosecute, it will have to deal with more than one or two people. Some people develop strong, easily understood reasons to justify their action. Then they increase their base of support by sharing these reasons with the media and in their community. Some people ensure that their act of civil disobedience draws public attention and is structured to win public support.

Alternatives to Working With an Attorney

Many homeschoolers have been pleased to discover that they could handle situations that they at first thought would require an attorney. They have been able to gather information from other homeschoolers, often working through WPA to find the people and information they needed. They have learned from the experiences of other homeschoolers and gained confidence from their support. For example, many homeschoolers have used the sample letters in this handbook to respond to demands from school officials that exceeded the authority these officials have been given under the law. Homeschoolers who resolve potential problems with officials in this way gain confidence, set a good example for other homeschoolers, and save on legal bills. Often they end up in a more secure position as well, because officials are generally less likely to bother people who are working from a position of strength and can defend themselves.

Mediation: Alternative Dispute Resolution

Increasingly people are choosing to resolve conflicts or settle disputes through mediation. Mediation involves disputing parties working together toward a resolution by listening to each other, trying to understand each others' perspective, and reaching an agreement everyone accepts. The discussion is facilitated by a neutral third party called a mediator. While mediation is not litigation, it is recognized by the courts in Wisconsin.

For more information on the process of mediation and ways to find a mediator, contact the Wisconsin Association of Mediators, 608-848-1970, www.wamediators.org

Working With an Attorney

If you are thinking about working with an attorney, the following suggestions may be helpful:

• Consider the alternatives above.

• **It is important to find an attorney who accepts and is willing to work for your principles, beliefs, and premises.** For example, if your major concerns are protecting parental and family rights and preserving the unity of the family, make sure your attorney will work with you for this. It is also very important that your attorney accepts and is prepared to defend your approach to homeschooling. This may be especially important if the attorney has experience with homeschooling, either personally or professionally or both. Homeschoolers have many different approaches based on their beliefs, philosophy of education, educational methods, etc. It may be a real problem to try to work with an attorney whose approach to homeschooling differs from yours. For example, some homeschoolers think standardized testing is a reasonable way to evaluate children, while others strongly oppose testing. It might not work well to have an attorney who accepted standardized testing defending homeschoolers who were fighting a court order to have their children tested.

• **The attorney needs to understand your local community.** Judges consider community practice in making their decisions, and the climate of opinion within a community can influence the outcome of a case. This is why local attorneys often are a better resource than "outside experts."

• **Make sure the attorney will listen to you, accept your input, and let you make decisions.** You are looking for an attorney who will work with you, not an expert who will simply take over the whole case and run it for you. Your involvement is crucial because you are the one who is most directly involved in the case and its outcome and because you are the one who knows what direction you want to go.

• **It is not essential that you find an attorney who has been personally involved in homeschooling** or who has read homeschooling law or worked with homeschooling cases. Your ideas and understanding of the law, plus this handbook and the resources it cites, are what an attorney needs to get started. (In fact, this handbook could save you significantly on legal fees if you were involved in a court case. Without it, an attorney would need to search for the information and develop the legal interpretations and strategies presented and referenced here.)

• Consider giving your attorney a copy of this handbook. Point out sections that are particularly important to you.

The information in this chapter about the complications, limitations, and risks of relying on laws may leave readers wondering what we can do to maintain our homeschooling rights and freedoms. In addition to taking responsibility for ourselves and working with other homeschoolers through WPA, we can work to gain support for homeschooling by educating the general public about homeschooling, working to win the hearts and minds of the people. Ways to do this are discussed in the following chapters.

Chapter 24

Issues Homeschoolers Need to Know About

These issues have been simmering for varying lengths of time. If they become active, front burner issues, you will need up-to-date information from WPA newsletters, special bulletins, fact sheets, and the website. Meanwhile, your help is needed to prevent them from becoming more serious. With the information below, you will be prepared to respond promptly whenever one of these issues comes up in casual conversation, through email lists and social media, at a support group meeting, on a radio talk show, in a media piece, in a speech by a public official, or wherever. If we all do what we can to educate other homeschoolers, legislators, the media, and the general public, we will have a better chance of preventing or at least minimizing problems from these threats to our homeschooling freedoms.

Background Information

• For our society to remain free, we citizens need to be alert for threats to our freedom. "Eternal vigilance is the price of liberty." We homeschoolers need to be especially concerned about the potential loss of our homeschooling freedoms because opponents of homeschooling look for opportunities to increase government regulation of homeschooling. We have to work to maintain our freedoms in the face of one of the most powerful interest groups in the US: the education establishment, which includes teachers, school administrators, teachers unions, textbook publishers, school boards, and others. Some issues discussed here might not be problems if we did not have active adversaries. But because of our position, we need to be extra alert. We need to bend over backward to make sure we don't give opponents of homeschooling opportunities to increase regulation of homeschooling.

• Parents have the right to educate their children according to their principles and beliefs. This right comes from nature or God, not from the state. We do not need laws to give us this right. We do need to prevent laws from being passed that would take this right away or significantly decrease it. And we need to educate the general public about homeschooling. In the long run, we must win the hearts and minds of the people in order to maintain our homeschooling freedoms. We need to be able to explain issues clearly and convincingly. Also, some of the points below include discussion of potential harmful backlash against homeschoolers.

• The general public is accustomed to public schools being regulated by the state, so they tend to assume that homeschools should be regulated as well, "just to be sure kids are getting a good education." They think homeschoolers who are doing a good job should have nothing to fear and should be willing to comply with regulations and have the state check up on them. Non-homeschoolers don't usually stop to think about all the reasons why public school standards should not be applied to homeschools, which are very different from public schools. (Homeschools have few students, so they can have a more flexible curriculum and allow children to learn at their own pace. The teacher knows them all well, so there is less need for testing. Homeschools don't receive tax money, so they don't have to answer to taxpayers.)

• Increased regulation by the state would affect what we homeschoolers do each day. It would force homeschools to be more like public schools in what knowledge, skills, and attitudes children are expected to learn, how they are expected to learn, what principles and beliefs they are expected to choose, etc. It would be a blow, especially to families who choose to homeschool because they want something different from the atmosphere, values, beliefs, and approaches to learning of the public schools.

• Avoiding or preventing state regulation of homeschooling is difficult to do, but it is much easier than getting rid of regulations if they are put in place. As pointed out above, the general public thinks that state regulation of homeschooling is not unreasonable, making it very difficult for homeschoolers as a small minority to find enough power and support to eliminate or reduce regulations. States like New York and Pennsylvania have had very difficult home-schooling regulations since the 1980s; homeschoolers have been unsuccessful in getting them changed.

• The legislative process is very difficult, if not impossible, to control. Once a bill is introduced, it can be drastically changed through amendments. Politics is messy. An old saying goes something like, "Two things you don't want to watch being made are sausage and legislation." Homeschooling legislation is especially risky because homeschoolers are a small minority that is opposed by large and powerful interest groups.

Several points are given in response to each issue so you can pick the one or ones that are most likely to be understood by the person with whom you are talking.

At the end of this chapter are suggestions for what we can do to minimize the problems caused by any or all of the issues discussed below. Although homeschoolers are a small minority, we have considerable strength when we work together on the grassroots level through WPA. Two examples: First, we managed to get one of the best homeschooling laws in the country in 1984, and we have managed to maintain it despite numerous challenges since then. (See Chapter 20.) Second, when corporations and school districts began marketing virtual charter schools in 2002, they referred to the schools as "homeschools." Homeschoolers working together through WPA countered this, and soon marketers were saying, "These are not homeschools."

Tax Credits and Other "Favors" From the Government

The problem: If the federal or state government used tax credits to reimburse home-schoolers for certain educational expenses approved by the government, it would be able to increase government regulation of homeschooling, force homeschools to become more like public schools, and reduce our homeschooling freedoms. Unfortunately, some individual homeschoolers and the Homeschool Legal Defense Association (HSLDA), a vocal national organization whose members are a small minority of the homeschooling population, support tax credits.

• At first glance, the idea of having more money for our homeschooling expenses may sound tempting. What homeschooling family wouldn't welcome more money to spend on curriculums, learning resources, classes, travel, and other educational opportunities? But recipients of government money are held accountable by the government. (For example, taxpayers want assurance that recipients of road contracts build satisfactory roads.) Therefore, government money would mean increased regulation of homeschools. There is no such thing as a free lunch.

• Experience shows tax credits don't work well for homeschoolers. As of March 2006, only two or three states had tax credits for homeschoolers. One of them, Minnesota, had very demanding homeschooling regulations, including required standardized testing and reporting to school officials, before tax credits were enacted. In Illinois, homeschoolers receive little benefit from the tax credits and face the threat of regulation because of them.

• Governments use money to gain authority they don't otherwise have. For example, during the 1970s, the federal government wanted states to reduce the speed limit to 55 miles per hour, but it did not have the constitutional authority to order them to. So it threatened to deny federal highway construction funds to any state that did not reduce its speed limit. Similarly but on a much smaller scale, governments could use money in the form of tax credits to get homeschoolers to become more like conventional schools by only allowing tax credits for educational expenses approved by the government. This would be a subtle and clever way for the government to gain control of homeschools.

• Tax credits are only reimbursements. They are not a means by which the government gives money to families so they can spend it on education. To receive tax credits, home-schoolers must first have money available and choose to spend it on expenses the government has approved.

• Tax credits mean the government collects less tax money, so they indirectly cost taxpayers and the government money. Therefore, they are designed to sound like a good deal but limit the amount anyone can receive, to prevent the government from losing too much money. Usually only people whose income is below a certain level can qualify for them. Often these people don't have enough money to spend in the first place, so it is difficult for them to qualify for the credits. On the other hand, people who can afford to spend a significant amount of money on education in the first place usually have incomes that are too large for them to qualify.

• Religious materials generally do not qualify for tax credits. Therefore, religiously based curriculums in basic subjects such as reading and math are unlikely to be eligible for tax credits. This could include such popular curriculums as A Beka, Alpha Omega, Bob Jones, Christian Liberty Academy, Christian Light, etc.

• Some supporters of tax credits argue homeschoolers are entitled to tax credits because we pay taxes that support public schools our children do not attend. However, citizens pay taxes to make services available to people who need or choose to use them. As homeschoolers, we pay for many services that we don't plan to use in addition to public schools, like jails, fire departments, police departments, etc.

• Some supporters of tax credits claim that homeschoolers do not need to be concerned because tax credits are not mandatory, so homeschoolers can decide not to claim the tax credits. Our concern is not being forced to pay lower taxes! Experience in other states and countries has shown that when homeschoolers become eligible for benefits, the benefits open the door to increased regulation of homeschooling, and the regulations are applied to all homeschoolers, not just those who accept the benefits. In other words, if tax credits led to increased regulation of homeschooling, we would not be able to avoid the new regulations by refusing to accept the tax credits.

Homeschoolers Playing on Public School Sports Teams

The problem: Some homeschooling athletes want to play on public school sports teams. Their desire is understandable, but their participation in public school sports could jeopardize the homeschooling freedoms of all of us. See "Sports" in Chapter 32.

Media Reports of Alleged Child Abuse

The problem: Once in a great while, a media report of a tragic case of child abuse in a family who claims to be homeschooling may prompt a call for legislation to increase regulation of homeschooling.

• Child abuse is not a homeschooling issue. In most, if not all, cases, serious problems preceded homeschooling, and the family had not been homeschooling for long. In some cases, it is unclear whether they were actually homeschooling or only claimed to be. Some may have been pushed into homeschooling.

• If a homeschooling family is suspected of child abuse, the problem can be handled as any other abuse case. Wisconsin already has statutes that provide for prosecution of parents who are charged with abusing their children. Child abuse and homeschooling are separate issues. No public school or private school (including homeschool) law can protect children from the tragedy of child abuse.

• Some people claim that if state regulation of homeschooling were increased, state officials would be able to identify homeschooling families with serious problems and prevent tragedy. However, in most cases, the family had already been reported to social services. If the family was officially homeschooling, this had not prevented them from being reported. School officials are not the only people who can and do report potential problems to social services. Family members, neighbors, members of the community, health care workers, etc., make such reports, and some professionals, such as physicians, are required by statute to do so. Increased regulation of homeschooling would not prevent child abuse, just as regulation of public schools does not prevent child abuse.

• Any group is likely to have a very few members with serious problems. An old legal maxim states, "Hard cases make bad law." In other words, a statute designed to take care of the worst possible case is almost certain to be long, difficult to enforce, and more likely to prevent good people from doing good than bad people from doing bad. It is unfair and solves nothing to punish conscientious homeschoolers by passing statutes that do not solve the problems of high-risk families anyway.

• Homeschoolers continue to be a target of the mainstream media. Most articles on homeschooling are positive, which is not surprising since the vast majority of homeschoolers do very well. However, we can expect this kind of sensational reporting from time to time. It highlights the importance of homeschoolers' continuing to be well informed and positive and active in their communities.

Federal Homeschooling Legislation

The problem: Homeschoolers have very little if anything to gain and a lot to lose from federal legislation. Unfortunately, HSLDA has repeatedly introduced such legislation.

• Any federal homeschooling legislation would require the government to define homeschooling so it's clear what's being discussed. Because legislators and other non-homeschoolers think of conventional schools when they think of education, and because they don't understand how different homeschools are from public schools, such a definition would inevitably force homeschools to become more like the public schools that many families chose homeschooling to avoid.

• Federal legislation would be an especially big mistake because the federal government has very limited authority in education, which is governed by the states instead. Federal homeschooling legislation would introduce a new source of homeschooling regulation (the federal government) and make it more difficult than ever to maintain our homeschooling freedoms.

• In 2003 and again in 2005, HSLDA introduced the Home School Non-Discrimination Act (HoNDA), a complicated bill they claim is intended to ensure that federal laws don't discriminate against homeschoolers. A detailed analysis shows that the bill is unnecessary and inaccurate. It is also unwise because it would open the door for a federal definition of homeschooling and federal regulation of homeschooling. For details about the problems with HoNDA, see the WPA website.

• If federal legislation were passed that the media and/or the general public thought granted special favors to homeschoolers, there would easily be a backlash against homeschoolers. Backlashes are especially hard for small minorities that lack broad support, like homeschoolers.

Virtual Charter Schools

The problem: Because virtual charter schools are public schools, they and their students have to comply with public school standards and requirements. However, because virtual charter school students study in their homes, legislators and the general public sometimes confuse them with homeschoolers. Unless a clear distinction is made between virtual charter schools and homeschools, homeschoolers are likely to be expected to comply with these standards and requirements.

Homeschooling parents take direct responsibility for their children's education. They choose the curriculum; daily, weekly, and yearly schedule; approach to learning; standardized tests (if any); requirements for graduation; religious and philosophical values; etc. By contrast, parents of public school students (including those enrolled in a virtual charter school or other public school program that allows them to study in their homes) turn the responsibility for their children's education over to the public schools. They agree to public school standards and requirements for the knowledge, skills, and attitudes children are expected to acquire. In most cases (including virtual charter schools), they follow curriculum chosen by the public schools. (Even in cases where parents are supposedly allowed to choose a curriculum, their choice must be approved by public school officials.) They comply with public school requirements for testing, graduation, etc. These differences are summarized in the accompanying chart.

If we don't maintain this distinction, we risk losing important homeschooling freedoms. Public school students who either study in brick and mortar schools or elsewhere are subject to state regulations that private school students, including homeschoolers do not have to comply with. If we don't maintain this distinction, regulations applied to public school students who study at home are likely to be applied to homeschoolers as well.

Maintaining this distinction is not easy. Many people incorrectly assume that anyone who studies at home is a homeschooler. When virtual charter schools began in Wisconsin in 2002, they claimed to be homeschools. However, homeschoolers working together through WPA informed people, wrote letters to the editor, attended informational meetings about virtual charter schools, and school board meetings to make the distinction clear. As of the publication of this book, virtual charter schools were generally identifying themselves as such and not as homeschools.

• Families whose children are enrolled in virtual charter schools sometimes ask to join homeschooling support groups. When groups ask WPA for suggestions about how to respond, WPA suggests that groups ask questions like: How would our group change if we allowed virtual charter school families to join? Do members of our group feel more free to raise concerns, discuss issues, and ask for support if they do not have to wonder if the person with whom they are talking is a homeschooler or a virtual charter schooler? With virtual charter schoolers in our group, would it be united and strong enough to take a position as a group, if need be, on homeschooling issues that come before the local school board or the Wisconsin Legislature?

Some support groups treat virtual charter schoolers as they do other public schoolers and welcome them as long as they are there to explore homeschooling. But if it becomes clear that they only want to participate in the activities, they could be asked to leave. The group's leaders are responsible for protecting it, looking out for its best interests, and taking action. If the virtual charter schoolers try to shift the group's orientation toward virtual charter schools (asking that activities be scheduled at their convenience, suggesting topics for parents' meetings that have more to do with virtual charter schools than homeschools, etc.), it would be even more important to act. Some groups suggest that they form their own group.

Testing

The problem: Both state governments and the federal government are increasingly using standardized tests to punish, reward, and hold accountable the schools they give money to. Homeschoolers need to be alert to ensure this practice is not applied to us. See Chapter 34.

• To prepare for and pass required tests, students need to follow a curriculum similar to those used in public schools and to adopt, at least temporarily, the test-makers' values and attitudes, which usually means giving up the opportunity to pursue an education consistent with their principles and beliefs. Required testing would force homeschools to become more like the conventional schools many of us chose homeschooling to avoid.

• Standardized tests are biased and unfair. They do not measure what a person knows; they only measure how a person performed on a given test on a given day. They are unfair to minorities, women, and anyone whose values, beliefs, and experiences differ from those of the test makers. They do not measure or give credit for physical skills, mechanical ability, creativity, integrity, etc. Creative thinkers and people who know a lot about a subject often have more difficulty because they see the complexities in supposedly simple questions.

• Standardized tests interfere with learning in a wide variety of ways. Any test is basically a vote of "no confidence." Taking such a test can be a frightening, intimidating experience for children. Tests force test takers to focus on oversimplified answers instead of questions and problem solving. Tests encourage students to focus on learning to take tests. This often reduces children's interest in learning since simple answers are not as interesting or mentally rewarding as problems. In emphasizing "right" and "wrong" answers, tests imply a kind of certainty that does not exist or cannot be measured. The learning process is much more complex, non-linear, and dynamic than tests can measure.

• Despite the severe limitations, defects, and unfairness of standardized tests, the results are taken seriously by schools, parents, and students and used to label children, justify additional testing, and control the choices parents have in where and how their children will be educated. Too often, one unfair and erroneous test leads to a child's being labeled "learning disabled" or seriously limited in some other way. Effects can be lifelong in terms of lost opportunities, self-confidence, and self-esteem.

• Government-mandated standardized testing means that the state, rather than parents, decides when children are ready for tests, what tests will be used, how and where tests will be administered, and what action will be taken based on the results.

• Wisconsin's homeschooling law is reasonable and holds parents accountable. Since 1984, nearly 100,000 of homeschoolers have entered conventional schools, gone to college, or entered the work force. Homeschools in Wisconsin have been successful in part because they have not been required by either the state or the federal government to take tests. They have been free to choose or develop a curriculum that works well for their family. There is no evidence that homeschoolers need to be required to take tests.

• If homeschoolers were required to take standardized tests, the tests would inevitably become high stakes tests with more potential problems for homeschoolers than conventional school students. This is because homeschoolers who supposedly do not score well enough could be forced to attend a conventional school, while conventional school students with low scores will not be forced to homeschool.

• If homeschoolers accept tax credits or other money from the federal or state government, they will voluntarily and unnecessarily give the government an opportunity to require testing of homeschoolers.

• Homeschoolers who ask to take state-mandated tests or who cite research based on homeschoolers' test scores send the misleading signal that homeschoolers are willing to be tested. It is much safer if homeschoolers who want to take tests use private testing services, which also allows parents to control what happens to test scores. Stories of homeschoolers who are doing well are better and more convincing evidence that homeschooling works than are test scores.

Growth of Homeschooling

Problem: Inaccurate media reports claiming homeschooling is still growing rapidly have regularly caused concern within the educational establishment and among some legislators and fueled proposals for increased regulation of homeschooling.

• Actually, as of March 2013 when this book was written, the rate of growth of homeschooling in Wisconsin had declined during nine of the past ten years. Homeschooling has leveled off at less than two percent of the school age population or about 18,000 students during the 2011-12 school year. The media and others have been slow to recognize this change and have continued to report that homeschooling is growing.

• The decline in the rate of growth is a national trend, not something that's happening just in Wisconsin.

• Homeschoolers can use the fact that we are a small number of students and are not growing rapidly to assure the educational establishment, legislators, and the media that they do not have to be concerned about us and do not need to further regulate us. If teachers, teachers unions, school administrators, school boards, the DPI, and other members of the educational establishment think homeschooling is still growing rapidly, they are likely to be more concerned about losing students, money, and jobs and to press for increased regulation of homeschooling. If they were convinced that homeschooling was growing slowly or possibly beginning to decline, they would probably be less intent on getting homeschoolers to enroll in public school programs and on trying to increase government regulation of homeschooling.

• Several factors may account for the decrease. Some people speculate that, given the alternative nature of homeschooling, the work involved, and the responsibility parents must assume, homeschoolers are unlikely to ever represent more than about two percent of the school age population, which is where we are now. In addition, the US economy has declined over the past several years, with middle and lower income families being most affected. This may mean that fewer families can afford to homeschool, which usually requires families to make a financial sacrifice so parents spend more time with their children.

• Although Wisconsin now has several virtual charter schools, they are not the primary cause of the decrease, which began before the schools opened.

Research on Homeschooling

The problem: Some homeschoolers and others want research on homeschooling that will "prove" that homeschooling works and homeschoolers excel. However, research and surveys could diminish our freedom in several ways.

• Research and surveys could contribute to increased state regulation of homeschooling. For example, research based on homeschoolers' scores on standardized tests could be used as evidence that homeschoolers consider such tests an acceptable way to measure and document learning. It could support arguments that homeschoolers should be required to take state-mandated standardized tests.

• The right of families to homeschool has a solid foundation. (See Chapter 22.) But by agreeing to be the subjects of research, homeschoolers would be implicitly agreeing that they need to be judged and assessed, that the foundations of homeschooling freedoms are not enough.

• Research and surveys promote the values of conventional education at the expense of the strengths of homeschooling. They do not give homeschoolers an opportunity to demonstrate the wide range of advantages to homeschooling. Instead, the way educational research and surveys are structured and organized, the variables they choose to measure, and the background and biases of researchers themselves are all heavily weighted in favor of conventional approaches to education. Such research and surveys are not an effective way to educate the public or legislators about homeschooling.

• Research weakens grassroots movements by promoting the idea of using quantitative measurements to convince others. A much more effective way to educate people about homeschooling is by telling our stories. See Chapters 9, 19, and 26.

• Research quantifies and dehumanizes people. It is an invasion of privacy. The emotional impact of filling out a survey is often much like that of taking a standardized test. The implication is that someone, somewhere knows what we should be doing, that there are right answers, or at least better answers, and that we might not be doing what we should.

For these and other reasons, WPA recommends that homeschoolers not participate in research or surveys on homeschooling. Instead, we can use rational, logical, legal, constitutional, moral, and practical arguments to support homeschooling, along with the more intangible reasons of the heart. It is much better for homeschoolers to provide such reasons and tell their stories than to participate in research or surveys on homeschooling.

Legislation to Prevent "Unqualified" Families From Homeschooling

The problem: Legislation to prevent "unqualified" families from homeschooling would give the government the power to decide who will be allowed to homeschool and who will not.

• There is no evidence that significant numbers of "unqualified" families or habitual truants are "escaping" to homeschooling.

• Allowing the state to determine who can homeschool would undermine parental rights and responsibilities and homeschooling freedoms. It would also interfere with homeschools that are thriving.

• "Hard cases make bad laws." In other words, a law designed to take care of the worst possible hypothetical case is almost certain to be long, difficult to enforce, and more likely to prevent good people from doing good than bad people from doing bad.

What We Can Do In Response to These Issues

• We can keep up to date by being a member of WPA, reading the WPA newsletter, and checking the WPA website.

• We can strengthen WPA's work by informing WPA as we learn of developments in our local communities or on the state or national level that could impact homeschooling freedoms.

• We can inform other homeschoolers about the issue in question. The more homeschoolers who understand the importance of a given issue, the better chance we have of minimizing the damage it could do. We can bring up issues in casual conversations, plan support group meetings to discuss them, etc.

• We can contact our state and federal legislators and inform them that we do not want favors from the government. This may surprise them, because they are accustomed to people asking for favors, not refusing them. We can share some of the points above and explain that we value our homeschooling freedoms and do not want to sacrifice them in exchange for favors.

• We can support WPA's work by being members, encouraging others to join and purchase a handbook, attending the annual conference, and making donations. This makes it possible for WPA to continue watching for challenges to our homeschooling freedoms, researching issues that arise, planning strategy, informing members, communicating with legislators when necessary, and doing other work that is necessary to maintaining homeschooling freedoms.

Chapter 25

Maintaining Unity and Respecting Diversity Among Homeschoolers

To maintain our rights and freedoms, we need to work together and remain united. Therefore, WPA is a group of people united to affirm parents' responsibility for their children's education and to protect the right of parents to educate their children at home if they so choose. WPA has avoided, and will continue to avoid, taking a stand on potentially divisive issues such as what approach to learning is best; what specific techniques should be used in homeschooling; whether a purchased curriculum should be used and if so, which one; and similar issues.

Wisconsin homeschoolers have many different loyalties and commitments. Our families are extremely important to us. That is one of the main reasons we are homeschooling. We feel strongly about our right to choose for our children an education consistent with our principles and beliefs. We have strong ideas and convictions about the particular approach to education that we have chosen for our families.

Sometimes our loyalties and commitments seem to conflict with each other. We have to figure out a way to order them so they don't interfere with one another. WPA has always been clear about how it approached these conflicting loyalties: We believe that political questions in general are not the most important questions in life. We don't think that the legal right to homeschool without undue state regulation is the most important issue we will ever face. But to be able to deal with the questions that really matter, questions of approaches to education and even larger questions of principles, beliefs, religious faith,and moral values and principles, we must have the political freedom and right to choose an education consistent with our principles and beliefs without undue regulation by the state. So WPA was organized and has always operated on the premise that we will all work together to maintain our right to homeschool, regardless of the reasons any of us as individuals has for exercising this right or the approach to education we choose. WPA has steadfastly refused to take any position on approaches to education, religion, and moral values. Instead it has fought for the rights of its members and others to make these decisions for themselves.

It seems backwards, but by putting a less important question first in time (that is, by first assuring our right to homeschool before dividing up into smaller groups whose members agree about approaches to education, religion, and moral values), we are really giving the most important questions the emphasis and priority they deserve. If we took the other approach, if we first split into smaller groups that agreed about educational and religious questions, we would not be able to withstand the political pressures from those who oppose homeschooling. We would soon be living under repressive legislation which would place unnecessary regulations on homeschoolers. (Look at states that have experienced this situation and the laws they have.) We all need time and energy to decide about educational and religious questions and act on them. But we would have to spend much of that time and energy fighting the results of repressive legislation, meeting ridiculous requirements that we "prove" to school officials that we are truly educating our children. (This would, of course, have to be according to their standards, and too bad for us if we happen to disagree with them!) Or we would be trying to stay out of court and possibly even jail.

In addition to the practical need to remain united, there is a more fundamental reason why WPA does not take an official position on curriculums, approaches to education, learning techniques, and related questions. We believe there is no one right answer for everyone. Each family must decide for itself what is most important and works best when it comes to the specifics of homeschooling. One of our objections to conventional schools is that they do not allow enough flexibility to meet the widely varying needs of different individuals. This is also why we are concerned about the increasing standardization and centralization of the public schools. So let's respect our differences, learn from each other, and remain united on the one principle that ensures our freedom, namely, the right of families to choose an education consistent with their principles and beliefs.

Another key to unity among homeschoolers is remembering that we need to work to maintain the right of all parents to homeschool if they choose to do so. It is not our responsibility as homeschoolers to ensure that all other homeschooling parents are doing a "good job" and that all homeschooling children are learning well. In fact, it is our responsibility to work to ensure that parents are not denied the right to homeschool because they are not high school graduates, or because their children have been labeled "learning disabled" by the schools, or because their children have been truant, or because they are single parents or have a low income, or for any other reason. A law or regulation that prevents any parent from homeschooling diminishes the rights and freedoms of all homeschooling parents.

Of course the possibility exists that the behavior of a few irresponsible homeschooling parents could diminish our rights and freedoms. However, instead of seeking laws or regulations that would prevent such parents from homeschooling, we would be much better off if we offered these parents support and accurate information about homeschooling. We can invite them to our support group meetings, tell them about resources we have found helpful, and share this handbook with them.

Although we come together with many different views on education and personal beliefs, we have a common bond and a common goal. Just as a quilt has a variety of textures, interesting shapes, and vibrant colors, our homeschooling community is rich in diversity. But there is a common thread that draws us together, nurtures us, and provides warmth. Today, we honor what brings us together so that we may celebrate as a community.–From Opening Remarks, WPA Conference, 2004

I don't know if you've noticed this, but Wisconsin seems to be a wee bit politically divided these days. Okay, deeply divided. I'm not here to pull you one way or another on that matter–I'm sure you've already decided how you'll vote on Tuesday. No, I'm here to celebrate an example of a much healthier community, the Wisconsin Parents Association.

I've been a member of WPA for a very long time–I think this is our 22nd conference–and from the beginning of my family's involvement I have been impressed with the range of people represented at these gatherings. Look around you. Scan the variety of workshops offered. Browse the wealth of materials at the Used Book Sale. Listen to the stories of today's graduates and their families. Talk with people you encounter in the hallways and bathrooms and workshop rooms. You will find examples of the wide spectrum of politics, religion, educational philosophy, income, family size, clothing, diet, interests and passions that people can choose. No two families are exactly alike. We could find all kinds of things to disagree about.

But WPA, as a healthy community, manages to hold all of us together. Despite our differences we come together to celebrate what we have in common. We come together and we gain energy and inspiration and encouragement from each other. We are better for each others' presence. We are stronger for our diversity. Rather than two or more opposing sides, what we have here is a circle, a strong, stable circle in which we all matter, all hold each other in life-giving tension. A community that welcomes otherness and empowers each personal voice builds the courage and expands the lives of its members. We are all valued here, like instruments in an orchestra. We depend on each other to share our perspectives, our stories, and to work together to keep homeschooling in Wisconsin the lovely free experience that it is.

We have in common that we cherish the freedom to homeschool in the way that works best for our families. We are family centered people who think of home as much more than a place to sleep and store our stuff. Homeschooling is a lifestyle, not just an educational choice, and the decision to homeschool usually leads to or stems from other "outside the box" choices. We have all had to learn to cope with the people who challenge those choices, who don't understand where we are coming from. My family isn't still technically homeschooling, since our youngest daughter is now a sophomore in college, but when I see another family with school-age children at the library or at a museum or out walking or playing during the school day, I know that we have much in common, that there are things we understand about each others' values and priorities and how we shape our days.

I'd like to share with you a poem written by the Arab American poet, Naomi Shihab Nye. It's about hospitality, about opening our ears and our hearts when we encounter the other.

Red Brocade

The Arabs used to say,
When a stranger appears at your door,
feed him for three days
before asking who he is,
where he's come from,
where he's headed.
That way, he'll have strength
enough to answer.
Or, by then you'll be
such good friends
you don't care.
Let's go back to that.
Rice? Pine nuts?
Here, take the red brocade pillow.
My child will serve water
to your horse.
No, I was not busy when you came!
I was not preparing to be busy.
That's the armor everyone put on
to pretend they had a purpose
in the world.
I refuse to be claimed.
Your plate is waiting.
We will snip fresh mint
into your tea.

If we can extend this level of hospitality to each other here at this conference and at home in our communities, we will be much stronger, richer, and healthier. We have a pretty great homeschooling law here in Wisconsin, and it is critical to each one of our families that we keep that reasonable law. We are free from egregious oversight by state or school authorities. We are free of testing mandates. Each family can tailor the homeschooling experience to fit each child in it. Our law gives us the flexibility that makes us such an intriguing mix of homeschoolers. We are not forced into sameness in our approach–and isn't the power to create our own unique learning paths one of the biggest reasons we homeschool? To maintain this law, WPA needs all of us to pull together, to look out for each other. As the March WPA newsletter said, "If your homeschool freedoms aren't secure, neither are mine."

I want all of you to be secure in your homeschool freedoms, secure enough to carry on learning joyfully and creatively, empowered to choose what homeschooling looks like for you.

Wisconsin only asks a few things of us: to file the PI-1206 form, and in doing so to declare that we meet the minimal requirements all private schools in Wisconsin must meet, even tiny ones like ours, and that we comply with the compulsory attendance law. Other than that, the options are wide open. Whether you use workbooks at the kitchen table, online materials, the public library, your farm or woods or stream, a neighbor with a telescope, a grandparent who knits or fixes cars or speaks another language; whether your child volunteers at an animal rescue or takes a college class or plays the ukulele or competes in Bible quizzes or writes a novel–I want you to choose what works, what will be true to each learner's needs and gifts, and to your family's understanding of how best to nurture the blossoming of each child.

So let's stay together in this circle. Let's look around and across at each other and know that our working together is what keeps Wisconsin homeschooling freedoms secure. Let's celebrate the way that WPA embraces all of us in all our rich variety, and appreciate those intrepid homeschoolers who founded this organization, whose vision made it what it is. Perhaps we can be an example to others and to ourselves of how to practice hospitality, how to make community, how to create harmony from many voices, and recognize that we are all in this together.–From Opening Remarks, WPA Conference, 2012.

Chapter 26

Winning Support and Dealing with Critics

The Importance of Public Opinion

In some ways, public opinion can be more important than laws and statutes in determining what rights and responsibilities a group of people will have. If there is strong public opinion in support of a group, officials will be reluctant to take action against them, even if the law would allow it. On the other hand, if a large or vocal segment of the general public is prejudiced against a group, it will probably be difficult for that group to receive fair treatment, even though such treatment is legally required. The more understanding, acceptance, and support homeschoolers have from the general public, the more secure our rights and freedoms will be.

Dealing with Critics

As homeschoolers we need to deal with skeptics and critics of homeschooling both in public settings and in our personal lives. The following suggestions might help in either of these situations:

• Generally we are better able to deal with critics calmly, without becoming defensive, when we are feeling confident ourselves. It often helps to remind ourselves about what our children are doing and what they are learning in addition to academics, such as how to get along with others, take responsibility, and talk with people of different ages. It might help to review records we are keeping and remind ourselves about how well homeschooling works. (See chapters 10 and 18.) It is better to share our doubts with people who are strong supporters of homeschooling than with critics.

• Homeschooling is a relatively new and different idea. People who have not had such experience often have a difficult time imagining how homeschooling could possibly work, especially in a culture dominated by conventional schools.

• We can try to make homeschooling seem reasonable and similar to experiences that non-homeschoolers have had personally or can relate to. Hearing homeschools are like one room schools helps some people understand. It sometimes helps to point out to non-homeschooling parents that they do many learning activities (like reading aloud, playing games, and visiting parks and museums) with their children when they are not in school. Homeschoolers just do them more.

• We can explain that children learn in many different ways. We can translate what our children are doing into conventional school terms. For example, interlocking building blocks are "math manipulatives," learning to cook is "home economics," and curling up with a picture book before bed is "learning to read."

• We can emphasize that each family needs to make its own decisions about education (and other aspects of family life and parenting). Homeschooling works well for our families, but we are not trying to convince other families that they should homeschool.

• If we avoid attacking the public schools or other conventional schools, non-homeschoolers are less likely to feel angry or defensive.

• Sometimes it helps to try to find out what critics are most concerned about and address those specific concerns. For example, many people say they can understand how children could easily learn basic subjects at home, but they don't see how they can learn to get along with a lot of other people. Once we have heard that, we can focus our comments on how homeschooled children gain social skills.

• It may help if we and our family appear as conventional as possible without compromising important principles.

• The mention of homeschooling or not having to attend school often raises very strong feelings. Without realizing it, people who ask about our homeschooling may really want to talk about themselves. With genuine interest, we can ask what school was like for them or what they think it would have been like if their parents had homeschooled them.

Dealing with Critics in Public Settings

• Generally speaking, the calmer we homeschoolers remain, the more positive the audience's response will be to us. It often helps to say, "Families have to make their own decisions about what approach to education will work for them."

• Regardless of what critics say, it helps to try to get across to the audience that we know from our own experience and from that of thousands of other families that homeschooling works. Increased state regulation of homeschooling is unnecessary and could be detrimental to homeschools. If we have made those points, we can feel good and not worry about the fact that we did not explain in detail things like what the law requires, how homeschooling children learn, or how they develop social skills. If we have convinced a few people that homeschooling might not be such a bad idea after all, we have accomplished a lot. We cannot expect to turn people into supporters of homeschooling overnight.

Dealing with Critics in Our Personal Lives

Criticism from friends, relatives, and acquaintances is frustrating for parents who are putting a lot of time and energy into their children's education. However, many families manage to homeschool and feel good about it despite criticism and lack of support. These families may begin by deciding that it is more important to choose an approach to education that works well for their children than to please other people and gain their approval. They realize that people can be good friends, neighbors, or relatives without understanding or agreeing with homeschooling.

When their homeschool is criticized, many parents listen carefully to try to understand the critic's real objections. Critics often fit into one of three groups. Some are open-minded enough to listen to information about homeschooling and possibly change their minds once they understand it better. In this case, it may help to share personal experiences and ideas and possibly articles, books, and websites.

A second group of critics has their minds definitely made up and is simply not interested in learning more about homeschooling. However, they may be willing to agree to disagree. They will continue their approach to education and will accept homeschoolers' decision to homeschool. This approach avoids a lot of pointless discussion and makes it possible to continue a relationship on relatively good terms.

Unfortunately a third group of people seems unable to accept the idea of homeschooling. Some homeschoolers find that they just have to give up, ask these people to stop talking about homeschooling, and, if they refuse, possibly even stop seeing them. It can be very frustrating to have a relationship end this way, but sometimes it seems the only choice. Many parents feel strongly that it is important to protect their children from undue criticism, teasing, ridicule, negative comments, lack of confidence, or informal testing. ("Can you read this word?" "Haven't you learned to multiply yet?" "How are you ever going to learn algebra?") Sometimes this means that parents have to speak very firmly to critics and possibly limit their children's contact with them.

Many homeschoolers find that time spent making connections with people who support homeschooling and trying to help others understand homeschooling is time well spent.

Telling Our Stories

Why Tell Homeschooling Stories

Telling our stories is important for a number of reasons, including the following:

• Stories are a dramatic, easily understood way to convey to others why we chose to homeschool and how well it works. The stories in Chapters 9 and 19 say that what happens to children in conventional schools does matter, even when they are things that some people might consider "not that important" or "things that happen to every kid growing up." Stories also show how well homeschooling works for children who had trouble learning in a conventional school. Sometimes skeptics can be shown that homeschooling does work by giving them specific examples.

• Homeschooling stories show the indispensable role of parents in children's lives and education, a point that is particularly important to make these days as more people are turning to experts and specialists rather than to parents as the people who know most about raising children. As the stories in this book show, it is not usually school personnel who say, "Things are happening in this school that are harming your child. We need to do something about it." Instead it is usually parents who say, "We have to do something."

• Stories give us an opportunity to give ourselves and our families the credit we deserve for what we are doing. They help children realize how much they are learning and doing and how important and legitimate it is.

• Stories are an effective way to educate legislators about homeschooling and the effects of both reasonable and unreasonable laws and regulations. For example, Wisconsin's current reasonable homeschooling law was passed in part because legislators listened when homeschoolers described the arbitrary and unfair ways in which they had been treated by Department of Public Instruction (DPI) officials to whom they had applied for approval of their homeschools. (See Chapters 19 and 20.) As a result, the Legislature decided not to give the DPI authority over homeschools.

• Some families find that telling stories helps them recover from difficult experiences they have had. It also helps if stories prevent others from having similar experiences or show them how they, too, could solve problems.

• Stories sometimes make it possible for listeners to understand how strongly they themselves have been influenced by their own personal school experiences and to begin finding ways to overcome negative ones. Few people question the power and influence that conventional schools have in our society. However, homeschooling stories help people realize that they can make choices and learn things outside conventional schools that they thought or were told they were unable to learn in school.

• Stories are an effective way to convey information about homeschooling without risking the problems of research and surveys. See Chapter 24.

Suggestions for Telling Homeschooling Stories

As homeschoolers we need to tell our homeschooling stories, or they will not be heard. However, we also have to be careful to protect our children's feelings and privacy. Making sure we have our children's permission before telling a story is important. Even then it is often better to say, "I know (or heard about) a nine-year-old homeschooler who..." instead of "When my son John was nine, he..."

When and where can we tell our stories? Among the possibilities are informal conversations, public meetings about homeschooling, radio talk shows, newspaper interviews, and at our place of worship. Also, send your stories to WPA. They are included as a regular part of the quarterly newsletter.

Some points to consider when telling stories:

• Concentrate on the positive aspects of homeschooling rather than the negative parts of conventional schools. Sometimes a story only makes sense if it includes something negative about a conventional school, but such details should be used only to make larger constructive points and only with caution because they may put listeners on the defensive.

• Stories that may be particularly helpful are those that show how much fun learning can be and how children learn in many different ways. Listeners frequently feel more comfortable with homeschooling after they have heard that in addition to academic studies, children can learn science by studying bugs in their backyard, math and nutrition by planning menus and shopping, and history by listening to grandparents talk about their childhood. Stories can also show how good parents are at helping their children learn, how well socialized homeschooling children are, how well children who have been labeled "learning disabled" can learn at home, how often children simply need the opportunity to learn at their own pace, how homeschooling strengthens families, what a wonderful opportunity homeschooling provides for parents to simply be with and understand their children, and how homeschooling builds confidence for families to take responsibility in other important areas of life.

• Whenever possible, relate homeschooling to experiences that listeners have had or are familiar with. Some people seem to understand better when homeschools are compared to one room schools. Sometimes it helps to point out that every family homeschools (in the sense that they do things together when children are not in school from which children learn); homeschoolers simply do this full-time.

• It may help if homeschoolers appear as conventional as possible without compromising important principles. Generally it works best to concentrate on one issue at a time, and not try to convince an audience of the importance of both homeschooling and, for example, good nutrition.

• If we have doubts about homeschooling or about our children's learning, it is usually better to share them with people we know who support homeschooling than to include them in stories we are telling to help skeptics or critics understand homeschooling.

For examples of homeschoolers' stories, see Chapters 9 and 19 and Stories in the index.

Chapter 27

Working with the Media

- **Responding to or Contacting the Media 199**
- **Preparing for an Interview 199**
- **During the Interview 200**
- **Following Up 201**
- **Responding to Negative Reports by the Media 201**

Responding to or Contacting the Media

Positive articles in the press and appearances on radio and television can educate the general public about homeschooling and win support. Therefore, it is usually a good idea to consider seriously and discuss with others any requests from the media, even though the idea of an interview might seem a bit overwhelming, especially the first time. On the other hand, it may be best to refuse to be interviewed if, for example, the publication is very radical (either left or right) or if the reporter is known to be very negative about homeschooling or has a reputation for quoting people out of context or being difficult to deal with.

It helps to figure out the reporter's objective or goal. Most articles and programs about homeschooling are either (1) human interest stories about a particular family, (2) general background pieces about homeschooling as an educational alternative, (3) explorations of one or more controversial issues that seem to involve homeschooling, or (4) a combination of these. Reporters often try to emphasize controversy because it makes stories seem more exciting. However, this may be more challenging to handle smoothly. If the reporter is focusing on controversy, you may prefer to respond to questions only in writing, so you have more time to consider your answers and less chance of being misunderstood and misquoted.

As in other areas, however, don't act hastily on your own, particularly on an important issue. Discuss your approach and strategy with other homeschoolers, including your WPA Regional Coordinator. Without this kind of communication, homeschoolers could make mistakes or work at cross purposes.

Preparing for an Interview

Keep in mind the background and perspectives of the reporter and the publication or station involved. Try to select homeschoolers from your area whose background, perspectives, and abilities would enable them to communicate effectively with the reporter, such as someone who regularly reads the publication or watches the program involved. Decide whether to include children and how you will respond if the reporter asks to include children. (Many children benefit from practice before an interview.)

Gather background information. Review your own experiences and talk with other homeschoolers. Make a list of the most important points you would like to try to include, such as:
• Homeschooling works. Children learn well at home, especially since they can follow their own interests and learn at their own pace. Homeschooling strengthens families.
• Homeschooled children participate in community groups and get along well with their peers and with people who are older and younger than they are.
• The current law works well and holds homeschoolers accountable. Increased regulation of homeschooling by the state (including testing children or reviewing and approving homeschoolers' curriculums) is not necessary and could be harmful to homeschools.
• Homeschoolers are less than two percent of the school-age population and are not a threat to public schools.
• Homeschoolers are a diverse group who choose to homeschool for many different reasons and use a wide variety of approaches to learning. There is no "typical" homeschooling family.

If possible, find out what kinds of questions the reporter is planning to ask. Commonly asked questions include:
• Why are you homeschooling? Is it for religious reasons? Do you use a curriculum? Describe a typical day in your homeschool. What makes you qualified to teach?
• Do you plan to continue homeschooling when your children are high school age? How will they get a high school diploma or get into college? Will they be able to get jobs?
• What about socialization? Aren't peer group experiences important? Shouldn't children meet people from different ethnic groups? Are your children going to be able to deal with the real world? What do your friends and relatives think of your homeschooling?
• What does Wisconsin law require of homeschoolers? Don't you think it would be a good idea for homeschoolers to be required to take standardized tests to be sure they are learning? If your children decided to go to school, how would the school figure out what grade they should be in? Doesn't the state have a responsibility to ensure that all children are receiving a good education? It sounds like your family is doing a good job, but what about the homeschoolers who aren't? What about child abuse among homeschoolers? What's so bad about the public schools?
• May I ask your children some questions? Questions children may be asked include: Do you think you are learning as much as children who go to school? Are you ever bored? Do you like having your mom and dad for teachers? Won't you be sorry not to be able to go to the prom?

Review pertinent sections of this book and other materials. Consider choosing some quotes to share with the reporter. If you quote others, the reporter can't argue with you personally on that particular point.

Give the reporter articles from the local, state, and national press on homeschooling, and background information from homeschooling authors, newsletters, magazines, and publishers. Read over the material first to be sure it doesn't make points that will work against homeschoolers. Think through how the material is likely to be used by the reporter.

During the Interview

Relax. As a homeschooler you have many reasons to feel confident. Try to be brief in your answers and make the most important points before going into detail. Remember that your comments will probably be condensed before they are printed or broadcast. Be polite and courteous, no matter how heated the discussion. Rudeness does not win friends, no matter how just the cause.

Speak only for yourself or the group you are specifically authorized to represent. (Being a member of an organization like WPA does not authorize you to speak for the organization.) Avoid making sweeping statements or speaking for all homeschoolers. Try to convey that homeschoolers have a wide variety of reasons for homeschooling.

Match your presentation to your audience. Think in terms of most people's ideas about conventional education and try to translate your ideas and experiences into terms they can understand. Keep your answers as basic and simple as possible, so you will be less likely to be misunderstood or misquoted.

Avoid negative comments about public schools, legislators, school boards, superintendents, etc. Reporters are often interested in advancing controversy, but this rarely helps our cause or public image and often hurts both.

Don't jeopardize relations with allies or potential allies by speaking for them or presenting a position that might embarrass them, forcing them to deny what you said or decreasing their trust in you and other homeschoolers.

Don't rely on or overemphasize our constitutional rights, which are very important but also complex and seldom accurately presented in the media. It may be better for homeschoolers to emphasize that we are a small minority, that we act responsibly, that our children do well academically and socially, and that the current law is working well.

Remember that you can refuse to answer a question and change the subject. You can also repeat an answer if you don't want to say more on a topic or be drawn into controversy.

Following Up

Few (if any) articles or news reports are perfect, and many people find it especially frustrating to try to convey anything substantive via television. If the article or program is basically accurate and positive, thank the reporter. Keep in touch with the reporter, sending articles that may be of interest, sharing information on further developments, etc. A reasonable reporter who is willing to listen can be a valuable ally.

If the article is inaccurate, unfair, or negative, write a letter to the editor and ask others to do the same. State your objections and counter-arguments clearly, but be polite. If possible, continue to send the reporter information about homeschooling.

Send WPA a copy of the article and your response (if any).

Responding to Negative Reports by the Media

If homeschoolers do not respond to negative and inaccurate reports about homeschooling, the public and the media get the facts wrong. Uncorrected information can be harmful. If the reporters and editors are not told about their errors, they are likely to assume that their reporting is accurate or at least acceptable, repeat their errors, and perhaps become emboldened to do more and worse reporting.

Some suggestions that may help when responding:

• Share your concerns with other homeschoolers. If possible, develop strategies that involve more than one person. Make sure that the people with the greatest likelihood of being heard are among those who respond.

• Respond as promptly as possible. The news media is most interested in and likely to publish or broadcast what it considers to be current information.

• Be as calm and polite as possible. Support your response with facts and logical statements. Consider using the index of this handbook to find facts and ideas that can be included.

• Consider talking with the reporter and editor to see how much they really know about what they wrote about. If they seem open to your ideas and perspectives, ask for an opportunity to write a guest column (rather than writing a letter to the editor) or appear on radio or television.

• Send WPA copies of the original publication or a report about the program and your response. They may be included in the WPA newsletter and other publications.

PART FIVE

UNDERSTANDING AND WORKING WITH LAWS

Chapter 28

Understanding Wisconsin's Homeschooling Law

History and Legislative Intent

In interpreting a law and deciding how it will be enforced, judges, public officials, and others often give serious consideration to the intent of the law. If it can be shown that one particular interpretation of the law conforms to the intent of the law, that interpretation is more likely to be accepted. Wisconsin's homeschooling law is intended to be a reasonable, workable law that protects the interests of the state and the rights of parents, children, and families. This is clearly different from the apparent intent of the educational establishment, including the Department of Public Instruction (DPI), now and in the past, to exercise control over private education, including homeschools, and to make private schools as much like public schools as possible. Fortunately for homeschoolers, the Legislature, not the educational establishment, passes laws. But if we don't keep in mind the intent of the legislation, we could lose valuable and important support for our reasonable homeschooling law.

The intent and meaning of Wisconsin's homeschooling law becomes clearer when it is seen in an historical context. Before May 1984, some homeschoolers in Wisconsin applied to the DPI to have their homeschool officially approved as part of the state's "home tutorial" program. (Many more homeschoolers declared their homes to be private schools and thereby operated legal homeschools independent of the DPI.)

On April 26, 1983, the Wisconsin Supreme Court declared Wisconsin's compulsory school attendance law "...void for vagueness since it fails to define 'private school.'" (*State v. Popanz*) In other words, the Court ruled that in order for it to be constitutional to prosecute homeschoolers for failure to comply with the compulsory school attendance law, the statutes first needed to be changed so people would have a clear understanding of what the law required of private schools, including homeschools. This meant, according to the court, that the state should first legislate a definition of a private school. In fact, the Popanz family had been charged with truancy although they considered their homeschool a private school.

1983 Assembly Bill 887 was drafted by a legislative committee that was dominated by the educational establishment and included no homeschoolers. It was introduced in December 1983. It defined home-based private educational programs (homeschools) as instruction elsewhere than at school and required that such programs be approved by the DPI as substantially equivalent to a public or private school. It prevented homeschools from qualifying as private schools and would have made homeschooling unreasonably difficult.

The seriousness of the bill and the strength of public reaction were demonstrated to the Legislature on January 25, 1984, when 2,500 people, the vast majority opposed to the bill, converged on the capitol for the first public hearing on the bill. Testimony presented the advantages and importance of homeschooling. Further testimony was presented before the Wisconsin Senate Health, Education, Corrections and Human Services Committee on March 13, 1984. It clearly showed that having the DPI review and approve homeschools was unacceptable because of the arbitrary and unfair way in which the DPI had dealt with homeschools. See Chapter 20.

Through amendments, AB 887 was changed into a reasonable and workable homeschooling law that was enacted as 1983 Act 512 on May 10, 1984. It includes the following provisions.
• The Legislature did not give the DPI authority to review and approve homeschools.
• The Legislature did not place the burden of proof on homeschoolers to show that they are in compliance with the law. Instead, the burden of proof is on the state, to show that homeschoolers are not doing what the law requires. (When there is substantial evidence that a homeschool is not in compliance with the law, the local truant officer can initiate actions leading to prosecution of the parents if necessary.)
• For reasons of privacy, the Legislature voted not to require parents to submit the names and ages of their children either to the DPI or to their local school district.
• A memo dated March 28, 1984, from Senator Marvin Roshell to all senators addressed the question of how the compulsory school attendance law would apply to private school students including homeschoolers. This was a central issue in the debate leading to this law, and the Legislature took special care to ensure that Wisconsin reinstated the compulsory school attendance law for private school students, including homeschools as private schools.

What Wisconsin's Homeschooling Law Does

Wisconsin's homeschooling law balances and protects the interests of the state and the rights of parents, children, and families.
1. The interests of the state: The state has an interest in seeing that children do not grow up to become a burden on the state. The US Constitution does not give the federal or state governments authority in the area of education. However, the US Supreme Court has ruled that because of the policing powers granted to the states by the Constitution, states can pass and enforce compulsory school attendance laws. Wisconsin's homeschooling law was passed to ensure that the state could enforce the compulsory school attendance law.

As an additional way of protecting the state's interests, private home-based educational programs in Wisconsin are subject to the same standards and requirements as all other private schools. Parents are held accountable and are subject to prosecution and fines and/or imprisonment if they fail to comply with the law.
2. Rights of parents, children, and families: Parents have the right to secure for their children an education consistent with their beliefs and principles. The state may not have a monopoly in education and may not demand a uniform education for all. This right is guaranteed by the First, Fourth, Fifth, Ninth, and Fourteenth Amendments to the US Constitution. It has been upheld by US Supreme Court cases such as *Pierce v. Society of Sisters* and *Farrington v. Tokushige*. Wisconsin's homeschooling law protects parental rights by requiring that the information reported to the DPI, while sufficient to protect the state's

interests, is not too burdensome; does not violate constitutional, parental, and religious rights; and does not violate the principle of innocent until proven guilty.

Children should be able to attend a quality educational program consistent with their needs and abilities. This means a range of alternatives must be available. Children should be able:

- to learn at their own pace, free from harmful competition and comparisons;
- not to be forced to take standardized tests (which dictate curriculum and can be unfair, biased, inaccurate, and inappropriate);
- not to be labeled as "learning disabled," "hyperactive," or other such terms and tracked, especially at an early age;
- to be a member of a family which is supported by the larger community and not torn apart by it; and
- to be helped and supported by parents and others.

Wisconsin's homeschooling law protects children by allowing homeschools enough flexibility that they can be true alternatives and thereby meet the educational needs of the children attending them.

Wisconsin's homeschooling law holds parents accountable. It provides for the enforcement of the compulsory school attendance law. On form PI-1206 which is submitted to the DPI, parents attest that, "The Program is not operated or instituted for the purpose of avoiding or circumventing the compulsory school attendance requirement under s. 118.15 (1)(a)." Homeschools must meet the same criteria as other private schools, including "875 hours of instruction" and "a sequentially progressive curriculum." Under the truancy law, s. 118.16 (c), the attendance officer may take action based on evidence of "intermittent attendance carried on for the purpose of defeating the intent of s. 118.15." In other words, although the statutes are quite clear that an attendance officer lacks authority for routine attendance checks on students attending home-based private educational programs, if there is reasonable evidence of truancy, the officer may request information concerning attendance from administrators of home-based private educational programs. Homeschooling parents who fail to comply with Wisconsin law are subject to prosecution for truancy, which is a criminal offense punishable by fines and/or imprisonment.

Wisconsin's homeschooling law defines homeschools as private schools. A major decision by the Legislature was to define homeschools by exactly the same criteria that define all other private schools, rather than defining them as "instruction elsewhere than at school," as the committee dominated by the educational establishment that drafted the initial legislation had proposed.

Statutes 115.01 (1g), 115.01 (1r), and 118.165 (1) clearly state that an educational program that meets all of the criteria under 118.165 "is a private school." Administrators of home-based private educational programs attest that they are meeting these criteria when they submit form PI-1206 to the DPI.

Homeschools are called "home-based private educational programs" in the law only to satisfy concerns that if homeschools were formally identified as schools, they might be eligible for federal or state funds that are paid directly to schools to cover the cost of things like school lunch programs and school bus service. However, private school students, including homeschoolers, are eligible for services provided by public schools, including courses in special education and other subjects. (See Chapter 32.) The other distinguishing features of a home-based private educational program, namely, that instruction is provided by a parent or guardian and that the school is limited to one family unit, could be applied as well to "homeschools" as to "home-based private educational programs."

It is clear that the Legislature intended that homeschools be defined as private schools. The Legislature was responding to a court decision involving a homeschooling family who had defined their homeschool as a private school. The court called for a definition of a private school. The DPI committee offered a definition that prevented homeschools from being defined as private schools. The Legislature, on the other hand, after four months of deliberation and debate, rejected the DPI definition of a homeschool and instead passed into law a definition that defines home-based private educational programs (homeschools) as private schools. This is an important point to understand since the DPI continues to disregard the fact that homeschools are in fact and in law private schools. Instead the DPI supports efforts to separate homeschools from other private schools and has proposed legislation that would regulate homeschools differently from other private schools. This is contrary to the intent and language of Wisconsin's homeschooling law.

Wisconsin's homeschooling law appropriately limits the state's role in regulating homeschools. There are important reasons why the Legislature acted well when it limited the DPI's role in relation to homeschools. First, according to Article X of the Wisconsin Constitution, "The supervision of public instruction shall be vested in a state superintendent and such other officers as the Legislature shall direct." Therefore, the DPI has authority over public education but not over private education. Private schools (including homeschools) exist and operate as separate and distinct from public schools. The DPI's role in homeschooling is to collect the required report forms. It does not have direct authority over or direct involvement in any private schools, including homeschools. It does not have authority to review and approve private schools, including homeschools.

Children vary widely in their strengths, abilities, interests, and needs. To ensure that children have access to educational programs that are well suited to them, a variety of programs must be available. Some children don't or can't learn well in a conventional school. Private schools, including homeschools, need flexibility so they can meet the needs of a wide variety of children. Regulation by the state makes it very difficult to be flexible. The state's commitment to increasing centralization and standardization demonstrates that it neither understands nor can fairly assess educational alternatives such as homeschools.

The homeschooling law places the burden of proof on the state, not on homeschoolers. The state must prove that homeschoolers are not complying with the law. It is not the responsibility of homeschoolers to prove that they are complying. This is consistent with the fundamental principle of common law that people are "innocent until proven guilty."

One Family Unit

Wisconsin's homeschooling statute states that "'Home-based private educational program' means a program of educational instruction provided to a child by the child's parent or guardian or by a person designated by the parent or guardian. An instructional program provided to more than one family unit does not constitute a home-based private educational program." (S. 115.01 [1r]) If a family wants to include children from other families in their homeschool, they need to organize a private school that is not a homeschool. (Remember that homeschools are private schools.) This is not difficult to do under Wisconsin law.

This statute was written to prevent people from organizing small private schools that are attended by children from more than one family and calling them homeschools. At the same time, the statute does not prevent homeschooling families from getting together to share resources or a homeschooling parent from organizing an activity such as a math club for kids from different families. Homeschooling parents are unlikely to be considered in violation of this statute if they provide children from other family units with instruction (such as music lessons) that is independent of the homeschool program they provide their own children.

So-called "homeschool cooperatives" (in which children from more than one family unit are provided with a significant portion of the required 875 hours of instruction by some of the parents or guardians or by people they hire) are not legally considered to be homeschools in Wisconsin, and therefore participants should not file form PI-1206 with the

Department of Public Instruction. (However, such families can form a small private school that is not a homeschool.) At the same time, "co-ops" that provide only a small number of hours of primarily extracurricular activities would not seem to be in violation of the statute.

The question could be raised: Is this part of the statute necessary? It maintains the important distinction between homeschools and conventional small private schools. It is needed to maintain a common understanding of homeschooling.

If you have questions, email WPA or call WPA's Voice Mail. WPA can provide general guidelines based on our interpretation of the statute, but there is no guarantee as to what precisely would result in a court case. In general, it seems safe to assume that the more an activity looks like a conventional school, with kids from more than one family attending classes for a significant period of time, the more likely it is to be seen as a conventional private school and to cause trouble.

Foundations of Wisconsin's Homeschooling Law

The foundations of our homeschooling rights and freedoms (and other rights and freedoms) are discussed in detail in Chapter 22. Here is a brief discussion of some of the most important foundations of Wisconsin's homeschooling law.

Wisconsin's current homeschooling law is based on important fundamental rights, legal principles, and legislative intent. As homeschoolers we need to keep this point firmly in mind so that we remember that our rights and freedoms exist independently of the state and are not given to us by the state, the educational establishment, or the schools. Therefore, we need to take responsibility for maintaining our rights and responsibilities. It is a big mistake to ask the state to protect our rights for us.

Although the US Constitution does not specifically mention education, parental rights in education are strongly supported by US Supreme Court cases such as *Pierce v. Society of Sisters* (268 US 510 [1925]) and *Farrington v. Tokushige* (273 US 284 [1927]). The court has ruled that parents have a right to secure for their children an education that is consistent with their principles and beliefs and that the state may not have a monopoly in education. Recent rulings by courts in various states have reaffirmed this.

The US Constitution does guarantee rights that are important to homeschoolers (as well as all other citizens, of course). The First Amendment guarantees freedom of religion, speech, and the press, and the rights of assembly and petition. The Fourth Amendment protects us from "unreasonable searches and seizures." The Fifth Amendment prevents us from being compelled to testify against ourselves, and protects our right not to "be deprived of life, liberty, or property, without due process of law." The Ninth Amendment says that certain rights are retained by the people even though they are not listed in the Constitution. This amendment is important for people who want to reclaim rights that the state has usurped by custom and even by statute, since they can argue that the state had no constitutional basis for taking away these rights in the first place. Under this amendment, courts have recently upheld parental rights in education and rights to privacy. The Fourteenth Amendment provides civil liberties that are important to homeschoolers.

More detailed information about these constitutional amendments is in Chapter 22. Other foundations of Wisconsin's homeschooling law include the legal principle of "innocent until proven guilty," the old legal maxim, "Hard cases make bad law," and the compulsory attendance law, all of which are discussed in Chapter 22.

Chapter 29

Other Wisconsin Laws
That Affect Homeschoolers

Compulsory School Attendance Law

Every state has a compulsory school attendance law. These laws have been upheld by numerous state and US Supreme Court cases, generally on the grounds that the state has an interest in seeing that citizens do not grow up to become a burden on the state. Enforcement authority comes from the policing powers granted to the states by the US Constitution. However, these laws require attendance, not education. This is a very important distinction. See Chapter 22.

Wisconsin's current compulsory school attendance law covers children from age 6 through 18, or until a diploma is earned. (See Appendix A for the text of this law.) This requirement has been tightened in two ways. First, it is now much more difficult for 16 and 17 year olds to gain exemption from the law. (See the text of the statute for ways in which this can be done.) Second, to earn a General Educational Development (GED) certificate or a High School Equivalency Diploma (HSED), people must be at least 18 1/2, or the class with which they entered ninth grade must have graduated. (See Chapter 12 for more on the GED and HSED.) Therefore, young people cannot meet the requirements of the compulsory school attendance laws by earning an equivalency diploma. The current law is narrow, rigid, and offers few options.

2009 Kindergarten Law

According to a law passed in 2009, children who are enrolled in a five-year-old kindergarten in a public or conventional private school are required to attend school regularly even if they are too young to be covered by the compulsory school attendance law. In addition, children cannot enroll in first grade in a public school unless they have completed five-year-old kindergarten or obtained an exemption from their local school district. (Certain exemptions are also granted to some children who moved to Wisconsin from other states.) For information about how this statute affects homeschoolers, see "Beginning Homeschooling a Child Who Is Enrolled in Kindergarten" in Chapter 5.

Truancy Laws

Truancy laws follow logically from compulsory school attendance laws. Wisconsin homeschoolers are subject to truancy laws and penalties. Unfortunately, truancy laws as of this writing are rigid and punitive. (See Appendix A for texts.) Truancy is a criminal offense punishable by a fine and/or imprisonment. A recent law defines a "habitual truant" as a student who is absent from school without an acceptable excuse for part or all of five or more days during a semester. Other recent legislation requires each county to establish a truancy committee that includes, among other people, a homeschooling parent. The committee is to draft a truancy plan and submit it to each school board. Truancy sweeps have also recently been authorized by law. See Chapter 31.

It may be helpful to homeschoolers to know that in Wisconsin local school boards are responsible for enforcing truancy laws. Local school superintendents do not enforce them unless the school board happens to select them as the attendance/truant officer. Homeschoolers engaged in discussions with local public school officials concerned about truancy questions should identify the district's attendance/truant officer. In certain situations it may be better to discuss truancy questions with the local school board than with the superintendent.

Public School Records of Homeschooled Children

See Chapter 32 for information on this statute (118.125) and suggestions for ways homeschoolers can obtain these records. The text of the law is in Appendix A. As part of increases in government collaboration, recent legislation allows freer exchange of records among agencies, which diminishes our privacy and increases prejudice that public officials have toward people who are already in one agency's data base. Therefore, it is a good idea for parents to get their children's records when they begin homeschooling.

School Census and Homeschools

School districts often contact homeschoolers to request information for the school census. See Chapter 31.

Wisconsin's Open Records Law

When dealing with state and local school officials and other public officials, Wisconsin homeschoolers may sometimes find it helpful to use Wisconsin's open records law, which is found under Public Records and Property, s. 19.21-19.39. (See Appendix A.) This law guarantees public access to public documents on the state level similar to the way the federal freedom of information act does on the federal level.

The Wisconsin law states that any document sent to or produced by a public employee is a public document unless it is specifically protected under the confidentiality provisions of the statutes. Since public school officials are obviously public employees, homeschoolers could use this law when necessary to get copies of documents these officials have produced or received. This might be important to do if public officials are doing research or surveys that affect homeschoolers, or collecting stories or anecdotal evidence about homeschoolers, especially if there is reason to think that these stories may be one-sided and present only negative evidence. In cases such as these, homeschoolers can use the open records law to gain access to the files, to documents produced by public officials (including reports they have written) and to letters sent to them (such as reports from neighbors). Then homeschoolers can work to correct incorrect or misleading information, to provide balance or clarification, or to plan other strategies for dealing with the situation.

However, even though homeschoolers have a legal right to these public documents, they should remember that public officials may react negatively or be resistant to giving the information. They are not accustomed to being subject to these statutes and may not even be aware of the openness the statutes require. Therefore, in requesting public documents, it may help if homeschoolers are polite but firm and cite or quote the statutes on which their request is based. Also, certain working drafts of documents are not subject to this law, and names and addresses may need to be removed from some documents before they are released.

Immunization

Wisconsin law requires that children admitted to an elementary, middle, junior or senior high school or into any day care center or nursery school present evidence that they have received certain immunizations. However, this requirement is waived if parents object to immunization "for reasons of health, religion or personal conviction." (See Appendix A.) Home-schoolers who are asked about immunization can explain that their homeschool is the school of record and has the evidence of immunization or the waiver on file.

Child Abuse and Neglect

Homeschooling and child abuse and neglect are two separate issues. Homeschooling laws do not, and should not, cover child abuse. (See Chapter 24.) Under Chapter 48 of the Wisconsin Children's Code, complaints of child abuse and neglect can be brought against parents and legal guardians of children, including homeschoolers, and others. However, Wisconsin statutes do not allow prosecution of parents and others for educational neglect. WPA has worked over the years to help ensure that a vague term like "educational neglect" is not added to Wisconsin statutes, especially when the law requires compulsory school attendance, not compulsory education, and provides ways parents can be charged with truancy.

People who have a complaint filed against them should be familiar with the statutory definitions of abuse and neglect and also be aware of how much power social service workers have. A family that is being investigated by social services because of their choices in education can point out that the law does not allow prosecution for educational neglect. (However, homeschoolers who are not complying with the homeschooling law can be charged with truancy.) See Chapter 31 for suggestions on how to respond if you are contacted by a social service worker and Appendix A for the text of the statutes on child abuse and neglect, truancy, and homeschooling.

Legal Rights of Wisconsin Parents

Parents in Wisconsin have important legal rights that we should be aware of, so we can use them and work to maintain them. (See Chapter 21.) Here are some of them.
• We have exemptions from certain requirements. For example:
—Parents can have children who are attending public schools exempted from state-mandated standardized tests. See Appendix A for the text of s. 118.30(2)(b)3.
—Parents who object to immunizations can have the immunization requirement waived for their children. See above.
• We have the legal right not to participate in a screening, a program, or a discussion, even though many people expect us to. It is important to remember that many of our strongest rights are those that we have retained and never given over to the government. This is especially important in education. The only real authority the government has in education is

based on compulsory school attendance laws. Here are some examples of educational programs that we are not required to participate in:

—Preschool screening is voluntary. Parents are not required to have their children screened. See Chapter 31.

—Attending kindergarten is also voluntary. Children do not come under the compulsory school attendance law until the year they are six by September 1. However, homeschoolers should be aware that because of a law passed in 2009, in order to enroll in first grade in a public school, including a charter school, in Wisconsin, a child must either complete five-year-old kindergarten or be exempted from this requirement. Therefore, if you homeschool your child for kindergarten and then want to enroll them in first grade in a public school or charter school, you will need to work this out with your local school district. If you homeschooled your child for kindergarten and want to homeschool for first grade, simply do so, remembering to file form PI-1206 at the appropriate time.

—Answering many of the questions asked by school officials and other educators, medical personnel, social service workers, etc. is voluntary.

—Virtually all screening, testing, and assessment of children requires parental permission. By refusing to give their permission, parents can prevent their children from being screened.

• We have important legal rights based on the fact that the compulsory school attendance law requires attendance but not education. See Chapter 22 for an explanation of this important distinction.

• Parents have access to information and records held by the government, including school districts. See Chapter 32 for information on pupil records and ways homeschoolers can obtain records from when their children attended public schools.

• Our right to privacy is protected by the federal Family Educational Rights and Privacy Act (FERPA). This act is the basis for the DPI's appropriate policy, "The DPI does not release the names of families who are currently providing a home-based private educational program," as stated on the homeschooling portion of its website. Homeschoolers can use FERPA to object to the release of the names of homeschooling families by their local school districts and other similar actions.

Chapter 30

Working with the Legislature

■ Identifying Federal and State Legislators 214
■ How a Bill Becomes a Law 215
■ Making Initial Contacts with Legislators 215
■ Contacting Legislators to Discuss a Specific Bill 216
■ How to Participate in a Legislative Committee Hearing 217

If we have a reasonable working relationship with our legislators, or at least know who they are and how to get in touch with them, we will be in a stronger position when we want to support or oppose a piece of legislation that is important to us or if we need to resolve a problem with a government agency or official. This chapter provides basic information on how a bill becomes a law, how to contact legislators and develop a working relationship with legislators, and how to testify at a legislative hearing.

Identifying Federal and State Legislators

State legislatures and the US Congress have jurisdiction over fairly distinct although somewhat overlapping areas of the government. The role of the federal government in education is very limited; the vast majority of laws concerning education are passed by state legislatures. It does not work well to ask the federal government to pass laws to take care of us or solve our problems, such as those that are supposed to protect parental rights. See Chapter 34.

Wisconsin citizens are represented in the Wisconsin Legislature by one representative who is a member of the Assembly and serves a two-year term and one senator who serves a four-year term. For their names, addresses, and phone numbers, call the Legislative Hotline at 800-362-9472 (in Madison, 266-9960). Or visit: http://legis.wisconsin.gov/pages/waml.aspx

In case it is needed, here is information about the US Congress. American citizens are represented by one representative who is a member of the US House of Representatives and serves a two-year term, and two senators who are members of the US Senate and serve a six-year term. There are eight congressional districts in Wisconsin, each represented by one US Representative. Everyone in Wisconsin is represented by the same two Senators. For the names of your US Representative and Senators, go to http://www.govtrack.us/congress/members.

Because we often contact legislators so we can share our ideas and concerns about legislation currently before the Legislature, this book presents a brief review of the legislative process before discussing ways of contacting legislators.

How a Bill Becomes a Law

Remember that laws are not the only (or even necessarily the best) means of maintaining rights and responsibilities (as discussed in Chapter 23). Also, it is seldom, if ever, a good idea for a small minority that does not have much money or power (such as homeschoolers) to try to initiate legislation and get it passed. It is difficult for a minority to get the necessary support for legislation. The process often backfires as the initial legislation is amended and the law that passes ends up working against, rather than for, its initial sponsors. Initiating legislation in one area can easily serve as a catalyst that opens other areas of the law to change, areas we do not want changed. In addition, much of the legislation that might be proposed regarding homeschooling would undermine our homeschooling freedoms. See Chapter 24.

Keeping these points in mind, let's consider the process by which a bill becomes a law in Wisconsin. A similar process is followed in passing federal legislation.

1. When legislators have an idea for a new law or a change in an existing law, they have it drafted as a bill. The Legislative Reference Bureau (LRB) drafts most bills, although the Legislative Council Service (LCS) does some.

2. One or more legislators introduces the bill by having the Chief Clerk of the Assembly or Senate, or both, record it, assign it a number, and, usually, assign it to a legislative committee. At this point the bill must become available to the general public; before this it can be kept a secret.

3. Hearings are not required, but at least one is held on most bills. The chairperson of the appropriate committee schedules the hearing, so chairpersons have considerable power in deciding whether a bill gets a hearing, how quickly this happens, and whether the full committee votes on it. Hearings are open to the public, and anyone may speak and/or register for or against the bill. The committee goes into executive session (closed to all but the committee) to amend and vote on the bill. This may happen on the same day as the hearing or later. If the bill is controversial or the hearing draws a large number of people, the chairperson will often delay the executive session. Amendments to the bill made by legislators during executive session or later can result in a much different bill than the one considered at the public hearing.

4. The Committee on Rules schedules the bill for floor debate in the Assembly or the Senate. A bill can die in this committee if it is not scheduled. Toward the end of a legislative session, this happens fairly often.

5. The bill is debated and voted on by the full Assembly or Senate and passed or defeated with or without amendments.

6. The bill goes to the other house of the Legislature and steps three, four, and five are repeated. If the bill is amended further in the second house, either it goes back to the first house so the new amendments can be considered or it goes to a conference committee to resolve the differences between the versions from the two houses. Once the same version of the bill passes both houses, it goes to the governor for signature.

7. The bill becomes law when signed by the governor. If the governor vetoes the bill, both houses of the Legislature must override the veto by a two-thirds majority for the bill to become law.

Making Initial Contacts with Legislators

Among the ways to contact a legislator are the following:

• Many legislators have open meetings with their constituents. Call the legislator's office in your district to find out when and where such meetings are held.

• A letter of introduction can be written. If e-mail your letter, mention in the subject that you are a constituent and include your street address and city or town in the message.

• Make an appointment to meet legislators at their offices either in your district or in the capitol in Madison.

• Invite legislators to speak to your support group. Groups that include more than one district sometimes invite a senator and several representatives.

Whatever approach is chosen, legislators will be more likely to support good homeschooling laws if they have had positive encounters with homeschoolers as real people, not just as statistics. A particularly good time to get to know legislators is while they are candidates for election or re-election.

Among the topics you may want to discuss with your legislators are the following.

• Wisconsin's homeschooling law is working very well. (Consider sharing some personal experiences and reasons you appreciate having such a reasonable law.)

• Thousands of homeschooled children in Wisconsin enter or re-enter conventional schools each year with no problem. This gives concrete evidence that the homeschooling law is working well.

• The law balances the state's interest in ensuring that children do not grow up to become a burden on the state, parents' rights to choose an education for their children that is consistent with their principles and beliefs, and children's rights to a quality education consistent with their needs and abilities. See Chapter 28.

• The law holds homeschooling parents accountable. See Chapter 28. Homeschools need to meet the same standards and criteria as other private schools. Each year they must submit a signed form to the Department of Public Instruction (DPI), attesting that they are in compliance with the law, are providing 875 hours of instruction and a sequentially progressive curriculum in the required subjects, and are not attempting to circumvent the compulsory school attendance law. Homeschoolers can be prosecuted for truancy, a criminal offense punishable by fines and/or imprisonment.

• There is no evidence that the homeschooling law needs to be changed. Further regulation would be harmful and would unnecessarily restrict the flexibility that homeschools need to operate effectively.

• Share with your legislator the information in Chapter 24. Explain the kinds of legislation that homeschoolers don't want. This will probably surprise many legislators and aides, because most people who contact legislators want them to do something, often introduce legislation. However, homeschoolers do not want government money because they realize that money would be accompanied by increased regulation by the government, a price they are not willing to pay.

Other sections of this handbook give more detail and support for these points and ideas for other topics to discuss. You may also find it helpful to ask your legislators whether they have questions or concerns about homeschooling. This book will help you be better prepared to answer questions. Offer to find answers to questions you can't answer and to send them more information if they are interested. Ask your legislators for their support in maintaining the current homeschooling law without change. Ask them what their position is on homeschooling and on Wisconsin's homeschooling law.

Contacting Legislators to Discuss a Specific Bill

When you hear about a bill relating to homeschooling or another topic that concerns you, it is time to act, whether or not you have previously contacted your legislators. The first step is to make sure that you have accurate information about the bill and what it will and will not do. Do not act quickly on the basis of rumors or scanty information, even if you hear there is a legislative emergency. Take time to make sure the information you have received is accurate and it comes from a reliable source. If possible, get a copy of the bill from www.legis.state.wi.us. Read and interpret the bill yourself and discuss it with others.

Check with other homeschoolers in your district to be sure you are working together and not at cross purposes. Email the information that you gather to WPA.

When you are confident that you have accurate information about the bill and know where you stand on the issues involved, contact your legislators. If you use email, mention in the subject that you are a constituent and include your street address and city or town in the message. In writing, you can begin by identifying yourself, your work, community, position, etc. State your concern or request, identifying the bill by number and general subject. Thank your legislators for any previous help. Briefly and factually state the main arguments to support your position. Choose arguments that your legislator is most likely to agree with even if they are not the most important points to you. It is fine to indicate how the bill would affect your family but even better if you can indicate how it would affect others as well. Assume that your letter will be read and acted upon. Be reasonable and courteous, and do not use threats. Do not use exaggerated or misleading information. Ask your legislators to tell you their views on the bill in question and to notify you when a hearing is scheduled. Close with a note of thanks and your full name

If your legislators respond favorably, send a letter of appreciation.

If you want to talk with your legislators, you can call their offices or call the Legislative Hotline (800-362-9472; in Madison, 266-9960) and ask to have them call you. Plan your call before you dial by listing the issues you want to cover and rehearsing if you like. When you call, identify yourself. If your legislators are busy or not available, you may talk with an aide, which is fine. Be friendly and courteous. Give the specific reason for your call, and say you would like your legislator to work for (or against) the bill. Stick to the facts. If your legislators or their aides disagree, listen carefully to determine their real objection. Explore disagreements but don't argue. If they ask a question you can't answer, offer to find out and call back. Ask your legislators if they will work and vote for (or against) the bill. Close with a thank you.

How to Participate in a Legislative Committee Hearing

Hearings are held to provide information and perspective on pending legislation for legislators and for the public record. Your attendance is very important, whether you speak or not. You can simply register for or against the bill on a form provided at the hearing. The following suggestions are for people who want to testify at a hearing.

• Learn as much as you can about the bill as soon as it is introduced. You can get a copy from your legislator. Or go to the Wisconsin Legislature's website at http://legis.wisconsin.gov/Pages/default.aspx and click on "Legislation" and choose "Legislative Documents." Find out the name(s) of the committee(s) that are holding the hearing. Legislator's websites have helpful information on their backgrounds, including their occupations, volunteer work, affiliations, interests, and the geographical area they represent.

• Contact WPA for its ideas. Find out who else is testifying and coordinate the subjects each of you will cover or select a few representatives from your group to testify. Review your draft testimony with others.

• Verify the date, time, and place the hearing will be held by calling the Legislative Hotline.

• When you arrive at the hearing, fill out a registration form indicating that you are speaking or registering "for" (if you support the bill), "against" (if you oppose it), or "for information only" (if you will be providing testimony and will not take a position either for or against the bill).

• Address the chairperson and committee members as "Mr./Ms./Mrs./Miss Chairperson and Members of the Committee." Thank them for holding the hearing and for the privilege of speaking. Be polite and respectful. Make your points briefly but with enough detail and emphasis to be understood and remembered. Time limits for speakers will be determined by the number of people who want to speak and the length of the hearing. Plan to speak for three to five minutes, but be prepared to shorten your presentation if requested.

• State that you are speaking for yourself only, unless you have been explicitly authorized to speak for a support group or another organization. Being a member of an organization such as WPA does not authorize you to speak for that organization or to claim to represent it. To promote unity among homeschoolers and to help ensure that unnecessary changes are not made in the current homeschooling law, avoid highlighting either your personal "credentials" (degrees, teacher certification, etc.) or your use of standardized tests or other standards of acceptability related to public schools. Such references may lead committee members to conclude that all homeschoolers should have these credentials or follow these practices and/or that homeschoolers would not object to the state's requiring such credentials or practices.

• Be prepared to answer questions from committee members and to respond to testimony from speakers who disagree with you and are critical of homeschooling. It may help you prepare for such questions to talk with other homeschoolers and read this book.

• Since hearings are public meetings, the information you give, including answers to questions, becomes a matter of record and may be used by the committee and others in developing a position on an issue. Therefore, it is a good idea to give a written copy of your testimony to the chairperson before or after your presentation and also to keep a copy for your records. It may prove useful if your testimony later becomes a matter of debate or is forgotten or not used. Include on the written copy the name of the committee holding the hearing; the bill number and topic; the date, time, and location of the hearing; and your name and contact information.

PART SIX

HOMESCHOOLING IN
A NON-HOMESCHOOLING
WORLD

Chapter 31

What to Know and Do When Public Officials Contact You

As homeschoolers we may be contacted by public officials for a number of reasons. These encounters are most likely to proceed smoothly if we understand what the law requires of us and what our rights are, and if we act in ways that help maintain our rights and responsibilities. Read Chapter 21 for important information on maintaining our rights. Chapters 3 and 28 have information on Wisconsin's homeschooling law, and Chapter 29 covers other Wisconsin laws that affect homeschoolers.

An Ounce of Prevention

It is worth thinking of ways that we as homeschoolers can reduce the chances of being contacted by officials and strengthen our position if we are contacted. Some suggestions:

• Be thoroughly familiar with Wisconsin laws concerning homeschooling, compulsory school attendance, and truancy. Have a copy available for quick reference. See Chapters 3, 28, and 29 for detailed discussions of these laws and Appendix A for texts of the laws. Many homeschoolers feel more confident and better able to deal with school officials once they understand the broader legal context for homeschooling, so see Chapter 22 for the foundations of Wisconsin's homeschooling law.

• Comply with the law, including filing form PI-1206 online with the Department of Public Instruction (DPI).

• Document your compliance with the law. Keep attendance records as required by Wisconsin law. (See Chapter 10.) Plan a calendar and schedule to ensure 875 hours of instruction per school year. For yourself, keep records; see Chapter 10 for suggestions.

• Meet your legislators. See Chapter 30 for suggestions.

• Promote a positive image of homeschooling in your community. See Chapter 26.

• Be discreet. As far as you can, without compromising important principles, appear as conventional as possible. WPA's goal is to secure the best possible education for children, not to reform our whole society. We know that children learn outside the home, for example, during field trips and regular visits to the library. But most non-homeschoolers expect children to be in school during conventional school hours. It may be prudent to make sure children are supervised during those hours. This of course does not require sitting at a desk for five hours without a break; students in conventional schools don't do that.

• Think before responding to questions from others, including neighbors, relatives, and school officials. As homeschoolers, we need to be able to translate what we are doing into terms that others will understand. For example, Wisconsin law requires that we have a curriculum. Since a curriculum is an educational plan, not necessarily a series of textbooks, and we have a plan for our children's education, we can say we have a curriculum. This plan may be a detailed course of study we have purchased; or it may be a detailed plan we have written ourselves; or it may be a more general plan we are following as we watch our children learn and encourage and support them. Whatever option we have chosen, we can and should say that we have a curriculum. To say, "We don't use a curriculum" would make us appear to be failing to comply with Wisconsin's homeschooling law, when in fact we are complying because we do have an educational plan that we have chosen to meet our family's needs.

Translating what we are doing into conventional terms like "school" and "curriculum" is part of our responsibility as homeschoolers. We are the ones who understand homeschooling and know from experience how much our children are learning and how well homeschooling works. Sometimes we may get tired of having to explain what we are doing. But we will be much better off, and we will be much less likely to get into difficulty with concerned neighbors and relatives and with school officials if we translate what we are doing into terms they understand.

Understanding the Perspectives of Public Officials

The more we understand the positions, responsibilities, and perspectives of officials, the more we will have a sense of what we are up against and be able to communicate effectively and work things out so our needs are met and our freedoms, rights, and responsibilities maintained.

As bureaucrats, public officials are parts of large, frequently inflexible institutions that they depend on for their jobs and feel some loyalty to. Some officials are well-intentioned and genuinely try to be helpful. (However, because of their experiences with and commitment to large institutions, they are unlikely to share our perspectives on many things. Also, it is their job to look out for the interests of the institution, which may very well conflict with what is best for our families or what we are trying to do.) However, many officials are just doing a job and are unlikely to stick their necks out for us. Some may not even care very much about us and our requests or problems. Most often, officials do not have final authority; sometimes they have very little authority. Their world is very proscriptive. Their job is to make and/or enforce rules. By contrast, requests from homeschoolers often involve basic issues of freedom, rights, and gaining exceptions to arbitrary rules. This may make it difficult for us to find common ground on which we can work with officials. Unfortunately, some officials who are very nice people when they are off the job can be difficult to deal with in their official capacities. Many officials, especially those with inaccurate or incomplete information regarding homeschooling, fear the officials or boards above them. They may say or think, "If I don't get this from you, I might be reprimanded or fired."

You may well know more about laws and regulations than an official you are dealing with. Homeschooling is probably only one small part of their job, something they don't deal with very often. They may be uninformed or have been misinformed by a superior. Also, they generally see themselves and are seen by others as authority figures. They are used to making statements they don't have to back up with facts or evidence. They expect people to obey. So don't be surprised or take it personally if an official reacts negatively or defensively to your question or request. Take responsibility for yourself and your family, be prepared, present the information you have, and politely but firmly stand your ground.

Screenings: Newborn, Birth to Three, Preschool, Mental Health, and Others

Types of Screenings

Screenings have increased tremendously during the last several decades. Children are screened in many ways, including the following:

• Newborns are routinely screened at birth.

• Screenings of children under three are done under programs such as Birth to Three and Child Find. The federal Individuals with Disabilities Education Act (IDEA) is used to justify many screenings, even though the law only requires that officials make screenings available and does not require that parents have their children screened. These programs were originally designed for children with disabilities. However, they have expanded to include children who do not have disabilities but only have developmental delays or even only potential developmental delays. The expansion seems strongly motivated by the fact that professionals, schools, and other institutions get more money from the government if they can find and treat more children. Some children who do not have real problems and some who would outgrow their so-called problems themselves given time, love, and support are no doubt being misdiagnosed by screenings and then subjected to treatment that may do more harm than good. Some parents choose to retain direct responsibility for their children rather than submitting them to screening and treatment, especially since money is likely to be one of the motivations behind the screening.

• Formal preschool screenings are conducted by school districts on children who the districts expect to enroll in the public schools. They are a scheduled one-on-one encounter with an evaluator who asks the child to do various tasks and reports on problems or potential problems the child supposedly has. They are discussed in detail below.

• Letters inviting parents to bring their children to informal preschool screenings make them sound like relaxed, informal get-togethers. However, during the events, evaluators observe children and decide what problems they may have. Much of the information below about formal preschool screenings applies to informal ones as well.

• Drug companies and others are pushing for increased mental health screening. Informal, unannounced screenings are conducted by health care workers on people of all ages, many of whom do not realize they are being screened.

Problems With Screening

• Numerous articles and books have been written on the problems with the diagnostic methods and techniques used to identify children with special needs and learning disabilities. Gerald S. Coles' *Learning Mystique: A Critical Look at "Learning Disabilities"* is a comprehensive study of the research and literature on learning disabilities. Dr. Coles, a psychiatrist, concludes that there is no reliable method or technique for identifying learning disabilities. Thomas Armstrong's *In Their Own Way: Discovering and Encouraging Your Child's Personal Learning Style* and Frank Smith's *Insult to Intelligence: The Bureaucratic Invasion of*

Our Classrooms demonstrate the severe limitations of the learning theory that supports most special education and programs for learning disabled children.

• Reports from screenings are often misleading and inaccurate. Inaccuracies arise from several sources. Any test or assessment inevitably reflects the values, background, and experience of its creators. Members of ethnic minorities and people who have chosen values different from the dominant culture are unfairly handicapped when assessed by mainstream standards. Is it really fair or accurate to say that children who don't do well on tests biased in favor of white, middle-class boys are abnormal?

Most people do not do their best in stressful situations. Young children who are appropriately shy around strangers and in unfamiliar settings often fail to perform tasks during preschool screening that they frequently do at home, leading assessors to underestimate their abilities.

To make matters worse, inaccurate assessments can become self-fulfilling prophecies when children conclude they are dumb.

• Many evaluators are biased, sometimes unintentionally. They focus on finding problems, not on identifying the few children who need and would benefit from available help and encouraging the rest of the families to continue what they are doing. Evaluators' training, mindset, and worldview tend to be dominated by the notion that many, many children need the help that their profession can offer. In addition, evaluators' prestige, salary, and job security depend on their finding new clients.

• Screening undermines children's confidence. It is a search for weaknesses, not strengths, and a vote of no confidence. To enable assessors to rank and label children, screenings include questions and tasks that few if any children will be able to handle in the time allowed. This increases some children's sense that "something must be wrong with me," that they have failed or at least done poorly.

• Screening interferes with children's learning and development. Each of us learns best at our own pace, quickly in some areas, more slowly in others. Learning happens much more easily and effectively when we discover things for ourselves instead of trying to follow a teacher's explanations that may not make sense or that we aren't ready to understand. But screening imposes arbitrary, one-size-fits-all standards that really don't fit anyone. Attempts to correct supposed deficiencies often make the situation worse. Supporters of screening often argue that early detection is necessary so problems can be corrected promptly. This leads to children being diagnosed with problems they would have outgrown given more time.

• Screening undermines parents' confidence in their children, themselves, and their ability to raise children. It says that parents are not competent and that experts are needed to assess children and tell parents what to do. In addition, parents know more about their children than people conducting screenings do. When parents are intimidated by screenings and give up on their own ideas and observations, we lose a very valuable resource for helping children grow and learn.

Although screenings are biased, unfair, and sometimes inaccurate, even parents and children who are skeptical about screenings have a very hard time not being influenced by the results, especially negative ones. People who think they need information from screenings are even more strongly influenced. For example, everyone encounters difficulties when trying to learn. People with self-confidence usually figure out how to resolve or get around the difficulty, or they seek help. But people who have been labeled learning disabled tend to give up much more quickly, saying, "The tests were right; I can't learn."

• By undermining confidence of both parents and children, screening makes it less likely that children will be able to develop their strengths and abilities. Ironically, it interferes with and hinders children's development, rather than giving them the help that proponents claim it does.

• Screening can lead to legal difficulties now and in the future. Parents who allow screening surrender a great deal of control. It is often harder to prevent additional screening once a child has been screened. Schools and other agencies may claim the initial screening shows that formal evaluations are necessary as a follow-up to the screening. As a result of screening, children are often diagnosed as having problems and labeled as learning disabled, etc. Such labels give schools legal authority they don't have if children have not been labeled. Even if children are not officially labeled, difficulties or potential difficulties that are supposedly found during screening and noted on children's records might cause problems in the future. Because of recent increases in collaboration and sharing of information among government agencies, information from screenings can easily spread and be used in numerous ways.

Even parents who really want to have their children screened should seriously consider whether the information from public school screening is worth the risk of legal difficulty. It is less risky to pay for a private assessment and consider the expense a relatively small price to pay to maintain privacy and control of their lives and minimize the risk of intervention by the state. However, parents must select private evaluators carefully to ensure that they will not submit results of the screening to the state, as some evaluators now do. And, of course, the basic risks of screening, such as inaccurate results and loss of confidence, apply to private assessments as well as public ones.

• Screening can lead to labels and treatments that damage children. Often the cure is worse than the disease. If there are areas in which children could use support and encouragement, the response of trained professionals may delay development by undermining children's self-confidence, increasing the pressure and embarrassment children feel, trying to make them learn in ways that are more difficult for them, and interfering with their natural learning style. For very dramatic information about the damage that can be done by special education, see Lori and Bill Granger's *Magic Feather: The Truth about "Special Education."*

What do screenings really accomplish? Educational bureaucracies and professional special interest groups decide what qualities, abilities, and skill levels are important and must be demonstrated by young children for them to be labeled normal. But what about families who value qualities different from those chosen by the government? What about children who are developing well but on a schedule different from the one prescribed? Sensitive children who are too overwhelmed by strangers in strange surroundings to demonstrate their real abilities? Geniuses who just don't fit the expected patterns?

Similar questions can be raised about the wisdom of using professional experts to assess children's strengths and limitations when parents have a wealth of information and are the real experts and know their children well. Although a big mystique has developed around the process of diagnosing and labeling all sorts of alleged disorders, most diagnoses are based on either common sense or unsubstantiated theories. Serious problems are pretty obvious, and some less serious problems that are diagnosed turn out, on closer examination, to be ridiculous.

• Some parents may say, "What if we don't have our children screened and we miss a problem that could have been corrected? If the kids are normal, the screening will confirm this, right?" Wrong. The likelihood that screening will turn up a serious but previously unidentified problem is slim and has to be weighed against the much greater chance that the screening will interfere with a child's natural development. Parents know a lot about their children, especially when they take responsibility for them and don't turn them over to experts. Screenings, on the other hand, can be inaccurate and often claim to identify problems that children would naturally outgrow given more time.

Preschool Screening

Parents are not required by state or federal law to have their preschoolers screened. However, federal law states that public or private schools that receive federal funding for special education must make their programs, including testing and screening, available to all children. This does not mean children must participate in these programs or screenings. It would be helpful to parents if screening announcements said something like, "We are required to inform you that free preschool screening is available for all children ages __ to __. Your child's participation in this screening is voluntary. If you are interested, please contact..." In 2012, WPA convinced the DPI to change its website from saying that school districts are required to screen all children to saying that they are required to offer screenings. However, letters that districts send to parents still usually give the impression that parents are required to have their children screened. One reason for this inaccurate message to parents is to that it protects the jobs of testers and school personnel who often have a strong self-interest and financial interest in finding children with special needs.

If you receive a letter from your school district announcing a screening or telling you to report for preschool screening, you can respond in one of several ways.

• You can continue to retain direct responsibility for your preschooler's development. To do this, observe your child, which you are no doubt already doing. Serious problems are generally obvious. If you feel you need more background information, try a book like Frank Smith's *Reading Without Nonsense.* He points out that: "Children who have learned to comprehend spoken language (not necessarily the language of school, but some language that makes sense in the world they live in) and who can see sufficiently well to distinguish a pin from a paper clip on the table in front of them have already demonstrated sufficient language, visual acuity, and learning ability to learn how to read." (page 9)

Many parents find it helpful to keep records of their children's learning and activities so they can see progress more clearly. A discussion with someone who knows your children and shares your values, perspectives, and approach to education can also be helpful.

• You can then ignore a letter telling you to bring your children in for screening, since you are not required by law to have them screened.

• You can tell others in your community the facts in this matter.

• You can also ask the author of such a letter to document it with legal references or issue a retraction or clarification.

Mental Health Screening

Increased mental health screening for children and adults is being encouraged by the federal government partly in response to strong marketing and lobbying by the pharmaceutical industry. Screenings can be done by school counselors and officials, doctors and other health care providers, employees of clinics and hospitals, social service workers, juvenile justice authorities, etc. People may not be told that the questions they are being asked are part of a mental health screening. The questions may sound reasonable, sometimes even complimentary.

For example, here are some questions from a widely used questionnaire designed to be answered by parents of children roughly 2 1/2 years old.

• Does your child cling to you more than you expect? Does your child seem too friendly with strangers? [Note that it's not easy to get the answers to these questions right. Children can't be either too clingy or too outgoing.]
• Does your child seem more active than other children her age?
• Can your child settle himself down after periods of exciting activity?
• Does your child follow routine directions? For example, does she come to the table or help clean up her toys when asked?
• Can your child move from one activity to the next with little difficulty, such as from playtime to mealtime?

Scoring on this screening makes it easy for a child to be referred for a mental health assessment. For example, there are 28 questions like the ones listed above. A score of 5 points is assigned each time a parent answers the question "sometimes." A score of 57 (in other words, a response of "sometimes" on 12 or more of the 28 questions) or higher leads to a referral.

Open-ended questions are also included, such as:
- Has anyone expressed concerns about your child's behaviors? If you checked "sometimes" or "most of the time," please explain.
- Do you have concerns about your child's eating and sleeping behaviors or about her toilet training? If so, please explain.
- Is there anything that worries you about your child? If so, please explain.

A questionnaire to be completed by parents of children ages 6 to 18 and widely used in schools includes questions such as the following:
- About how many close friends does your child have? (Do not include brothers & sisters)
- Do any of the following describe your child now or within the past six months?
    - Clings to adults or too dependent
    - Daydreams or gets lost in his/her thoughts
    - Doesn't seem to feel guilty after misbehaving
    - Feels too guilty
    - Fears going to school
    - Feels or complains that no one loves him/her
    - Bites fingernails
    - Not liked by other kids
    - Overweight
    - Prefers being with older kids
    - Prefers being with younger kids
    - Showing off or clowning
    - Too shy or timid

Problems Raised by Mental Health Screening

• Those who define mental illness and decide who is mentally ill have enormous power. Unlike physical illness where symptoms are often clear and uncontroversial, the definition of mental illness depends on one's approach to life, self-interest, history, and belief system. In other words, essentially anyone could be labeled mentally ill depending on the definitions chosen.

• Labeling people as mentally ill is a way of blaming individuals, parents, and families rather than social service agencies, schools, the economy and financial inequalities, racism, etc.

• These mental health screening programs are set up so that drug companies, public school districts, social service agencies, prison systems, some professionals in the mental health field, etc., stand to gain financially. Such financial incentives obviously make it more likely that people will be misdiagnosed and unnecessarily labeled and treated.

• Screening preschoolers and children in elementary schools is justified by the argument that early detection will prevent more serious problems from developing. However, sometimes early detection catches a person in a weak moment or makes a mountain out of a mole hill, turning a behavior that a child would have outgrown given some time, support, and love into an emotional disturbance, undermining the confidence of the child and their family, and becoming a self-fulfilling prophecy.

• Much controversy surrounds the treatment of mental illness. The use of drugs is promoted by drug companies to increase their profits. Drugs are chosen by some patients, families of patients, and professionals because they seem easier to use and seem to give faster results than therapy or other approaches. They are promoted by HMOs and insurance companies because they are sometimes cheaper than other approaches. However, many people question whether drugs really work and are concerned about their safety. Many of these drugs have not been tested thoroughly. Many consumers do not like taking drugs and object to their side effects. Many people object to drugging people.

• The groundwork for labeling many people mentally ill has been laid in the fourth edition of the *Diagnostic and Statistical Manual of Mental Disorders* (DSM-IV), an 886-page book published in 1994 by the American Psychiatric Association. (Note: The DSM-V is scheduled to be released in May 2013.) According to the DSM-IV, a very wide range of behavior can be defined as abnormal and indicative of mental illness. For example, in an article in *Harpers,* L. J. Davis reviewed the DSM-IV's description of several adolescent disorders (including Attention-Deficit/Hyperactivity Disorder and Oppositional Defiant Disorder) and concluded, "A close reading of the text reveals that the illnesses in question consist of failure to listen when spoken to, talking back, annoying other people, claiming that somebody else did it, and (among a lot of other stuff familiar to parents) failure to clean up one's room. According to the DSM-IV, adolescence is a mental disorder." ("The Encyclopedia of Insanity-A Psychiatric Handbook Lists a Madness for Everyone" by L. J. Davis, *Harpers,* February, 1997).

• Mandatory mental health screening would provide a legally sanctioned way for professionals to interfere with homeschooling or possibly prevent some families from homeschooling. Some children have, quite understandably, reacted to difficulties in school (such as problems with teachers, bullying, and labeling) by becoming anxious or developing other behaviors that are listed in the DSM-IV. Many parents have found that simply removing their children from school and homeschooling them has solved the problem and was far superior to labeling the children mentally ill and treating them with drugs.

Sharing Our Concerns About Screenings With Others

It's worth considering several points that may be raised by people who either support increased screening or feel that they do not need to be concerned about it, including legislators and their aides.

• Some may claim that mentally ill people really do need help. It's true that there are people who need or want help, and they should certainly get it. However, they are far more likely to be harmed than helped by a program of mental health screening strongly influenced by drug companies intent on increasing their profits, supported by professionals who have received money and other favors from drug companies, and promoted by lawmakers who have received lots of money from drug companies.

• Some people may argue that they aren't afraid to be screened because neither they nor their children are mentally ill. But as pointed out above, the symptoms listed in the DSM-IV are general, broad, and widespread. It may be difficult to get through a screening, especially one conducted by someone who has a strong financial incentive to label as many people mentally ill as possible.

• Other people may argue that the current screenings are only demonstration projects aimed at marginal groups like prisoners, young people in the juvenile justice system, and families involved with social services. In April 2002, President Bush launched the New Freedom Commission on Mental Health. The commission conducted a "comprehensive study of the United States mental health service delivery system" and developed six goals "as the foundation for transforming mental health care in America." The report states, "The early detection of mental health problems in children and adults-through routine and comprehensive testing and screening-will be an expected and typical occurrence."

Experience has shown that many programs are started with assurances that they are only for a small group in need and then spread to a much wider group. For example, IDEA, originally for children with disabilities, has resulted in the screening of nearly all preschool children, the labeling of 10% of the school age population, and the wide use of Ritalin and other drugs. These drugs are now being seriously questioned, but they continue to be used, despite their obvious costs to children, families, and taxpayers, largely because professionals and institutions are committed to the program and the drugs.

• When we are asked questions like those above or asked to complete questionnaires, we can find out what our rights are. We can ask which questions or questionnaires are mandatory, which we can refuse to answer, and how the information we provide will be used. If the person asking us the questions cannot answer our questions in this regard, or if they insist that we have to answer questions we don't feel comfortable answering, or if we are told that information is mandatory but we don't want to provide it for reasons of privacy or anything else, we can ask to see the statute that requires that we provide such information.

• See Appendix C for the WPA resolution on mental health screening adopted on May 7, 2005.

• Do an Internet search for information about and critiques of the DSM-V, scheduled for publication in May 2013. For example, look for articles by Marcia Angell, a Senior Lecturer at Harvard and a former editor of the *New England Journal of Medicine.*

School Census

Wisconsin law (s. 120.18, in Appendix A) requires school districts to report to the DPI each year the total number by age of people between the ages of 4 and 20 who live in the district, regardless of where they attend school. Therefore, along with other residents of their school district, homeschoolers often receive a letter, phone call, or personal visit from public officials requesting information for the school census. Sometimes the district asks for the names and birth dates of everyone between the ages of 4 and 20. Before providing this information, homeschoolers should consider the following:

• In 1984, in the process of passing Wisconsin's homeschooling law, the Legislature decided that to protect their children's privacy, homeschoolers should not be required to report to the DPI their names and ages. Therefore, form PI-1206 requires the number of children by gender and grade level, including the options to report children as "ungraded, 1-8" and "ungraded, 9-12." This is consistent with the intent of the Legislature and the specific requirements of the homeschooling law and is reasonable.

• School districts do not need to know children's names and ages. They report the gender and grade levels and/or ages of children, but ages can be estimated from grade levels. (Parents of homeschooled children listed as "ungraded" can either provide their grade level or a range of levels.) It would be more helpful for school districts and the state to know children's grade levels, rather than their ages, since planning for school facilities and finances is based on the number of children in each grade.

• We are in a much better position to maintain our rights and freedoms if we make it a practice not to give the state any more information than is necessary for the orderly functioning of the government. This protects families' rights to privacy and is consistent with the statutes and the U.S. Constitution. It helps to ensure that the government has enough power to govern but does not unreasonably interfere with people's lives. Voluntarily providing a bureaucracy with more information than is required by law sets a precedent and may lead to this information eventually being required.

• Two laws are in conflict here. The homeschooling law tells parents they do not have to report their children's names and ages. The school census law requests numbers and ages. Since the homeschooling law was specifically designed for homeschoolers and determines what requirements they must meet, it seems logical that they should obey the homeschooling law rather than the census law, which only involves homeschoolers in a minor way. Moreover, the census law allows school districts to do surveys and make estimates, so they can easily complete their reports without having the names and ages of homeschooled children.

• The number of children by age is only one part of the report each district sends to the DPI. Also included are the names and monthly salaries of teachers, an itemized account of money received and expended by the school district, and the amount and type of school district debt. The law also states, "If the school district clerk neglects to make the annual report, the clerk shall be liable to the school district for the whole amount of money lost by the school district because of such neglect." Clearly the report deals primarily with finances of public school districts. Information about privately educated homeschoolers is a very small part of it.

In addition to requesting names and ages of homeschooled children, some school districts use the school census as an opportunity to request additional personal information about homeschooled children and their families. Such requests clearly exceed the districts' legal authority and the intent and purpose of the school census. Providing such information could set unwise precedents, invade families' privacy, and diminish their rights.

WPA therefore suggests that homeschoolers respond to school districts' requests for school census data by providing the same information they provided on form PI-1206, adding a grade or range of grades for children identified as ungraded on the form. Parents can simply give a copy of the form to the census taker. Homeschoolers who think a problem or battle is going to develop over this approach might prefer simply to give names and ages of their children, realizing that such action may contribute to the bureaucracy's beginning to require such information. This approach is consistent with WPA's general approach of cooperating with school districts and the DPI whenever there is clearly a need and legal requirement for such cooperation and of acting on principle to protect homeschoolers' rights as private educators whenever necessary.

Consider this example from a WPA member who received a census form from her school district. The form requested for "ALL Children (age 19 and under): Name, Male/Female, Date of Birth, Race, Social Security #, School, Grade, Homeroom." Accompanying the form was a letter which read,

> We are aware that you home teach your children. However, we do need their names, gender, race and date of birth for our records. The Department of Instruction [sic] requires us to complete several reports each year and many of them require information on the total number of students living in the District as well as students enrolled in the schools in the District.

The mother shared her response with WPA:

> I responded to this letter and census. At first I wasn't sure what to do. I knew something wasn't quite right with these questions. The WPA handbook was a real help. I wrote a nice letter explaining the law, Act 512, the school census law, and the Fifth Amendment right to privacy. I sent them a copy of PI-1206 for their reference. I said I was sorry, but all I could supply them with was gender and grades, and that they had my permission to estimate my children's ages. If I hadn't had all this wonderful information, I probably would have filled out the form and sent it back, just to keep the peace.

Other Forms from Local School Districts

Occasionally school districts send various other forms to homeschoolers. WPA strongly encourages homeschoolers not to fill out any forms except PI-1206 (which is filed with the DPI) and not to supply local school officials or other public officials with any information (except information for the school census, discussed above) unless they are sure that the form and the information are required by law. This is important because:

• Providing information sets a precedent. Any time citizens give a bureaucracy more information than is required by law, the bureaucracy's power and control are increased. By their nature, bureaucracies grow and spread. One of the most effective ways they do this is by repeatedly asking for small, seemingly harmless pieces of information. If citizens comply without giving the matter much thought, before long the bureaucracy may have gathered an impressive amount of information. It is important for citizens to resist this encroachment on their rights and liberties.

• Officials frequently request information although they do not have the legal authority to do so. When people refuse to supply this information, they are acting in a way that helps maintain their rights and freedoms. See Chapter 21.

• Although the information seems innocent and insignificant, it may be used to support a claim by local public school officials or the DPI that they should have (or actually do have) authority to require this information. Sometimes supplying a piece of information can legally be construed as an indication that a bureaucracy has authority over the individual supplying the information. Or it can be used as a justification for the bureaucracy's demanding such authority.

WPA also recommends that homeschoolers exercise caution in responding to requests for information about their homeschool from researchers working for the DPI, a university, or any other organization. Such information can end up being distorted, misinterpreted, quoted out of context, and misused. See Chapter 24 for more information on research.

If you have questions about a form or other request for information that you have received from a public official, or if you need help dealing with such a request, contact your WPA Regional Coordinator, email WPA, or call the Voice Mail.

For information and suggestions on responding to offers made to homeschoolers by public school officials, see "Offers from Public Schools to Homeschoolers" later in this chapter.

Unauthorized Requests from School Officials

Occasionally school officials request a copy of homeschoolers' curriculums, school calendars, etc., either to review or to file. Wisconsin law does not require homeschoolers to provide such information, and WPA strongly recommends that they not. When homeschoolers comply with such requests, they are doing more than the minimum that the law requires, setting dangerous precedents, and increasing the power of school officials over homeschoolers. Such requests can often be handled by letter. See the sample letter below.

As an example, consider the experience of a Wisconsin family who had been homeschooling for more than ten years when they received the following letter from the assistant principal of their local school district.

September 12, 2008

Parent of XXXXXXXXXXXX

Please remember that requests with the DPI for Home Based instruction need to be filed each year. According to our records, we do not have a current request on file. Until we receive this form, your son/daughter is required to be in school.

If we do not hear from you within the next week, we will consider him/her truant and will be filing a truancy referral with Social Services.

If you have moved out of our school district please let us know so we can remove him/her from our roll.

Please contact us at the high school, to let us know your plans. We would be glad to assist you in this matter in any way we can.

Sincerely,
XXXXXXXXXXXXXXXX
Assistant Principal

At first glance this might seem like a reasonable request: the school district simply wants homeschoolers to notify them at the beginning of the school year that they are homeschooling. (Even so, the threat of truancy charges is harsh and impolite.) However, the letter contains several significant errors.

• Under Wisconsin law, it is the truant officer's responsibility to prove that students are truant. It is not up to parents or students to prove that they are innocent.

• Form PI-1206 does not request anything. It is designed to report enrollment as of the third Friday of September.

• The school district presumably does not contact all private school students and all students who were enrolled during the previous year but have not enrolled this year. Therefore, this action is clearly discriminatory and does not treat homeschools as the private schools that they are.

Consider, too, the consequences that would result if homeschoolers voluntarily complied with this request which exceeds the school district's legal authority.

• Compliance with the request would place homeschools under the authority of public schools by setting the precedent that school officials have the authority to direct the timing and reporting of homeschools.

• Compliance would separate homeschools from other private schools. Homeschools would then be more vulnerable to school district power in the community and in the Legislature.

• Other school districts would follow suit and require that homeschools report to them at the beginning of the school year.

• School districts might claim additional authority that they have not been given by law. They might set rules about when students can begin homeschooling or other such matters.

In other words, if parents don't know the law and their rights and don't take action to protect them, rights and freedoms can be diminished, even though Wisconsin has a reasonable homeschooling law.

Fortunately in this case the situation was resolved. The family realized the official was exceeding their legal authority and called WPA. Both the assistant principal and the DPI were contacted. A DPI official agreed with WPA's assessment of the situation and interpretation of the law. The assistant principal complied with the family's request for a written statement that the matter had been resolved by sending the following letter.

September 25, 2008

Dear XXXXXXXXXXXXX

Thank you for your understanding when we spoke this morning. I want [sic] apologize again for any misunderstanding. It is not our intent to file truancy on your son.

The letters that went out were intended to simply verify which students are being home-schooled or are enrolled elsewhere. In the future, we will not contact students who were home-schooled the previous year before the October 15 deadline for filing with the DPI.

Thank you for your understanding on this issue. If we can be of any assistance in the future, please feel [sic] to call.

Sincerely,
XXXXXXXXXXXXXXX
Assistant Principal

This letter does several important things. First, it states in writing that the school does not intend to file truancy charges against the family, thus eliminating the threat. Second, the school district agreed not to do something like this in the future. The district also refers to filing the form rather than making a "request" of the DPI.

As homeschoolers, we need to be prepared to use this information with our school districts, if necessary; to share it with other homeschoolers; and to encourage homeschoolers not to set precedents by complying with demands from school officials that are not required by law.

Sample Letter to a School Official Who Requests Documents

Your street address
City, state, zip code
Date

Dr. or Mr. or Ms. (full name of official)
_____ School District
Street address
City, state, zip code

Dear Dr. or Mr. or Ms. (last name):
    I am writing in response to your letter dated _____, in which you requested _____
_____.
    This is to advise you that in accordance with the laws governing a home-based private educational program, I have filed form PI-1206 with the Department of Public Instruction (DPI) and am in compliance with the laws referenced above. In addition, the laws do not grant either local school districts or the DPI the responsibility or authority to monitor a home-based private educational program. This is clear from the laws themselves; from the legislative discussion and debate leading to the passage of the laws; from the Legislative Council's memorandum on the law; and from meetings and correspondence concerning the administration of the laws that included the DPI, public school officials, legislators, and homeschoolers.
    We are aware that the attendance officer has authority under the truancy statute to initiate action when there is reasonable evidence of "intermittent attendance carried on for the purpose of defeating the intent of S. 118.15." However, your request does not concern a truancy matter.
    After much discussion, the Wisconsin Legislature passed the "Definition of a Private School" law to ensure that home-based private educational programs were not subject to review or approval by public school officials. This is consistent with parental rights in education, provisions of the U.S. and Wisconsin Constitutions, and the distinction between public and private schools.
    Therefore, I respectfully decline your request for _____.

Sincerely,
Your signature
Your full name
Home-Based Private Educational
Program Administrator

It is in educating ourselves about the complicated legal issues that arise and then speaking out that we will maintain our easy-to-live-with law. The school district administration in my own town is an individual who dislikes homeschoolers and whose actions try to erode our rights. This spring, he sent a registered letter to a new member of my homeschool group, a family that has just moved here from out west. In it he said that the application to homeschool needed additional information before it could be approved. They needed to call his office immediately. The parents were not rattled, much.

The mother consulted the WPA handbook to see just what they needed to report for a school census. Then she read the law itself. No, it was not fun to read. Yes, it takes a while to read and understand. Yet the more she read, the more clearly she knew her legal foundation, the angrier she got at this upstart. She wrote back, not phoned. She corrected that the PI-1206 form is a notification of intent and not an application, that no approval was needed, that some of the information will come on the annual school district census, and that most of it is not required by any law or regulation. Another member of the group is checking to see what letter, if any, is sent to families who enroll in one of the conventional private schools midyear. Conserving our rights continues each day and in a thousand places. —From Opening Remarks, WPA Conference, 2000

Offers from Public Schools to Homeschoolers

Public school officials are increasingly making special offers to homeschoolers. Some request meetings with homeschoolers to discuss ways public schools could serve homeschoolers. Some offer use of school computers, libraries, and other facilities. Some offer to supervise families' homeschooling programs, providing curriculum, conferences with parents, testing, resources, and perhaps money to cover educational expenses. Others try to convince homeschoolers to enroll in virtual charter schools. (See Chapter 24.)

These offers may sound tempting, but it is important to be aware of problems they raise.

• Most offers are motivated by money. Some school officials think that they can increase both their enrollments and their budgets by offering special programs to homeschoolers that will draw them into public schools so they can be counted as enrolled students.

• Homeschoolers who accept offers from public schools also have to accept the schools' requirements, approaches to education, values, etc. Money and services have strings attached. There's no such thing as a free lunch. Officials use this opportunity to require things like review and approval of homeschoolers' curriculums, testing (including state-mandated testing), and reports documenting what students have learned. So homeschoolers who accept these offers are surrendering some of their homeschooling freedoms.

• The freedom of other homeschoolers is undermined when some homeschoolers accept offers from public schools. First, their compliance with increased regulation sets a precedent that other homeschoolers are likely to be expected to follow. Second, the general public begins to think of these homeschoolers as typical, especially since they are more visible and easy to locate, so they are more likely to be the subject of media stories and research studies. This promotes the idea that homeschooling should be an arm of the public schools, rather than part of private education and therefore independent.

If school officials invite you to a meeting to discuss ways the school district could help you and other homeschoolers or send you a survey to get ideas for programs they could offer that would draw homeschoolers into the public schools, think before you respond. Most homeschoolers do not want to participate in public schools. They prefer to maintain the flexibility they have when they don't have to attend classes every day. They don't want their children to be required to take the state-mandated tests that public school students have to take. They may not want their children strongly influenced by the culture and values of public school. They may also realize that the more homeschoolers participate in public schools, the more opportunity the schools have to increase their power and authority over homeschoolers.

Many homeschoolers who are invited to a meeting with their school district administrator decide to go to the meeting to explain clearly that they don't want public school services. This is important. If the only people who attend such meetings are the few homeschoolers who do want to participate in such activities or are new to homeschooling and don't understand the consequences, school officials may assume that homeschoolers want such "opportunities" and may increase their efforts to provide them. If you receive such an invitation, please seriously consider attending to explain your opposition to public school control of homeschooling. If you receive a survey asking for ideas for services your school district could provide homeschoolers, you can send it back with a letter explaining that you do not want such services and that school districts' use of the names and addresses of parents for purposes other than record keeping is a violation of the federal Family Educational Rights and Privacy Act (FERPA).

Contact by a Social Service Worker

Homeschoolers are very seldom contacted by social service workers. However, because such contacts can have serious consequences, the following comments and suggestions are provided.

In Wisconsin, as in most other states, county or state social service workers have legal authority to intervene in the lives of families in response to a complaint that someone makes to social services. (The family is unlikely to know who made the complaint. In fact, the identity of the people who make complaints is protected by law.)

Social service workers have a lot of power and authority. Some common civil liberties and parts of due process are suspended in situations where they are investigating complaints against families. Social service workers do not need to have formal evidence or an indictment in order to be legally authorized to question parents and children. Results of questioning by social service workers can be serious, too, including removing children from their families. Therefore, contacts from social service workers need to be taken seriously and handled carefully.

Usually if homeschoolers are suspected of failing to comply with the homeschooling law, the case is handled by truant officers, as described below. However, social service workers who are investigating a family for other reasons may begin asking questions about their homeschool. It is usually best for homeschoolers to try to keep homeschooling separate from whatever other investigations are being conducted. They can explain that Wisconsin statutes do not allow parents to be charged with "educational neglect." (See Chapter 29.) They can also remind the social service worker that parents whose children are attending public schools are not questioned about curriculum, hours of attendance, testing, etc. These are questions about education and should not enter into complaints of abuse or neglect. Homeschoolers who are contacted by social service workers often find it helpful to discuss the situation with other homeschoolers or their WPA Regional Coordinator, email WPA, or call the Voice Mail.

Generally, any complaints that are received by social services need to be investigated, regardless of their source or credibility. If a social service worker contacts you by letter or phone or comes to your house, you can usually explain that you are busy with your children and ask that an appointment be scheduled to discuss the questions. This gives you a chance to prepare for the interview by thinking about questions you might be asked and how you want to respond. You can also schedule the appointment outside school hours and find someone to be with your children while you talk.

More Serious Situations

Even if you have received threatening letters from your school district or the district attorney, have been investigated by social services, have been scheduled to appear in court on truancy or other charges, are involved in a custody dispute, or are involved in another

RECORD OF DISCUSSIONS CONCERNING HOMESCHOOLING

**For use with public school officials, DPI, District Attorney, the media
(newspapers, radio, TV), etc.**

This form filled out by:

Name _____

Address _____

_____

Phone (___) _____ Date _____

Email _____

**Support person(s) with me at time of contact
(spouse, friend, attorney, etc.):**

Name _____

Address _____

_____

Phone (___) _____ Date _____

Email _____

I was contacted about homeschooling by or I contacted:

Name _____

Title _____

Agency _____

Address _____

_____

Phone (___) _____ Date _____

Email _____

Name _____

Title _____

Agency _____

Address _____

_____

Phone (___) _____ Date _____

Email _____

Contact was made by [ ] phone [ ] letter [ ] email [ ] in person [ ] other _____

Contact took place on (date) _____ at (time) _____AM/PM

   at (location) _____

Reason for contact _____

_____

Summary of what happened _____

_____

_____

Attach letters, longer summaries, media coverage, etc.

serious situation, you still have choices and can make decisions that will help the outcome of your difficulty be as satisfactory as possible. Here are some suggestions:

• Don't panic. Staying as calm as possible will improve your chances of working things out.

• Review key chapters in this book, including Chapter 29. The texts of many important laws are in Appendix A and interpretations of laws can be found by consulting the index.

• Make a written record of what has happened so far, if you have not already done so. Be as specific as possible about dates, names and titles of people involved, what they have said and what you have said, etc. The form titled "Record of Discussions Concerning Homeschooling" in this chapter can be copied and used and will give you ideas for what to write down.

• Ask for help from people you know, your WPA Regional Coordinator, and your support group, or email WPA or call the Voice Mail. It often helps to seek help as soon as you realize there is a problem rather than waiting or allowing threats, claims, or court dates to go unanswered or become pressing before preparing yourself and taking action.

• Don't expect to be able to simply turn your case over to attorneys or rely on them to be well prepared to defend you, especially if you have little or no money and must rely on court appointed attorneys. But even if you do have money to hire an attorney, be prepared to educate your attorney and help them plan how your case will proceed. Consider giving your attorney a copy of this book. See Chapter 23.

• In most cases, don't agree to have your children screened, tested, or evaluated. See Chapter 24 for problems with testing and the section on screening earlier in this chapter.

• Read the law yourself and think about possible solutions, even if you think you don't have time or wouldn't understand the law.

• Find character witnesses who can testify on behalf of you, your children, and your family, if necessary. Develop a local support system of people who agree with what you are trying to do.

• These more serious problems tend to have long histories of conflicts and often a good bit of emotion. Homeschooling is often not the real issue but only a convenient lightning rod. In such a situation, discussions about homeschooling are often not only a waste of time but also provide an opportunity for the other party to hear your arguments and build a case against you and your homeschooling.

Recording Contacts with Public Officials

Whatever the outcome of your contact with truant officers or other public officials, it is a good idea to make a record, using the form here (which can also be used for contacts with the media, etc.) or something similar. Readers may copy this form as needed. This documentation is important for several reasons. First, if the contact develops into a conflict, documentation will be important. Second, documentation will help others who are assisting you. (These may include friends, other homeschoolers, the media, your legislator, an attorney, etc.) Third, documentation lets the people who are contacting you know that they are dealing with someone who knows what rights people have under the law and who will be thorough in dealing with officials and agencies. This may deter officials who might otherwise try to take advantage of a situation without due cause, but it does not threaten officials who are on solid, professional footing.

How Truancy Laws Affect Homeschoolers

Truancy affects homeschoolers in several very different ways. Despite the differences, these ways are discussed together here because they all center around truancy issues. Following an overview and some general comments about truancy, the following situations are discussed in detail.

1. Individual homeschooling families can be charged with truancy.

1a. If a family is starting homeschooling and local school officials think the family has not complied with the law, including filing form PI-1206, they sometimes threaten to charge the family with truancy.

1b. Sometimes when children were so unhappy with school that they became truant, families decide to homeschool. (This can work well when the family is serious about taking on the responsibilities involved in homeschooling.) After they begin homeschooling, they can still be prosecuted for truancy that was allegedly committed before they began homeschooling. In other words, families can't escape truancy charges simply by beginning homeschooling.

1c. If a school truant officer has substantial evidence that a family is not complying with Wisconsin's homeschooling law, the officer can charge them with truancy. It is important to remember that the state must prove that the family is not complying. Consistent with the principle of "innocent until proven guilty," homeschoolers do not have to prove their innocence by demonstrating that they are complying.

2. Some truancy issues undermine the freedoms of all homeschoolers.

2a. Curfews threaten civil liberties and homeschoolers' ability to work and learn outside their homes during school hours.

2b. Truancy sweeps also threaten civil liberties and homeschoolers' ability to work and learn outside their homes during school hours.

2c. Legislation has been considered that would prohibit habitual truants from homeschooling. Such a law would undermine the freedoms of all homeschoolers.

3. Some homeschoolers serve on county truancy committees.

Background Information on Truancy

To deal effectively with all these concerns, it helps to have some background on truancy in general.

• Truancy laws tend to reflect our society's negative attitude toward young people and the legislation that has been passed as part of the war on crime. Some violate young people's civil liberties.

• Truancy may be caused by:

—Many different kinds of stress, from a variety of sources, that many families and children face today.

—An educational system that tries to force parents and children to comply with mandates rather than offering them choices and incentives.

—Lack of alternative educational programs that would allow students to make maximum use of their widely varying talents, abilities, and learning styles.

—Labeling students with demeaning terms and self-fulfilling prophecies indicating that they are "learning disabled" and require "special education," and then tracking them.

—Lack of parental participation in their children's education caused in part by the widespread but mistaken notion that professionals and institutions know better than parents do what children need and by the attitudes of many school personnel toward parents.

—Wisconsin statutes that force students to remain in school until age 18.

—The redefinition of truancy in strictly quantitative terms. According to a recent Wisconsin statute, a habitual truant is anyone who misses part or all of five days of school in a semester without an acceptable excuse. Some school districts count someone who is ten minutes late to class absent. Truants could include children who went on a five day trip with their family, or those who were sick or injured and unable to afford a doctor's visit to get an official and valid excuse. Until this law was passed, truancy was decreasing. After the law was passed, some districts reported a 300% increase in "truancy." This redefinition also makes it easier to prosecute truants.

—Other legislation eliminated the possibility of legally dropping out of school at age 16 with the agreement of parents and the local school board. Since students cannot earn a GED certificate or an HSED until they are 18 1/2 or until the class with which they entered ninth grade has graduated, there is no legal way to get out of school before a student turns 18 or graduates. Therefore, teens who refuse to attend school become truants.

• Forcing reluctant young people to attend school does not work. It make things more difficult for the school personnel and other students. Fines and denying truants drivers licenses or hunting licenses don't turn them into willing students, either. Do we really want to send teens or their parents to jail for truancy?

• Significant numbers of students who do well academically are also truant, reinforcing the point that schools may be a significant part of the reason for truancy.

• Approximately 85,000 Wisconsin students are reported to the DPI by school districts as "habitual truants" each year. However, very few are prosecuted for truancy, partly because prosecutors have more important cases to deal with and neither punishment nor trying to force kids to go to school works.

• One solution to truancy would be to offer young people constructive alternatives to school, such as on-the-job training, volunteer service programs, independent study, and college classes.

Specific Truancy Situations

1. Individual homeschooling families can be charged with truancy.

1a. If you are starting homeschooling and local school officials are threatening to charge you with truancy because your children are not attending school any more and the officials think you have not complied with the homeschooling law, read Chapter 2. If you are not in compliance, do what is required now. If you are in compliance, explain that to officials, perhaps showing them the appropriate pages in Chapters 2, 3, and 4. Or if you prefer, send a letter like the example in Chapter 4.

1b. If you are being charged with truancy because your children did not attend classes before you started homeschooling, read Chapter 2 and follow the instructions to make sure they are not still truant. Since truancy charges are seldom prosecuted, you have a reasonable chance of not being taken to court, especially if officials see that you know what the homeschooling law requires and are complying with it.

1c. If a truant officer is threatening to charge you with truancy because they claim that you are not complying with Wisconsin's homeschooling law:

• Don't panic. Take time to think. Remember that the state has to prove that you are not complying with the law. You do not have to prove you are innocent.

• Be polite.

• If the truant officer comes to your home, talk with them at the door. It is generally better not to invite the officer into your home, at least at first.

• Either on the phone or at the door, explain that you are busy teaching your children and that you know the law and are in full compliance. If the truant officer has further questions, ask them to write to you or make an appointment to talk with you at a convenient time. Whatever approach to homeschooling you are using, remember you do not have to prove that you are complying with the law. You do not have to show your curriculum, school calendar, or other materials. The only record you might have to show a truant officer is your attendance record. (See Chapter 10.)

If the truant officer insists on talking with you on the spot, you will have to decide what seems best to do. Among the alternatives:

• If you have done the preventive work outlined above and know you have at least some support (from the local school superintendent, for example) and perhaps even know the truant officer, it may be best in the long run to cooperate by inviting him or her in and showing your daily attendance records (which will demonstrate that you are complying with the compulsory school attendance law). Perhaps the truant officer is under pressure from other people and will be able to satisfy their concerns with this kind of cooperation from you. If the officer wants a copy of your attendance record and you are willing to cooperate, offer to make a copy yourself and send it; don't give them the original.

• As another alternative, if the truant officer seems somewhat less than friendly, you can refuse to talk and refuse to allow them in your home.

• If the officer is not satisfied with just seeing your attendance records, it may be very tempting to talk further about your homeschooling program. However, this approach should only be used as a last resort for several reasons.

—Sharing more information very seldom solves the problem. Often officials respond by making additional requests. Before the current homeschooling law was passed in 1984, some homeschoolers tried to gain approval of their homeschools from the DPI. They found the DPI difficult to deal with, arbitrary, and unreasonable. Often when they cooperated with the DPI's requests for more information, officials then demanded even more. See Chapters 19 and 20.

—Truant officers are usually looking for problems rather than successes. They have been trained to behave in a bureaucratic and legalistic manner. They often do not understand the law, parental rights in education, or the principles of due process. Curriculums different from those used in public schools tend to raise more questions in a truant officer's mind than they answer.

—Giving the truant officer more information sets a dangerous precedent. It is another example of the way in which we can diminish our rights and freedoms by doing more than the minimum that the law requires.

If you do decide that it is worth taking these risks and talking further with the truant officer, remember that legally you don't have to prove anything or gain approval. You are talking in a spirit of cooperation. It generally is better not to discuss areas that are not mentioned in the law. For example, if the truant officer asks about your educational background, you could refuse to discuss that. Don't be intimidated. Feel free to stick with an answer you want to give, no matter how many times you have to repeat it. Silence can also be effective if you don't want to discuss something.

You may want to record the conversation. Begin the recording by having everyone present identify themselves and acknowledge that a recording is being made. You may want to have a witness present, a neighbor, for example.

If the truant officer sends you a follow-up letter, respond but remember you don't have to give more information than the law requires. The law does not require a certified teacher, a curriculum equivalent to that used in the local public schools, school hours at any set time, or many other things that truant officers often expect because of their experience with public schools.

If an interview with the truant officer is set up, the above suggestions may be helpful.

See the example earlier in this chapter for the way one family dealt with the threat of truancy charges.

2. Truancy issues that undermine the freedoms of all homeschoolers
2a. Curfews

Daytime and nighttime curfews that prohibit young people from being in public places are sometimes proposed as ways of solving problems of truancy and juvenile crime. However, curfews undermine civil liberties, are difficult to enforce fairly, and promote submission of citizens to the power of the state. Therefore, people from every political persuasion oppose curfews.

2b. Truancy sweeps

Some communities have started truancy sweeps in which police take into custody young people who are not in a school building during regular school hours and do not appear to have a valid excuse for being out of school. Wisconsin's truancy statutes allow the use of these sweeps.

Truancy sweeps present homeschoolers with challenging, complex, and contradictory issues. The very idea of police taking children into custody simply because they are not in a specific building during school hours is an appalling demonstration of fundamental problems within our society. The idea of cooperating in any way with such actions may feel like too great a moral compromise. In addition, the specter of children undergoing the traumatic experience of being taken into custody is very troublesome.

If you are faced with the possibility of a truancy sweep, you have several options, all of which have drawbacks.

• Children can stay with their parents or other adults or in safe places during school hours, thereby minimizing their chances of being included in a truancy sweep. However, this limits children's independent learning opportunities during conventional school hours. And it implies acceptance of the loss of the freedom to choose where we will be during school hours, a freedom that should be ours and our children's.

• Some homeschooling families think carefully about where their children are during conventional school hours and tell neighbors, librarians, and others that they are homeschooling.

• Children can carry a copy of your completed PI-1206 form and present such evidence to any official who questions them, thereby hopefully avoiding the experience of being taken into custody. However, it is inconvenient for children to have to carry these papers. Much more serious, carrying papers implies we are willing to comply with requirements for registration and identification, and we risk losing important freedoms.

• Parents can help their children learn how to act in ways that do not attract negative attention or arouse suspicion and how to respond in ways that are likely to minimize difficulty if they are questioned by officials for not being in school. Often the best approach may be to answer questions directly and politely and offer a phone number at which a parent or another responsible adult can be reached to confirm the information supplied by the young person.

2c. Legislation that would prohibit habitual truants from homeschooling

Early in 1997, SB 106 was introduced to prohibit habitual truants from homeschooling. WPA strongly opposed this bill for several reasons, including the following:

• SB 106 was unnecessary. Wisconsin's homeschooling law has worked since 1984. Evidence has not been presented that truants are flocking to homeschooling and should be prevented from doing so. Under existing law, people who have been charged with truancy and who then begin homeschooling can still be prosecuted for previous truancy charges. Homeschoolers who do not comply with the requirements of the homeschooling law can be prosecuted. In addition, there is already a wide range of truancy laws.

• By giving the state the authority to determine who is eligible to homeschool, SB 106 would have seriously threatened homeschoolers' independence of the state educational bureaucracy. It does not make sense to undermine the thousands of homeschools that are working well in the hopes of keeping out a few families for whom homeschooling might not work well.

• SB 106 violated two fundamental principles of American jurisprudence that the homeschooling law is based on. One is parents' right to choose for their children an education consistent with their principles and beliefs. The second is "innocent until proven guilty." If homeschoolers do not comply with the law, they can be charged with truancy and prosecuted. To give the state the authority to determine who is eligible to homeschool would violate both these principles. It would give the state more authority than parents in determining how children should be educated.

Over 400 homeschoolers attended a legislative hearing on SB 106 on April 9, 1997. The bill died in committee.

3. County truancy committees

Legislation passed in 1988 and 1998 established county truancy committees, each of which is to include one homeschooling parent, to draw up a truancy plan and submit it to the school board. See Appendix A. These committees influence the policies that are adopted by their county and can make recommendations to the Legislature for new truancy legislation.

Here are some important points that homeschoolers and others can use in trying to develop reasonable truancy policies and in issuing minority reports when they disagree with statements issued by committees they are serving on.

• See the points made above.

• Schools play a role in why students are truant. This should be factored into determining both the causes of truancy and what can be done to prevent and deal with it.

• According to Wisconsin statutes, school districts may provide alternative programs for students who can demonstrate that they want and need one. (See Appendix A.)

• The Fourth Amendment to the US Constitution protects citizens from unlawful search and seizure. Truancy policies should be consistent with this civil liberty as well as the fundamental idea that people are innocent until proven guilty.

• Compulsory school attendance laws require attendance but not compulsory education. See Chapter 22.

• Students cannot legally be forced to homeschool.

• "Hard cases make bad law." Truancy policies designed to catch and punish a few serious offenders are much more likely to prevent good young people from being fairly treated than they are to solve serious hard-core truancy problems.

Send WPA information you get about your county's truancy committee and reports of your experiences if you get involved with your committee.

In sum, when dealing with truancy issues,

• Protect yourself from truancy charges by filing form PI-1206 with the DPI at the appropriate time. See Chapter 4.

• Oppose curfews and truancy sweeps because they unnecessarily limit freedom of movement and, more importantly, violate civil liberties of young people.

• If necessary, prepare your children for possible truancy sweeps. Talk with them. Consider having them carry a copy of your completed PI-1206 form.

• Oppose legislation that would prevent habitual truants from homeschooling because it sets a dangerous precedent of allowing government to decide who can homeschool. It is also unfair to young people in trouble.

• If you are the homeschooling representative on your county's truancy committee, get information from WPA, and issue minority reports when appropriate.

Chapter 32

Dealing with Public Schools

Solving Problems Through Effective Communication with Public School Officials

Most homeschoolers find homeschooling in their homes and communities works very well, and they don't want to be involved in conventional public schools. However, some homeschoolers choose to get involved, perhaps because they want shared services, because their children are entering or re-entering the public schools, or for other reasons. They often work easily and cooperatively with their local public schools. Here are some suggestions for developing good working relations with public schools, for homeschoolers who are interested in doing so.

• Do background research. Find out your local school's or school district's current policy on entry/re-entry, shared services, or whatever you are interested in. Be prepared to talk with several different people before you find someone who can answer your questions. Try to track the policy to its source. If it is a written policy, get a copy. If it is not written, find out as much as you can from the people responsible for enforcing it. If you are told that something is "required by law," get the number of the statute and a copy of the statute itself, from either the person you are talking with, your local library, or the Internet.

If you are working to change existing policy or if the problem you are working on is covered by statute, be sure to read and interpret these policies or statutes yourself. Often, people with the most at stake in an issue (in this case, you) have the clearest, most reasonable perspective, despite the commonly held notion that they aren't objective. Do not accept anyone else's interpretations, even if they are the basis for years of practice. Just because people are getting paid to interpret or enforce a policy doesn't mean they are right. One of our greatest strengths as homeschoolers is our experience with alternative perspectives and practices. Use your expertise in this area.

• Ask other homeschoolers to help you answer questions such as:

–What is your goal? What policy or outcome do you want?

–What factual evidence and supporting arguments can you use?

–In what ways would your proposal benefit the other party (such as the public school)? The more you can convince them that your proposal will benefit them, or solve problems for them, the better your chances.

• Present your proposal and supporting arguments. If you need the approval of a group, such as your school board, consider contacting individual members, beginning with the one you expect to be most supportive of your ideas, before asking to make a presentation to the whole group.

–Include in your presentation factual information that will help other people feel comfortable about homeschooling. Share positive articles. Be polite, reasonable, and as conventional as possible. Stick to the issue.

–If you reach an impasse before you reach an agreement, ask yourself and your adversary what other alternatives exist that might be acceptable. Don't be afraid to suggest new ideas that may at first seem impossible.

–Once a positive policy is in place, work to see that you and other homeschoolers act responsibly in accord with it.

Developing a good working relationship with your local school board can pay big dividends. An example is described in Mary Penn's article "Board nixes homeschool monitoring," which appeared in the *Sauk Prairie Star* on October 26, 1989. Ms. Penn reported on the discussion of a school board resolution "which would have enabled school district personnel to visit and evaluate local homeschooling situations."

Board member Tony DeGiovanni said, "Personally I do not think we need to take on that responsibility. I don't know how a person would evaluate a home school. If the state wants them to follow guidelines, I think that is their problem. I think we are ill prepared to measure what is going on in a home school."

Board member Walter Dickey said the philosophy of home schooling is not to educate so students can pass certain tests, so standardized testing could prove meaningless in a home schooling situation. "If the state feels it is a problem they should legislate it," Dickey said.

"If it is not a big problem, say four to five students go to the high school and are not at grade level, I think they should leave it alone," DeGiovanni said.

Val McAuliffe objected to what she sees as the "inflammatory" wording of the resolution. McAuliffe said any movement to regulate home schooling means the district has its own education problems to deal with.

The resolution died for lack of a motion.   [Reprinted with permission.]

Entry/Re-Entry into a Conventional School

Many public schools in Wisconsin use common sense and deal with the entry/re-entry of homeschoolers on an individual basis, without formal written policies. This approach has worked well, and homeschoolers who have used a variety of curriculums and approaches to learning have successfully entered public schools thanks in part to good communication among parents, students, teachers, principals, and/or superintendents.

However, entry/re-entry sometimes causes concern.

• Parents of homeschoolers who are considering entering or re-entering a conventional school want to be sure they are prepared and make a smooth transition.

• School officials who are critical or skeptical of homeschooling sometimes allude to problems homeschoolers may cause if they enter conventional schools. These concerns are vague and undocumented. There have been no significant problems, despite the fact that nearly 100,000 homeschooled students in Wisconsin have entered conventional schools since 1984.

• School districts sometimes pass entry policies that discriminate against homeschoolers by requiring that they meet requirements not placed on transfer students from other public and private schools. These requirements may include testing, a trial period, or a demonstration of social maturity. They have been judged discriminatory by attorneys working for local school districts, by an attorney working for the Wisconsin Association of School Boards, and by local school officials. For example, many of these requirements were included in a February 1986 proposed entry/re-entry policy in the Sparta school district. Homeschoolers in that district pointed out the discriminatory nature of the policy. A local newspaper reported:

> The [Sparta school] board requested a legal view of their proposal which [Ralph] Osborne [a Sparta attorney] presented at the March meeting. He said the policy could be considered discriminatory and was asked to prepare another policy for Tuesday's meeting. Osborne said the new policy treats all students equally. He added that he thinks it would meet any tests of constitutionality. To create the proposal, he consulted with an attorney of the Wisconsin School Board Association and studied the policies incorporated in other school systems. (*Monroe County Democrat*, April 24, 1986, page 2.)

Many parents whose children have entered school have found the following suggestions helpful:

• At least several months before your children will enter school, begin establishing a good working relationship with school personnel. Visit the school with your children, sit in on classes, and talk with teachers and the principal. Being familiar with the school is often reassuring to children, and you can ask about policies concerning records, credits, tests, and psychological counseling and screening. You can also request further information from the district superintendent and the school board. It is particularly important to find out how children's grade placement will be determined. Among the questions to ask: What criteria will be used? (Possibilities include age, test results, curriculum the student used while homeschooling, review of the children's records and credits, interviews of children and parents, assessment of social maturity.) Which criteria are most important and/or mandatory? Which could be waived or de-emphasized? Who makes the final decision?

• Are the criteria reasonable, non-discriminatory, and acceptable to you? If not, try to change them or have them waived. For suggestions, see below.

• Wisconsin law requires that public schools administer standardized tests to students who are attending public schools. (Parents of public school students can have them exempted from the state-mandated standardized fourth, eighth, tenth, and twelfth grade tests. See Appendix A for the text of s. 118.30[2][b]3) Although state law does not require that entering students take tests, some school districts require them. This is a discriminatory policy if it is not applied to all students; see below for more details. Some parents object to standardized tests for entering students and work hard to prevent their children from having to take them. (See Chapter 24 for information on standardized tests.) If tests are unavoidable, some parents arrange to have them administered in a setting in which their children are comfortable and stay with younger children. Sometimes the tests can be postponed until the children have been in school for several months. Many parents also find it beneficial to have their children practice taking sample tests of the same type from the same company as those they will take at school.

• Be careful about signing any authorizations or waivers, especially concerning psychological testing and screening. Some controversial tests cannot be administered without parental permission. It is important to find out exactly what tests will be administered, why, and what will be done with the results before signing away your rights and your children's.

• Many parents work hard to give their children extra support while they are adjusting to school. They communicate frequently with the teacher(s), are available to help with homework, and act as their children's advocates whenever necessary. Extra time and effort often pay big dividends in a smooth transition and good adjustment for their children.

The following questions are sometimes asked about entry/re-entry policies.

On what basis should homeschoolers evaluate proposed entry policies?

If homeschoolers cannot convince their local school board that a formal entry policy is unnecessary, they need to be sure that any policy that is adopted does not discriminate against homeschoolers. The only valid requirements for entry of homeschoolers are those which are also placed on other transfer students (whether from public or private schools) and for promotion of students from one grade to the next within the school. Examples of specific requirements which are sometimes placed exclusively on homeschoolers are:
• Achievement of a certain score or percentile on a standardized test in order to be placed in a specific grade.
• Completion of a probationary period during which former homeschoolers must prove themselves.
• Demonstration of social maturity, including a certain degree of socialization or appropriate interaction with one's peers.

What arguments can be used against discriminatory policies?

• There is no concrete evidence to justify discrimination against homeschoolers. Since 1984, nearly 100,000 former homeschoolers have entered or re-entered conventional schools without problems.
• The Wisconsin Constitution requires that public schools provide services for all children, and it states that children may not be denied on the basis of discriminatory practices.
• The Fourteenth Amendment of the U.S. Constitution guarantees equal treatment under law and protects citizens against discrimination. (See Chapter 22.)
• Such policies violate the principle of "innocent until proven guilty" by assuming there is something wrong with homeschoolers until they have proven otherwise. The policies also disregard due process.

Shared Services: When Homeschoolers Participate in Public Schools

The term "shared services" refers to situations in which students from other public school districts or from private schools, including homeschools, participate in classes or activities at a public school. WPA supports homeschoolers' right to shared services, even though the vast majority of homeschoolers do not want them.

Homeschoolers' right to shared services is founded on Article X (pronounced Article 10), Section 3 of the Wisconsin Constitution. It reads, "The legislature shall provide by law for the establishment of district schools, which shall be as nearly uniform as practicable; and such schools shall be free and without charge for tuition to all children between the ages of 4 and 20 years." There are no restrictions. Neither the statutes nor the Constitution says that students who want to receive shared services from a given public school must be full-time students in that or any other public school. Neither says that students can only have shared services if the public schools have enough money. Neither says that shared services are only available for students approved by the school district or the DPI. Neither says that homeschoolers do not qualify for shared services. Therefore, none of these is a valid reason for denying homeschoolers access to shared services.

On the basis of this constitutional guarantee, homeschoolers have participated in public school classes and activities. Homeschoolers who want shared services find it works well to begin with the general steps in "Problem Solving Through Effective Communication With Public School Officials" earlier in this chapter. Find out your local school's policy.

Taking courses in a public school (updated March 2015)

Homeschoolers who want to take courses in a public school can cite s. 118.53. (For the text of this statute, see page 273.) It states that school boards "shall allow" homeschoolers to take up to two courses each semester provided they meet the general standards for admission and "the minimum standards for admission" to a given course in grades kindergarten through 8 or, for high school courses, "if the school board determines that the pupil qualifies for admission to those courses." The requirement that "the pupil qualifies for admission" is generally understood to mean that they have to meet prerequisites for courses they want to take. In other words, they would not be allowed to take German II without German I or its equivalent. The law also says that the school board has to determine that "there is sufficient space in the classroom."

Receiving services from elementary and middle schools

According to the Question and Answer section of the DPI's website as of December 2012, *Can my child participate in extracurricular activities and clubs offered by the local public school?*

Other than the part-time attendance option described in Section III, school districts are not required to provide any services to homeschooled students nor to permit homeschooled students to participate in any school district activities. However, school districts are not prohibited from allowing participation by homeschooled students. You will need to contact your school district directly to inquire about its policies.

Receiving special education and related services from public schools

Some of the greatest need for shared services comes from families who want speech or other therapy for their children and have decided the therapy offered by the public schools would be helpful. Private therapy can be very expensive and too often is not covered by insurance.

Final decisions about shared services are made by local school districts, but the DPI advises them, and many districts follow the DPI's advice. Unfortunately, the DPI's website contains this information:

28. Is my school district required to provide special education and related services for my child while he/she is enrolled in a home-based private educational program?

No, school districts are not required to provide special education and related services to children with disabilities enrolled in home-based private educational programs.

However, since neither federal nor state law prohibits districts from providing special education services to home-schooled children, school districts may provide any special education and related services to these children that they deem appropriate. If a public school district chooses to provide these services, the costs are not aided by DPI under federal or state categorical aids.

Public school districts are required to provide the service of identifying and evaluating all children in the district who may have a disability. If a child is found to have a disability, the district must offer a placement that would provide the child a free appropriate public education. Generally, this placement means the child would be enrolled in a public school.

If you suspect that your child may have a disability, you can request that he/she be evaluated by the public school. The district will then perform a publicly-funded evaluation and, if your child is found to have a disability, offer your child a placement to meet his/her educational needs.

However, families who want shared services for special needs children can still request them from local school officials, supporting their request with the following information.

• Homeschools are private schools, so homeschoolers should have the same access to shared services that other private school students have. Unfortunately, the DPI claims that homeschools are not private schools. You may need to use the information in "What Wisconsin's Homeschooling Law Does" in Chapter 28 to try to convince officials that homeschools are , in fact, private schools.

• School officials should take seriously both Article X of the Wisconsin Constitution and their responsibility to make their own decisions about what is right, regardless of what the DPI advises them.

• School districts that want to be reimbursed for providing services to homeschoolers can get the money they are due by including homeschoolers in the district's annual plan for providing services to private school students. Because homeschools are private schools, as explained in the first point above, homeschoolers can be counted as private school students. Of course, if the district identifies the students as homeschoolers, or asks the DPI if it is all right to include homeschoolers as private school students, the DPI will most likely refuse. This is why it is important that the district realize that the DPI can only give advice, and the district has final responsibility for complying with the Wisconsin Constitution and the statutes.

Some families decide it is worth their effort to contact their school district, even though officials may not be very receptive and some can be unreasonable. Few are as vengeful as the district that ended the speech therapy they had been providing for a family's oldest child when she turned six and began homeschooling and also refused to provide therapy for their three year old because "you probably will homeschool her when she turns six."

WPA is opposed to working to get legislation requiring districts to offer shared services either to homeschoolers who want them from elementary or middle schools or those who want them for special needs children. Introducing legislation on shared services (or any other topic related to homeschooling) would raise the possibility of increased regulation of homeschooling. The Wisconsin Constitution and current statutes already allow shared services, as explained above. The problem is not that we don't have appropriate statutes. The problem is that the DPI and school officials do not follow them. Therefore, even if we were successful in getting a law passed, it would not necessarily prevent powerful agencies from disobeying it just as they are disobeying current statutes. In addition, the roadblock in getting services for special needs children is the DPI's refusal to acknowledge that homeschools are private schools, even though legislation passed in 1984 makes it clear that they are. Also see Chapter 23 for general information on avoiding legislation and court cases if at all possible.

Sports

A few homeschoolers occasionally ask whether they can play on public school sports teams. The question is not unreasonable; public school sports are important to some people. However, a complex set of reasons, including Wisconsin Interscholastic Athletic Association (WIAA) regulations, make it difficult and risky for homeschoolers to do this. Fortunately, homeschoolers can participate in sports in a number of other ways, some of which have significant advantages over public school sports.

First, consider high school sports. At present, high school sports are governed by the WIAA. WIAA rules limit participation in school sports to students who are enrolled full-time as defined by the DPI. (Even homeschoolers who took two courses under the shared services law discussed above would not qualify to participate in sports.) The question has been raised: Could WIAA rules be changed? However, a closer look reveals that WIAA rules are not the major factor that prevents homeschoolers from playing public school sports.

If homeschoolers played on public high school teams, they would undoubtedly be required to demonstrate their eligibility by taking tests, providing evidence of academic work they have done, etc. One reason is that all other team members are required to have a certain grade point average or in some other way prove they meet academic standards. Why

A Homeschooling Mother's Perspectives on Shared Services:

Public schools are required by statute to offer up to two courses per semester to home-schooled students in the 9th through 12th grades. Friends assume that I think that this is a wonderful opportunity. I do not agree.

Homeschooling is more than just a choice of location for learning. Homeschooling is family life. Homeschooling is learning all the time, in all places and under all conditions. Homeschooling is about family control of our family life.

Our experience with high school came several years ago when we had exchange students live as part of our family. We wanted to continue to have a close family life, but the institutional schedule the exchange students had to follow drove our family's schedule-when we woke and ate and slept, or when we had to be home from an outside activity to meet the one returning from school. We certainly could not leave town to visit the Smithsonian for a few weeks if school were in session. Everyone was affected by just one person involved in the school.

We chose to homeschool in the first place because we felt that we wanted our children to have more control over when, how or on what to spend time and effort learning. In school, tests are used to evaluate what was learned and then, mistakes or not, holes in understanding or not, the class moves on. In our homeschool, we can spend as much or as little time as needed to master any particular subject to our standards. Outside of school I have learned that success comes not from avoiding failure or getting it all right on the first try. I triumph from continuous, successive actions, picking myself up from mistakes and working onward.

The subjects taught in a high school are subjects that have been useful in some way to the larger society-and those subjects still exist in that larger society. Short conversations with a commercial artist give my son insight into his drawing, but he must draw to improve. A college student majoring in Spanish gives a homeschooler I know refinements to her accent, but she must use her Spanish to continue to improve. The high school physics lab may have a $400 air table to study friction, but only one day is scheduled for thirty students to use it; the oil and ice my youngest uses to examine friction is inexpensive enough to allow him to think about the process and play around with it until he can understand it thoroughly.

There might be some things which we cannot do, but there are so many more benefits to controlling our learning, it is no sacrifice to give them up. I do not intend to ever send my children to a conventional school.

should homeschoolers be an exception? Also, it would undoubtedly be argued that without such requirements for homeschoolers, athletes who did not meet the high school's academic standards could begin homeschooling as a way to get around the academic standards and continue playing.

In addition, it would probably be argued that some oversight of homeschooling athletes would be needed to prevent misuse of the situation. For example, a young person could homeschool for one year, claim that homeschooling had not worked out, and re-enter the public schools to repeat that grade. This would give them the advantage of being a year older and more mature than others in their grade. (This is not a far-fetched scheme. It happened in Fond du Lac, Wisconsin.)

The major problem for homeschoolers is that setting such a precedent for public school regulation of homeschoolers is very likely to lead to increased regulation of all homeschoolers. Once a mechanism has been established for determining whether homeschoolers meet the academic standards required for athletes, whether that is standardized testing or review and approval of curriculum and records or some other approach, there will be pressure to apply the same process to all homeschoolers. Some school officials and others want to increase state regulation of homeschoolers. Homeschoolers working through WPA have countered this pressure since 1984.

Backlash against homeschooling could result from homeschoolers playing on public school sports teams. There is a lot of competition for spots on teams. Some people would resent having kids who didn't even attend the school filling highly desired positions.

In several states, homeschoolers have made arrangements to play sports. However, homeschoolers in these states were already under much greater government regulation than we are in Wisconsin, so procedures were already in place for them to demonstrate their academic competence through review of their curriculum and in other ways. (See Chapter 21 for a comparison of homeschooling requirements in Wisconsin and other states.) In other words, homeschoolers in these states had already lost a great deal of the freedom that we in Wisconsin have. We have much more to lose than they did.

The situation is somewhat different for homeschoolers who want to play on public elementary or middle school teams. Most elementary and middle schools are not members of WIAA, although increasing numbers of middle schools are joining. Therefore, a few homeschoolers have made arrangements to play on elementary and middle school teams without having to comply with WIAA's rule that they meet the DPI's definition of a full-time student in that school and without having to prove to the school that they meet academic requirements for team participation.

However, even here homeschoolers need to be careful. A story from a Wisconsin family is not unusual. A fifth grader was invited to play on the local school's basketball team. The venture started well. But soon parents of other girls on the team began pressuring school officials who responded by requesting a report card as proof that the girl had the required grade point average. The family complied. Then officials requested copies of the family's curriculum and school calendar. The family refused.

Homeschoolers who are strongly committed to sports can develop their interest and skills in ways other than being on public school teams. Among the possibilities:

• Some communities have sports teams and programs homeschoolers can join. Where teams don't already exist, homeschoolers can participate in organizing them. The Amateur Athletic Union (AAU) provides a multi-sport program for all ages and organized athletic competition. It may be contacted at 407-934-7200 or http://aausports.org/.

• Some private schools will allow families to homeschool and pay a fee just to play sports.

• Playing sports in college without having played them in high school is another option.

• Homeschoolers can participate in sports camps.

• Homeschoolers can choose individual sports that do not require a team, such as running and swimming.

• To be sure, none of these alternatives is the same as strongly competitive high school team sports. If that is what is most important to homeschoolers, they can attend a public or conventional private high school and consider it part of the cost of playing sports. Homeschoolers and their families need to make their own decisions and balance the advantages and disadvantages. One drawback is that there are 50 million students in kindergarten through twelfth grade and only 8,500 professional athletes in all sports in this country.

Nonetheless, some people may argue that it is not fair to ask homeschoolers who really want to play high school sports not to pursue this option. One logical response is that homeschoolers who want to play sports can find other ways to do so, such as those mentioned above. But if the participation of a few homeschoolers in public school sports leads to increased government regulation of all homeschoolers, those who want to homeschool without unnecessary regulation would not be able to do so.

Therefore, WPA asks homeschoolers who may want to try to change WIAA regulations so they can play high school sports to think seriously about the cost to themselves, their families, and other homeschoolers in Wisconsin. Obviously, it is not easy to give up something that is very important, but as shown above, other alternatives exist. And many homeschoolers have made sacrifices to gain and maintain our homeschooling freedoms. We need to continue to make sacrifices, some of us more than others, to continue to maintain them.

Update on Sports — September 2015

In May 2015, a legislative provision to allow homeschoolers to play public school sports (and participate in extracurricular activities) was inserted into the Wisconsin Budget Bill by a vote of the Joint Committee on Finance within hours of the first public notice. No hearing was held. Despite strong efforts by homeschoolers working through WPA to remove the provision, including a petition signed by over 1,100 people within 10 days, the provision became law. For the text, see p. 273.

As WPA has forecast for the past 15 years, this statute leads to issues that affect all homeschoolers as the parties involved (the few homeschoolers who want to play public school sports, Wisconsin's 430 public school districts, and the WIAA) work out requirements for homeschoolers to play sports. The vast majority of homeschoolers who are unlikely to want their children to participate in public school sports still need to be aware of homeschoolers who are participating, how this is being received in their community, what they are being required to provide and demonstrate to qualify for sports, etc. The very few homeschoolers who want to participate in public school sports need to be very careful about how they respond to the requirements put forth by school districts and the WIAA.

Public School Records of Homeschooled Children

Parents who begin homeschooling after their children have attended a conventional school should get either the original set or at least a copy of their children's records, especially in light of recent legislation that has weakened provisions that protect the privacy of pupil records. In addition, collaboration among government agencies has increased the kinds of records that can be released to government agencies. Parents who obtain the original set of records are protecting their family's privacy and reducing the chances that information from their children's time in conventional schools will be transferred to other agencies and used against the family. Parents who obtain a copy of their children's pupil records at least know most of what is contained in the records and can take action to have inaccurate and unfair records corrected and to do as much as the law allows to protect their privacy and prevent the records from being released to individuals or agencies.

When requesting original pupil records or copies of them, it helps to understand that Wisconsin statute 118.125 defines several different categories of records, including behavioral records, directory data, progress records, and pupil physical health records. Some records are included in more than one category. See Appendix A for the text of this statute.

When a non-homeschooler is withdrawn from a public school, statutes require that the original set of pupil records be transferred within five days of a written notice from the school to which a student is transferring. See statutes 118.125(3) and 118.125(4) in Appendix A.

Local school boards are required to have rules and regulations concerning the maintenance and confidentiality of pupil records. Parents who want to get their children's records might find it helpful to get a copy of these from their school district to see how they could be used by the parents.

There appear to be two different ways that homeschooling parents can obtain pupil records. The first, simplest, and most straightforward is to write to the school superintendent as a parent and request a complete copy of your children's records. Requests from parents are supported by three provisions in the statutes:

118.125(2)(a) A pupil, or the parent or guardian of a minor pupil, shall, upon request, be shown and provided with a copy of the pupil's progress records.

118.125(2)(b) An adult pupil or the parent or guardian of a minor pupil shall, upon request, be shown, in the presence of a person qualified to explain and interpret the records, the pupil's behavioral records. Such pupil or parent or guardian shall, upon request, be provided with a copy of the behavioral records.

118.125(2)(e) Upon the written permission of an adult pupil, or the parent or guardian of a minor pupil, the school shall make available to the person named in the permission the pupil's progress records or such portions of the pupil's behavioral records as determined by the person authorizing the release. Law enforcement officers' records obtained under s. 48.396 (1) or 938.396 (1) or (1m) may not be made available under this paragraph unless specifically identified by the adult pupil or by the parent or guardian of a minor pupil in the written permission.

Copies of "directory data" records are not specifically provided for in the statutes, but given the language of the statutes, the intent is clearly that parents are to have copies of these records as well. What is not as clear is how and where the personal notes and records used for psychological treatment by certain teachers and school personnel are maintained, or how parents could obtain either the original set or copies. Due to recent amendments to this statute, it is also unclear what happens to health records. Furthermore, confidentiality of records is no longer protected unless parents take action and formally deny access to the records. Even then courts and agencies now have access to information that until recently parents could prevent from being released.

The second way homeschooling parents can obtain pupil records, and the way to get the original set of records (rather than getting a copy and leaving the originals with the school), is to write to the local school superintendent as the administrator of a home-based private educational program, including a copy of PI-1206 for the current school year. Request that the original and complete set of records be transferred to your home-based private educational program, since statute 118.165 defines such a program as a private school, and since your homeschool is now the school of record as shown on the enclosed PI-1206 form and you are the administrator.

The school district may be more willing to give you your children's original records if you request them in a formal letter you have signed as "Administrator." You could point out to the district that the law says they need to send the records within five days of receipt of your request.

School districts may hesitate to transfer original records to administrators of home-based private educational programs. Districts may claim that such administrators may not be qualified to interpret or use certain behavioral records. For these and/or other reasons, school districts may claim that they cannot transfer the original set of records to home-schools because they are not "schools." However, homeschools in Wisconsin are private schools. They are subject to the compulsory school attendance law and carry out the functions of a school. Therefore, administrators of these private schools have the right to request the original set of pupil records, and public and other private schools should provide them.

Public School Student ID Numbers

In response to federal legislation such as No Child Left Behind Act, the DPI has created a statewide system for assigning ID numbers to public school students and using them to collect, store, sort, and use more personal data about students than the state has ever collected before. Called the Wisconsin Student Number Locator System (WSLS), this system undermines privacy and freedoms by allowing government officials and others access to personal information about students and families. Because of collaboration statutes passed during the 1990s, the data can be shared with other government agencies such as public health departments, law enforcement agencies, the courts, social service agencies, etc. An innocent adult applying for a job that requires a background check, a motorist charged with a traffic violation, or a parent reported to social services by an anonymous person could all find information collected during their years in public school included in materials being used against them.

The DPI has assured WPA that homeschoolers should not be assigned public school student ID numbers, even if they take one or two courses in a public school. The DPI has also informed school districts that private school students, including homeschoolers, are not to be included in the database. It has posted on its website as one of the questions and answers dealing with the ID system the following: "Which students count as enrolled for WSLS purposes?" The DPI's answer: "A student is 'enrolled' in your district if the student receives his/her primary PK-12 educational services either (1) directly from district employees or (2) from a third party (not another Wisconsin district) under the direct supervision of your district." It is clear that since homeschoolers receive their primary PK-12 educational services from their homeschools and not from a public school district, they should not be included. However, because school officials are often misinformed or uninformed, we need to take responsibility for ensuring that our children are not wrongfully assigned a student ID number and included in the statewide ID system. It is easy to imagine a well-intentioned clerk who thinks that every student in the building should be in the system and therefore includes homeschoolers taking one or two courses or participating in a program sponsored by the district such as a summer recreation program.

If your children are involved in any public school courses or programs, during the process of registering them you can send a letter of understanding to the school district administrator with a copy to the principal or program director. Give the names of the children involved, explain that they should not be included in WSLS, and state that it is your understanding that they will not be. Request that the district notify you within 10 days if your children are already included.

If homeschooled children have already been assigned an ID number, perhaps because they attended a public school at some point or they were assigned one by mistake, it is important to get them out of the system. Email WPA or call the Voice Mail for suggestions.

Inform other homeschoolers, especially those taking public school courses or participating in public school activities. If homeschoolers are included in the statewide database, it will set a precedent and make it more difficult to maintain the current policy.

Parents of public school students can reduce damage from their inclusion in the database by formally notifying their school district in writing that none of the directory data for their children may be released. Such notification requires the school district to activate the No-Release Indicator in the WSLS. The WSLS should then restrict access to the student's directory data, but it will not totally prevent it from being released to certain people. For more information, contact the DPI official responsible for administering the WSLS and/or visit the DPI web pages dealing with WSLS.

Chapter 33

Protecting Your Family's Privacy

We strengthen our position as homeschoolers when we act in ways that protect our privacy. Developing the habit of not giving away information about our family pays big rewards, especially if many of us do it. We are not paranoid, and we don't have anything to hide. We simply want to maintain as much control as we can over our lives and our personal information.

Why Privacy Is Important

• The more people and institutions know about us, the more power they have over us. Privacy is especially important for homeschoolers because homeschooling itself is sometimes a red flag. The more red flags we have, the greater the chance we will be regarded with suspicion and/or investigated. Because of legislation on collaboration passed in the 1990s, government agencies (including law enforcement, social services, county health, and courts) can share much more information than was previously allowed, so all those flags could end up in one file.

• Our children's futures may be influenced by the information about them that is in databases.

• Prevention is much, much better than cure. Once you have released information, it is very difficult, if not impossible, to get it back.

• Computers sort, use, misuse, flag, and spread information at frightening speed. If any incorrect information about your family is entered in a database, it is very difficult to catch up with it and correct it.

• Protecting your privacy helps prevent identity theft. It also reduces annoying marketing calls and junk mail.

• As citizens of a democracy, we need to take responsibility for maintaining our freedoms and our privacy. When citizens do so, it helps keep the government in check.

Developing the Habit of Protecting Privacy

Developing the habit of refusing to give information, and teaching our children to do so, will make a big difference. Here are some suggestions.

• Be aware of the many ways information about your family is being collected through birth certificates, preschool and mental health screenings, social security numbers, medical records, drivers licenses, taxes, mortgages, credit cards, Internet use, etc.

• Ask the following questions before providing any information:

1. Is this information absolutely necessary? Some is legally required, like that on form PI-1206. Some is necessary for your own safety and well-being, like telling a doctor what medications you are taking. Some is simply on a form and is not required.

2. How will the information be used?

3. Is it likely to be spread or shared with companies and organizations?

4. Can I really trust the organization, institution, or business I'm giving the information to? It's not usually enough to trust the individual you are communicating with. They probably are just doing their job and don't have a real understanding of how the information will be used.

• Know your rights and exercise them. Refuse to give information that is not required. Otherwise, if people voluntarily give information, we don't even need laws to allow the government and other organizations to collect, store, sort, use, and misuse information about us and other families.

• Read privacy notices that banks, insurance companies, and other institutions are required by federal statute to send every year. If they offer a way you can restrict the information they share, do so.

• Have only the minimum information printed on personal checks. Do not include your phone number, social security number, drivers license number, or other information.

• Ask unwanted telemarketers to put you on their "do not call" list.

• Tell your federal and state legislators that you oppose legislation that allows the government and/or other institutions access to people's private information and that you favor legislation that protects privacy.

• Don't just say, "What's the point? They could get my address, phone number, or whatever other information is being requested from the Internet or some other source." If you don't give them the information, they will have to work to get it, which they may not bother to do. You also send the message that privacy is important.

• Carefully dispose of papers that have private information.

Specific Ways to Protect Our Privacy

Newborns

A mother in Wisconsin who is getting a birth certificate and social security number for her newborn is asked for personal information about herself and her husband, including things like their social security numbers, employment a year before the birth, the highest grade each of them completed in school, the month that the mother's prenatal care began, cigarette and alcohol use, weight gain or loss during pregnancy, etc. This information is certainly not needed to record a birth or issue a social security number for the baby. The fact that it is asked for just after a birth makes it easier to collect-what new parent feels like worrying about a form at such a special time?

WPA recommends that new parents ask which questions are required and which are optional and refuse to answer the optional ones.

Immunization Records

We can have information about members of our family removed from the Wisconsin Immunization Registry (WIR). The WIR can be accessed by health professionals, insurance companies, schools, hospitals and clinics, and state and county agencies dealing with health and human services. To have records removed, file a separate Wisconsin Immunization Registry Exclusion form (HCF 5102) for each person. To request forms, write to the

Wisconsin Immunization Program, 1 W. Wilson, P. O. Box 2659, Madison, WI 53701-2659. Parents who do not want their children's records included in WIR in the first place can indicate this when they provide information for their children's birth certificates.

Screenings

Preschool screenings, informal mental health screenings by professionals, and other screenings give the government a lot of information about our families. Parents are not legally required to take their children to preschool screenings, even though the letters that announce such events often say they are "required by law." (School districts are required by law to provide screenings; families are not required to have their children screened.) We can avoid them by refusing to participate. More difficult to avoid are informal mental health screenings by health care providers and others. Often they do not announce that they are screening us. It is worth our while to be alert for such screenings and to refuse to answer the questions. See "Screenings" in Chapter 31.

Social Security Numbers

Be especially careful with social security numbers, given their importance and the amount of information that is connected to them. Unless you have very good reason, do **not** give a social security number for anyone in your family to anyone except an employer for whom you are working, a financial institution from whom you will be getting interest which may be taxable (which means your social security number is required by statute), or, if you want a drivers license, the Department of Motor Vehicles. (Wisconsin statutes require that people getting drivers licenses give their social security number or sign a form stating they are withholding it for religious reasons.) Do not put your social security number on a job application, even if there's a blank for it or a clerk asks you for it. Do not have it printed on your checks. (If it's on checks you don't want to waste, cross the number out before using the checks.) Do not use it as a student ID number. (Many institutions request it because it's an easy way to keep track of you. However, if you explain that you don't want it used that way, they will usually assign or let you choose an alternative number.)

Drivers Licenses The Wisconsin Department of Motor Vehicles (DMV) releases personal information about licensed drivers. For $250, anyone can purchase a computerized file with the names and other personal information about the four million licensed drivers in Wisconsin (except those who have opted out of the database). To opt out, file form MV 3592 at DMV locations or at http://www.dot.wisconsin.gov/drivers/optout.htm

Conventional School Records

If your children have attended a conventional school and are now homeschooling, it's a good idea to get the originals of their school records or at least copies of them, especially if there were problems. Negative school records can follow children into adulthood. See "Public School Records of Homeschooled Children" in Chapter 32.

Public School Student ID Numbers

See "Public School Student ID Numbers" in Chapter 32.

Family Educational Rights and Privacy Act

Our right to privacy is protected by the federal Family Educational Rights and Privacy Act (FERPA). This act is the basis for the DPI's appropriate policy, which is described in the homeschooling portion of its website.

31. Will the Department of Public Instruction release my name and address to outside organizations or individuals?

Consistent with the state's pupil records law and its policies, the Family Educational Rights and Privacy Act (FERPA) and the open records law, the Department of Public Instruction does not release the names of families who have enrolled their children in homeschool programs.

Homeschoolers can use FERPA to object to the release of the names of homeschooling families by their local school districts and other similar actions. The code reference for the statute is Title 20, Chapter 31, Subchapter III, Part 4, Section 1232g. See Appendix A for the text.

Department of Defense Database and Military Recruitment

The Department of Defense announced in May 2005 that it was creating a database of young people ages 16-25 for military recruiting and other "routine" purposes. Many homeschoolers do not want to be included. They prefer to contact the military themselves if they are interested. If you want, you can try to stay out of the database by writing a letter to your local school district explaining that they do not have the authority to release contact information about homeschoolers and you do not want them to release any information about you that they might have.

If you are already in the database, you can contact Joint Advertising and Marketing Research & Studies (JAMRS), the company that manages it, and ask to "opt out," which means requesting that your data not be released. (It will be moved to a "suppression file;" it will not be deleted from the database.) However, this presents a dilemma. If you are not already in the database, you will be providing more information than the database managers already have. WPA has been unable to find an effective way to determine whether someone is in the database, although people who are being contacted by military recruiters probably are. When a young person turns 18, they are required to register and therefore information about them is probably in the database. Requesting suppression, however, is still possible.

For more information, including sample letters and forms that can be sent to your local school district and JAMRS, do an Internet search for "JAMRS military recruitment opt-out."

Telemarketers

To prevent telemarketers from contacting you, contact Wisconsin's No Call List at 866-966-2255 or complete a form at https://nocall.wisconsin.gov/web/home.asp Contact the National Do Not Call Registry at 888-382-1222 or https://www.donotcall.gov/.

Companies That Market to Homeschoolers

The DPI appropriately refuses to release the names of homeschoolers who have filed form PI-1206 to colleges and universities, the media, marketers, and other. (See "Family Educational Rights and Privacy Act" above.)

Companies like Tri-Media Online (http://www.trimediaonline.com/products/home-school-families-list) collect lists of homeschoolers and their contact information to sell to marketers and others. These companies often gain access to homeschoolers' names, addresses, phone numbers, email addresses, and other data by various means, including homeschoolers' online purchases, trial downloads of products, responses to offers to be put on lists that provide information, etc. Sometimes it pays to contact these companies directly. For example, call Tri-Media (1-800-874-4062 extension 110) to find out if they have your name and/or to have your name deleted or, better yet, made inactive, since deleting will not guarantee your name will not be re-entered when you make another purchase.

Privacy Resources

For comprehensive information about privacy, your rights, laws, and effective measures to take to protect your privacy, contact Privacy Rights Clearinghouse at https://www.privacyrights.org/ or Electronic Privacy Information Center (EPIC) http://epic.org/

Chapter 34

Current Developments That Affect Homeschoolers

Note: For more recent information about the topics in this chapter, see WPA newsletters and the WPA website at www.homeschooling-wpa.org.

Developments occurring outside homeschooling affect homeschoolers. Some are discussed here so that we homeschoolers can better understand changes that are happening and act in ways that will minimize the negative effects they have on us. Sometimes we can have a significant effect on what is happening. More often, unfortunately, the changes are too large and powerful and beyond our control. Then our best response is to work to maintain the rights and freedoms we have, perhaps also trying to secure exemptions from laws and regulations so that parents and families will still have as much choice as possible. It sometimes seems that the magnitude of these changes and the swiftness with which they are occurring make it more important than ever that we continue to homeschool and work to maintain our homeschooling rights and freedoms, which offer us a way to make our own decisions, maintain greater control over our lives, and live according to our principles and beliefs.

Increases in State-Mandated Testing and Assessment

Use of state-mandated standardized tests is increasing, partly because federal education legislation, including No Child Left Behind, requires that schools test students to qualify for federal funds.

Among the problems with federal testing of students:

• Standardized tests are biased and unfair. They do not measure what a person knows; they only measure how a person performed on a particular test on a given day. They are unfair to minorities, women, and anyone whose values, beliefs, and experiences differ from those of the test makers. They do not measure or give test takers credit for physical skills, mechanical ability, creativity, integrity, etc. Creative thinkers and people who know a lot about a subject often have more difficulty because they see the complexities of supposedly simple questions.

• Tests dictate curriculum and how subjects are covered. To prepare students, schools need to teach what is on the tests. This means that tests required by the federal government will lead to federal control of the curriculum in schools throughout the country. Federal testing of homeschoolers would force homeschools to become more like the conventional schools many of us have chosen to avoid by homeschooling.

• Federal testing erodes local control of education and the role of local school boards, communities, and individual states in education. It moves the US toward federal control of education, something that is inconsistent with freedom of education.

• Compulsory attendance laws require attendance, not education. This distinction is crucial. If the government were to require compulsory education, we would lose our freedom of education and learning. Testing required by either the federal or state governments increases the government's role in education and moves us closer to compulsory education because tests dictate what students must learn.

• Testing required by the federal government represents a major increase in federal control of education. According to the US Constitution, the states, not the federal government, have the policing authority to make laws that govern schools. But through No Child Left Behind and other legislation, the federal government is claiming it has the authority to require testing to ensure that students in schools that accept money from the federal government meet federal standards and goals.

• The bipartisan support for and lack of opposition to federal testing requirements indicate that the general public either supports testing or does not care enough to oppose it. It is unsettling, to say the least, to observe the readiness with which people are sitting by while the federal government plays an increasing role in education.

In Wisconsin, as in other states, state-mandated tests are now required of public school students in the fourth, eighth, and tenth grades plus a twelfth grade graduation test. Such tests have a strong effect on children's futures and give the state increased power and authority over education. Fortunately, parents worked hard through WPA to have included in the legislation a provision that allows all parents to have their children exempted from these tests. See Chapter 29.

Vouchers and School Choice Programs

At first glance, a voucher system may appear to offer advantages: some of the money that would normally be spent on public schools would instead be transferred to qualifying private schools chosen by parents. (However, students would be required to take state-mandated tests, and religious-based curriculums would not be covered.) Some parents may be pleased with the idea of the government paying for private school tuition. However, in reality it is clear that vouchers would not be allowed to be used for homeschooling unless the government had strong control over homeschools, unless strong regulations were strictly enforced, and unless homeschoolers could prove that their children were getting an equivalent education. Therefore, many homeschoolers conclude that the only way we could participate in a voucher system would be to pay for it with our freedom and oppose submitting to further regulation in exchange for vouchers.

Virtual Charter Schools

See Chapter 24.

Collaboration

Legislation has increased collaboration among government agencies, allowing them to exchange confidential information and records. This undermines the privacy of individuals and families. It also may cause officials to be prejudiced against families who are already on record with other agencies for doing things that the officials consider to be questionable, like homeschooling. WPA recommends that families try to minimize the records that are kept on them. For example, when parents do not take their children to preschool screening, they prevent the establishment of a record with screening and test results. See "Screening" in Chapter 31 and "Privacy" in Chapter 33.

Legislation Supposedly Designed to Protect Parental Rights

In recent years, legislation has been introduced in the US Congress and many state legislatures in a misguided attempt to protect parental rights and responsibilities in education, health care, religion, and other areas. To be sure, parental rights and responsibilities need to be maintained, especially in light of recent attempts to protect children by increasing the power and authority of the government, particularly in the areas of education and social services. However, either state or federal legislation to protect parental rights is a serious mistake that will not only fail to protect our rights but will also cost parents and families an enormous amount of freedom and contribute to the current erosion of the legal, social, and moral position of families in our society.

Parental rights and responsibilities in education are basic and fundamental and come from nature or God, not from the government. If we allow the government to pass a law or a constitutional amendment which gives it authority in education, we will be diminishing the rights we have independent of the state and increasing the control the state has over our children's education.

One of the important lessons from these initiatives is that it is virtually impossible to write a law that protects parental rights in areas that are considered fundamental, such as education and health care, without first passing laws that require parents to take responsibility for their children. (To be sure, parents are responsible for their children. However, they do not want or need to have the government grant this responsibility to them and then check to make sure they are doing the right thing.)

Even more serious, if the government passed legislation that required parents to assume responsibility for their children, parents would have to demonstrate to the government that they were being responsible by acting in ways that were consistent with the beliefs, standards, and choices of those people who have the most power in our society. Therefore, the government would decide what kind of education and health care would be required, how families would be monitored to ensure that they were complying with the law, and how they would be dealt with if a government official decided that they were not complying. These legislative initiatives, supposedly designed to protect parental rights, actually diminish basic freedoms that are the foundations of a democratic society.

Increases in Programs Targeted at Children from Birth to Three

Child development specialists, social workers, medical personnel, and professional educators are focusing increased attention on children from birth to age three. Some of these so-called "experts" are well-intentioned, but many are influenced by the fact that their prestige, careers, job security, and salaries all benefit from the increased emphasis. Government involvement in this area is also increasing. One prime example is the federal Individuals with Disabilities Education Act (IDEA). Part C of this program covers "Early Intervention Program for Infants and Toddlers With Disabilities." The program is designed to find and treat children from birth on who

(1) Are experiencing developmental delays . . .in one or more of the following areas: (i) Cognitive development, (ii) Physical development, including vision and hearing, (iii) Communication development, (iv) Social or emotional development, (v) Adaptive development; or (2) Have a diagnosed physical or mental condition that has a high probability of resulting in developmental delay. (b) The term may also include, at a State's discretion, children from birth through age two who are at risk of having substantial developmental delays if early intervention services are not provided.

These criteria would give the state grounds for intervening in just about any family with young children. Among the people who are to report suspected problems are parents and families; medical personnel (including those attending births); and employees of social service agencies, mental health programs, WIC, day care centers, preschools, Head Start, and public school programs.

In addition, government records would be established for children identified under such programs. Since collaboration increases the exchange of information among government agencies, once a file is established on children in a family, the chances increase that the file will be expanded with other information about the family.

These programs could cause problems for families that have young children and are considering homeschooling, including the following:

• The programs undermine families by decreasing parents' confidence. The programs often take so-called problems that don't really exist, that are really a normal part of development for many children who outgrow them if given time and support, and turn them into self-fulfilling prophecies. In addition, they increase the power and authority of the state and professionals in families' lives by increasing the extent to which they are taking over the traditional roles of the family.

• If children are diagnosed as having disabilities or labeled as being at risk, officials may pressure parents not to homeschool, claiming that these children need expert help that is available only through specialists and conventional schools. Of course, many families have shown that such children certainly can be homeschooled. In fact, they often learn better at home than in conventional schools. See Chapter 9.

WPA recommends that families be alert for ways in which they could get drawn into such programs and seriously consider not having their children screened or tested unless there is a very clear need. For more information, see "Screening" in Chapter 31.

What We Can Do To Counter These Developments

• Be informed. We need to choose our sources of information carefully. The mainstream media reports and reflects the views of the government, professional interest groups, and big corporations. Therefore, much of the information we receive from mainstream radio, television, newspapers, and magazines is strongly biased in favor of the very developments we oppose and is unlikely to be helpful to us. Many people prefer to get their information from independent sources such as the WPA newsletter.

• Share our concerns with others. We need to help as many people as possible understand what is happening and decide what they want to do in response to the direction in which our society is moving.

• Act in ways that support and communicate to others what we believe. We can refuse to have our children tested at preschool screenings or in other situations.

• Act in ways that will maintain our rights and responsibilities. See Chapters 20 and 21.

• Continue to homeschool. By homeschooling we are living according to our principles, maintaining strong families, strengthening an important educational alternative, living meaningful lives, and preparing our children and ourselves for the future.

Conclusion:

Strengthening Homeschooling

Among the ways you can strengthen both your own homeschool and the homeschooling movement are the following.

• Relax and enjoy learning with your family.

• Find approaches to learning that work well for everyone in your family and encourage family members to develop their strengths, talents, and special interests.

• Make connections with other homeschoolers.

• Make sure your own house is in order. Comply with Wisconsin law, including filing form PI-1206 online. Act in ways that reflect positively on homeschooling.

• Know your rights and responsibilities under the law. Understand the basic foundations of homeschooling freedoms, including the difference between compulsory school attendance and compulsory education.

• Comply with only the minimum requirements of the law. Don't set dangerous precedents by agreeing to officials' requests that are not required by law.

• Resist the temptation to use personal credentials ("I'm a certified teacher") or status ("I'm recognized as an exemplary homeschooler"), even to get out of difficult situations with school officials, reporters, and others. Using credentials or status may make it difficult for other homeschoolers who do not have the same credentials or status, which are not necessary for homeschooling anyway.

• Join with other homeschoolers in WPA, an inclusive, statewide, grassroots homeschooling organization that encourages all homeschoolers to work together to protect the right of every family to choose for their children an education consistent with their principles and beliefs. Send information to WPA on developments in your local community and on your experiences both homeschooling your children and working to maintain rights and responsibilities. Support WPA with your participation, membership, and donations. Attend the WPA conference. Encourage other homeschoolers to join.

• Respect diversity among homeschoolers.

• Help new homeschoolers and people considering homeschooling get accurate information so they can comply with the law and act in ways that will help maintain our rights and responsibilities. Encourage them to get a copy of this book.

• Get to know your legislators. It is important that legislators get to know homeschoolers as individuals and families, not just names and statistics. The outstanding work we do in educating our children and our commitment to homeschooling are best communicated through personal contact. Legislators who know homeschoolers as individuals are less likely to view homeschoolers merely as a political faction.

• Take responsibility for developments in your local community and the state. Don't assume that someone else is going to identify and solve problems. Each of us needs to be alert to what is happening that affects or could affect homeschooling at the community and state level. WPA learns of important events from individual homeschoolers, not through a top-down chain of command. Establish and use communication channels, including WPA Regional Coordinators, to help us all be informed.

• Avoid acting hastily on your own. Before making a move, particularly on an important issue, discuss your concerns and proposed strategy with other homeschoolers, including your WPA Regional Coordinator. Without this kind of communication, we could easily make serious mistakes or work at cross-purposes, threatening each other's effectiveness.

• Promote a positive image of homeschooling through newspaper articles, letters to the editor, calls to radio talk shows, etc. Telling our stories is also an important part of gaining support for homeschooling.

• Accentuate the positive. Celebrate your family and who your children are and what they do.

Appendix A
Laws Relating to Homeschooling in Wisconsin

DESCRIPTION	STATUTE HEADER	STAT. #	PAGE
Homeschooling law*	Wisconsin Act 512 1983	Various	266
Compulsory school attendance	Compulsory school attendance	118.15	270
2009 Kindergarten law	Five-year-old kindergarten	118.15(1)(am)	270
Homeschooling law*	Private schools	118.165	271
	Private school determination by state superintendent	118.167	271
	Definitions	115.001(3g)	271
	Definitions	115.001(3r)	271
	Attendance	118.15(4)	271
Age of pupils	Age of pupils	118.14	270
Immunization	Immunization	252.04	272
Open records law (freedom of information)	Public records and property	19.21--19.35	268
Courses in public schools	Admission to high school	118.145	270
Public school ID system	Pupil identification numbers	118.169	271
Public school assessment and exemption	Pupil assessment	118.30	271
Public school graduation	Public school graduation standards criteria for promotion	118.33	271
School census	Annual school district report	120.18	271
Student discrimination	Pupil discrimination prohibited	118.13	269
Student records	Pupil records	118.125	268
Wisconsin State Constitution	Article X. Education	Article X	272
Homeschoolers in military	Military enlistment statute (US)	Sec. 532	273
Taking courses in public schools	Attendance by pupils	118.53	273
Playing public school sports	Participation in interscholastic athletics & extracurricular activities	118.133	273

*Wisconsin's homeschooling law, 1983 Act 512 appears on pages 266-267. When put into statute form, it became s.118.165, s.118.167, s.115.001 (3g), s.115.001 (3r), and s.118.15(4).

NOTES:
(1) Selected parts of the statutes are printed on the following pages.
(2) The Wisconsin statutes included here are up to date as of April, 2013. Many statutes are revised each year. Major changes in these and related statutes will be reported in WPA newsletters. (Actually, important proposed changes will be discussed there before they become law.) If you need to be sure that you have the most recent version of the statutes, get a current copy from the Internet.
(3) The sections of the law that relate most directly to the content of this book are printed in a larger type. Also, bold type was added for emphasis.

1983 Wisconsin Act   **512**

AN ACT *to repeal* 118.255 (1) (am) and 121.51 (3); *to amend* 115.30 (3) and 118.15 (1) (a); *to repeal and recreate* 118.15 (4); and *to create* 115.01 (1g) and (1r) and 118.165 of the statutes, *relating to* establishing criteria for defining private schools and home-based private educational programs.

The people of the state of Wisconsin, represented in senate and assembly, do enact as follows:

SECTION 1.   115.01 (1g) and (1r) of the statutes are created to read:

115.01 (1g)   PRIVATE SCHOOL. "Private school" means an institution with a private educational program that meets all of the criteria under s. 118.165 (1) or is determined to be a private school by the state superintendent under s. 118.167.

(1r)   HOME-BASED PRIVATE EDUCATIONAL PROGRAM. "Home-based private educational program" means a program of educational instruction provided to a child by the child's parent or guardian or by a person designated by the parent or guardian. An instructional program provided to more than one family unit does not constitute a home-based private educational program.

SECTION 2.   115.30 (3) of the statutes is amended to read:

115.30 (3)   On or before each October 15, each administrator of a public or private school system or a home-based private educational program shall submit, on forms provided by the department, a statement of the enrollment on the 3rd Friday of September in the elementary and high school grades under his or her jurisdiction to the department which shall prepare such reports as will enable the public and private schools and home-based private educational programs to make projections regarding school buildings, teacher supply and funds required. The administrator of each private school system and home-based private educational program shall indicate in his or her report whether the system or program meets all of the criteria under s. 118.165 (1).

SECTION 3.   118.15 (1) (a) of the statutes is amended to read:

118.15 (1) (a)   Except as provided under pars. (b) and (c) to (d) and sub. (4), unless the child is excused under sub. (3) or (4) or has graduated from high school, any person having under control a child who is between the ages of 6 and 18 years shall cause the child to attend school regularly during the full period and hours, religious holidays excepted, that the public or private school in which the child should be enrolled is in session until the end of the school term, quarter or semester of the school year in which the child becomes 18 years of age.

SECTION 4.   118.15 (4) of the statutes is repealed and recreated to read:

118.15 (4)   Instruction in a home-based private educational program that meets all of the criteria under s. 118.165 (1) may be substituted for attendance at a public or private school.

SECTION 5.   118.165 of the statutes is created to read:

118.165 Private schools. (1) An institution is a private school if its educational program meets all of the following criteria:

(a)   The primary purpose of the program is to provide private or religious-based education.

(b) The program is privately controlled.

(c) The program provides at least 875 hours of instruction each school year.

(d) The program provides a sequentially progressive curriculum of fundamental instruction in reading, language arts, mathematics, social studies, science and health. This subsection does not require the program to include in its curriculum any concept, topic or practice in conflict with the program's religious doctrines or to exclude from its curriculum any concept, topic or practice consistent with the program's religious doctrines.

(e) The program is not operated or instituted for the purpose of avoiding or circumventing the compulsory school attendance requirement under s. 118.15 (1) (a).

(f) The pupils in the institution's educational program, in the ordinary course of events, return annually to the homes of their parents or guardians for not less than 2 months of summer vacation, or the institution is licensed as a child caring institution under s. 48.60 (1).

(2) An institution may request the state superintendent to approve the institution's educational program as a private school. The state superintendent shall base his or her approval solely on the criteria under sub. (1).

SECTION 5m. 118.167 of the statutes is created to read:

118.167 Private school determination by state superintendent. If an association that regulates or accredits private educational institutions in this state submits an affidavit to the state superintendent attesting that the institution meets or exceeds all of the criteria under s. 118.165 and the state superintendent finds that the institution does meet or exceed all of the criteria under s. 118.165, the state superintendent shall determine that the institution is a private school. If at any time the state superintendent finds that an institution determined to be a private school under this section no longer meets the criteria under s. 118.165, he or she may withdraw the determination.

SECTION 6. 118.255 (1) (am) of the statutes is repealed.

SECTION 7. 121.51 (3) of the statutes is repealed.

SECTION 8. **Cross-reference changes.** In the sections of the statutes listed in Column A, the cross-references shown in Column B are changed to the cross-references shown in Column C:

(1) PRIVATE SCHOOL DETERMINATION.

A	B	C
Statute Sections	Old Cross-References	New Cross-References
115.34 (2)	s. 121.51 (3)	s. 115.01 (1g)
340.01 (56)(a) 1	s. 115.01 (2) or s. 121.51 (3)	s. 115.01 (2)

PUBLIC RECORDS AND PROPERTY [Note: See Wisconsin Statutes 19.21–35.]

118.125 Pupil records.
(1) DEFINITIONS. In this section:
(a) "Behavioral records" means those pupil records that include psychological tests, personality evaluations, records of conversations, any written statement relating specifically to an individual pupil's behavior, tests relating specifically to achievement or measurement of ability, the pupil's physical health records other than his or her immunization records or any lead screening records required under s. 254.162, law enforcement officers' records obtained under s. 48.396 (1) or 938.396 (1) (b) 2. or (c) 3., and any other pupil records that are not progress records.
(b) "Directory data" means those pupil records which include the pupil's name, address, telephone listing, date and place of birth, major field of study, participation in officially recognized activities and sports, weight and height of members of athletic teams, dates of attendance, photographs, degrees and awards received and the name of the school most recently previously attended by the pupil.
(be) "Law enforcement agency" has the meaning given in s. 165.83 (1) (b).
(bL) **"Law enforcement unit"** means any individual, office, department, division, or other component of a school district that is authorized or designated by the school board to do any of the following:
1. Enforce any law or ordinance, or refer to the appropriate authorities a matter for enforcement of any law or ordinance, against any person other than the school district.
2. Maintain the physical security and safety of a public school.
(bs) "Law enforcement unit records" means records maintained by a law enforcement unit that were created by that law enforcement unit for the purpose of law enforcement.
(c) "Progress records" means those pupil records which include the pupil's grades, a statement of the courses the pupil has taken, the pupil's attendance record, the pupil's immunization records, any lead screening records required under s. 254.162 and records of the pupil's school extracurricular activities.
(cm) **"Pupil physical health records"** means those pupil records that include basic health information about a pupil, including the pupil's immunization records, an emergency medical card, a log of first aid and medicine administered to the pupil, an athletic permit card, a record concerning the pupil's ability to participate in an education program, any lead screening records required under s. 254.162, the results of any routine screening test, such as for hearing, vision or scoliosis, and any follow-up to such test, and any other basic health information, as determined by the state superintendent.
(d) "Pupil records" means all records relating to individual pupils maintained by a school but does not include any of the following:
1. Notes or records maintained for personal use by a teacher or other person who is required by the state superintendent under s. 115.28 (7) to hold a certificate, license, or permit if such records and notes are not available to others.
2. Records necessary for, and available only to persons involved in, the psychological treatment of a pupil.
3. Law enforcement unit records.
(e) "Record" means any material on which written, drawn, printed, spoken, visual, or electromagnetic information is recorded or preserved, regardless of physical form or characteristics.
(2) Confidentiality and disclosure of pupil records. All pupil records maintained by a public school shall be confidential, except as provided in pars. (a) to (p) and sub. (2m). The school board shall adopt policies to maintain the confidentiality of such records and may adopt policies to promote the disclosure of pupil records and information permitted by law for purposes of school safety.
(a) A pupil, or the parent or guardian of a minor pupil, shall, upon request, be shown and provided with a copy of the pupil's progress records.
(b) An adult pupil or the parent or guardian of a minor pupil shall, upon request, be shown, in the presence of a person qualified to explain and interpret the records, the pupil's behavioral records. Such pupil or parent or guardian shall, upon request, be provided with a copy of the behavioral records.

[Note: See Wisconsin Statutes for (2) (c)–(cm).]
(d) Pupil records shall be made available to persons employed by the school district which the pupil attends who are required by the department under s. 115.28 (7) to hold a license, law enforcement officers who are individually designated by the school board and assigned to the school district, and other school district officials who have been determined by the school board to have legitimate educational interests, including safety interests, in the pupil records. Law enforcement officers' records obtained under s. 938.396 (1) (c) 3. shall be made available as provided in s. 118.127. A school board member or an employee of a school district may not be held personally liable for any damages caused by the nondisclosure of any information specified in this paragraph unless the member or employee acted with actual malice in failing to disclose the information. A school district may not be held liable for any damages caused by the nondisclosure of any information specified in this paragraph unless the school district or its agent acted with gross negligence or with reckless, wanton, or intentional misconduct in failing to disclose the information.
(e) Upon the written permission of an adult pupil, or the parent or guardian of a minor pupil, the school shall make available to the person named in the permission the pupil's progress records or such portions of the pupil's behavioral records as determined by the person authorizing the release. Law enforcement officers' records obtained under s. 48.396 (1) or 938.396 (1) (b) 2. or (c) 3. may not be made available under this paragraph unless specifically identified by the adult pupil or by the parent or guardian of a minor pupil in the written permission.
(f) Pupil records shall be provided to a court in response to subpoena by parties to an action for in camera inspection, to be used only for purposes of impeachment of any witness who has testified in the action. The court may turn said records or parts thereof over to parties in the action or their attorneys if said records would be relevant and material to a witness's credibility or competency.
(g) 1. The school board may provide any public officer with any information required to be maintained under chs. 115 to 121.
2. Upon request by the department, the school board shall provide the department with any information contained in a pupil record that relates to an audit or evaluation of a federal or state-supported program or that is required to determine compliance with requirements under chs. 115 to 121.
(h) Information from a pupil's immunization records shall be made available to the department of health services to carry out the purposes of s. 252.04.
(hm) Information from any pupil lead screening records shall be made available to state and local health officials to carry out the purposes of ss. 254.11 to 254.178.
(i) Upon request, the school district clerk or his or her designee shall provide the names of pupils who have withdrawn from the public school prior to graduation under s. 118.15 (1) (c) to the technical college district board in which the public school is located or, for verification of eligibility for public assistance under ch. 49, to the department of health services, the department of children and families, or a county department under s. 46.215, 46.22, or 46.23.
[Note: See Wisconsin Statutes for (2) (j)–(p).]

(2m) CONFIDENTIALITY OF PUPIL PHYSICAL HEALTH RECORDS.
(a) Except as provided in par. (b), any pupil record that relates to a pupil's physical health and that is not a pupil physical health record shall be treated as a patient health care record under ss. 146.81 to 146.84.
(b) Any pupil record that concerns the results of an HIV test, as defined in s. 252.01 (2m), shall be treated as provided under s. 252.15.
(3) MAINTENANCE OF RECORDS. Each school board shall adopt rules in writing specifying the content of pupil records and the time during which pupil records shall be maintained. No behavioral records may be maintained for more than one year after the pupil ceases to be enrolled in the school, unless the pupil specifies in writing that his or her behavioral records may be maintained for a longer period. A pupil's progress records shall be maintained for at least 5 years after the pupil ceases to be enrolled in the school. A school board may maintain the records on microfilm, on an optical disk, or in electronic

format if authorized under s. 19.21 (4) (c), or in such other form as the school board deems appropriate. A school board shall maintain law enforcement officers' records obtained under s. 48.396 (1) or 938.396 (1) (b) 2. or (c) 3. separately from a pupil's other pupil records. Rules adopted under this subsection shall be published by the school board as a class 1 notice under ch. 985.

(4) **TRANSFER OF RECORDS. Within 5 working days, a school district and a private school participating in the program under s. 118.60 or in the program under s. 119.23 shall transfer to another school, including a private or tribal school, or school district all pupil records relating to a specific pupil if the transferring school district or private school has received written notice** from the pupil if he or she is an adult or his or her parent or guardian if the pupil is a minor that the pupil intends to enroll in the other school or school district or written notice from the other school or school district that the pupil has enrolled or from a court that the pupil has been placed in a juvenile correctional facility, as defined in s. 938.02 (10p), or a secured residential care center for children and youth, as defined in s. 938.02 (15g). In this subsection, "school" and "school district" include any juvenile correctional facility, secured residential care center for children and youth, adult correctional institution, mental health institute, or center for the developmentally disabled that provides an educational program for its residents instead of or in addition to that which is provided by public, private, and tribal schools.

(5) **Use for suspension or expulsion.** (a) Except as provided in par. (b), nothing in this section prohibits a school district from using a pupil's records in connection with the suspension or expulsion of the pupil or the use of such records by a multidisciplinary team under ch. 115.

(b) Law enforcement officers' records obtained under s. 48.396 (1) or 938.396 (1) (b) 2. or (c) 3. and records of the court assigned to exercise jurisdiction under chs. 48 and 938 or of a municipal court obtained under s. 938.396 (2g) (m) may not be used by a school district as the sole basis for expelling or suspending a pupil or as the sole basis for taking any other disciplinary action against a pupil, but may be used as the sole basis for taking action against a pupil under the school district's athletic code.

(6) Application to existing records. Any records existing on June 9, 1974 need not be revised for the purpose of deleting information from pupil records to comply with this section.

(7) Disclosure of law enforcement unit records. A school board shall treat law enforcement unit records of juveniles in the same manner as a law enforcement agency is required to treat law enforcement officers' records of juveniles under s. 938.396 (1) (a).

History: 1973 c. 254; 1977 c. 418; 1979 c. 205; 1981 c. 20, 273; 1983 a. 189; 1985 a. 218; 1987 a. 27, 70, 206, 285, 337, 355; 1987 a. 399 s. 491r; 1987 a. 403 ss. 123, 124, 256; 1989 a. 31, 168; 1989 a. 201 s. 36; 1989 a. 336; 1991 a. 39, 189; 1993 a. 27, 172, 334, 377, 385, 399, 450, 491; 1995 a. 27 ss. 3939, 3940, 9126 (19), 9130 (4), 9145 (1); 1995 a. 77, 173, 225, 352; 1997 a. 3, 27, 205, 237, 239; 1999 a. 9, 149; 2003 a. 82, 292; 2005 a. 344, 434; 2005 a. 443 s. 265; 2007 a. 20 ss. 2712, 9121 (6) (a); 2009 a. 11, 28, 209, 302, 309; 2011 a. 32, 105, 260.

A public school student's interim grades are pupil records specifically exempted from disclosure under s. 118.125. A failure to specifically state reasons for denying an open records request for records that are specifically exempted from disclosure does not compel disclosure of those records. State ex rel. Blum v. Board of Education, 209 Wis. 2d 377, 565 N.W.2d 140 (Ct. App. 1997), 96-0758.

A court need not wait until trial to disclose pupil records under sub. (2) (f) and may instead base its decision on the review of deposition testimony. Sub. (2) (f) refers to an action, which is a much broader term than trial. A witness who has been deposed has testified in the action. Anderson v. Northwood School District, 2011 WI App 31, 332 Wis. 2d 134, 796 N.W.2d 874, 09-1881.

A court may not disclose confidential records under sub. (2) (f) merely because they are relevant to a plaintiff's claim. The court's gatekeeper role is to protect the privacy of the pupil whose records are sought, releasing only those records that may concern a specific witness's credibility or competency. Anderson v. Northwood School District, 2011 WI App 31, 332 Wis. 2d 134, 796 N.W.2d 874, 09-1881.

Pupil information that local education agencies are required to release to the department of public instruction under the reporting provisions of ch. 89, laws of 1973, may be provided, with or without permission, without violation of the state or federal confidentiality statutes. 65 Atty. Gen. 1.

"Pupil records" are "public records" under 19.32 (2) but are subject to special statutes that limit access and direct maximum and minimum periods of maintenance before destruction. 72 Atty. Gen. 169.

Access to student records in Wisconsin. 1976 WLR 975.

118.126 Privileged communications.
(1) A school psychologist, counselor, social worker and nurse, and any teacher or administrator designated by the school board who engages in alcohol or drug abuse program activities, shall keep confidential information received from a pupil that the pupil or another pupil is using or is experiencing problems resulting from the use of alcohol or other drugs unless:

(a) The pupil using or experiencing problems resulting from the use of alcohol or other drugs consents in writing to disclosure of the information;

(b) The school psychologist, counselor, social worker, nurse, teacher or administrator has reason to believe that there is serious and imminent danger to the health, safety or life of any person and that disclosure of the information to another person will alleviate the serious and imminent danger. No more information than is required to alleviate the serious and imminent danger may be disclosed; or

(c) The information is required to be reported under s. 48.981.

(2) A school psychologist, counselor, social worker or nurse, or any teacher or administrator designated by the school board who engages in alcohol or drug abuse program activities, who in good faith discloses or fails to disclose information under sub. (1) is immune from civil liability for such acts or omissions. This subsection does not apply to information required to be reported under s. 48.981.

History: 1979 c. 331; 1985 a. 163; 1987 a. 188, 339.

118.13 PUPIL DISCRIMINATION PROHIBITED.
(1) Except as provided in s. 120.13 (37m), no person may be denied admission to any public school or be denied participation in, be denied the benefits of or be discriminated against in any curricular, extracurricular, pupil services, recreational or other program or activity because of the person's sex, race, religion, national origin, ancestry, creed, pregnancy, marital or parental status, sexual orientation or physical, mental, emotional or learning disability.

(2) (a) Each school board shall develop written policies and procedures to implement this section and submit them to the state superintendent as a part of its 1986 annual report under s. 120.18. The policies and procedures shall provide for receiving and investigating complaints by residents of the school district regarding possible violations of this section, for making determinations as to whether this section has been violated and for ensuring compliance with this section.

(b) Any person who receives a negative determination under par. (a) may appeal the determination to the state superintendent.

(3) (a) The state superintendent shall:
1. Decide appeals made to him or her under sub. (2) (b). Decisions of the state superintendent under this subdivision are subject to judicial review under ch. 227.
2. Promulgate rules necessary to implement and administer this section.
3. Include in the department's biennial report under s. 15.04 (1) (d) information on the status of school district compliance with this section and school district progress toward providing reasonable equality of educational opportunity for all pupils in this state.

(b) The state superintendent may:
1. Periodically review school district programs, activities and services to determine whether the school boards are complying with this section.
2. Assist school boards to comply with this section by providing information and technical assistance upon request.

(4) Any public school official, employee or teacher who intentionally engages in conduct which discriminates against a person or causes a person to be denied rights, benefits or privileges, in violation of sub. (1), may be required to forfeit not more than $1,000.

History: 1985 a. 29; 1987 a. 332; 1991 a. 131; 1995 a. 27 s. 9145 (1); 1997 a. 27; 2005 a. 346; 2007 a. 97.

118.14 Age of pupils. (1) Except as provided in s. 120.12 (25): (a) No child may be admitted to a 4-year-old kindergarten unless he or she is 4 years old on or before September 1 in the year that he or she proposes to enter school.

(b) No child may be admitted to a 5-year-old kindergarten unless he or she is 5 years old on or before September 1 in the year he or she proposes to enter school.

(c) No child may be admitted to the 1st grade unless he or she is 6 years old, on or before September 1 in the year he or she proposes to enter school.

(2) A resident over 20 years of age may be admitted to school when in the judgment of the school board the resident will not interfere with the pupils of school age.

(3) (a) Except a provided in par. (b), if a school board establishes a 4-year-old kindergarten program, the program shall be available to all pupils eligible for the program under sub. (1) (a) or s. 120.12 (25).

(b) A school board that was operating a 4-year-old kindergarten program in the 2007-08 school year that did not comply with par. (a) shall make a 4-year-old kindergarten program available to all pupils eligible for the program under sub. (1) (a) or s. 120.12 (25) by the beginning of the 2013-14 school year.

History: 1977 c. 418, 429; 1983 a. 36; 1985 a. 29; 1997 a. 240; 2007 a. 226.

118.145   Admission to high school.

(1) The school board of a district operating high school grades shall determine the minimum standards for admission to high school.

(2) A certificate or diploma or other written evidence issued by a school board showing that the pupil has completed the course of study in the elementary grades of the school district in which the pupil resides shall entitle the pupil to admission to high school. Such certificate or diploma or a certified copy thereof or a certified copy of a list of graduates shall be filed with the school district clerk of the school district operating the high school.

(3) If the superintendent of a private school or of a tribal school files with the department the course of study for elementary grades prescribed by such school and if such course of study is substantially equivalent to the course of study prepared for elementary grades by the department, a certificate or diploma or other written evidence issued by the superintendent of the private school or tribal school showing that the pupil has completed such course of study shall entitle the pupil to admission to a public high school. The certificate or diploma or a certified copy thereof or a certified copy of a list of graduates shall be filed with the school district clerk of the school district operating the high school.

(4) The school board of a school district operating high school grades shall allow a pupil enrolled in a private school, a pupil enrolled in a tribal school, or a pupil enrolled in a home-based [private] educational program, who has met the standards for admission to high school under sub. (1), to take up to 2 courses during each school semester if the pupil resides in the school district in which the public school is located and if the school board determines that there is sufficient space in the classroom.
NOTE: A missing word is shown in brackets. Corrective legislation is pending.
History: 1975 c. 39, 199; 1995 a. 27 s. 9145 (1); 1997 a. 27, 240; 2009 a. 302.

118.15   Compulsory school attendance.

(1) (a) Except as provided under pars. (b) to (d) and (g) and sub. (4), unless the child is excused under sub. (3) or has graduated from high school, any person having under control a child who is between the ages of 6 and 18 years shall cause the child to attend school regularly during the full period and hours, religious holidays excepted, that the public, private, or tribal school in which the child should be enrolled is in session until the end of the school term, quarter or semester of the school year in which the child becomes 18 years of age.

(am) Except as provided under par. (d), unless the child is excused under sub. (3), any person having under his or her control a child who is enrolled in 5-year-old kindergarten shall cause the child to attend school regularly, religious holidays excepted, during the full period and hours that kindergarten is in session at the public or private school in which the child is enrolled until the end of the school term.

(b) Upon the child's request of the school board and with the written approval of the child's parent or guardian, any child who is 16 years of age or over and a child at risk, as defined in s. 118.153 (1) (a), may attend, in lieu of high school or on a part-time basis, a technical college if the child and his or her parent or guardian agree, in writing, that the child will participate in a program leading to the child's high school graduation. The district board of the technical college district in which the child resides shall admit the child. Every technical college district board shall offer day class programs satisfactory to meet the requirements of this paragraph and s. 118.33 (3m) as a condition to the receipt of any state aid.

(c) 1. Upon the child's request and with the written approval of the child's parent or guardian, any child who is 16 years of age may be excused by the school board from regular school attendance if the child and his or her parent or guardian agree, in writing, that the child will participate in a program or curriculum modification under par. (d) leading to the child's high school graduation.

2. Upon the child's request and with the written approval of the child's parent or guardian, any child who is 17 years of age or over may be excused by the school board from regular school attendance if the child and his or her parent or guardian agree, in writing, that the child will participate in a program or curriculum modification under par. (d) leading to the child's high school graduation or leading to a high school equivalency diploma under s. 115.29 (4).
[Note: See Wisconsin Statutes for 118.145 (1) (c) 3–cm 1-5.]

(d) Any child's parent or guardian, or the child if the parent or guardian is notified, may request the school board, in writing, to provide the child with program or curriculum modifications, including but not limited to:

1. Modifications within the child's current academic program.

2. A school work training or work study program.

3. Enrollment in any alternative public school or program located in the school district in which the child resides.

4. Enrollment in any nonsectarian private school or program, or tribal school, located in the school district in which the child resides, which complies with the requirements of 42 USC 2000d. Enrollment of a child under this subdivision shall be pursuant to a contractual agreement under s. 121.78 (5) that provides for the payment of the child's tuition by the school district.

5. Homebound study, including nonsectarian correspondence courses or other courses of study approved by the school board or nonsectarian tutoring provided by the school in which the child is enrolled.

6. Enrollment in any public educational program located outside the school district in which the child resides. Enrollment of a child under this subdivision may be pursuant to a contractual agreement between school districts.

(dm) The school board shall render its decision, in writing, within 90 days of a request under par. (d), except that if the request relates to a child who has been evaluated by an individualized education program team under s. 115.782 and has not been recommended for special education, the school board shall render its decision within 30 days of the request. If the school board denies the request, the school board shall give its reasons for the denial.

(e) Any decision made by a school board or a designee of the school board in response to a request for program or curriculum modifications under par. (d) shall be reviewed by the school board upon request of the child's parent or guardian. The school board shall render its determination upon review in writing, if the child's parent or guardian so requests.
[Note: See Wisconsin Statutes for 118.145 (12) (f)–(3).]

(4) Instruction in a home-based private educational program that meets all of the criteria under s. 118.165 (1) may be substituted for attendance at a public or private school.
[Note: See Wisconsin Statutes for 118.145 (4m)–(6) and History.]

Requirements for Pupils Enrolled in Five-Year-Old Kindergarten

118.15 (1)(am) Except as provided under par. (d), unless the child is excused under sub. (3), any person having under his or her control a child who is enrolled in 5-year-old kindergarten shall cause the child to attend school regularly, religious holidays excepted, during the full period and hours that kindergarten is in session at the public or private school in which the child is enrolled until the end of the school term.

118.33 (6) (c) 1. Except as provided in subds. 2. and 3., beginning on September 1, 201 1, a school board may not enroll a child in the first grade in a school in the school district, including in a charter school located in the school district, unless the child has completed 5-year-old kin - dergarten. Each school board that operates a 5-year-old kindergarten program shall adopt a written policy speci - fying the criteria for promoting a pupil from 5-year-old kindergarten to the first grade.

2. Each school board that operates a 5-year-old kindergarten program shall establish procedures, conditions, and standards for exempting a child from the requirement that the child complete kindergarten as a prerequisite to enrollment in the first grade and for reviewing the denial of an exemption upon the request of the pupil' s parent or guardian.

3. A school board that operates a 5-year-old kinder - garten program shall enroll in the first grade a child who has not completed kindergarten but who is otherwise eligible to be admitted to and to enroll in first grade as a new or continuing pupil at the time the child moves into this state if one of the following applies:

a. Before either commencing or completing first grade, the child moved into this state from a state, country, or territory in which completion of 5-year-old kindergarten is a prerequisite to entering first grade and the child was exempted from the requirement to complete 5-year-old kindergarten in the state, country , or territory from which the child moved.

b. Before either commencing or completing first grade the child moved into this state from a state, country , or territory in which completion of 5-year-old kindergarten is not a prerequisite to entering first grade.

118.165 Private schools.
(1) An institution is a private school if its educational program meets all of the following criteria:
(a) The primary purpose of the program is to provide private or religious-based education.
(b) The program is privately controlled.
(c) The program provides at least 875 hours of instruction each school year.
(d) The program provides a sequentially progressive curriculum of fundamental instruction in reading, language arts, mathematics, social studies, science and health. This subsection does not require the program to include in its curriculum any concept, topic or practice in conflict with the program's religious doctrines or to exclude from its curriculum any concept, topic or practice consistent with the program's religious doctrines.
(e) The program is not operated or instituted for the purpose of avoiding or circumventing the compulsory school attendance requirement under s. 118.15 (1) (a).
(f) The pupils in the institution's educational program, in the ordinary course of events, return annually to the homes of their parents or guardians for not less than 2 months of summer vacation, or the institution is licensed as a child welfare agency under s. 48.60 (1).
(2) An institution may request the state superintendent to approve the institution's educational program as a private school. The state superintendent shall base his or her approval solely on the criteria under sub. (1). History: 1983 a. 512; 1989 a. 336; 1995 a. 27; 1997 a. 27.
118.167 Private school determination by state superintendent. If an association that regulates or accredits private educational institutions in this state submits an affidavit to the state superintendent attesting that the institution meets or exceeds all of the criteria under s. 118.165 and the state superintendent finds that the institution does meet or exceed all of the criteria under s. 118.165, the state superintendent shall determine that the institution is a private school. If at

any time the state superintendent finds that an institution determined to be a private school under this section no longer meets the criteria under s. 118.165, the state superintendent may withdraw the determination. History: 1983 a. 512; 1995 a. 27; 1997 a. 27.
115.001(3g) Home-based private educational program.† "Home-based private educational program" means a program of educational instruction provided to a child by the child's parent or guardian or by a person designated by the parent or guardian.† An instructional program provided to more than one family unit does not constitute a home-based private educational program.
115.001(3r) Private school.† "Private school" means an institution with a private educational program that meets all of the criteria under s. 118.165 (1) or is determined to be a private school by the state superintendent under s. 118.167.
118.15(4) Instruction in a home-based private educational program that meets all of the criteria under s. 118 .165 (1) may be substituted for attendance at a public or private school.

118.169 Pupil identification numbers. A school board, and the governing body of a private school, may assign to each pupil enrolled in the school district or private school a unique identification number. The school board or governing body shall not assign to any pupil an identification number that is identical to or incorporates the pupil's social security number. This section does not prohibit a school board or governing body from requiring a pupil to disclose his or her social security number, nor from using a student's social security number if such use is required by a federal or state agency or private organization in order for the school district or private school to participate in a particular program. History: 1997 a. 128.

118.30 Pupil assessment. (1) The state superintendent shall adopt or approve examinations designed to measure pupil attainment of knowledge and concepts in the 4th, 8th and 10th grades. [Does not apply to private school students, including homeschoolers.]

118.30(2)(b)3. Upon the request of a pupil's parent or guardian, the school board shall excuse the pupil from taking an examiniation administered under sub. (1m) [that is, the state-mandated 4th, 8th, and 10th grade examinations].

118.33 High school graduation standards; criteria for promotion.
(1) (a) Except as provided in par. (d), a school board may not grant a high school diploma to any pupil unless the pupil has earned:
1. In the high school grades, at least 4 credits of English including writing composition, 3 credits of social studies including state and local government, 2 credits of mathematics, 2 credits of science and 1.5 credits of physical education.
2. In grades 7 to 12, at least 0.5 credit of health education.
(am) The state superintendent shall encourage school boards to require an additional 8.5 credits selected from any combination of vocational education, foreign languages, fine arts and other courses. [These standards do not apply to private school students, including homeschoolers.]

120.18 Annual school district report.†
120.18(1) Annually at such time as the department prescribes but after the end of the school year and no later than September 1, the school district clerk of a common or union high school district shall file a verified annual school district report with the department, on forms supplied by the department. The school district clerk shall send a copy of the annual school district report to the school district administrator and shall notify the person in charge of each school in the school district that the reports are on file in the school district clerk's office. Accounting and financial information provided by the school district in the annual report shall be prepared from the system of accounts prescribed by the department. If the school district clerk neglects to make the annual report, the clerk shall be liable to the school district for the whole amount of money lost by the school district because of such neglect. The annual report shall contain:

120.18(1)(a) (a) The school count, showing the numbers and ages of persons who are at least 4 years old but not yet 14 years old and who reside in a school district operating only elementary grades, showing the number and ages of persons between the ages of 14 and 20 residing in a union high school district and showing the number and ages of persons between the ages of 4 and 20 residing in any other school district. Children cared for at a charitable or penal institution of this state may not be included in the report. The school district clerk may employ a competent person to take the school count. **The count may be determined by using any of the following methods:**
120.18(1)(a)1. 1. **Conducting a school census on the preceding June 30.**
120.18(1)(a)2. 2. Adding the number of persons under this paragraph who were residents of the school district and were enrolled in the school district on the 3rd Friday of September of the previous school year; plus the number of persons under this paragraph who were residents of the school district and who **were enrolled in private schools, tribal schools, home-based private educational programs,** or other school districts on the 3rd Friday of September of the previous school year; **plus the number or an estimate of the number** of those persons under this paragraph who were residents of the school district and not enrolled in the school district, private schools, tribal schools, home-based private educational programs, or other school districts on the 3rd Friday of September of the previous school year.
120.18(1)(b) (b) **The number of children between the ages of 4 and 20 taught in the schools of the school district during the school year.**
120.18(1)(c) (c) The number of children attending the schools of the school district during the school year under the age of 4 and over the age of 20 years.
120.18(1)(d) (d) The number of school days taught, including holidays, and the number of hours of direct pupil instruction provided in each school, by teachers legally qualified to teach.
120.18(1)(e) (e) The names of all teachers employed by the school district during the school year; the number of days taught by each, including holidays; the monthly salary paid to each; and the time allowed each teacher for attendance at an educational convention for which no wages were deducted.
120.18(1)(f) (f) The amount of money received during the school year, designating separately the amount received from the school fund income, from taxes levied by the county board, from taxes voted by the school district and from all other sources and the manner in which such money was expended, showing separately the expenditure of school money received from the state.
120.18(1)(g) (g) The amount and character of school district debts.
120.18(1)(gm) (gm) Payroll and related benefit costs for all school district employees in the previous school year. Payroll costs for represented employees shall be based upon the costs of wages of any collective bargaining agreements covering such employees for the previous school year. If, as of the time specified by the department for filing the report, the school district has not entered into a collective bargaining agreement for any portion of the previous school year with the recognized or certified representative of any of its employees, increased costs of wages reflected in the report shall be equal to the maximum wage expenditure that is subject to collective bargaining under s. 111.70 (4) (mb) 2. for the employees. The school district shall amend the annual report to reflect any change in such costs as a result of any collective bargaining agreement entered into between the date of filing the report and October 1. Any such amendment shall be concurred in by the certified public accountant licensed or certified under ch. 442 certifying the school district audit.
120.18(1)(i) (i) A description of the educational technology used by the school district, including the uses made of the technology, the cost of the technology, and the number of persons using or served by the technology. In this paragraph, "educational technology" has the meaning given in s. 16.99 (3). **120.18(1)(s)** (s) Such other facts and statistics in relation to the public, private or tribal schools, in the school district as the department requires.
120.18(3) (3) The state superintendent may promulgate rules to implement and administer this section.

120.18 History History: 1975 c. 189, 224; 1989 a. 31; 1993 a. 16; 1995 a. 27 s. 9145 (1); 1997 a. 27, 87; 2001 a. 16; 2003 a. 33; 2005 a. 252; 2009 a. 302; 2011 a. 10.

252.04 Immunization program.
(1) The department shall carry out a statewide immunization program to eliminate mumps, measles, rubella (German measles), diphtheria, pertussis (whooping cough), poliomyelitis and other diseases that the department specifies by rule, and to protect against tetanus. Any person who immunizes an individual under this section shall maintain records identifying the manufacturer and lot number of the vaccine used, the date of immunization and the name and title of the person who immunized the individual. These records shall be available to the individual or, if the individual is a minor, to his or her parent, guardian or legal custodian upon request.
252.04(2) (2) Any student admitted to any elementary, middle, junior, or senior high school or into any child care center or nursery school shall, within 30 school days after the date on which the student is admitted, present written evidence to the school, child care center, or nursery school of having completed the first immunization for each vaccine required for the student's grade and being on schedule for the remainder of the basic and recall (booster) immunization series for mumps, measles, rubella (German measles), diphtheria, pertussis (whooping cough), poliomyelitis, tetanus, and other diseases that the department specifies by rule or shall present a written waiver under sub. (3).
252.04(3) (3) **The immunization requirement is waived if the student, if an adult, or the student's parent, guardian, or legal custodian submits a written statement to the school, child care center, or nursery school objecting to the immunization for reasons of health, religion, or personal conviction.** At the time any school, child care center, or nursery school notifies a student, parent, guardian, or legal custodian of the immunization requirements, it shall inform the person in writing of the person's right to a waiver under this subsection.
252.041 **Compulsory vaccination during a state of emergency.**
252.041(1)(1) Except as provided in sub. (2), during the period under which the department is designated as the lead state agency, as specified in s. 250.042 (2), the department, as the public health authority, may do all of the following as necessary to address a public health emergency:
252.041(1)(a) (a) **Order any individual to receive a vaccination unless the vaccination is reasonably likely to lead to serious harm to the individual or unless the individual, for reasons of religion or conscience, refuses to obtain the vaccination.**

252.041(2) (2) The department shall promulgate rules that specify circumstances, if any, under which vaccination may not be performed on an individual.
252.041 History History: 2001 a. 109.

Wisconsin State Constitution
ARTICLE X. EDUCATION [Selected sections] Superintendent of public instruction. SECTION 1. [As amended Nov. 1902 and Nov. 1982] The **supervision of public instruction** shall be vested in a state superintendent and such other officers as the legislature shall direct; and their qualifications, powers, duties and compensation shall be prescribed by law. The state superintendent shall be chosen by the qualified electors of the state at the same time and in the same manner as members of the supreme court, and shall hold office for 4 years from the succeeding first Monday in July. The term of office, time and manner of electing or appointing all other officers of supervision of public instruction shall be fixed by law. [1899 J.R. 16, 1901 J.R. 3, 1901 c. 258, vote Nov. 1902; 1979 J.R. 36, 1981 J.R. 29, vote Nov. 1982] District schools; tuition; sectarian instruction; released time. SECTION 3. [As amended April 1972] The legislature shall provide by law for the establishment of district schools, which shall be as nearly uniform as practicable; and such schools shall be free and without charge for tuition to all children between the ages of 4 and 20 years; and no sectarian instruction shall be allowed therein; but the legislature by law may, for the purpose of religious instruction outside the district schools, authorize the release of students during regular school hours. [1969 J.R. 37, 1971 J.R. 28, vote April 1972]

HOUSE REPORT 112–329 – **NATIONAL DEFENSE AUTHORIZATION ACT** – FOR FISCAL YEAR 2012 – CONFERENCE REPORT TO ACCOMPANY H.R. 1540 **SEC. 532. POLICY ON MILITARY RECRUITMENT AND ENLISTMENT OF GRADUATES OF SECONDARY SCHOOLS.**
(a) EQUAL TREATMENT FOR SECONDARY SCHOOL GRADUATES.
(1) EQUAL TREATMENT.—For the purposes of recruitment and enlistment in the Armed Forces, the Secretary of a military department shall treat a graduate described in paragraph (2) in the same manner as a graduate of a secondary school (as defined in section 9101(38) of the Elementary and Secondary Education Act of 1965 (20 U.S.C. 7801(38)).
(2) COVERED GRADUATES.—Paragraph (1) applies with respect to person who—
(A) receives a diploma from a secondary school that is legally operating; or
(B) otherwise completes a program of secondary education in compliance with the education laws of the State in which the person resides.
(b) POLICY ON RECRUITMENT AND ENLISTMENT.—Not later than 180 days after the date of the enactment of this Act, the Secretary of Defense shall prescribe a policy on recruitment and enlistment that incorporates the following:
(1) Means for identifying persons described in subsection (a)
(2) who are qualified for recruitment and enlistment in the Armed Forces, which may include the use of a non-cognitive aptitude test, adaptive personality assessment, or other operational attrition screening tool to predict performance, behaviors, and attitudes of potential recruits that influence attrition and the ability to adapt to a regimented life in the Armed Forces.
(2) Means for assessing how qualified persons fulfill their enlistment obligation.
(3) Means for maintaining data, by each diploma source, which can be used to analyze attrition rates among qualified persons.
(c) RECRUITMENT PLAN.—As part of the policy required by subsection (b), the Secretary of each of the military departments shall develop a recruitment plan that includes a marketing strategy for targeting various segments of potential recruits with all types of secondary education credentials.
(d) COMMUNICATION PLAN.—The Secretary of each of the military departments shall develop a communication plan to ensure that the policy and recruitment plan are understood by military recruiters.
[Note from WPA: Statutory language (2) (B) could have been interpreted to mean that homeschool graduates have equal footing with graduates of public and other private schools. However, the Department of Defense's June 6, 2012, policy memorandum that implements this statute, requires that homeschool graduates also pass the Armed Forces Qualification Test (AFQT) with a score of 50 or higher in order for their diplomas to qualify for Tier 1 status.]

118.53   Attendance by pupils enrolled in a home-based private educational program.
(1) In this section, "course" means study which has the fundamental purposes of developing the knowledge, concepts, and skills in a subject.
(2) In addition to the standards for admission under ss. 118.14, 118.145 (1), and 120.12 (25), the school board of a district shall determine the minimum standards for admission to a course offered by the school district in grades kindergarten through 8.
(2m) A school board shall allow a pupil enrolled in a home-based private educational program who has not met the minimum standards for admission into high school under s. 118.145 (1) to attend up to 2 courses at a public school in the district during each school semester if the school board determines that the pupil qualifies for admission to those courses and if there is sufficient space in the classroom.
(3) A school board shall allow a pupil enrolled in a home-based private educational program, who has met the standards for admission under sub. (2), to attend up to 2 courses at a public school in the district during each school semester if the school board determines that there is sufficient space in the classroom.
(4) A pupil enrolled in a home-based private educational program and attending a public school under this section may attend one course in each of 2 school districts, but may not attend more than 2 courses in any semester.
History: 2013 a. 20, 211.

118.133   Participation in interscholastic athletics and extracurricular activities.
(1) INTERSCHOLASTIC ATHLETICS.
(a) A school board shall permit a pupil who resides in the school district and is enrolled in a home-based private educational program to participate in interscholastic athletics in the school district on the same basis and to the same extent that it permits pupils enrolled in the school district to participate.
(b) Upon request, the home-based educational program in which the pupil is enrolled shall provide the school board with a written statement that the pupil meets the school board's requirements for participation in interscholastic athletics based on age and academic and disciplinary records. No person may provide a false statement under this paragraph. The school board may not question the accuracy or validity of the statement or request additional information.
(2) EXTRACURRICULAR ACTIVITIES. A school board shall permit a pupil who resides in the school district and is enrolled in a home-based private educational program to participate in extracurricular activities in the school district on the same basis and to the same extent that it permits pupils enrolled in the school district to participate.
(3) PARTICIPATION FEES. A school board may charge a pupil who participates in interscholastic athletics or extracurricular activities as permitted under this section participation fees, including fees for uniforms, equipment, and musical instruments, on the same basis and to the same extent that it charges these fees to a pupil who is enrolled in the school district.

Appendix B
About Wisconsin Parents Association

Wisconsin Parents Association (WPA), a statewide, inclusive, grassroots organization, was founded in response to a crisis. Late in 1983, legislation designed by the Department of Public Instruction (DPI) and other members of the educational establishment was introduced in the Wisconsin Legislature. Homeschoolers were about to be put under the DPI's control and authority.

On January 6, 1984, a diverse group of 70 homeschoolers founded an organization to include all homeschoolers. Its mission was to support and defend the right of families to choose an education consistent with their principles and beliefs. The organization decided to work for legislation that made no compromises: no state-mandated standardized testing, no review and approval of homeschoolers' curriculums, no progress reports to school districts, no special qualifications required of parents. Parents would be held accountable in a reasonable way, and the interests of the state would be respected.

Members of the new organization quickly encouraged homeschoolers to attend a legislative hearing on January 25, 1984. When 2,500 people came, nearly all opposed to the bill, legislators took note. At a March 13 hearing, WPA presented information from homeschoolers who had had difficulty with the DPI. Amendments turned the legislation around. After much effort by homeschoolers working together through WPA, one of the best homeschooling laws in the country was created. Since then, WPA has maintained its strong reputation in the Legislature.

But WPA's work was just beginning. The DPI quickly exceeded its authority by putting more requirements on the first PI-1206 form than the law allowed. WPA's meeting with DPI representatives and legislators forced a correction that made the form consistent with the new law.

To meet homeschoolers' need for support and information, WPA opened a post office box. Later voice mail was added. WPA's first annual conference was held in June, 1984 so homeschoolers could meet, celebrate, and learn from each other. The first edition of this handbook, a slender, 35-page, typed volume, was published in 1985. Over the years, the courage and work of thousands of homeschooling families have turned it into the book you are holding. WPA has also educated the general public and the Legislature about homeschooling and established a favorable climate for homeschooling in Wisconsin.

Since 1984, WPA has had to counter numerous challenges, including resolutions introduced by the Wisconsin Association of School Boards (WASB), an inaccurate study of homeschooling by the University of Wisconsin (the "Lufler Report"), and a Legislative Council study. The last took five months, cost taxpayers $100,000, and resulted in a rare decision to not introduce legislation following such a study and the recognition that changes to the homeschooling law were unnecessary. WPA also has put out many brush fires, as school districts around the state at first tried to require more of homeschoolers than the law allows and more recently to entice them into the public schools. Several unwise and apparently self-serving actions by a national homeschooling organization have required action. All this work continues.

WPA works hard to prevent problems and prepare members to counter them when they arise. Among the many issues WPA has researched and written about are standardized testing, preschool screening, collaboration among government agencies, mental health screening, family privacy, virtual charter schools, and government regulation of homeschooling.

What are WPA's main activities today?

• **Help for individuals:** WPA responds to homeschoolers' emails, calls, and letters, whether they need help getting started, dealing with school officials, or meeting everyday challenges of homeschooling. WPA gives homeschoolers the information and resources they need to be able to make the best decisions for their families.

• **Information:** Through newsletters, fact sheets, emails, a website, this handbook, annual conferences, Facebook, and responses to individual inquiries, WPA gives homeschoolers the information and support they need to homeschool and to respond intelligently to threats to homeschooling freedoms. Background information from WPA prepares people to make good decisions and respond reasonably in a crisis.

• **Tracking and analysis:** Members and allies of WPA send information they have collected from their local communities and other sources, and share experiences they have had homeschooling and dealing with officials, legislators, and others. WPA gathers, organizes, and analyzes an enormous amount of information, much of which has been distilled into this book. The information is then given to members and others who need it so they can make decisions and take action.

• **Conferences:** Since 1984, WPA's annual spring conference has provided information, inspiration, and opportunities to meet other homeschoolers.

• **Freedom:** Wisconsin's current homeschooling freedoms are in large part due to the work of homeschoolers involved in WPA. Over and over again, WPA members have taken specific action that has maintained Wisconsin's reasonable homeschooling law.

• **Making connections:** WPA works with local support groups to help homeschoolers meet and support one another.

• **Self-representation:** Parents work together through WPA to represent themselves and their own best interests when action is needed, rather than relying on individuals or groups, however well-intentioned, who present themselves as experts or representatives of homeschoolers.

WPA Membership

Consider joining WPA, if you are not already a member. Members receive a quarterly newsletter, special bulletins and emails as needed, and discounts on conferences and handbooks. More importantly, members support WPA, which receives no state or federal funding. Without faithful and committed members, WPA could not continue to be an effective means for families to work together. In turn, WPA members have the satisfaction of knowing they are part of an organization of families committed to reclaiming and maintaining their rights and responsibilities.

How To Contact WPA and its Regional Coordinators

Email WPA at wpa@homeschooling-wpa.org, call the Voice Mail at 608-283-3131, go to www.homeschooling-wpa.org, or write to WPA, P O Box 2502, Madison WI 53701-2502.

WPA also has a network of Regional Coordinators who answer questions, help homeschoolers find support groups and connect with other homeschoolers, and provide a link to WPA and its resources. For the name and phone number of the Regional Coordinator nearest you, see the WPA newsletter or website or call the WPA Voice Mail.

Appendix C
WPA Resolutions Adopted at Annual Meetings

TOPICS OF ALL RESOLUTIONS

Note: Selected resolutions that are marked with * appear on the following pages. Full text of all the resolutions is available on the WPA website.

1. WPA and Choice in Education 4/88 *
2. Wisconsin's Home Schooling Law 4/88
3. State-Mandated Standardized Testing 4/88 *
4. Home Schooling, Private Education, and the DPI 4/88 *
5. State Review and Approval of a Home-Based Private Educational Program's Calendar and Curriculum 4/89
6. Teacher Certification of Home Schooling Parents 4/89
7. Entry and Re-entry Into Public Schools 4/90
8. Home Schoolers Taking Courses in Public Schools 4/90
9. Unity Among Home Schoolers 4/90 *
10. The Primary Role of Parents in Education 4/91
11. Opposition to State Control of Education and the Family 4/91
12. State goals in education 4/92
13. America 2000 and Wisconsin 2000 4/92
14. Education Vouchers 4/92 *
15. Outcome-Based Education 4/93
16. Government Collaboration 4/93
17. Maintain the Distinction Between Public and Private Schools 4/93
18. Screening, Evaluating, and Labeling Children 4/94 *
19. The Federal Government and Homeschooling 4/94 *
20. Privacy and Homeschooling 4/94
21. The Independence of the Homeschooling Movement 4/95
22. Families First 4/95
23. Homeschooling, Educational Reform, Freedoms, and Money 4/95
24. Maintaining Wisconsin's Homeschooling Law 5/96
25. Maintaining the Fundamental Foundation of Parental Rights and Responsibilities 5/96
26. Attempts by the State to Determine Eligibility to Homeschool 4/97

27. School-To-Work Programs 4/97
28. Day-Time Curfews, Truancy Sweeps, and ID Cards for Homeschoolers 5/98
29. The Real Cost of Tax Credits for Homeschoolers' Educational Expenses 5/98
30. Impact on Homeschooling Freedoms of Homeschoolers' Qualifying for Public School Sports Teams 5/98 *
31. High Schools' Mock Trial Involving a Homeschooler 5/98
32. Graduation Test 5/99
33. Legislation That Undermines Homeschooling Freedoms 5/99
34. Laws Designed to Prevent Certain Families from Homeschooling 5/00
35. Survey Research on Homeschooling 5/00
36. Standardized Testing Required by the Federal or State Government 5/01
37. Homeschools Defined by Law as One Family Unit 5/01
38. Public E-Schools 5/02
39. Government Imposed Immunizations 5/02
40. Education Vouchers, Educational Investment Accounts, and Tax Credits and Deductions for Education 5/03 *
41. Maintaining the Distinction Between Public Schools and Homeschools (and Other Private Schools) 5/03
42. The Media and Homeschooling 5/04
43. Student Identification Database Systems 5/04*
44. Mental Health Screening 5/05 *
45. No Child Left Behind 5/05
46. History of Homeschooling in Wisconsin 5/06
47. Institutionalizing Young Children 5/07
48. Maintaining the Basic Principles of Homeschooling 5/08
49. Importance of Parents to Children's Development and Learning and a Family's Well Being 5/09 *
50. Prevent Further Erosion of the Role of Parents in Children's Early Years 5/10
51. New Kindergarten Statute and Homeschooling 5/11
52. Encouraging Homeschoolers to File Form PI-1206 Online in Accordance With the Law 5/12

*SELECTED RESOLUTIONS
(For all, see WPA's website)

1. WPA and Choice in Education
Whereas the Wisconsin Parents Association (WPA) is a state-wide association that watches, promotes, and defends the rights of parents, families, and children; and

Whereas WPA recognizes that there is no one best way to educate children since their talents and abilities are so varied; and

Whereas home schoolers are a very diverse group with widely varying income levels, approaches to education, religious and philosophical beliefs; and

Whereas the one thing home schoolers have in common is their commitment to establishing and maintaining their parental rights to educate their children according to their beliefs and principles;

Be it resolved that WPA and its members will support parents in their choice in education.   April 1988

3. State-Mandated Standardized Testing
Whereas standardized tests are only one way of measuring the mastery of a specific set of facts; and

Whereas standardized tests can become a means of determining and controlling the curriculum, teaching methods, and structure of a school or program; and

Whereas there is increasing evidence that standardized tests do not measure what they claim to measure; and

Whereas standardized tests can be used to label children, to justify additional testing, and to require child placement out of the home; and

Whereas state-mandated standardized testing provides that the state rather than the parent would decide when children are ready for tests, what tests will be used, how and where tests will be administered, and what to do about the results;

Be it resolved by members of the Wisconsin Parents Association (WPA) that WPA is opposed to state-mandated standardized testing and will work to prevent it from being mandated for Home-Based Private Educational Programs. April 1988

4. Home Schooling, Private Education, and the DPI
Whereas the United States by its constitution, tradition, and custom has long recognized, practiced, and provided for the parent to have the primary right in and responsibility for a child's education; and

Whereas the distinction between public and private education, including home-based private education, is established by custom, tradition, and statute and is fundamental to the exercise of choice in education and to the avoidance of a state monopoly in education; and

Whereas Article X of the Wisconsin Constitution grants the State Superintendent of Public Instruction authority over public, not private, education; and

Whereas the Wisconsin legislature has passed a law (1983 Act 512) that requires Home-Based Private Educational Programs to meet educational requirements and be in compliance with the compulsory school attendance law, a law that balances the state's, parent's, and children's rights and responsibilities in education;

Be it resolved by members of the Wisconsin Parents Association (WPA) that WPA views the Department of Public Instruction (DPI) to have no authority to regulate private education, including Home-Based Private Educational Programs.

Be it further resolved that the WPA will not initiate or propose matters to the DPI that would recognize, foster, or grant such regulatory authority by the DPI over private education.   April 1988

9. Unity Among Home Schoolers
Whereas home schoolers come from all walks of life; they home school for a number of different reasons; and they use a variety of curriculums and approaches to education; however, they all have one thing in common, namely, their determination to preserve the right to choose for their children an education consistent with their beliefs and principles; and

Whereas the Wisconsin statutes defining private schools (including home schools) resulted from the hard work of the full range of home schoolers and people involved in other small private schools in this state; and

Whereas home schoolers have organized themselves as Wisconsin Parents Association (WPA) to watch and protect their parental rights in education, especially home schooling rights and responsibilities; and

Whereas WPA has steadfastly refused to take any position on approaches to education, religion, moral values, and has fought for the rights of its members and others to make their own decisions in these matters; and

Whereas it is not necessary for home schoolers to agree on educational approaches or religious and moral beliefs and principles in order to work together to secure and preserve the rights and freedoms all home schoolers need in order to make choices; and

Whereas home schoolers are a small minority and are opposed by powerful political interest groups and organizations; and

Whereas Wisconsin has a reasonable home schooling law; and

Whereas the unity of home schoolers on home schooling legislative issues has earned home schoolers respect in the Wisconsin Legislature and has worked to prevent unnecessary regulation of home schoolers; and

Whereas WPA is a grassroots organization which relies on the strength of its own local members rather than "experts," especially out-of-state experts who become involved in state legislative matters;

Be it resolved by members of Wisconsin Parents Association (WPA) that WPA affirms its goal of assuring reasonable home schooling laws by working together as a united group that is open to all home schoolers; and

Be it further resolved that WPA opposes any state or national efforts that would split home schoolers into factions and thus weaken the ability of home schoolers to ensure reasonable home schooling laws. April 1990

18. Screening, Evaluating, and Labeling Children

Whereas a growing number of government programs screen, evaluate, and label children at earlier and earlier ages; and

Whereas the power of these programs is growing and spreading because they often involve a number of different public and private agencies, organizations, and professionals now working together through new programs to promote collaboration among government agencies; and

Whereas the definition of "children with special needs" has been broadened so that many children who are following their own unique timetables but are well within the range of normal development are now being labeled as "developmentally delayed," or "learning disabled," or some such label; and

Whereas these labels are very destructive because they undermine the confidence of children and parents and become self-fulfilling prophecies; and

Whereas these programs are technically voluntary and require parental permission for children to participate and be evaluated, BUT increasingly parents who allow their children to be evaluated and placed in such programs are unable to get their children out of the programs unless they enroll in a private program or a private school (including homeschools); and

Whereas pressure is being put on parents and the general public to believe that institutions and so-called experts know how to evaluate, label, and train very young children; and

Whereas requiring children to participate in programs and/or schools at early ages is not generally good for children or their families; in fact, there is growing evidence that these programs are detrimental to children and their families; and

Whereas requiring young children to participate in such programs could lead to including younger children in the compulsory school attendance law; and

Whereas requiring participation in such programs could expand the authority of these programs, of the schools in general, and of "professional experts" and further reduce the role and respect given to parents and the family;

Be it resolved by the members of the Wisconsin Parents Association (WPA) that WPA and its members will work to inform parents about their rights and responsibilities in education; to inform parents about the problems associated with screening, evaluating, and labeling of children, including very young children; and inform parents about how they can get their children out of such programs. April 1994

30. Impact on Homeschooling Freedoms of Homeschoolers' Qualifying for Public School Sports Teams

Whereas homeschoolers have regained significant freedom of thought and belief by working to establish and maintain ourselves as private schools independent of public schools; and

Whereas Wisconsin has a reasonable homeschooling law that homeschoolers have worked hard to get passed and to maintain; and

Whereas homeschoolers are a very small minority but large and powerful interest groups are pressing for increased state regulation of homeschooling; and

Whereas, in order for Wisconsin Interscholastic Athletic Association (WIAA) rules to be changed so that homeschoolers could participate on public school sports teams, homeschools would have to comply with the Department of Public Instruction (DPI)'s policies and regulations, including the DPI's definition of a full-time student, standards for acceptable curriculum, determinations of scholastic standing in terms of grades and credits through testing, and other demonstrations of qualifications that are consistent with public school standards and approaches to education; and

Whereas if just a few homeschoolers convinced the WIAA to change its rules to allow homeschoolers to play on public school teams, this would result in state oversight and intrusion into homeschools; and

Whereas, once in place, such state regulation of homeschools could easily spread to other areas of homeschooling and over time to all homeschoolers; and

Whereas young people who want to play sports can either choose from among opportunities available outside public schools or can enroll in public schools, but families who want to homeschool can only do so under the laws and regulations of the state of Wisconsin (which would be less favorable to homeschoolers if WIAA rules were changed to allow homeschoolers to play on public school sports teams);

Be it resolved by members of the Wisconsin Parents Association (WPA) that WPA will continue to work through its members to maintain Wisconsin's reasonable homeschooling law and will oppose initiatives that would increase state regulation of homeschooling in exchange for the opportunity for a few homeschoolers (who were interested and judged to be qualified) to play on public school sports teams; and

Be it further resolved that WPA will work through its members to inform parents and the general public and legislators of the unacceptability and risks of such initiatives. 5/98

40. Education Vouchers, Educational Investment Accounts, and Tax Credits and Deductions for Education

Whereas education vouchers, educational investment accounts, and tax credits and deductions for education that are being proposed at the federal and state levels of government would allow the government to define education and impose its values, judgments, and often its testing on people; and

Whereas such education vouchers would not be given to families but only to the institutions that families select from among those the state has certified as eligible to receive money from the state through vouchers; and

Whereas such education vouchers can easily lead to state control of education and further control of families; and

Whereas legislation providing for educational investment accounts and tax credits and deductions tied to educational expenses sets the terms of who, what, and under what conditions one qualifies for such tax breaks, including defining key terms such as teacher, educator, homeschool, private school, educational expense, etc.; and

Whereas defining, interpreting, and applying such key terms provides federal and state governments with the authority to further regulate private schooling including homeschools; and

Whereas monitoring (including auditing) the use of such tax breaks, credits, and deductions can further define and regulate homeschools; and

Whereas there are other publicly funded services that we as citizens pay taxes for (such as fire departments and prisons) but hope we will not use their services for ourselves; and

Whereas there are better and more direct ways for the state and federal governments to assist families in funding private education (including home schooling), such as reducing taxes to families and increasing tax deductions and credits for dependents;

Be it resolved that members of Wisconsin Parents Association (WPA) that WPA opposes education vouchers, educational investment accounts, and tax credits and deductions for education that would require the surrender of educational freedom, and, instead, WPA supports measures that would strengthen families either by decreasing their tax burdens and thus leaving them money to use for private education or by returning money directly to families, thus allowing families true choice in how moneys are spent for education.   May 2003

44. Mental Health Screening

Whereas an increasing number of federal and state mental health screening programs are being established to screen preschool and school children as well as young children, teens, and adults; and

Whereas the questions asked during the screenings are so general and ambiguous that nearly anyone could be identified as mentally ill or in need of further testing; and

Whereas doctors, workers in health clinics, school personnel, social service workers, juvenile justice authorities, etc. are all being encouraged to conduct such screenings, and people may not realize that they are being screened; and

Whereas screenings are especially targeted at groups considered marginal to the mainstream of our society because of their practices, small numbers,

and/or anti-social behavior (categories in which homeschoolers could easily be included); and

Whereas certain institutions and professionals are either suspicious or critical of homeschooling or have vested interests in stopping people from homeschooling; and

Whereas mental health screenings could be used as an effective way to curtail homeschooling; and

Whereas the pharmaceutical industry is spending large sums of money to encourage professionals and legislators to promote mental health screening; and

Whereas the drugs that are being administered through these programs to people who are diagnosed as "mentally ill" through these screenings have been shown to be harmful to people;

Be it resolved by members of Wisconsin Parents Association (WPA) that WPA will work to inform its members, homeschoolers throughout the state, and the general public about the importance of recognizing mental health screenings in whatever setting they occur, to inform them of their rights and responsibilities as parents and as patients, to question and/or refuse such screenings, and to oppose legislation that encourages or requires mental health screening that leads to highly subjective identification of mental illness and use of drugs for treatment.   May 2005

49. Importance of Parents to Children's Development and Learning and a Family's Well Being

Whereas major studies over the past 40 years have consistently shown parents and families, rather than schools or teachers, to be the determining factor in whether a child succeeds academically and socially; and

Whereas day care and preschool have been shown to lead to anti-social and aggressive behavior; and

Whereas child care can have serious harmful results for the child, parents, and the family (For example, an abstract from a recent major study of universal child care includes these findings: "Finally, we uncover striking evidence that children are worse off in a variety of behavioral and health dimensions, ranging from aggression to motor-social skills to illness. Our analysis also suggests that the new childcare program led to more hostile, less consistent parenting, worse parental health, and lower-quality parental relationships."[1]); and

Whereas screening practices designed to determine a child's need for special education and/or to assess a child's mental health have been shown to be unscientific and flawed, resulting in many children being inappropriately labeled and treated; and

Whereas the academic gains made by children who attend kindergarten have been shown to disappear by third grade; and

Whereas universal day care or preschool as well as mandatory kindergarten are among the polices being promoted by the federal and state governments; and

Whereas such programs may become more widely accepted and practiced and, as a result, people will accept as normal certain practices that are not only harmful and expensive but over time may be required, thereby undermining parents' rights and responsibilities in many areas of family life; and

Whereas for many years there has been a movement among a wide range of professions (such as specialists in child development, teachers, social workers, psychologists, psychiatrists, family and juvenile court judges, and many researchers studying areas covered by these professions) to turn more and more children and families into their clients or sources of income; and

Whereas many of these professional groups as well as individual professionals identify the family itself, especially parents, as the cause of problems in the family and with children; and

Whereas these same professional interest groups have lobbied for and secured laws and procedures that grant these professionals the authority to use "the best interests of the child" rather than "the best interests of the family" as the standard in making decisions regarding a child's placement, education, health care, religious practice, etc.; and

Whereas the media reports on social issues involving children and parents rely almost exclusively on studies and research done by the professional interest groups with little, if any, independent investigation; and

Whereas these professions have established associations that promote their professions and practices often with large budgets and lobbyists; and

Whereas by and large parents are not organized as parents, do not have lobbyists, and do not have significant representation in the world of academic experts and researchers or in the media; and

Whereas the growing trend regarding child care and learning is to further empower professionals and institutions at the expense and undermining of parents and families; and

Whereas homeschoolers have demonstrated how effective ordinary parents can be in educating and socializing children as well as preparing them for employment and higher education;

Be it resolved by members of Wisconsin Parents Association (WPA) that WPA will work to educate parents, legislators, the media, and the general public about the essential role parents play in their children's learning and development and the harm that can be caused to children, parents, and families by early institutionalization of children and/or professional screening and treatment. 5/09

(1) *Universal Child Care, Maternal Labor Supply, and Family Well-Being* by Michael Baker – University of Toronto and National Bureau of Economic Research, Jonathan Gruber – Massachusetts Institute of Technology and National Bureau of Economic Research, and Kevin Milligan – University of British Columbia and National Bureau of Economic Research. Published by the National Bureau of Economic Research. Working Paper No. 11832 Issued in December 2005. Also, published by *Journal of Political Economy,* University of Chicago Press, vol. 116(4), pages 709-745, 08. May 2009

Bibliography

Allen, David. *Getting Things Done: The Art of Stress-Free Productivity.*

Amdahl, Kenn and Jim Loat. *Algebra Unplugged.*

Armstrong, Thomas. *In Their Own Way: Discovering and Encouraging Your Child's Personal Learning Style.*

Beechick, Ruth. *The Three R's: Grades K-3 and You Can Teach Your Child Successfully: Grades 4-8.*

Blatner, David. *The Joy of Pi.*

Bolles, Richard. *What Color Is Your Parachute? A Practical Manual for Job-Hunters and Career Changers.*

Cain, Susan *Quiet: The Power of Introverts in a World That Can't Stop Talking.*

Coles, Gerald S. *The Learning Mystique: A Critical Look at "Learning Disabilities."*

Elias, Stephen. *Legal Research: How to Find and Understand the Law.*

Enzensberger, Hans. *The Number Devil: A Mathematical Adventure.*

Goodwin, Corin Barsily and Mika Gustavson. *Making the Choice: When Typical School Doesn't Fit Your Atypical Child.*

Griffith, Mary. *The Unschooling Handbook: How to Use the Whole World As Your Child's Classroom.*

Guedj, Denis. *The Parrot's Theorem.*

Gurian, Michael. *The Minds of Boys: Saving Our Sons From Falling Behind in School and Life.*

_____. *The Purpose of Boys: Helping Our Sons Find Meaning, Significance, and Direction in their Lives.*

Hakim, Joy. *A History of US.* 3rd edition, revised.

Henkel, Jane R. *Recent Court Cases Examining the Constitutionality of Other States' Laws Regulating Home Schools.* (Available on the WPA website.)

Hirsch, E. D., ed. *What Your Kindergartener Needs to Know: Fundamentals of a Good First Grade Education.* (Series goes through Sixth Grade)

Holt, John. *How Children Learn,* revised edition.

_____. *Learning All the Time.*

_____ and Patrick Farenga. *Teach Your Own: The John Holt Book of Homeschooling.*

Illich, Ivan. *Deschooling Society.*

Jacobs, Harold. *Elementary Algebra.*

_____. *Geometry: Seeing, Doing, Understanding,* 3rd edition.

_____. *Mathematics: A Human Endeavor,* 3rd edition.

Jones, Claudia. *Parents Are Teachers, Too: Enriching Your Child's First Six Years.*

Juster, Norton. *Phantom Tollbooth.* 50th anniversary edition.

Kealoha, Anna. *Trust the Children: An Activity Guide for Homeschooling and Alternative Learning.*

Llewellyn, Grace. *The Teenage Liberation Handbook: How to Quit School and Get a Real*

Life and Education.

McKee, Alison. *Homeschooling Our Children, Unschooling Ourselves.*

Meltzer, Tom and Paul Foglino. *Cracking the CLEP.*

Osen, Lynn M. *Women in Mathematics.*

Pappas, Theoni. *The Joy of Mathematics.*

_____. *Math for Kids and Other People Too!*

Phillips, Richard. *Numbers: Facts, Figures and Fiction.*

Reimer, Luettta & Wilbert Reimer. *Mathematicians Are People, Too: Stories from the Lives of Great Mathematicians,* Volume 1 and 2.

Rivero, Lisa. *Creative Homeschooling,* 2nd edition.

Ross, Michael E. *Sandbox Scientist: Real Science for Little Kids.*

Rupp, Rebecca. *Home Learning Year by Year: How to Design a Homeschool Curriculum from Preschool Through High School.*

Russell, William F. *Family Learning: How to Help Your Children Succeed in School by Learning at Home.*

Sax, Leonard. *Why Gender Matters: What Parents and Teachers Need to Know About the Emerging Science of Sex Differences.*

Seife, Charles. *Zero: The Biography of a Dangerous Idea.*

Sher, Barbara with Annie Gottlieb. Wishcraft: *How to Get What You Really Want.*

Stenmark, Jean Kerr, Virginia H. Thompson, and Ruth Cossey. *Family Math.*

Using a Law Library, published by HALT, Inc.

Vorderman, Carol. *How Math Works.*

Wessling, Suki. *From School to Homeschool: Should You Homeschool Your Gifted Child?*

Whitehead, John W., and Wendell R. Bird. *Home Education and Constitutional Liberties: The Historical and Constitutional Arguments in Support of Home Instruction.*

Wilde, Sandra and David Whitin. *Read Any Good Math Lately? Children's Books for Mathematical Learning, K-6.*

Wise, Jessie and Susan Wise Bauer. *The Well-Trained Mind: A Guide to Classical Education at Home.*

Zaslavsky, Claudia. *Number Sense and Nonsense: Building Math Creativity and Confidence Through Number Play.*

Index